Reclaiming the
Prophetic Mantle

*Preaching the
Old Testament
Faithfully*

Contributors for
Reclaiming the Prophetic Mantle

Michael Duduit is Editor, *Preaching* magazine. He also serves as Director of Development at Samford University, Birmingham, Alabama.

Kenneth A. Mathews is Associate Professor of Divinity, Beeson Divinity School, Samford University.

Robert D. Bergen is Department Chairman and Associate Professor of Religion, Hannibal-LaGrange College, Hannibal, Missouri.

George L. Klein is Graduate School Dean and Professor of Old Testament and Hebrew, Criswell College, Dallas, Texas.

Dan G. Kent is Professor of Old Testament, Southwestern Baptist Theological Seminary, Fort Worth, Texas.

Duane A. Garrett is Professor of Old Testament and Hebrew, Canadian Baptist Seminary, Cochrane, Alberta.

Robert B. Sloan is The George W. Truett Professor of Evangelism and Associate Professor of Religion, Baylor University, Waco, Texas.

David S. Dockery is Dean of the School of Theology and Associate Professor of New Testament Interpretation, The Southern Baptist Theological Seminary, Louisville, Kentucky.

G. R. Beasley-Murray is Senior Professor of New Testament Interpretation, The Southern Baptist Theological Seminary.

David E. Garland is Professor of New Testament Interpretation, The Southern Baptist Theological Seminary.

Al Fasol is Professor of Preaching and E. Hermond Westmoreland Professorship of Preaching, Southwestern Baptist Theological Seminary.

C. Richard Wells is Associate Professor of Divinity, Beeson Divinity School, Samford University.

James Emery White is Consultant for Preaching and Worship, Baptist Sunday School Board, Nashville, Tennessee.

Kenneth S. Hemphill is Church Growth Specialist, Home Mission Board of the Southern Baptist Convention.

RECLAIMING

THE
PROPHETIC
MANTLE

Preaching The Old Testament
Faithfully

Edited by

GEORGE L. KLEIN

BROADMAN PRESS
NASHVILLE, TENNESSEE

© Copyright 1992 • Broadman Press
All Rights Reserved

4260-20
ISBN: 0-8054-6020-9

Dewey Decimal Classification: 251
Subject Heading: PREACHING // BIBLE. OLD TESTAMENT
Library of Congress Catalog Number: 91-39141
Printed in the United States of America

Library of Congress Cataloging-in-Publication Data

Reclaiming the prophetic mantle: preaching the Old Testament faithfully / George L. Klein, editor.
   p. cm.
   Includes bibliographical references and index.
   1. Bible. O.T.—Homiletical use. 2. Bible. N.T.—Relation to the Old Testament I. Klein, George L., 1955- .
   BS1191.5.R43 1992
   251—dc20
                                                   91-39141
                                                   CIP

Contents

PREFACE

Marcion lives! Marcion, a second-century A.D. theologian, believed that the God of the Old Testament and the God of the New were not one and the same. He argued that the God of the Old was a malevolent Creator/Judge, while the God of the New was a loving Redeemer. Consequently, Marcion rejected the Old Testament as the Word of God and maintained that any reference to the Old in the New Testament should also be excluded from the canon. Although his views were condemned and have been generally rejected ever since (among the notable exceptions, for instance, was Adolf von Harnack), the shadow cast by this second-century theologian still falls over Christians today.

Most believers today would join the ancient church in rejecting Marcion's views on the Old Testament, upholding an orthodox affirmation of the Old Testament's place within the canon. However, these same Christians' reliance upon the Old Testament is often unintentionally deficient.

The reasons for neglecting the Old Testament today are many, and only a few can be addressed within this volume. For instance, differences of culture, theology antecedent to Christ, and even the rigors of the Hebrew language all contribute to the problem. This work attempts to address the hermeneutical differences which exist within the Old Testament itself as well as between the Old and New Testaments.

Perhaps the single most important assumption of this book is that the Old Testament is God's Word, with relevant, even mandatory messages for the church today. To be sure, it is often difficult to understand precisely what an Old Testament text meant to its original audience, let alone to today's hearers. However, it is our conviction that preachers must discover these messages for the well-being of their own congregations. One can lose one's way in search of God's truth, and, accordingly, we are grateful to the contributors for their wise advice on the path(s) we should follow.

Many deserve acknowledgement for their contributions to this volume. To Mike Smith and David Dockery go my thanks for their helpful suggestions concerning the ultimate shape of the work.

To my family go my appreciation for their encouragement.

Especially, I wish to thank the contributors who have brought their expertise to bear on crucial facets of the problem of proclaiming the Old Testament.

My deepest desire is that this work will help those doing the work of the ministry to handle the full counsel of God with greater hermeneutical and expositional skill.

To God be the glory!

GEORGE L. KLEIN

INTRODUCTION

The Church's Need for Old Testament Preaching

Michael Duduit

As we approach the 21st century, advances in technology seem to be announced almost daily. Innovations which would have seemed at the farthest reaches of science fiction just a century ago are today considered commonplace—from lasers used in a physician's office to semiconductors which give life to our desktop computers. The science textbook published less than five years ago has already been made obsolete by further discoveries.

In this brave new world of science and technology, communication is no longer measured in days or weeks but in milliseconds. Images of war now rush onto our television screens in America even as they are occurring on the other side of the globe. Fax machines, satellites, and computer technology have made the global village a reality.

For men and women living in such an age—pressed on all sides by technological innovation and social change—what possible relevance could be found in a collection of religious writings written three or four millennia ago? Does the Old Testament still have any meaning or value even to the Christian church in the 21st century?

The question of the Old Testament's value to the church is not a modern question at all. Little more than a century following the death and resurrection of Christ, Marcion had already advocated the elimination of the Old Testament (and much of the New) from the church's accepted Scriptures.

9

Though Marcion's teachings were branded heretical by the church in his own era and would be rejected out of hand by many contemporary Christian theologians, in practice, the church has often preached and taught as if Marcion had prevailed in the second century.

Even among evangelicals, the Old Testament is often treated as secondary in value when selecting texts for preaching. As editor of a professional journal for preachers, I annually receive hundreds of sermon manuscripts from ministers in a variety of Protestant denominations. Though the Old Testament makes up some two-thirds of the canon, less than one-tenth of the sermons submitted to *Preaching* are based on Old Testament texts.

Even among ministers who use a lectionary in guiding their worship and preaching—in which an Old Testament, a Gospel, and an Epistle text are suggested for each Sunday of the year—it is not at all uncommon to find the Old Testament primarily used for public reading, with the vast majority of preaching texts drawn from the New Testament.

It is easy enough to understand why Christian preachers would turn overwhelmingly to the New Testament for preaching texts. We turn to the Gospels as we preach about Jesus—His life, His teachings, His death, and resurrection. We look to Acts to preach about the remarkable development of that early church, and we draw on Paul's letters for their inspired teaching about the Christian faith and its application in human life. It is natural to turn to the books of the New Testament for preaching.

Yet it is also important—indeed, it is necessary—for us to draw heavily on the Old Testament in our preaching if we are to have balanced and effective pulpit ministries. Allow me to suggest several reasons for this.

The Old Testament Aids Us in Understanding the New Testament

Can you imagine enrolling in a foreign language class two-thirds of the way through the term? You would hear the same lessons as the rest of the class, but those words would have little meaning to you because you did not receive the foundational material on which the later lessons are based. For example, unless you learn the basic grammar of a language, it will be impossible for you to move immediately into the advanced elements of the language. You need to build on a solid foundation.

Trying to understand and preach the New Testament without a solid diet of Old Testament preaching and study is similar. We will overlook or misinterpret much of the New Testament without a clear understanding of the Old Testament.

How can we properly understand the role and significance of John the Baptist without understanding the prophetic tradition found in the Old Testament? How much more insight into Jesus' teaching about his own identity is possible when we have read Old Testament passages about the promised Messiah. Can the apostolic preaching be understood without some knowledge of God's dealings with His people as related in the Old Testament? Is it possible to preach effectively from Paul's Letter to the Romans unless a congregation has some foundation in the Jewish religious system as described in the Old Testament? Effective New Testament preaching is virtually impossible without an appropriate balance of Old Testament preaching.

The Old Testament Is Vital for Theological Understanding

When Paul told his young colleague Timothy that "all Scripture is God-breathed," he refers directly to the writings of the Old Testament, since many of the New Testament books were not yet written. Those which already existed were circulating as independent letters when Paul wrote.

As the inspired Word of God, the Old Testament is far too important to neglect in our preaching ministries. That was certainly Paul's message to his young preacher friend in the passage cited above. Paul emphasized, "All Scripture is God-breathed and is useful for teaching, rebuking, correcting, and training in righteousness" (2 Tim. 3:16, NIV).

As inspired Scripture, Paul said, the Old Testament is "useful for teaching." The Old Testament writings are absolutely essential for us to have a balanced biblical theology. Our theological understanding of creation and the Fall is drawn from the Book of Genesis, as is much of our doctrine of humanity. The foundation of our doctrine of salvation is laid in the pages of the Old Testament.

It is in the Old Testament we learn about the nature of God—that He is Spirit and yet personal, that He is powerful, holy, and righteous, yet also characterized by love and mercy. While the ultimate revelation of God is found in Jesus Christ, our understanding of Christ is rooted in what we know of God in the Old Testament. The Old Testament provides us with a comprehensive treatment of sin—its origin, its nature, its results. Without the books of the Old Testament we would not have an understanding of the biblical theme of covenant. Vital concepts of worship and ethics are also rooted in the Old Testament.

Clearly, much of the theological basis for Christian proclamation is drawn from the pages of the Old Testament. For us to neglect these books in our preaching is to abandon our congregations to theological shallowness and mediocrity. The Old Testament is inspired by God and is "useful for teaching" (2 Tim. 3:16, NIV) for every preacher who seeks to proclaim the "whole counsel of God" (Acts 20:27, RSV).

The Old Testament Offers Practical Insights for Christian Living

It is ironic that so many evangelical preachers spend an inordinate amount of their time dealing with Pauline texts, ostensibly because they are so practical in nature and filled with applications for contemporary Christians. Ironic because nowhere does one find a greater treasure of practical guidance for the people of God than in the pages of the Old Testament. No wonder that Paul (in 2 Tim. 3:16) stressed that the Scriptures are valuable for "rebuking, correcting and training in righteousness" (NIV).

Those who struggle with temptation and sin in their own lives can relate to character after character in the Old Testament—real people who faced real temptations, sometimes successfully, sometimes not. We can learn from Adam and Eve, who lost paradise because of the illusion of sin's satisfaction. We learn from David, who allowed a moment of weakness in his sexual life to stain his character and produce heartbreak for him and for others.

Christians who seek faith to follow God's will for their lives can draw courage from Abraham, who left the comfortable and familiar to venture out into an unknown future. Those who feel their own resources are inadequate can gain great insight from God's dealings with Gideon—reducing the army of 32,000 to just 300, then using that handful to vanquish the Midianites. Those who would be tempted to exploit others will be confronted forcefully by the prophetic challenge of Amos. Those who are in the midst of trials can find strength in the story of Joseph.

As we deal with practical issues of Christian living in our preaching, we will find excellent illustrations in the Old Testament for almost every topic we may touch. Many of the best sermon illustrations we will ever use will come directly from the lives of Old Testament characters.

Though technology changes, human nature remains remarkably consistent through the centuries, and the same issues and temptations with which the ancients grappled are the points of conflict with which members of our congregations struggle today. The Old Testament is packed with practical insights that will add new life to our preaching ministries.

The Old Testament Deals With Life's Great Questions

Why is it that some books become classics while others are relegated to the back rooms of library annexes? The great books that survive through the ages are those which deal with the significant issues of humanity. The works of Plato, Aristotle, Augustine, Dante, Shakespeare, and Goethe are still read and studied today because they deal with the deeper issues of human existence. No wonder we refer to them as "classics."

No collection of books fits that definition more completely than the Old Testament. The most significant issues faced by humanity are explored in its pages. Where did we come from and why are we here? Is there any better response to that question than the powerful phrase that opens the book of Genesis: "In the beginning God created the heaven and the earth?"

Humanity has always sought to know if there is something beyond the temporal world of its own existence. The pages of the Old Testament ring out the affirmation that there is One beyond this world, yet One who relates to us personally. Furthermore, no matter how many writers have tried to deal with the issue of human suffering, none has done so more profoundly than the writer of Job.

It is all too easy to fall into a pattern of preaching on the hottest issue of the day, and our sermons can become little more than presentations of the latest pop psychology covered with a thin veneer of piety. If we are to meet the deepest needs of the men and women in our congregations, it is essential that we move beyond the superficiality of such sermons to deal with the great questions of human existence. No place will we find greater resources for such preaching than in the Old Testament.

The Old Testament Leads Us to Jesus

As those called to proclaim the gospel, our greatest and highest priority is to lead men and women to faith in Jesus Christ. As we preach, we will find that the Old Testament is a priceless tool in that vital task.

It is no wonder that Paul told his young protégé Timothy: "from infancy you have known the holy Scriptures, which are able to make you wise for salvation through faith in Christ Jesus" (2 Tim. 3:15, NIV). As we have already observed, the only Scriptures Timothy had known were the books of the Old Testament. It was this priceless collection that prepared him to place his faith in Christ as Lord and Savior.

The earliest Christian preachers certainly knew that the Old Testament pointed to Christ. On the day of Pentecost, as Peter preached the first post-resurrection sermon to the crowd assembled on the streets of Jerusalem, he used the Old Testament to aid in their understanding of the gospel. Peter's sermons contained references to the prophet Joel and the psalmist/king David.

A few days later, as Peter and John went to the temple and healed the lame man at the gate (Acts 3), Peter's ensuing sermon contained direct references to Abraham, Isaac, and Jacob and pointed to "what he had foretold through all the prophets" (3:18, NIV) in order to help his listeners understand what God has done in Christ.

In Stephen's great sermon in Acts 7, he traced the history of God's dealing with the Jewish people as recorded in the Old Testament. Stephen used extensive Old Testament references to describe the people's past unwillingness to respond to God's love, culminating in the ultimate rejection of God by crucifying His Son.

When Paul spoke in the synagogue at Antioch (Acts 13), he drew on several Old Testament examples of God's provision for His people in order to proclaim Christ as God's greatest gift. Even in Athens, speaking to the Greek intellectuals (Acts 17), Paul used Old Testament allusions to lead the crowd to Christ; for instance, his statement that the Lord "does not live in temples built by hands" (17:24, NIV) is a reference to 2 Chronicles 2:6, which asks, "But who is able to build a temple for him, since the heavens, even the highest heavens cannot contain him?"

Clearly, the earliest Christian preachers understood that the Old Testament was foundational to their proclamation of the gospel. The same was true of the Gospel writers. The genealogies in Matthew and Luke are relatively meaningless apart from some knowledge of Old Testament history. Both writers make it clear that Jesus was descended from David, confirming that Jesus' heritage was in accordance with the Old Testament expectation for the coming Messiah.

This use of the Old Testament is further reinforced in the narratives concerning Jesus' life and teaching. As a boy in a faithful Jewish home, Jesus had been immersed in the teachings of the Old Testament. In His own life and teaching, Jesus made frequent references to Old Testament characters and incidents.

Following His baptism at the hands of John, Jesus went into the wilderness where He faced satanic temptation and where He fasted forty days and forty nights (Matt. 4:2). Is it only coincidental that when Moses was in the presence of the Lord at Mount Sinai, "Moses was there with the Lord forty days and forty nights without eating bread or drinking water" (Ex. 34:28, NIV)? In the midst of that wilderness experience, as Satan brought before Him three different temptations, in each situation Jesus responded by quoting from the Old Testament.

After healing the leper, Jesus told the man to "show yourself to the priest, and offer the gift that Moses commanded"—a reference to Leviticus 14:2ff. In sending His disciples out to preach, Jesus told them to go "to the lost sheep of Israel" (Matt. 10:6, NIV)—a reference most likely drawn from Isaiah 53:6, "We all, like sheep, have gone astray" (NIV). Over and over, Jesus drew on the Old Testament in illustrating His own message.

Jesus also seems to have understood His own identity in terms of the "suffering servant" of Isaiah. It is little wonder that the church has drawn on passages such as Isaiah 53 to express the reality of Christ's sacrifice for us:

> He was despised and rejected by men,
>   a man of sorrows, and familiar with suffering.
> Like one from whom men hide their faces
>   he was despised, and we esteemed him not.
> Surely he took up our infirmities and carried our sorrows,
>   yet we considered him stricken by God,
>   smitten by him, and afflicted (Isa. 53:3-4, NIV).

Such a passage offers a powerful basis for Christian preaching, since it so clearly communicates Jesus' own awareness of His mission. Just as they were for Peter and Stephen, for Paul and for Timothy, the books of the Old Testament are the Word of God which will lead us to Jesus.

Conclusion

We are grateful for the New Testament writings which tell us of Jesus Christ—His birth, life, teachings, death, and resurrection. We are grateful for the marvelous stories of those earliest days of the Christian church and the models provided by bold, committed men and women who gave their all to Christ and willingly paid any price to be faithful to Him. We are grateful for the exhortation and instruction that enables us to live more effective Christian lives. It is no surprise that we are drawn to the New Testament in our teaching and preaching.

Yet if we limit ourselves to the New Testament, we will miss much of God's revelation to us. The pages of the Old Testament provide important truths about God, about our world, about ourselves. These pages tell us of our lostness, of the divine law we have broken, and the judgment that is rightfully ours. Thankfully, the same pages also tell us of a God who loves us and will not let us go, of His love and mercy that reaches out to us even when we would reject it, of a Promised One who will come to save us from our own rebellion and self-destruction.

Great preaching is to be found in the precious pages of the Old Testament. May God's Spirit help you and your congregation to discover it anew.

PART 1

Preaching from Different Old Testament Genres

1

Preaching Historical Narrative

Kenneth A. Mathews

The Christian proclamation is anchored in the Hebrew Scriptures and therefore requires the Christian preacher to interpret his message in continuum with the historic redemption of God's people, believing Israel (1 Cor. 15:3-4; Luke 24:44-46). The revelatory character of God's historic salvation was preeminently expressed through Hebrew narrative as it interpreted the ancient traditions of Israel's faith. The Christian minister is compelled to preach Old Testament narrative, not only to emulate Paul who proclaimed the "whole counsel of God" (Acts 20:27, RSV) but, more importantly, to preach the redemptive theology of the Scriptures which includes a *narrative* theology. By narrative theology, we mean biblical theology that is conveyed through the medium of narrative discourse.[1]

The cosmic ordering of the universe, the covenant call of Abraham as the father of our faith (Rom. 4:11; Gal. 3:7), the creation of national Israel, the establishment of David's anointed lineage, the subsequent demise of Jerusalem, and the return of a believing remnant from its Captivity are all *narrated* events which are interpreted theologically by the authors and compilers of Israel's two canonical histories. The Primary History, consisting of Genesis through Kings in the Hebrew Bible, is a continuous account tracing the rise and fall of national Israel during which God formed a believing people. The Secondary History, which includes 1-2 Chronicles and Ezra-Nehemiah, retells the story from a later vantage point and goes beyond the first history by recounting what happened to the faithful few who returned from

Babylon. The unity of the testaments is reflected by the New Testament's continuing narration in which its theology of the Gospel accounts and the church's rise in the Book of Acts are bound up with Israel's history. The apocalyptic narratives of John's Revelation depict the final, victorious days of the kingdom of God, bringing the Bible's account of God's redemptive acts in history to a satisfying denouement. The very nature of the gospel message which is revealed, realized, and encountered in history demands that Christian expositors give themselves to preaching the historical narratives of the Old Testament.

Narrative's prominence in the Old Testament is not only seen by these two great histories but also by the shorter accounts of the Hebrews' heroes (for instance, Jonah, Dan. 1–6) and heroines (for instance, Ruth, Esther). Narratives are even embedded among the poetic oracles of the Hebrew prophets where they lend continuity and structure (for instance, Isaiah).[2]

Before we can properly discuss preaching narrative texts, we will address three critical issues that are related to interpreting historical narrative: (1) the relationship of historical narrative to history, (2) the literary characteristics of biblical narrative, and (3) the theology of Hebrew narrative.

Hebrew Historians and Their Accounts

The very expression "Hebrew historians" points up a continuing debate among scholars. Were the Hebrew authors historians? Are the narratives they produced history? Are they prose fiction or historicized fiction?[3]

History and Hebrew Historiography

The terms *history* and *fiction* are colloquially used as synonyms for "true" and "false," but this assumption oversimplifies the issues involved and leads to misunderstanding. When rightly understood, we will discover that history writing makes use of fiction and fiction writing can make use of history.

"History" may refer to the inquiry of past events and their causes (historiography) or it may be shorthand for the literary genre, history writing (as opposed, for instance, to poetry or law). Since our essay concerns history writing, that is, historical narrative, we begin by explaining how it is generally understood. "Narrative" is the telling of a series of related events that are coherent in reference.[4] Usually, narrative includes description of these events and an explanation, either stated or implied, for the events. Narrative is subcategorized into parable, short story, hero story, and many others; thus, the subgenre designated *historical* narrative is a significant reflection on the claims of a narrative composition to be a product of historiography.

Actually, there is no such thing as "history" apart from history writing. All events and artifacts require interpretation. Those interpretive records result from a process of selection and arrangement by the author. Historians, assuming that they write history (whether good or bad) and not propaganda, intend to present a discourse that corresponds to real events and persons. Historians claim this for their work and expect to be judged accordingly. Fiction writing, on the other hand, may make use of actual events or persons (for instance, Tolstoy's *War and Peace*), but it does not submit itself to judgment on the same basis as historical narrative. No reader would judge fiction writing as "good" or "bad" on the basis of whether its account corresponds to authentic events and persons.

The difference in the two kinds of writing lies, first, in their commitment to reality. Fiction writing begins with an idea or character and not an inherited plot. It has freedom to add and subtract at whim; anything conceivable falls within the possibility of the novelist. The historian, on the other hand, begins with a given series of events and cannot freely disregard or distort them.[5] The reader assumes that historians are attempting to give authentic accounts. If, however, the historian falsifies an account intentionally, then the product is not authentic, even if it is "documentary-like" in presentation.

Second, historians claim that their records are authentic and therefore submit their writings to a judgment of their facts.[6] They do this by referring to collaborating evidence, such as appealing to contemporary eyewitnesses and public records. Hebrew historians, for instance, refer to contemporary witnesses and invite the reader to consider palace and temple records for verification or amplification.[7] History writing, unlike fiction, can be found falsified, its accuracy of the facts disputed, and can be subject to varying interpretations. Fiction cannot be falsified or disputed since it is not epistemologically based.[8]

The distinction between history writing and fiction writing is, therefore, not literary form but intention. The dichotomy between fiction as "literary" and history as documentary occurred in the 19th century when modern historians moved their discipline away from the study of rhetoric to reflect a scientific based inquiry. However, fiction and history writing as literature have much in common. They enjoy the same aesthetic considerations in their presentations and make use of the same literary and linguistic conventions. They have the same task of explaining why or how some event took place. History writing makes use of literary plots like that of fiction where a theme is developed in a series of interconnected cause-effect chains. Fiction is not indicated merely by the presence of contrived settings and events since we know that fiction writing often employs a context of historical happenings. Nor is history recognized by the absence of invention since it too utilizes selection, arrangement, and interpretation.[9] Both history and fiction create their own worlds and presuppose that the reader is equipped to enter that world, recognizing and employing the appropriate interpretive rules of each. Therefore, it is wrong to question the historiography of a literary work solely on the basis of its formal similarities to fiction writing.

Furthermore, biblical narrative should not be judged exclusively by the conventions of modern historians. Even though they followed practices different from modern expectations, the ancients were not any less interested or capable of presenting real events than modern historians. The major difference is the modern historian's attribution of all events to human causation so as to meet the contemporary definition of scientific inquiry. Biblical narrative permits a fuller explanation, however, acknowledging a dual causation for events in which providence and humanity work together in the historical process.

Another difference is that modern historiography integrates more documentation; its style tends to be straightforward prose while biblical narrative is more metaphorical and picturesque. Biblical narrative makes use of documentation, too, but also claims accessibility to private knowledge not ordinarily derived from public sources. It has private conversations between people and even gives the inner thoughts and motivations of a person. For example, the narrator of Genesis reveals Judah's inner fears concerning the marriage of his youngest son Shelah to Tamar: "For he thought, 'He may die too, just like his brothers'" (Gen. 38:11, NIV).

Because of formal features corresponding in fiction writing and the element of private knowledge, many scholars conclude that biblical narrative must be deemed fictionalized history. This prejudice on the part of modern scholars has resulted in attributing to historical narratives the Western literary categories of novella (Ruth), family saga (Abraham saga), legend or hero story (Samson), historical story (Saul's selection as king), and the like.[10] A parade example is David's Succession Narrative (2 Sam. 9–20; 1 Kings 1–2) which until this century was generally recognized by all critical scholars as history, albeit limited to a "court history" of David. Studies in the latter half of this century have reflected a different opinion. The elements of literary artifice, particularly private conversations between characters (for instance, the bedroom scene of Amnon and Tamar, 2 Sam. 13) have led scholars to consider the author a novelist.[11] This conclusion underestimates the genuine antiquarian interests of the writers of Samuel and Kings who have been shown to be historians and not fanciful novelists.[12]

But what about narratives, such as the patriarchal accounts of Genesis, where there is literary ornamentation and public sources are not invoked? As we have shown earlier, it is modern supposition that fiction has literary artifice and history writing is plain prose. This is not a dependable absolute even in typologizing modern literature and should not be imposed on the Bible. Certainly, biblical narratives such as Genesis must be regarded as literature, since they partake of "literariness," but they are not solely literary art without a claim to history.[13] The authenticity of their writings and their theological assertions depend on the historicity of their accounts.

Neither does the accessibility of private knowledge nullify an author's claim to historicity. The reader presupposes that the authors are under divine inspiration, giving them access to private information (even the thoughts of God!), just as the reader assumes that God exists. This is the "rule" of reading to which the author and reader are agreed. Biblical writers do not surrender their claim to historicity by giving private knowledge but appeal to a different source of knowledge. Unlike modern literature where the omniscience of the narrator signals a work of fiction, for biblical narrative it gives authenticity to the tradition's claim to knowledge since it is based on God-given revelation.[14]

A related concern is the comparison of Hebrew narrative to the practice of Greek and Roman historians, such as Thucydides (ca. 460) and Polybius (ca. 202), who created dialogue for their accounts.[15] The same practice has been attributed to biblical authors, calling into question the value of their reporting.[16] At once we may take issue with likening Hebrew historiographers from an earlier period to Greek convention; we simply do not know how this was practiced by the Hebrews. However, even if we grant similarity in practice, to doom Greek and Latin historians as fabricators of dialogue is a misrepresentation of their use of dialogue. C. W. Fornara has argued that Thucydides' practice must be interpreted in light of his scrupulous character

as a historian. Thucydides preferred verbatim speech, considering dialogue as important in the writing of history as accurate
reporting of events, but if the actual wording were inaccessible,
he endeavored to give the substance of the speech. Modifications
were permitted when necessary but always retaining the tenor
of the dialogue if possible. This approach was followed by Greek
and Latin writers as the accepted convention, although individuals admitted departing from it. In remarks concerning Herod-
otus, Fornara questions the critics' line of thinking:

> We are asked to believe that Herodotus could undertake to write
> a vast history with as much accuracy and inquiry as he could
> manage, and yet at crucial moments spin off one speech after an-
> other merely according to his own notions or desires.[17]

History writers in one way or another must write speech for
their characters either by giving synopsis, abbreviating or orna-
menting, but it is unwarranted to conclude that unbridled fancy
was the norm for biblical writers. The sayings of Jesus, when a
comparison of the parallel accounts in the synoptic Gospels is
made, clearly show that the Evangelists varied the particular
wording of Jesus' sayings for theological or rhetorical reasons.
The writers gave the substance of Jesus' sayings if not always
the exact words.[18] Differences in the Synoptic sayings are best
explained as the consequence of ancient conventions in reporting speech rather than the fabrications of the early church as
has been claimed by some New Testament scholars.[19] Modern
practice, too, permits synopsis under certain restrictions; this is
illustrated by television reporters who, after a presidential address to the nation, summarize what the audience just heard,
introducing their synopsis by "the President said." The audience knows to interpret "the President said" as metaphorical for
the substance of the address. Where we should fault the modern commentator and the ancient historian is if they concoct
material for what never occurred or distort what had occurred.

In sum, we conclude that the narratives of the Hebrew Bible
are history writing and are trustworthy accounts, when they are
not prejudged on the basis of modern categories of historiography.

Hebrew Historiography and Theology

How then did Hebrew historiography serve the theology of
the biblical writers? First, historical narrative enhanced the
Hebrews' understanding of the nature of God as Lord of history
and creation. The arena of God's revelation is human history;

to know and understand God is to know Him in the workings of human affairs. Unlike Israel's neighbors whose gods were cosmic but tied to the cyclical patterns of nature, the God of Israel expressed Himself in the context of history. This was considered true by the Gentiles concerning pagan deities to a limited extent, to whom were attributed the territorial gains or losses of a nation, but pagan gods were impotent when directing the outcome of universal history. Historical narrative presents God in His dealings with humankind where He predicts and brings to pass historical event. Behind every human cause lies the divine hand of God's all-causality.

Preachers, therefore, who lapse into preaching ancient history or even the history of Israel's religion miss the biblical writers' intentions. Biblical narrative presents *theology*—that is, a proclamation about God—told by means of narrative as opposed to philosophical discourse or sermon. The theology of the biblical writers, however, was shaped by their religion and also the experiences of Israel's history.[20] The study of Israel's religion and the history of the ancient Near East are therefore preparatory for the preacher to understand a narrative's theology but they are not its theology.

Second, history writing requires subjective filtering of sources; biblical historians were not objective reporters. The biblical writers had an ideological agenda; they attributed to God whatever occurred in Israel's history (and all cosmic history). Because of God's covenant demands, the Hebrew historians understood that the determination of the outworkings of history included an ethical factor. The God of Israel, who is morally upright and just, weighed a people by the scales of righteous living and, in the case of ancient Israel, by the measure of covenant fidelity.

Human causation was not avoided; it was common to attribute history to human cause as well as divine. The tension of divine sovereignty and human responsibility is retained by the writers who show how history is in the frail hands of human agents but undergirded by the directing arm of God.[21] The biblical account shows, on the one hand, how political events in the Near East affected the collapse of Jerusalem where Israel's kings made diplomatic and military blunders in the face of Egyptian and Babylonian pressures. Yet, it gives priority to the divine perspective which tells the destruction of Jerusalem as the result of its sin by an avenging covenant-keeping God. Babylonian records corroborate this event in Israel's life, but they cannot validate Scripture's theological interpretation of it.

Since the theology of the historian is dependent upon the reality of the event, any discovery of its nonhistoricity would undermine the narrative's theological claims.[22]

Preachers are not explicating bare historical facts but preaching texts which are interpretations of God's acts. Scripture *is* the revelation of God which brings both event and its inspired interpretation together. Historical events by themselves are not God's revelation since they require an authoritative illumination of that event's significance.[23] What the preacher must keep foremost in mind is that biblical narrative has a "theological quality" that is paramount.[24]

History writing is not complete but selective. Every historiographer must decide what is relevant to the account, sorting out what pertains to the particular thesis. The Bible never claims to be a complete account, only a true and trustworthy one. We can be happy that the Hebrew historians discriminate or we would have a very laborious history to read. Furthermore, we would not know which events are more important since every event would be given attention.

Third, history is multifaceted in perspective and may be told from various viewpoints that are complementary, such as political, social, religious, and economic perspectives. As we indicated earlier, the Hebrew historians were not writing a political history per se. This is illustrated by the account of Omri, father of Ahab, who was still honored as a formidable king for years after his death.[25] In spite of Omri's accomplishments, he is hardly mentioned in Kings where only eight verses are given to his reign (1 Kings 16:21-28). Ahab receives far more attention not only because his reign is contemporaneous with Elijah but also because Ahab's career better illustrates the author's thesis of God's vindication (as in the case of Naboth). This explains why there is little overlap between the Bible and ancient sources. Simply put, the Hebrew writers were not interested in writing a history of the ancient Near East nor of Israel's political and economic history. Theirs was a telling of events designed to express their theological understanding of how history works.

Preaching the text, then, means preaching the theological perspective of the biblical writer rather than some ancillary perspective—although granted it may have some social or scholarly interest. The dimensions of social and economic concerns are contributive to a fuller picture, but they are not the window through which the preacher views the narrative. To preach a political or economic history of Israel would misrepresent the intention of the text.

To conclude, we have shown that historical narrative is narrative theology in which the biblical writers as prophets of God presented a theological interpretation of history.[26] They fashioned their accounts creating an aesthetically pleasing literature.[27] This demands that the biblical preacher consider the literary features of the narrative, to which we turn next, in order to appropriate the inspired writer's theological purposes.

Hebrew Narrative and Its Features

Narratology is diverse in methodology and value for the preacher. We have limited our discussion to those facets of narrative theory which we believe will best aid the homiletician.[28]

Meaningful communication includes both a coherent message and an appropriate form designed to convey that message. The author selects a discourse type, such as epistolary or narrative discourse, which has conventional "rules" of structure and arrangement that make the message intelligible. Communication presupposes competent readers who knows the "rules" which govern the genre, enabling them to interpret the message correctly. Meaning cannot be conveyed apart from form, since form always bears the shape and structure of the message. Form therefore is integral to meaning.[29] Both parable and historical narrative are narrative genres; but reading parable, for example, Jotham's fable of the bramblebush king (Judg. 9:7-15), requires the interpreter to apply different reading conventions. This is clearer when we consider the widely disparate hortatory (Malachi) or epistolary (Pauline letters) discourse types.

Interpreting narrative includes a knowledge of how narrative genre works; a reader through experience unconsciously comes to expect how a story should be told and what makes for a good story. The reason why narrative is readily understood by readers of the Bible, even the very young, is that stories are commonplace in most cultures. However, to be "better" readers of biblical narrative, we will want to analyze it consciously with the view of grasping its focus for preaching. As we discuss the primary features of narrative below, we will apply them to a correlative reading of Genesis 22:1-19, the account of Isaac's sacrifice or *Akedah* as it is popularly known in the Jewish tradition.

Narrative Structure

Every narrative has a deliberate arrangement of constituent parts. How those parts fit together and interrelate will expose the building blocks of the narrative, enabling the expositor to discover the unity, themes, and emphases of the passage. The "structure" of a passage may be viewed from different levels—including the surface and semantic levels.[30] The latter is the conceptual, informational level which groups meaningful units of communication while the surface structure is the phonological, grammatical, and syntactical elements of the language which are subservient to the semantic. The surface features of the language will demarcate the meaning units and signify the prominent information of the composition.[31] This is why the reader must be aware of the narrational techniques that mark out the climax and the prominent points of the story.[32]

Narrative discourse will have a plot made up of a sequence of events that moves toward a closure. The cohesion of a narrative depends on the storyline as it runs its course through the account. These events are linked by a series of stimulus-response relationships given usually in a specific temporal-spacial setting. The common stimulus-response pairings are: (1) problem-resolution and (2) occasion-outcome. Problem-resolution occurs when the story advances a problem and tells how the problem is resolved. Occasion-outcome concerns what happened and what was the outcome of that happening. In many cases, there is both resolution and outcome in a narrative; it is common to have interlocking stimulus response chains where the response of one becomes the stimulus of the next.[33]

Because narrative has time orientation, there will be a time-line or event-line which provides the backbone of movement in the plot's advancement. A *simple* plot builds up to a high point of tension until its release at the climax of the account where the story turns toward resolution or outcome. The climax of a *complex* plot will be retarded by complicating tensions that prolong the story's event-line. The climax or peak is signaled by *sudden* changes in the surface (grammatical-lexical) structure of the text where the common (expected) discourse features of the narrative shift to another set of features. Among these, for example, are: shifts from non-discourse to speech, change of story-telling pace from short, quick sentences to long, slow ones, variation in verbal tenses and person, and repetition of information.[34] These shifts mark the peak both for a network of stories and for individual episodes (embedded narratives) which make up the plot.

For example in the Joseph cycle (Gen. 37–50), the climax (or peak) is Joseph's rise to power (chap. 41) and the denouement (or peak) is the revelation of his identity (chaps. 43–45). Genesis 41:14-45 is the focus of the story where Joseph is installed as vice regent of Egypt. This section has a "sandwich" construction that begins and ends with a staccato of quick acting verbs providing an unusual amount of detail (41:14 and 41:37-45); the middle is the slow, protracted dialogue between Pharaoh and Joseph (41:15-36), resulting in Joseph's ascension. Ultimately, Joseph's rise means the salvation of Jacob's family; the denouement contains Joseph's invitation for Jacob to descend to Egypt, as he explains: "God has made me lord of all Egypt" (45:9, NIV).[35]

Natural prominence in narrative discourse is the climax of the story and the last resolution/outcome. A narrative naturally tends to move from the less to the more important information. If authors want to indicate prominence elsewhere in the account, they must use additional devices, such as repetition, inverted parallelism (*chiasmus*), opening and closing parallelisms (*inclusio*), and deictic particles (for instance, [*hinneh*] "behold"). We will discuss these devices later.

Usually, a narrative in the Bible contributes to a larger narrative plot. Stories are tied together to form a complex of narratives (for instance, the Abraham cycle, Gen. 11:27–25:11) which in turn form the plot of a book (for instance, Genesis) that is included in a still larger canonical shape (for instance, the Pentateuch and Genesis–Kings). Therefore, the plot of an account must be interpreted in light of the expanding whole; the broader circles of context must come to bear in addressing the significance of the original narrative. To treat a narrative in total isolation from its literary contexts diminishes its significance for the reader. A series of narratives may include actions that recur as parallel or analogous accounts. The arrangement of such parallel stories encourages the reader to consider a parallel plot as a commentary; such parallel events contribute to a theme or motif of the whole composition (for instance, the wife-sister deception of Abraham and Isaac [Gen. 12; 20; 26] contributes to the "deception" motif common to the patriarchal narratives as a whole).

When we consider the narrative structure of the sacrifice of Isaac, we must first set it in its narrative context. The sacrifice of Isaac occurs in the Abraham sequence, as its prominent episode,[36] which tells of God's promises to the patriarch and his descendants. The Abraham cycle contributes to the theme of Genesis, the "blessing" of God upon His creation (1:22,28), by showing how this blessing intended for all nations is to be channeled through the family of Abraham (12:1-3 *et al.*).[37] The Abraham series is arranged as an inverted parallelism (known as *chiasmus*); chapters 12 and 22 are corresponding parts (BB'). The explication of the promises, which were first given in chapter 12, stands at the center (EE'):[38]

A Genealogy of Terah (11:27-32)
   B Start of Abraham's Spiritual Odyssey (12:1-9)
      C Sarai in foreign palace; ordeal ends in peace and success; Abram and Lot part (12:10–13:18)
         D Abraham comes to the rescue of Sodom and Lot (14:1-24)
            E Covenant with Abraham; Annunciation of Ishmael (15:1–16:16)
            E' Covenant with Abraham; Annunciation of Isaac (17:1–18:15)
         D' Abraham comes to the rescue of Sodom and Lot (18:16–19:38)
      C' Sarah in foreign palace; ordeal ends in peace and success; Abraham and Ishmael part (20:1–21:34)
   B' Climax of Abraham's Spiritual Odyssey (22:1-19)
A' Genealogy of Nahor (22:20-24)

By this arrangement, the sacrifice of Isaac (B') is naturally prominent since it gives the outcome of the Abraham cycle. This pericope brings to conclusion as many as seven motifs developed within the cycle.[39] The primary tension in the Abraham sequence is the barrenness of Sarah and absence of the promised descendant (12:1-3). The resolution comes with the birth of Isaac who is chosen as the recipient of God's blessings (chap. 21), but the solution is complicated by the protracted tension of the story when God commands the sacrifice of the promised lad (chap. 22). The command (22:2) is reminiscent of God's first instructions to Abram (Gen. 12:1):

Genesis 12:1, "Leave [*lek-leka*] your country . . . "
Genesis 22:2, "Go [*lek-leka*] to the region of Moriah . . . "

The sacrifice of Isaac, where God commands Abraham to "take your son," begs to be interpreted in light of the first command to leave "your father's house." It has long been recognized that the two accounts show striking parallels in language and arrangement.[40] The point of the intended parallel is that Abraham receives the command of God again in chapter 22 with the renewed opportunity to obey; whereas in the first calling he was to leave his father behind, now he must leave his son behind on Mt. Moriah.[41] During his sojourn in Canaan, too, the spiritual pilgrimage of the patriarch was as much "up and down" as the hilly terrain of the land he traversed. "Is

Abraham trustworthy of the promises?" the reader ponders. "Has he learned obedience through the travails of Canaan's experiences?" The "test" then places Abraham as at the beginning to respond to God in complete obedience.

The structure of the narrative is arranged around the recurring exclamation, "Here am I" [*hinneni*] (vv. 1b,7,11); the closure for each section is the parallel use of "together" [*yahdaw*]:

Opening—the "test" (1a)
- "Here am I" [*hinneni*] (1b-6)
    "and the two of them went on *together*" [*yahdaw*] (6)
- "Here am I, my son" [*hinneni beni*] (7-8)
    "and the two of them went on *together*" [*yahdaw*] (8)
- "Here am I" [*hinneni*] (9-19a)
    "and they went on *together* for Beersheba" [*yahdaw*]
    (19a)
Closing (19b)

The peak occurs at 22:11-12 when the angel of the Lord intervenes with new instructions: "Abraham! Abraham!" "Here I am," he replied (NIV). The repetition of the name "Abraham" and the shift from the narration of verses 9-11a to the heavenly dialogue of verses 11b-12 contribute to indicating the peak. The reply of Abraham in verse 11 is the climactic third occasion of the verbless sentence, "Here (am) I." The arresting sequence of two verbal jussives further distinguish the peak: "*Do not lay* a hand on the boy" and "*Do not do* anything to him" (v. 12, NIV). Also, there is the use of the verbal participle [*yere*] rather than the perfective form of the verb: "that you *fear* God." The denouement is the "second time" the angel speaks from heaven (22:15-18) wherein the language of the covenant, so important to the Abraham cycle (12:1-3; chaps. 15–17), is rehearsed and the promises confirmed. This practice is known as "back reference" which brings to the foreground prominent information which has been previously given. Also, the denouement consists of the longest speech in the narrative, slowing the tempo to a snail's pace, and is conspicuous by a formal oath: "I swear by myself" (v. 15, NIV). The prominence of the denouement is indicated also by its location in the Abraham cycle; it is the last of 35 speeches delivered by God (or angel of the Lord).[42]

Scenes

Narrative structure, as we have seen above, is made up of scenes or episodes that are interconnected. Cinematography provides a closer analogy to Hebrew narrative than modern literature.[43] As in modern cinemas, selective scenes dominate the plot, being prolonged by dialogue. Gaps occur between the scenes but the cohesiveness of plot structure implies intervening events which the viewer supplies through imagination. Supportive scenes are usually shorter but still integral to the continuity of the film. Narrative makes use of the same techniques by giving scenes with picturesque qualities, enabling the reader mentally to view the event. Detailed description, however, is limited only to where necessary for understanding the plot. Therefore, where elaborate description of settings occur, the expositor must be aware of its special emphasis. Most likely, these details will come into play in the outcome of the plot.

The scenes of Genesis 22 are indicated by change in participants and dialogue. Abraham appears in every scene as the main referent, giving coherence to the whole:

Scene one: God's command to Abraham (1-2)

Scene two: Abraham's journey and instructions to his servants (3-5)

Scene three: Abraham and Isaac's dialogue (6-8)

Scene four: Abraham's offering of Isaac and the voice from heaven (9-12)

Scene five: Abraham's offering of the ram and the voice from heaven a second time (13-19)

Time and Distance

Related to plot is the narration's management of time and distance. In a single phrase, decades and miles can be covered by the narration. The action of the event-line can be pushed ahead or retarded at the will of the author. Narrative slows the pace through its creation of scenes which focus on characters and their dialogue. If we compare the event-line to a railroad track, the railroad line's stops along the route would be the dialogical scenes. As a consequence, time and distance covered in a story may be illusory since the author protracts the dialogical over the narrational. Biblical narrative prefers subtle shifts in time and place without drawing attention; the reader as a result does not sense abrupt changes.[44] The expositor should give greater care to dialogue since the narrational element in establishing its setting is supportive of the dialogical. In the case of Genesis 22, the journey of Abraham to Moriah is three days but is covered in only two verses without detail (22:3-4). The remainder of the chapter concerns only the brief portion of the third day when the sacrifice of Isaac occurred. The silence of the three-day journey serves to heighten the first words of the patriarch which show his commitment to carry out the task (22:5).

Characters and Characterization

Unlike modern novels or the ancient epic, the characters of the Bible are rarely described physically or psychologically.[45] Characters in the Bible are more often described according to their intellectual and moral features. Jacob is "the deceiver" and Nabal "the fool." In Homer's *Odyssey*, the heroes are given full description with explicit information; biblical characters are described only in terms of what is necessary for the plot. In the case of Genesis 22, there is no physical description. Isaac is identified as Abraham's son ("your son, your only son," v. 2, NIV) because the familial relationship is critical to the story.[46] When such description occurs, the expositor should give special attention to it. For instance, the description of Esau at birth as "red" and hairy (Gen. 25:25) anticipates the account two ways: (1) the "red stew" which Esau exchanges for his birthright (25:30) and (2) his hairy body which Jacob simulates in the deception of his father Isaac when Esau lost his blessing (27:23,36).

Characterization more often occurs by the actions and dialogue of the participants. Dialogue by or concerning a character is the chief way narrative characterizes the participants; dialogue and internal monologue provide insight into the motivations and actions of characters. However, we must be forewarned that the Bible often presents ambiguous or unclear characterizations. Rarely does the narrator baldly sum up a character for the reader. Ambiguity results from the true-to-life portraits of its characters that the Bible draws. It never shies from presenting the multidimensional aspects of a protagonist. Abraham was both failure and success; he was an untrustworthy deceiver, on the one hand, and yet showed exceptional faith on the other. The author shows the developing character of a protagonist by such contrasts. Also, characters may take differing points of view which creates contrasting portraits. Biblical narrative encourages the reader to compare and contrast characters through similar descriptions, dialogue, and situations. For example, the comparison of the two Gentile women, Tamar and Ruth, and the contrast in how they come by their children are implied by their similar circumstances and also by the elders' blessing on the house of Boaz (compare Ruth 4:12).

Characters fill different functional slots. In Genesis 22, the main characters are God and Abraham, with the angel of the Lord and Isaac having supporting roles. The angel of the Lord is interpreted as one and the same as God (22:12); yet, the angel functions distinctly as God's authoritative mouthpiece who evaluates the response of Abraham and confirms the promises. Isaac is overshadowed by the role of Abraham; this is true for Isaac in general since he plays only a transitional figure between Abraham and Jacob. He serves as a foil for Abraham, offering a different viewpoint of the patriarch's actions.

Some characters are no more than props which give the scene its fullness. The two servants who accompanied Abraham and Isaac to Moriah are unnamed and silent. We know nothing about or from them. However, they are still crucial to the account, because they provide Abraham the audience for voicing his faith in God's goodness: "We [Abraham and Isaac] will return to you" (22:5, NASB). They appear at the end of the story, accompanying Abraham to Beersheba, to round out the narration (22:19). Minor characters also may provide a foil against which the protagonist can be more forcefully characterized. For example, Orpah and the Nearer-kinsman are foils for the righteous Ruth and Boaz; the wicked sons of Eli are foils for Samuel.

It is not surprising that the central "character" of the Bible is God. He is present in every scene either overtly or by implication. As the most important figure, the expositor's attention should be focused on God's role in the narrative. Because biblical narrative is proclamation, giving a prophetic interpretation of God's acts in history, the biblical writers were not writing a psychological portrait of a human character or drawing moral lessons from human experience. A study in human character was not the intent of biblical narrative any more than it was to study a narrow slice of human history. No human character or action supplants the lead of God in a biblical story. Human characters are not models to be emulated. L. Toombs rightly says:

> They [biblical characters] are not to be presented as recipes for anyone else's existence, as if one could prepare the cake of his personality by combining abstract virtues gathered from theirs. Rather, they show us the kinds of issues which arise in an existence lived in history under God's demand and invite us to see how these issues take shape in our own experience.[47]

Character studies as sermons which preach the positive and negative attributes of an individual are wrongheaded because they divorce the character from the larger plot of God's salvific work, distract from the intent of the author, and ignore the principle of progressive revelation. Biblical characters are elements of a much larger plot and are in that sense minor characters giving way to God and His kingdom. From the biblical writer's theological understanding of human history, we learn about the nature of God and His expectations for individuals and nations. Our foremost question should be, "What is God doing in this scene?"[48] Otherwise, we run the danger of reducing biblical narratives to morality plays! For these reasons, the virtue of mutual trust shown by Abraham and his son Isaac should not distract the preacher. The passage is not intended as a divine paradigm for father-son relationships. It concerns God's faithfulness as response to Abraham's enduring love.

Narrator

The narrator is the voice telling the story and the narratee is the audience addressed. The narrator, speaking in the third person, usually remains in the background and is satisfied with establishing the circumstances of the story. He rarely gives an authoritative judgment or offers commentary, leaving the subtle influences of literary patterning and dialogue to inform the reader. He controls the story, even without commenting, by manipulating the scenes and managing the information shared. When the narrator speaks, his voice functions as the author's and presents the point of view subconsciously taken by the reader. Whenever narration offers a value judgment concerning an event or person the expositor must take special note of its importance (for example, "But Er, Judah's firstborn, was wicked in the Lord's sight; so the Lord put him to death" Gen. 38:7, NIV).

Narration may choose to tell the account as an independent observer of the events or occasionally from the perspective of a character (for example, " . . . but his brothers were not able to answer him because they were terrified at his presence" Gen. 45:3, NIV). Sometimes the narrator speaks in the first person as a character in the story (compare Nehemiah and Ecclesiastes). Also, the narrator may speak from outside the story, interrupting its natural flow, by supplying parenthetical information to clarify aspects of the account (for example, "Now Jacob did not know that Rachel had stolen the gods," Gen. 31:32, NIV) or to place the reader in a better position to interpret the actions or dialogue of the participants.[49]

A significant feature of biblical narrative is the privileged information of the narrator. He is often omniscient, knowing private conversations and the thoughts of God Himself. The narrator does not stand above God, giving or denying knowledge where he pleases, but rather has an authority derived from God. The existence of an omniscient narrator is consistent with the Hebrews' reverence for God's knowledge; the narrator's omniscience indicates that the account is the uttering of God's prophetic word.[50]

In Genesis 22 the narration is limited but nonetheless critical. The narrator informs the reader at the outset that God's command is a "test" of Abraham (22:1). This frees the reader to concentrate on the interaction between Abraham and God rather than wrestle with the entangling perplexity of how God could resort to human sacrifice. Since the audience is privy to heaven's intentions, it is in a better position to interpret God's command than even Abraham who, as far as the narrative is concerned, never discovered that it was a "test" (except by implication when God changed His mind about the matter). The narrator therefore shares with the reader a viewpoint different from those of the participants (see discussion below); consequently, the reader adopts the standpoint of God and narrator.

Point of View

Related to the role of the narrator is the matter of viewpoint. Point of view is critical for interpretation, because it is the lens through which the reader sees the events recounted. The viewpoint which dominates the text is that of the narrator. There are four aspects of viewpoint by which the narrator may shape the story.[51] (1) Ideological: this refers to the narrator's evaluation of the event whose opinion reflects the ideology of the Bible. (2) Spatial and temporal: this aspect refers to the narrator's location with respect to the telling of the event. The narrator may be close, as an observer or as one of the characters, or distant; he may be telling it as a contemporary or from long after the event. (3) Psychological: this position indicates how the event is perceived. The story may be told objectively as an impartial observer or subjectively by presenting the standpoint of a character or by the narrator giving the thoughts of a person. (4) Phraseological: this refers to the surface features (language techniques) of the story to indicate whose viewpoint is being expressed.

As we indicated in our discussion of characterization, dialogue enables the inclusion of points of view differing from that of the narrator. In fact, many times the narrator offers no opinion at all and readers are left to form their own judgment or adopt the point of view of a character. Varying viewpoints in a story become a seedbed of dramatic irony and ambiguity which give the story a multifaceted dimension. By contrasting outlook within a story, the author is able to highlight one perspective over others.[52]

In the case of Genesis 22, we have four points of view; some coincide but the four voices are different. First, the narrator interprets God's instruction to Abraham as a test of loyalty (22:1); this viewpoint, of course, is the perspective adopted by the reader. Second, Abraham is unaware of the test and expresses his view in terms of God's loyalty. He implies that God is faithful when he says that the boy will return from the mount (22:5) and that God will provide a lamb for offering (22:8). This is the lesson that Abraham learned from the experience as indicated by the naming of the site "the Lord will provide." Third, Isaac has still less insight; he is perplexed by his father's actions since he is not aware, though perhaps suspicious, of Abraham's intentions. The absence of the customary animal offering evokes Isaac's question about the legitimacy of the worship. His view reflected normative Hebrew worship as practiced among the Israelite readers of this story. Isaac's view elicits Abraham's perspective on the matter (22:8). The fourth outlook is God's own voice, since we take the angel of the Lord and God as one and the same (22:12) which, by approving Abraham's action, complements the narrator's perspective. The structural arrangement of the narrative highlights the divine view since it occurs at the climax (22:11-12) and denouement (22:15-19).

Key-wording

Key-wording, also known as *Leitwort* ("lead word"), is the repetition of the same word or the convergence of words which are related in sound or form in strategic locations within a narrative.[53] This technique is used to enhance the thematic unity of a story or to accept a motif developed within a narrative. Stitching *Leitworten* across stories ties common themes and motifs, contributing to the unity of a complex of plots (for instance, "blessing" in Genesis, occurring about 70 times). For example, Genesis 22 spotlights the motif "father–son" by the high incidence of those words sprinkled throughout the passage. This relationship impacts the severity of the test; does Abraham love his son more than God? The threefold reiteration of "your son, your only son" (22:2,12,16, NIV) points up the importance of the boy for the larger concern of the covenant. Actually, Isaac was not Abraham's "only" son; Ishmael, however, did not count in the covenant reckoning! Consequently, Isaac was Abraham's unique and irreplaceable son. The poignancy of the passage is underscored by the one variation in this appositive, "whom you love" (22:2, NIV).

The nature of Semitic language encourages the word-play of alliteration, assonance, and pun. The triliteral feature of Hebrew words, whose various parts of speech (verbs, nouns, adjectives) are built around the same letters, give them a similarity in sound and appearance. Pun occurs when words similar in sound but different in meaning are used. An example of punning in our passage is the repeated "he looked up" (*wayyar*ᵓ, vv. 4,13) and the similar sounding "fear" (*yere*ᵓ, v. 12) and "provide/provided" (*yir*ᵓ*eh/yera*ᵓ*eh*, v. 14). When Abraham "looked up" to see the mount afar off, he showed his "fear" of God by obedient journey; when he "looked up" to see the ram, he received God's "provision."

Repetition

Biblical scholars in the last century commonly explained repetitions as evidence of putative literary sources. Since the rise of rhetorical criticism in the last quarter-century, scholars are explaining repetitions as rhetorical devices for aesthetic reasons or as functional devices for structuring purposes, giving unity and coherence to narrative as well as indicating prominence.[54] Repetition may occur with just one word, as we saw with *Leitwort* above, or at the higher levels of phrase, sentence, paragraph, and whole episode. This feature is so pervasive in Hebrew style that the patterns are many times quite sophisticated in their intricacy. They have a rich variety which prevent monotony and produce change in a less conspicuous way. For the Western reader, they appear redundant and have been in some expositions wrongly excised from the text.[55]

The most common use of repetition is for emphasis. We have seen this already in the Abraham-Isaac story in which the "father–son" motif is highlighted by repetition. Also, parallel lines as a use of repetition can mark out the beginnings or closings of different units. The parallel expressions of "and the two of them went on together" (vv. 6,8) and "and they went on together" (v. 19) establish the closing boundary for their respective section. Furthermore, repetition, as an *inclusio* device, may be used to set the parameter of a literary unit. The *inclusio* marks out the beginning and end of a unit (sometimes a whole discourse) by repeating words, phrases, or just an idea. The expression "There was no king in those days and every man did what was right in his own eyes" occurs in Judges 17:6 and 21:25 to distinguish chapters 17–21 as a unit. The formula, in a modified form, occurs again within the unit twice (18:1; 19:1) where it ties the two stories together. As a structuring device, repetition is used to arrange the macrostructure of a book or discourse. For example, the elevenfold recurrence of "this is the history of" in Genesis structures the book (2:4; 5:1; 6:9; 10:1; 11:10,27; 25:12,19; 36:1,9; 37:2).

Repetition in dialogue among characters is an effective tool for characterization. Subtle alterations of a quotation by a participant may be indicative of a change in perspective on the part of a character. God's instructions to Adam concerning the trees of the garden (Gen. 2:15-17) are repeated with slight differences by the serpent and the woman so as to give the command of God their own interpretation (Gen. 3). In the sacrifice of Isaac, the angel of the Lord commends Abraham in two speeches, repeating "you have not withheld from me, your son, your only son" (22:12,16, NIV), but the second is prefaced with the oath "I swear by myself" (22:16, NIV). This formal oath confirms the covenant promises to Abraham and sets Abraham's response of faith in the broader context of Genesis' theme of blessing (22:16-18).

Finally, repetition occurs for theological reason; the biblical writers believed that the divine word was accomplished through the actions of human experience. A predictive word or expressed command of God was repeated, sometimes verbatim, by the narrator or a character to show that it had been realized. This reflects the Old Testament's view of the "word" as the dynamic force which brings to pass history's happening (for instance, the command of Ex. 7:17-18 and the almost verbatim narration of its accomplishment in Ex. 7:20-21).[56]

Chiasmus

A special form of repetition of parallelism, known as *chiasmus* (or inverted parallelism), is a mirrored repetition where the second half corresponds to the first (A B B' A'). The name *chiasmus* is derived from the capital Greek letter *chi* which is formed by crossing two lines (similar to the arabic letter "X"). *Chiasmus* is an ubiquitous feature of ancient writing, practiced in the ancient Near East and the Greco-Roman world.[57] Its simplest use is at the word level (particularly in poetry); it also is utilized for structuring narrative episodes, whole books, and even collections of books.[58] It provides cohesion and produces a feeling of rounded completion as a composition reaches its outcome. Chiastic structures are also prominence marking devices.

Genesis 11:1-9 demonstrates how *chiasmus* both shapes the account and indicates the prominent idea:

A "The whole earth had one language" (v. 1)
  B "there" (v. 2)
    C "each other" (v. 3)
      D "Come let us make bricks" (v. 3)
        E "Let us build for us" (v. 4)
          F "a city and a tower" (v. 4)
            G "the Lord came down" (v. 5)
          F' "the city and the tower" (v. 5)
        E' "which mankind had built" (v. 5)
      D' "come . . . let us mix up" (v. 7)
    C' "each other's language" (v. 7)
  B' "from there" (v. 8)
A' "the language of the whole earth" (v. 9)[59]

The center leg is without parallel and therefore is the focal point of the arrangement, emphasizing God's judgment on the nations and the irony that God "comes down" to witness their feeble efforts to "reach up" to heaven. The technique of key-wording creates a mirrored effect where words in the first half of each leg are repeated in its matching line (for instance, "language," "build"). However, these paralleling words primarily serve to highlight the exception to this pattern which is in lines D and D' where "let us make bricks" and "let us confuse" do not parallel. There is subtle play between the two where the Hebrew letters of *lbn* ("let us make bricks") and *nbl* ("let us confuse") are inverted. The motif of reversal is indicated by the chiastic arrangement and the inversion of word sounds. The message is clear: what the nations are building up will be torn down by God.[60]

In summary, the primary literary features important to interpretation are the climax and denouement of the event-line, narration and dialogue indicating point of view, and repetition techniques (such as key-wording, *inclusio, parallelism*, and *chiasmus*) to emphasize motifs, mark boundaries, and indicate the theme.

Theology and Narrative

We have already commented on the issue of theology and history and how narrative facilitated the Hebrew understanding of God as Lord of history. Now, we turn to the ways narrative served the theology of the authors. Four major theological ideas are presupposed in narrative's way of doing theology. First, Hebrew narrative depicts a God who has chosen to do nothing apart from human participation. Narrative shows how God accomplishes His purposes through human instrumentality in the natural processes of this time-space continuum. Because of the sinful limitations of human beings, there is an ongoing tension as to whether God's designs will ultimately triumph. Narrative is able to give these very real but diverse perspectives of human frailty and divine ability within an integrated whole. God is never treated as abstract or distant from the earthly setting.

Second, narrative reflects the "apparent" ambiguity of God's actions in the context of the vicissitudes of life.[61] The paradox of good and evil as it manifests itself in the rise and fall of individuals and nations is enhanced by narrative's commitment to telling actual events. God remains mysterious through it all; he is not a slave to human expectation. In Genesis, God tested Abraham to learn of his faith; when he passed the test, God said, "Now I *know* you love me more than your son your only son." God's knowledge is presented in a very "human" way; the tension of the account as to whether Abraham is in fact a worthy recipient of the promises is maintained by God discovering it along with the reader.

Third, narrative enhances the theology of the "word." The whole universe as well as Israel is ordered by God's spoken word. Narrative's emphasis on God's promises, foresight, and commands illustrates in the setting of human history how God's word is true, trustworthy, and effectual. What God predicts comes to pass because He alone has the authority to bring His will to completion. The concept of the effectual, spoken "word" embodies a critical difference between Israel's theology and the pagan Near East.

Finally, historical narrative bears witness to God as the architect of a universal kingdom which was foreshadowed by Israel's monarchy. Israel's kingdom was born in history through the election of Abraham, the constitution of Israel, and the appointment of David's royal house. The kingdom of God, although manifested in history, was not primarily a physical realm but rather a spiritual dominion in the hearts of a believing remnant. The destruction of Jerusalem therefore did not nullify the reign of God. The religion of Israel was never so closely identified with Israel's political state or religious institutions so that it could not survive their destruction. The kingdom persevered and its presence in the earth was proclaimed by Christ and the apostles; this kingdom is also future when it will culminate in the reign of Christ and His saints at the parousia. This concept of the kingdom of God gives both testaments a unity that undergirds all of revealed Scripture. The questions of the interpreter must be: How does this passage contribute to understanding God's kingdom purposes for His people? How does this passage contribute to the soteriological and eschatological dimensions of His theocratic rule?

Preaching in a Narrative Way

Learning to read ancient texts in light of their genre and particular rules of interpretation has impacted recent homiletical theory. There is an increasing awareness that the literary form of presentation contributes to the text's meaning. T. Long comments:

> Texts are not packages containing ideas; they are means of communication. When we ask ourselves what a text means, we are searching for the *idea* of the text. We are trying to discover the total impact upon a reader—and everything about a text works together to create that impact.[62]

We have commented that the "meaning-form" complex of communication cannot be divorced in our interpretation of a composition, neither should it be neglected in preaching. Radical *biblical* preaching is preaching theological content but also permitting the literary form of the biblical text to govern how the sermon is conceived.

The traditional pattern of logical argumentation in preaching is not appropriate for all biblical forms; narrative texts do not lend themselves easily to this kind of Aristotelian logic. To preach narrative the same way as expository discourse, the preacher must impose a line of argument foreign to the nature of the passage. This approach diminishes the power of the original writing since it neglects the *form*-meaning complex. It also detracts from the theology presupposed by the Hebrew authors who chose narrative as the best vehicle to convey their understanding of God and His work. D. Wardlaw warns that discursive preaching of narrative restricts the hearing of the text. Rational argumentation, he says, is not the way people in reality deal with the issues of life; narrative encourages change through experience and complements logic.[63] The contemporary audience, we believe, is entitled to hear and experience biblical narrative as close as possible to how their ancient counterparts enjoyed it.

Therefore, narrative theology requires narrative preaching. By narrative preaching, we do not mean simply retelling the story by synopsis, nor do we call for a contemporary story, whether told out of the preacher's own experience or drawn from lessons in history or literature. Narrative preaching is explicating the passage by an *informed* reading, that is, following the event-line and exposing how the narrational-theological features of the text reveal the underlying spiritual universals that are applicable to the modern audience.

This narrational-theological retelling depends on the interdependent factors of: (1) historical awareness, (2) literary context(s), and (3) theological perspective(s).[64] These factors do not work independently of one another; they mutually feed one another and nurture the impact of the passage on the reader.

(1) Historical awareness recognizes that the biblical text has temporal and spacial expression that must be understood by the expositor. To preach a text freed from historical moorings will be too reader-oriented, permitting the text to float. This counters the very theological presupposition that the passage rests upon, namely, that history is important and that God's revelation is dependent both on historical event and the telling of that historical event. Therefore, the historical element will impact the theological meaning derived from the passage. For the Abraham-Isaac account, the expositor must be informed about the nature of patriarchal societies in the ancient Near East, the traits of patriarchal and Canaanite religions, and the historical/geographical reference of the setting. In short, an informed reading requires the preacher's willingness to view this account in its own historical-cultural milieu as best as it can be reconstructed.

(2) Literary contexts also inform our reading of the text. *Internally*, the passage must be interpreted as narrative with its peculiar set of techniques and reading rules. The expositor must harness the structure and detect the guideposts that reveal the text's emphases—not his own! This discovery by the informed reader occurs through literary analysis. We have shown above how these features are evidenced in the story of Abraham and Isaac.

A passage must also be placed hermeneutically in the concentric circles of its *external* literary reference. In spite of the continued efforts by critical scholars to trace the complex workings of literary composition, which always includes faceless and nameless editors, we are only sure of its extant canonical shaping. The present state of the text is the heritage of the church and is the proper subject of the Christian preacher. Thus, literary analysis also impacts our theological perspective on the text as it grows in significance by new canonical contexts. Ultimately, the preacher must be Christocentric in his handling of the text. The unity of the Scriptures and the timeless principles of God's kingdom require this of the expositor. Also, because of this genetic unity a Christocentric hermeneutic is possible without the preacher manipulating the text by allegory or other methods of interpretation.

The circles of literary reference include: (1) the immediate context of the passage, (2) its role in the complex of stories in the book, (3) its contribution to the Old Testament, and (4) the Christian proclamation of the New Testament. The circles of context take in the whole canonical setting, each new circle adding to the significance of the passage for each new hearing. The canonical shaping will provide the pattern for what the contemporary audience should receive.

In this way, too, the Abraham story has a new hearing in today's contemporary audience. Genesis 22 as a pericope of the Abraham cycle traces the last steps of the patriarch's faith as he responds to God's covenant revelation of promise. All along, however, the reader wonders if Abraham is an appropriate channel of blessing upon the nations since he stumbles in the face of Pharaoh and King Abimelech and out of desperation settles for Hagar's child. In the end, Abraham is trustworthy and God secures the promises for the succeeding generations of Isaac and Jacob. The second circle of context is the "books of Moses" in which the revelation at Sinai is primary (Ex. 20). The patriarchal story was penned to inspire the faith of Abraham's prodigious seed, Israel, as they entered into covenant with the God of their fathers. The third context is the Old Testament in which Genesis is foundational to Israel's interpretation of God; the commitment of God to Abraham perpetually encouraged Israel's hope of a final triumphant restoration. Finally, the Christian community is also Abraham's offspring, "the father of all who believe" (Rom. 4:11,16, NIV) and the promises of God have their realization in those related to Christ (Gal. 3:16).

(3) Last, the passage must be considered from its theological perspective. A narrative's theology is the implied theology underlying the narrative expression. A narrative does not commonly announce its purpose; it must be derived from the general tenor of the work and particularly by the outcome of the story. This is where the context of pericope and book will help the informed reader see how a passage contributes to the intentions of

the whole composition. Once this has been determined, for instance blessing in the account of Genesis, the expositor welcomes larger "theological settings" to shape the theological contribution of the narrative. We are saying then that there must be expanding circles of theological context as well as the literary. The two work in tandem. The principles of progressive revelation and *sensus plenior* open the passage to speak to the mediatorial and universal aspects of the kingdom message.[65] The whole of Scripture is preached through the windows of each biblical passage.

In Genesis 22, the expositor asks, what does the passage say about God and God's provision of blessing? God's people and His kingdom purposes? From these questions will emerge the underlying universals that bind text and audience in any era. This is because God, God's message, and the human condition are constants.[66] The mode of expression, the models, and the historical settings are time bound but the principles are transcendent. The Old Testament is relevant to contemporary hearers by virtue of its inherent universals as revelation from God. Translation into our cultural norms is the final step where such kingdom principles as promise and obedience, judgment and grace, faith, and repentance are dressed in the modern experience of Christian discipleship.

The threefold structure of Genesis 22, the peak, and denouement indicate a three-stage movement in the story's event-line: (1) the occasion of the testing, (2) the response of faithful obedience, and (3) the outcome of God's approval. As we saw, the account parallels the initial call and promise of Genesis 12 and answers at last the gnawing question as to the nature of Abraham's once-wavering faith. The apostle James (2:21-23) understood the text in this same way and applied it as illustrative of how faith and works are necessarily compatible. The narration declared at one place, "Abraham believed God and it was reckoned to him for righteousness" (Gen. 15:6). That righteousness, which was wrought by faith, was effectually exercised unto salvation when Abraham responded to God's testing. The underlying spiritual universals of this story are reflected in our sermon outline below:

I. God tests His saints so as to confirm their faith through enduring obedience.

II. The righteous obey the Lord, trusting in His ultimate provision for deliverance.

III. The Lord rescues His saints, fulfills His promises, and rewards the righteous.

The principle of the test may be expressed this way: does the saint love the promises of God more than the God of the promises? The response: the righteous must rely on the Lord as trustworthy and yield to Him all that they are and value. The approving and securing word: the Lord blesses His people now and in the world to come.

Notes

1. G. Fackre ("Narrative Theology: An Overview," *Interpretation* 37:4 [1983]: 340-52) defines narrative theology as "discourse about God in the setting of story" (p. 343).

2. In Isaiah's structure, the narrative is a transition, linking the two poetic sections: poetry (chaps. 1–35), narrative (chaps. 36–39), and poetry (chaps. 40–66).

3. These designations are used by R. Alter (*The Art of Biblical Narrative* [New York: Basic Books, 1981]) to describe biblical narrative which he understands to be the "imaginative reenactment of history"; since biblical historiography does not require "documentable facts," he distinguishes it from modern historiography and prefers the term prose fiction (pp. 23-24, 33).

4. Historical narrative has a setting and participants which are related by "a sequential chronological framework of events" (J. Beekman, J. Callow, and M. Kopesec, *The Semantic Structure of Written Communication* [Dallas: Summer Institute of Linguistics, 1961], 37). An inclusive definition of narrative is "the presence of a story and a story-teller" (R. Scholes and R. Kellogg, *The Nature of Narrative* [New York: Oxford University Press, 1966], 4).

5. W. Martin, *Recent Theories of Narrative* (Ithaca, NY: Cornell University Press, 1986), 72.

6. M. Sternberg, *The Poetics of Biblical Narrative* (Bloomington: Indiana University Press, 1987), 23-35, esp. 31.

7. For instance, an eye-witness to Jericho's destruction (Josh. 6:26); compare public records, for instance, the book of Jashar (Josh. 10:13; 2 Sam. 1:18), the annals of Solomon (1 Kings 11:41), the annals of the kings of Israel and the annals of the kings of Judah (1 Kings 14:19,29). There are the corroborating data of extrabiblical sources as well, such as the Assyrian and Babylonian chronicles. B. Halpern (*The First Historians: The Hebrew Bible and History* [New York: Harper & Row, 1988]) in his study of the historiography of Deuteronomy to Kings (the so-called Deuteronomic Historian) concludes that the authors of Samuel and Kings appealed to two chronicles and a synchronistic king list as well as various regal lists and sources for their writing (see chap. 9). He observes, "External texts afford control over the history, chiefly during the Divided Monarchy, the time for which H(Dtr) [that is, the compiler of Deuteronomy to Kings] had most ample documentation. Almost uniformly, biblical claims are corroborated" (p. 207). This kind of appeal to documentation is not common to all biblical narrative; Halpern does not claim, for instance, that the patriarchal narratives are history. See our response below.

8. Ibid., 10.

9. Martin, *Recent Theories*, 72-74 and Sternberg, *Poetics*, 23-35. Sternberg concludes that there are no universals concerning the *literary* forms of fiction and history that may be a satisfactory basis for differentiating the two (p. 30).

10. G. Coats' *Genesis with an Introduction to Narrative Literature* (FOTL 1; Grand Rapids: Eerdmans, 1983) is a form-critical study representative of this

practice; the narratives are "works of ancient literary art" which are studied for their own sakes, having limited value for the historian in reconstructing accurately the period they recount (p. 3). The form categories, defined and discussed in his introduction, are drawn from Western literature (pp. 3-10; for instance, the sacrifice of Isaac [Gen. 22:1-19] is regarded "legend"). B. Long's form-critical study of historical literature includes the subgenres, "historical story" and "history." He defines "historical story" as a "self-contained" narrative close in kind to the popular narratives of legend and tale but differs by its purpose to recount events rather than to entertain or educate. "History" is an extensive composition consisting of numerous sources assembled around a theme (*1 Kings with an Introduction to Historical Literature* [FOTL 9; Grand Rapids: Eerdmans, 1984], 6-8). Long distinguishes "history" from historical story primarily on the basis of its use of public sources.

11. For instance, R. N. Whybray, *The Succession Narrative* (SBT 9; London: SCM, 1968), 10-19.

12. Halpern (*The First Historians*, 181, 207-40) concludes that, though the Hebrew historians were at times inaccurate and self-contradictory in their accounts, the way they used their sources indicates a commitment to writing history and not fantasy, refusing to concoct events for their own ideological purposes. We differ with Halpern's assessment that the historians could not keep their facts straight, but the importance of his study for our purposes is that the writers of Israel's monarchic history were historians.

13. Compare the discussion of T. Longman, "Storytellers and Poets in the Bible: Can Literary Artifice Be True?" *Inerrancy and Hermeneutic* (ed. H. M. Conn; Grand Rapids: Baker, 1988), 137-49.

14. Sternberg, *Poetics*, 32-34.

15. Thucydides comments on his procedure: "With reference to the speeches in this history, some were delivered before the war began, others while it was going on; some I heard myself; others I got from various quarters; it was in all cases difficult to carry them word for word in one's memory, so my habit has been to make the speakers say what was in my opinion demanded of them by the various occasions, *of course adhering as closely as possible to the general sense of what they really said*" (italics mine) (1:22). J. H. Finley ed., *The Complete Writings of Thucydides: The Peloponnesian War* (Crawley trans.; New York: Random House, 1951).

16. Alter (*The Art of Biblical Narrative*, 35-36) views narrative's dialogue as part of the biblical writer's "imaginative reenactment of history." He believes the biblical writers created the moral and psychological aspect of characters by inventing interior monologue. In his view, this exceeds the practice of Thucydides who created dialogue to represent varying positions among characters. Alter favorably compares the relationship of the biblical author and Israelite history with Shakespeare and English history. Halpern (*The First Historians*, 9, 243) takes a more conservative position; he agrees that dialogue is the historian's reconstruction, but which neither the author nor audience interpreted as literal, rather understanding it as metaphorical representation. He argues that because the modern critic fails to recognize this distinction, the biblical writers have been falsely interpreted as writers of fiction.

17. C. Fornara, *The Nature of History in Ancient Greece and Rome* (Berkeley: University of California Press, 1988), 143-68, quotation from p. 164.

18. See the discussion of I. H. Marshall, *I Believe in the Historical Jesus* (Grand Rapids: Eerdmans, 1977), 186-94.

19. C. Blomberg (*The Historical Reliability of the Gospels* [Downers Grove, IL: InterVarsity, 1987]) categorizes the variations in Jesus' sayings within the

synoptic Gospels. Blomberg defends the authenticity of the Gospels by explaining that ancient convention in reporting speech best resolves "apparent" contradictions rather than attributing them to authorial confusion or later church tradition (pp. 113-52). He comments, "Even defenders of Scripture's infallibility freely admit that the evangelists usually record only Jesus' *ipsissima vox* (actual voice) rather than his *ipsissima verba* (actual words)" (p. 118). E. Earle Ellis, taking a different approach, suggests that the Evangelists were prophets who by the Spirit uttered the words of the Risen Lord which were no less authentic than the teachings of Jesus' earthly life ("Reading the Gospels as History," *Criswell Theological Review* 3:1 [1988]: 11-15).

20. "If biblical theology is honey, its religious ideas are the honeycomb, and history is the hive in which both are created," G. Wenham, "History and the Old Testament," *History, Criticism & Faith* (ed. C. Brown; Leicester/Downers Grove, IL: InterVarsity, 1976), 20.

21. Such a theology of history creates the "paradoxes of history" where, for example, the judgment of the wicked is not always proportionately administered. This gave rise to the speculative tradition of Israel's wisdom as seen in Job and Ecclesiastes (H. Butterfield, *Christianity and History*. [History and Historiography; ed. R. Winks; New York: Garland, 1985 repr./Schribner's, 1949], 59-62).

22. The validity of the writers' theological claims were grounded in authentic historical event; see the discussion of Wenham, "History and the Old Testament," 29-30.

23. At the same time, the word of promise and anticipation is corroborated by the reality of the event to which it testifies. See. J. Goldingay, "'That You May Know That Yahweh is God': A Study in the Relationship Between Theology and Historical Truth in the Old Testament," *Tyndale Bulletin* 23 (1972): 58-93.

24. This description of narrative is used by R. E. Clements ("History and Theology in Biblical Narrative," *Horizons in Biblical Theology* 4-5 [1982-83]: 45-60) who warns that pursuing historical questions of the text is only tendential to the meaning of the passage and usually of little consequence in interpreting biblical narrative.

25. The Moabite Stone, inscribed 25 years after the reign of Omri (886-874 B.C.) refers to Israel as the "house of Omri." Omri's political success included the building of the strategically located capital of Samaria and the trade alliances with the rising maritime powers of Phoenicia.

26. The rabbis interpreted the history of Joshua through Kings as the prophetic word of God, referring to them as the Former *Prophets*.

27. Jacob Licht speaks of two aspects of biblical narrative: historiography and aesthetics. The biblical writer, he says, was historian and story teller. The what of the account is the historiography and the manner of telling is the aesthetic. We agree strongly with Licht's warning, however, that the distinction may "seem forced" and therefore they are best considered "aspects" of an integrated whole (*Storytelling in the Bible* [Jerusalem: Magnes, 1978], 13-19).

28. For bibliography and survey, consult T. Longman, *Literary Approaches to Biblical Interpretation* (Grand Rapids: Zondervan/Academie, 1987); also, R. Culley, "Exploring New Directions," *The Hebrew Bible and Its Modern Interpreters* (ed. D. Knight and G. Tucker; Philadelphia: Fortress/Chico, CA: Scholars, 1985), 167-200. Among literary critics, the best-known work is R. Alter (*The Art of Biblical Narrative*); see also the evangelical scholar, L. Ryken, *How to Read the Bible as Literature* (Grand Rapids: Zondervan/Academie, 1984).

29. Beekman, Callow, and Kopesec, *Semantic Structure*, 6-15.

30. S. Bar-Efrat, "Analysis of Structure," *Vetus Testamentum* 30:2 (1980): 154-73, distinguishes four levels of narrative structure: (1) verbal (words and phrases), (2) narrative technique (how it is arranged), (3) narrative world (characters and events), and (4) conceptual content (themes and ideas).

31. Beekman, Callow, and Kopesec, *Semantic Structure*, 32-33.

32. The relationship of surface features and semantics in biblical Hebrew has been attempted on a firmer scientific basis in the textlinguistic proposal of R. Longacre, *The Grammar of Discourse* (New York: Plenum, 1983) and "Interpreting Biblical Stories," in *Discourse and Literature: New Approaches to the Analysis of Literary Genres* (ed. T. van Dijk; Philadelphia: John Benjamins, 1985), 169-85. His theory is applied to the Joseph pericope in *Joseph: A Story of Divine Providence* (Winona Lake, IN: Eisenbrauns, 1989). In particular, R. Bergen has shown how discourse linguistics reveals the prominence markers in our sample passage ("The Role of Genesis 22:1-19 in the Abraham Cycle: A Computer-Assisted Textual Interpretation" *Criswell Theological Review* 4 (1990): 313-26). Since our essay is for the general reader who may not have facility with Hebrew, this paper will not refer in depth to the language's specifics.

33. Beekman, Callow, and Kopesec, *Semantic Structure*, 37-38, 135.

34. Longacre, *Joseph*, 18.

35. Ibid., 22-23, 34-35, 49.

36. Bergen, "Role," 313-17.

37. For a discussion of the theme of "blessing" in Genesis, see J. Goldingay, "The Patriarchs in Scripture and History," *Essays in on the Patriarchal Narratives* (eds., A. R. Millard and D. J. Wiseman; Leicester: InterVarsity/Winona Lake, IN: Eisenbrauns, 1983), 1-34, esp. 3-27. Also, A. Ross, *Creation and Blessing* (Grand Rapids: Baker, 1988), 65-69; C. Westermann, *Blessing in the Bible and the Life of the Church* (Philadelphia: Fortress, 1978).

38. See G. Rendsburg, *The Redaction of Genesis* (Winona Lake, IN: Eisenbrauns, 1986), 27-52 (esp. 28-29) which discusses and adds to U. Cassuto's analysis in *From Noah to Abraham* (Jerusalem: Magnes, 1964). Rendsburg considers chaps. 23–25 of the Abraham cycle as transitional to the Jacob sequence.

39. See Bergen ("Role," 322-25): (1) Abraham tested, (2) heir denied, (3) Abraham the altar builder, (4) separation from family, (5) family, (6) blessing, and (7) possession of the land.

40. See N. Sarna, *Understanding Genesis* (New York: McGraw-Hill, 1966), 60-61; Rendsburg, *Redaction*, 31-35.

41. The text is tantalizingly silent about the return of Isaac. The passage leaves it to the reader's imagination that Isaac was among those who went on to Beersheba (22:19a).

42. Bergen, "Role," 320.

43. A. Berlin, among others, draws the analogy between cinematography and how the reader views the events through the narrator's lens (*Poetics and Interpretation of Biblical Narrative* [Sheffield: Almond, 1983], 44).

44. Licht, *Storytelling in the Bible*, 102-3, 120.

45. Cf. Alter, *Art of Biblical Narrative*, 114-30; Berlin, *Poetics*, 23-42; Longacre, *Joseph*, 141-57.

46. E. Auerbach, *Mimesis* (Princeton: University Press, 1953), 10-11.

47. L. Toombs, "The Problematic of Preaching from the Old Testament," *Interpretation* 23 (1969): 308.

48. See the discussion of C. G. Kromminga, "Remember Lot's Wife: Preaching Old Testament Narrative Texts," *Calvin Theological Journal* 18 (1983): 32-46.

49. Berlin, *Poetics*, 57-58.

50. Sternberg, *Poetics*, 89.

51. Berlin in *Poetics*, 55-56 summarizes this discussion by B. Upensky, *A Poetics of Composition* (Berkeley: University of California Press, 1973).

52. Berlin, *Poetics*, 66-68.

53. Cf. Alter, *Art of Biblical Narrative*, 92-97.

54. The high incidence of repetition in the Flood account (Gen. 6–9) has been commonly analyzed as evidence of a reworking of several disparate literary sources; alternatively, the repetitions have been explained as a coherence device by G. Wenham, "The Coherence of the Flood Narrative," *Vetus Testamentum* 28 (1978): 336-48; and R. Longacre, "The Discourse Structure of the Flood Narrative," *Journal of the American Academy of Religion* 47 (1979): 89-133.

55. Licht, *Storytelling*, 74, 86.

56. See Alter's discussion for this example, *Art of Biblical Narrative*, 90-91.

57. J. Welch, ed., *Chiasmus in Antiquity* (Hildesheim: Gerstenberg, 1981).

58. 1–2 Chronicles and the memoirs of Ezra–Nehemiah are joined by the repetition of the Cyrus edict which closes 2 Chronicles (36:22-23) and begins Ezra (1:1-3a). The rabbis, however, rearranged the books by placing Ezra-Nehemiah before 1–2 Chronicles in the Hebrew canon. By doing so, the Cyrus edict begins and closes the collection (Ezra–Neh–Chronicles), producing an *inclusio* and a loose chiastic parallelism. Compare Y. Radday, "Chiasmus in Hebrew Biblical Narrative," *Chiasmus in Antiquity* (ed. J. Welch; Hildesheim: Gerstenberg, 1981), 84-86, which shows the "chiastic tendencies" of the Pentateuch.

59. See G. Wenham, *Genesis 1–15*, vol. 1 in *Word Biblical Commentary* (Waco, TX: Word, 1987), 235.

60. The chiastic structure and implications were first observed by J. P. Fokkelman, *Narrative Art in Genesis* (Assen: Van Gorcum, 1975), 15, 22, 29-38; see also Ross, *Creation and Blessing* 234-37.

61. Alter, *Art of Biblical Narrative*, 153-54.

62. T. Long, *Preaching and the Literary Forms of the Bible* (Philadelphia: Fortress, 1989), 12.

63. D. Wardlaw, "Introduction: The Need for New Shapes," *Preaching Biblically: Creating Sermons in the Shape of Scripture* (ed. D. Wardlaw; Philadelphia: Westminster, 1983), 18-20.

64. S. Greidanus (*The Modern Preacher and the Ancient Text* [Grand Rapids: Eerdmans/Downers Grove, IL: InterVarsity, 1988], 213-21) calls for "holistic interpretation" in preaching, which includes literary, historical, and theological facets.

65. For a discussion of these principles of interpretation, see W. S. LaSor, "The *Sensus Plenior* and Biblical Interpretation," *Scripture, Tradition, and Interpretation* (eds. W. W. Gasque and W. S. LaSor; Grand Rapids: Eerdmans, 1978), 260-77.

66. L. Toombs ("Problematic of Preaching," 302-14) comments that the problem of relevancy begins with the false supposition of preachers that they must *make* the text relevant; the proper task of the preacher is to *show* how the text is relevant. Toombs emphasizes the ancient human condition as the key and he includes the purposes and grace of God as critical to relevancy. We emphasize the relevancy in what the text says about God and His relationship to human history, while recognizing that the historical conditions of the first audience must have some analogy to the present audience to have relevancy.

2

Preaching
Old Testament Law

Robert D. Bergen

Introduction

The glory and pride of Israel was the Law—the Torah—that God gave to Moses in the Sinai wilderness. Songs praised it, festivals celebrated it, and lives were measured by it. Torah was, in the words of the apostle Paul, "the embodiment of knowledge and truth," which enabled one who knew it to be "a guide for the blind, a light for those who are in the dark, an instructor of the foolish," and "a teacher of infants" (Rom. 2:18-20, NIV). But what authority should Old Testament law possess within the Christian church today? To what extent should it dictate the daily conduct of a Christian's life? Before exploring answers to these questions, it is necessary to provide some definitions, boundaries, and background for the discussion.

Definition of Old Testament Law

Old Testament vocabulary is rich with terms referring to the written materials and oral traditions that have guided Israelite society since its inception. The most important term is *torah*. Found 221 times in the Bible, this word is often translated as "law," "instruction," or "teaching."[1] Within the context of Israelite religious life Torah came to refer to the written and oral instruction originating with Moses during Israel's Sinai experience. Though other ordinances were added by later leaders, these supplemental materials possessed only secondary authority to those attributed to Moses.

The Pentateuch was the written portion of the Torah of Moses and corresponds to the biblical books of Genesis, Exodus, Leviticus, Numbers, and Deuteronomy. While it may seem a bit surprising that these books should be called *Law*, since they contain far more narrative than actual legislation, Israelites recognized that both the stories and the legal materials contained valuable guidelines for living a God-pleasing life.

Eight other Hebrew terms were used to refer to the legal materials associated with Moses' Sinai revelation. These are: *mispat, miswa, hoq/huqqa, dabar, piqqud, edut, aseret haddebarim*, and *berit*. The first five of these were used somewhat interchangeably to refer to the large number of "commandments," "judgments," or "regulations" given by God to the people of Israel. The next two terms are used to refer specifically to the Ten Commandments (Ex. 20:1-17; Deut. 5:6-21). The final term, normally translated "covenant," is a general word that can refer to the entire body of legislation.

Jewish society also considered the Mosaic and rabbinical oral traditions to be authoritative, and thus law. However, within the present discussion the term "Law" will be used in a narrow sense to refer only to the judicial portions of the Pentateuch.[2]

Characterization of Old Testament Law

Based on a tradition extending back into pre-Christian times, Jewish rabbis have recognized the existence of two distinct sets of laws in the Pentateuch: those which apply to non-Jews, and those which apply specifically to the Israelite community. The Noachide laws, those intended to guide the behavior of Gentiles, are derived from divine statements made to Adam and Noah in the first nine chapters of Genesis. In the earliest periods of Judaism no unanimous agreement existed as to exactly what those laws were, but today the Noachide laws are usually understood to be the following: prohibitions against idolatry, sexual sin, eating from a living animal, human bloodshed, blasphemy, and theft; and the establishment of a legal system, presumably to enforce the previous commands.[3]

For members of the Israelite community the demands were much more rigorous. A total of 613 laws applicable to Jews were identified in the Pentateuch. These regulations are sometimes divided into three broad categories according to the issues they address: moral, civil, and ceremonial.

According to this scheme, moral laws are those that address the matter of personal values: respect for God, human life, parents, marriage, personal property, and reputation.[4] Civil laws are those that deal with such issues as the maintenance of public safety and welfare; rights of widows, orphans, slaves, and foreigners; property rights; and restitution for theft or injury.[5] Ceremonial laws address issues relating to the cultus: sacrifices, holy days, priesthood, dietary regulations, and purity rites.[6] A more traditional Jewish understanding of the Law recognizes six different legislative categories: Seeds, Festivals, Women, Damages, Holy Things, and Purifications.[7]

The Israelites did not attempt to separate "religious" laws from "secular" ones, as though one was distinguishable from or perhaps more important than the other. For the Israelite community of faith, all the laws found in the Pentateuch were sanctioned by God, and therefore each was to be obeyed with diligence.

The Influence of Law in Old Testament Society

The Law of Moses became the standard by which human, but particularly Israelite, conduct was judged. The writers of Scripture evaluated each period of their national history on the basis of the people's obedience to the Mosaic law. The biblical record indicates that Israel's adherence to the Torah was uneven at best.

After receiving these divinely mandated laws, Israel seems to have wasted no time in breaking them. Even while still at Mount Sinai, site of the original covenant revelation, they violated the prohibition against idolatry (Ex. 32:1-25). Throughout Moses' lifetime Israel continued to have difficulties complying with the provisions of the Law (Num. 15:32-36; 25:1-5).

Though leadership changes within nations have often been accompanied by changes in public policy, Moses' successor Joshua retained the Sinai covenant as the legal standard for the fledgling nation Israel (Josh. 1:7). The Torah's ordinances guided the Israelites during the critical period of the conquest of Palestine (Josh. 8:30-35). Joshua also made provision for Israel to follow the mandates of Mosaic law even after his death (Josh. 24:1-27).

However, in the years immediately following him, no strong leader arose in Israel to consolidate the tribes and enforce Mosaic laws. Instead, for the next considerable period of time a series of judges exercised only sporadic, localized influence in teaching and enforcing the judgments of God. Concern for adherence to the Torah decreased, resulting in social, political, and spiritual degradation. Social obligations toward the weaker members of society were neglected (Ruth 4:6; compare Lev. 25:25; Deut. 25:5-6); covenantal standards of sexual conduct were openly violated (Judg. 19:2,22-26; 1 Sam. 2:22); tribal leadership condoned the kidnaping of Israelites by Israelites (Judg. 21:16-23); and idolatrous and covetous practices were institutionalized by members of the priestly tribe of Levi (Judg. 17:5-13; 1 Sam. 2:13-17).

These covenant violations were not overlooked by Yahweh, who "was very angry with Israel and said, 'Because this nation has violated the covenant . . . I will no longer drive out before them any of the nations Joshua left when he died'" (Judg. 2:20-21, NIV). The biblical writer, in fact, portrayed the period of the judges as an object lesson in the tragic consequences of disobedience to Yahweh's revealed will. Violation of the Torah produced economic loss (Judg. 6:3-6), foreign oppression (Judg. 3:8,14; 4:2-3; 10:7-8; 13:1), and loss of life (Judg. 9:5,49; 12:6).

In describing the reigns of the forty-three monarchs who ruled united Israel and the divided kingdoms, the theological historian who wrote Samuel and Kings measured each person and nation using the same yardstick applied during the period of the judges. Rulers and kingdoms were evaluated on the basis of their adherence to the founding principles of Israel.

David was reckoned as the greatest king in Israelite history because he was a man after God's own heart who walked in God's ways and obeyed His statutes and commands (1 Sam. 13:14; 1 Kings 3:14). His son Solomon's apostasy, expressed through disobedience to the Torah in the latter part of his reign (1 Kings 11:1-8) served as the underlying cause for the division of Israel into two kingdoms (1 Kings 11:9-13).

The creation of the new political entities of Judah and Israel after the death of Solomon provided an opportunity for return to Mosaic law and a renewed period of blessing and promise (1 Kings 11:29-33,37-38). Yahweh promised to make the dynasty of Jeroboam I, first monarch of the Northern Kingdom, as enduring as that of David's, if Jeroboam I would commit his life to obedience to the Mosaic law (1 Kings 11:38). However, instead of initiating a national return to the Torah, Jeroboam I substituted some of its key aspects with policies of his own (1 Kings 12:31-33). Jeroboam I's enactments, which amounted to a rejection of the law of Moses, were so offensive to the biblical writer that they became the standard by which the wickedness of all future Northern kings was judged.[8] Because the nation continued to follow Jeroboam I's policies in preference to the Torah, national destruction and exile became inevitable (2 Kings 17:7-23).

Judah, the Southern Kingdom, did not avoid the cursed effects of disobedience either. Though its national history extended some 140 years beyond that of the Northern Kingdom and was evaluated more positively, disobedience to the covenant established at Sinai ultimately brought a catastrophic end to the nation. As Josiah, the last king of Judah to be favorably evaluated by the biblical writers, noted: "Great is the Lord's anger that burns against us because our fathers have not obeyed the words of this book" (2 Kings 22:13, NIV). Accordingly, the Babylonians brought the existence of Judah to an end through a series of mass deportations and, in 586 B.C., the destruction of the capital city Jerusalem.

Orthodox members of the exilic community, reflecting on Israel's tumultuous history, concluded that the Israelite people's only hope for survival and prosperity lay in their obedience to the revealed Law of the Lord. Consequently, when provided with an opportunity to reestablish a political state in Palestine, they made it one strictly regulated by the dictates of the Torah.[9] The Old Testament historical accounts conclude with the picture of a Jewish state firmly controlled by religious conservatives determined to prevent a disastrous repetition of divine judgment on a Torah-rejecting people.

The Role of Old Testament Law in the First-Century Church

Throughout history Christians have looked to the pages of the New Testament for direction in determining normative beliefs and practices. Working on the assumption that an understanding of the New Testament's use of Pentateuchal law is an essential beginning point for deciding how to use this Law in the church today, we will make some general observations and then investigate selected New Testament passages.

Three Basic Views

As it turns out, one of the more debated topics in contemporary New Testament scholarship regards the status that the first-century Christian community granted to the Torah.[10] Three basic positions have been set forth in modern study regarding the Bible's understanding of the relationship of Mosaic law to the Christian faith. These may be described by the terms discontinuity, continuity, and mediating.

Scholars who hold to the discontinuity position suggest that no essential relationship exists between Mosaic law and Christianity. For them, Christ through his atoning work abolished the law. The primary text used to support this position is Romans 10:4. Other passages which seem to confirm this view include Romans 3:21; 2 Corinthians 3:17-18; Galatians 2:18; Ephesians 2:14; and Philippians 3:2-11.[11]

Other experts emphasize an essential continuity between Mosaic law and Christianity. Preferring to interpret Romans 10:4 to mean that Jesus is the *fulfillment* (*telos*) of the Law, they understand Christ to be the culminative fruit produced by the Old Testament root. The most important verse used to support this view is Romans 3:31. Other pertinent Pauline passages include Romans 2:12-13; 3:21,27; 7:10,12,14; 8:2,4; 13:8-10; 1 Corinthians 7:17-24; 9:21; Galatians 3:24; 5:13-14; and 6:2.[12]

Still other scholars take a mediating position on the question of the relationship between Christian faith and Mosaic law. These individuals often suggest that since the time of Christ, law no longer operates as a means of obtaining favor from God; however, portions of it continue to possess authority as an expression of God's will. Usually the Ten Commandments and other ethical portions of the Torah are thought to have a binding force on Christians today.[13]

Exegesis of Key Passages

The New Testament writers wove much of their literary fabric using threads pulled from the spindle of Mosaic law. Almost every page of the New Testament contains either direct or indirect reference to regulations found in the Torah. Because of this, the present study cannot provide an exhaustive treatment of the New Testament's use of these laws. However, a brief treatment of a few of the key passages will provide some help in determining what role the law of Moses played in the first-century church.

Matthew 5:17-22.—In this passage Jesus portrayed himself as an ally, not an opponent of Mosaic law. His stated purpose in ministry was "to fulfill" (*plērōsai*) the law (v. 17). In the context of Matthew, "the gospel of Christian Rabbinism,"[14] this statement seems to mean that Jesus came to proclaim and be the fullness of the law's intent.[15] Stern warnings were issued for anyone who violated the commands and encouraged others to do the same (v. 19; compare 23:2-3).

In His remarkable commentary on the Sixth Commandment of the Decalogue, Jesus indicated that the divine purpose of this prohibition included not only the avoidance of the physical act of murder but also the mental process which produced it (vv. 21-22). In this passage Jesus did not nullify the claim of Mosaic law; instead, He clarified it. The demands of God upon individuals reached even to the hidden aspects of each being.

Matthew 22:34-40.—This brief pericope, recorded also in the Gospels of Mark (12:28-34) and Luke (10:25-28), reveals the innermost mechanism controlling Jesus' interpretation of the law. Though Jesus was obviously aware that hundreds of strictures were present in the Torah, yet He indicated here— somewhat surprisingly, perhaps—that not all of them were of equal importance. In fact, all the imperatives present in divine revelation were actually secondary spinoffs derived from the commands to love God and to love one's neighbor as oneself.

Jesus' words imply that every law in the writings of Moses— and elsewhere in Hebrew Scriptures—must be understood as a command to express some facet of love for God and humanity. All Mosaic law was fundamentally a call to live a life of love. Furthermore, it was impossible to separate the command to love God from the command to love people. Therefore, any interpretation of a commandment that hindered people from expressing love for others and oneself was a false interpretation.

That this radical approach to law was what the first-century church understood Jesus to be teaching is evident from the apostolic writings. "Dear friends, let us love one another, for love comes from God. Everyone who loves has been born of God and knows God" (1 John 4:7, NIV; compare 2:7-11; 3:11; 4:11). "Love is the fulfillment of the law" (Rom. 13:10, NIV); in fact, "the entire law is summed up in a single command: 'Love your neighbor as yourself'" (Gal. 5:14, NIV; compare 6:2; Jas. 2:8).

Mark 2:23-3:5.—Perhaps the most obvious sign of submission to Mosaic law was observance of the sabbath through a temporary cessation of labor (compare Ex. 20:8-11). Jesus challenged the prevailing ideas of what this command meant through two confrontations with the Pharisees recorded in this passage.

In the first situation, Jesus affirmed the right of individuals to attend to human needs on the sabbath. When questioned about His disciples' apparent violation of the harvesting prohibition (compare Ex. 34:21), Jesus pointed to a revered Israelite leader who also violated a requirement of the Torah in order to satisfy legitimate human needs. He implied that since David was not condemned for his violation, his actions must not have transgressed the fundamental spirit of the law. Jesus, as Lord of the sabbath, then suggested by way of clarification that the primary intent behind God's creation of the sabbath was to benefit people, not to handcuff them (2:28).[16]

In 3:1-5 Jesus demonstrated the positive purpose of the sabbath by using that day to heal a man with a shriveled hand. In the midst of a synagogue service, Jesus publicly challenged the Pharisees with a pair of rhetorical questions. With them He suggested that the sabbath is a time to act, not rest; it is a weekly call to affirm and save life. With these actions and teachings, Jesus dealt a blow to centuries of encrusted misunderstandings regarding proper conduct on this day.

Jesus did not here disclaim the validity of the Fourth Commandment of the Decalogue; He merely demonstrated its underlying purpose. Like all other ordinances in the Torah, this regulation must be interpreted in light of the twin commands to love God and to love one's neighbor as oneself (12:29-31). The sabbath was given as an act of divine love and must be used in the spirit it was given.

Acts 15:1-21.—In this tension-filled narrative a decisive confrontation occurred between rival factions of the first-century Christian community. The issue separating them was the place of Pentateuchal law in the Christian life. More specifically, the basic question was, What role does obedience to Mosaic law play in the process of salvation? An influential portion of the first-century Christian community taught that submission to the law was part and parcel of salvation (vv. 1,5). For them, it seems, Torah was the Holy Place into which people had to pass in order to come to Christ, the Holy of Holies.

Convinced otherwise by personal experience and divine revelation, Paul, Barnabas, and Peter argued vehemently against this view. In keeping with prophetic promises, God had given His Spirit to Gentiles who had never submitted to the demands of Jewish law (vv. 7-9,12-18). Circumcision and other physical evidences of acquiescence to the law were therefore fundamentally irrelevant to right relationship with God. People were saved only through faith in Jesus Christ, not through obedience to the law (v. 11). Since Torah regulations had no power to save, demanding adherence to them as a prerequisite for coming to salvation in Christ amounted to using law as a weapon of damnation. Such a use of law was totally contrary to the teaching of Christ. Therefore, obedience to the Torah would not be required of Gentiles prior to their acceptance into the Christian community.

However, a delicate balance needed to be struck in this matter. Though it was true that Gentiles did not need to submit to Jewish laws before becoming Christians, it was still true that they should use law as a means of expressing love for humanity. Jews believed Gentiles needed to submit to the Noachide laws of the Pentateuch.[17] Therefore, in order to avoid offending unsaved Jews and Pharisaic Jewish Christians, thereby driving them away from Christianity, Christ's law of love dictated that Gentiles should submit to these minimal regulations (vv. 20-21).

Romans 3:19-22.—The apostle Paul, who studied under the great rabbi Gamaliel, probably knew the teachings of the Torah as well as any Christian ever has. He was uniquely qualified to discuss the relevance of Pentateuchal law to the church. In the present passage Paul concisely stated two reasons for the church to utilize Mosaic law.[18] First, law is valuable in that it creates a consciousness of sin within those who know it (v. 20). Furthermore, it testifies to God's gift of righteousness that comes through faith in Jesus Christ (vv. 21-22).

Paul thus understood law's function to be pedagogical and Christological. By presenting unambiguous standards of behavior, Old Testament law invites those who study it to measure their lives against divinely set standards. Doing so naturally quickens the moral sensibilities of those who study it. Ultimately, it also condemns them, because no one totally succeeds in fulfilling it. Additionally, law also points to Christ. Principles are taught, patterns are established, and tensions are created by these regulations that prepare its readers for submitting to the call of Christ.

The Torah demands personal righteousness, but it cannot produce it (v. 19). Therefore, Mosaic law ultimately forces those who study it to look outside the law for help. Righteousness can be obtained only from the Giver of the law, not from the law itself. Jesus Christ is God's provision for the law's demand of righteousness. As Paul states, "righteousness from God comes through faith in Jesus Christ to all who believe" (v. 22, NIV).

Hebrews 9:1–10:4.—The Book of Hebrews, the longest sermon recorded in the New Testament, draws heavily upon Mosaic law to support its thesis that Jesus Christ was both the high priest and atoning sacrifice establishing a new and superior covenantal relationship between God and humanity (compare especially 9:6-27).[19] Central to the logic in this book is the contention that Mosaic "law is only a shadow of the good things that are coming" in Christ—"not the realities themselves" (10:1a, NIV). That is, the law—at least its cultic legislation—was given to Israel to symbolize and prefigure the life and ministry of Christ. The sacred tabernacle was only an inferior copy of "the greater and more perfect tabernacle that is not man-made," which Christ Himself entered (vv. 11-12, NIV). Gifts and sacrifices prescribed in the Torah were "only a matter of food and drink and various ceremonial washings—external regulations applying until the time of the new order" (9:9-10, NIV). The daily slaughter of animals at the temple foreshadowed the fact that "Christ was sacrificed once to take away the sins of many people" (9:28, NIV).

Christ came to do what the law, itself a secondary or derived reality, could not do. Since "it is impossible for the blood of bulls and goats to take away sins" (10:4, NIV), obedience to the law could not save an individual. At best, adherence to Torah regulations could produce an outward cleanness (9:13). On the other hand, Christ "appeared once for all at the end of the ages to do away with sin by the sacrifice of himself" (v. 26, NIV). Indeed, "the blood of Christ, who through the eternal Spirit offered himself unblemished to God, cleanse(s) our consciences from acts that lead to death" (v. 14, NIV).

Summary of the New Testament Position

A conscientious reading of the New Testament yields three primary impressions concerning the first-century church's view of Mosaic law. First, the church believed that the Torah was a divine gift that possessed great value. The New Testament writers warmly embraced and affirmed its ethical and social teachings. The church of the first-century clearly accepted its behavioral guidelines as authoritative and normative.

At the same time, the New Testament teaches that Mosaic law is utterly incapable of providing spiritual regeneration. Obedience to the regulations handed down at Sinai does not produce personal righteousness or right standing before God. That righteousness can come only through a personal relationship with Jesus Christ.

Related to the previous point, the New Testament writers clearly understood the law—especially in its ceremonial legislation—to prefigure and anticipate the life and ministry of Jesus Christ. The legal demands associated with the cultus established a pattern which prepared individuals to understand the deeper meaning of Christ's coming.

Suggested Uses of Old Testament Law
for the Church Today

The previous study suggests that the law of Moses did indeed play a significant shaping role in both Old and New Testament societies. We will now explore inappropriate and appropriate functions of the Torah for the Christian community today.

Inadequate Perspectives

Fully Valid.—If one accepts the teachings of Jesus and the apostles as authoritative, then he or she must evaluate the role of Mosaic law fundamentally differently than a first-century Jew would have. Circumcision, dietary restrictions, animal sacrifices, and the keeping of the sabbath and other prescribed holy days were an essential part of the Torah's demands on God's Old Testament community. Yet the New Testament repeatedly affirms that these play no necessary role in Christian living.[20] At a *minimum*, therefore, we must recognize that the ceremonial requirements of the law are no longer in force for one who follows Christ.[21]

Valueless.—It might seem logical to conclude that since "Christ is the end of the law," the Torah possesses no value for the Christian. However, this conclusion would also be inaccurate. The personal qualities of respect for authority, life, marriage, and property enjoined in the Ten Commandments stand at the core of all Western and Middle Eastern law codes today. The moral laws of the Torah provide a time-tested blueprint for integrated personal and social living. Unlike secular codes of behavior, these rules claim to be supremely authoritative, having been established by the God of the universe. For one who accepts it, this claim to divine authority gives biblical law a binding strength surpassing that of all other systems.

For the Christian there is another reason to recognize the value of Old Testament law. A careful reading of the New Testament suggests that Christ Himself believed that at least some of the laws of Moses have eternal value.[22] Even Jesus' well-known "but I tell you" statements in Matthew[23] do not curb the force of Mosaic law; they actually affirm and extend certain of its demands. Furthermore, it should also be noted that leaders of the first-century Christian community seem to have had no qualms about keeping the law. As E. E. Ellis notes concerning the apostle Paul:

He had his young Jewish colleague Timothy circumcised, and he carried out a religious vow; he emulated the custom of diaspora synagogues by taking an offering to Jerusalem, celebrated the Pentecost festival there, and participated in purification ceremonies at the temple. He knows that, since Christ has come, these practices are theological adiaphora (for Jewish Christians), nevertheless he apparently finds a practical value in them.[24]

For Paul the Christian, it seems, the primary purpose of keeping the law was evangelistic. Obeying the dictates of Mosaic law was useful and good so long as it was done to establish or maintain relationships in which the gospel might be shared (1 Cor. 9:20).

Proper Uses of Old Testament Law

Beyond the evangelistic use of the law suggested by Paul's example above, I propose that there are six specific ways that Old Testament law can be used today by individual Christians and the Christian community at large.

Behavioral.—The Torah is not a road map charting a magical path of conduct that leads to external life. However, it does serve as an invaluable guide to existence on this side of eternity. Its value is multiplied in a society that encourages individuals to practice "values clarification" without providing adequate guidance in the undertaking. Many people who become Christians without previous religious training are especially in need of an unambiguous standard of conduct by which to guide their lives. The clear, concise guidelines contained in the Torah, particularly the Decalogue, provide a compass directing the morally ignorant toward God-pleasing conduct.

I believe that Christians involved in discipling recent converts ought to make certain that each new convert has studied—and even memorized—the Ten Commandments. Other sections of the law that deal with moral and civil responsibilities should also be included in an adequate discipleship program.

Analogical.—God revealed the law of Moses to a preindustrial, tribal society. The laws were ideally suited to the social structure and needs of their civilization. But because of changed social, technological, and political conditions, many of the laws do not directly apply to western society today. For example, the ordinance regarding habitually violent oxen that gore slaves (Ex. 21:32) does not relate to a situation that normally occurs in our culture.

However, this law might be made relevant to contemporary situations through the power of analogy. The modern counterparts to oxen and slaves might be machinery and employees. If taken this way, then the law can be understood to provide guidelines concerning the responsibilities of employers to employees, or perhaps manufacturers to consumers. Similarly, the command not to sacrifice children to Molech (Lev. 18:21) might be taken by analogy as a prohibition of child abuse or a demand for the proper religious instruction of children.

Though Mosaic law must be used in this way with caution, in some instances it can prove useful in addressing contemporary issues for which no explicit New Testament teaching exists. Because the Torah presents a collection of ancient precedents for dealing with more-or-less analogous modern situations, it can provide some insight into divine counsel.

Christological.—Following the example set by Jesus Himself (Luke 24:27), the Christian community has always interpreted the Torah as a work relating to the person and work of Christ. In fact, the apostle Paul seems to suggest that the very purpose of Mosaic law was to prepare to accept Jesus as the Messiah: "the law was put in charge to lead us to Christ" (Gal. 3:24a, NIV; compare Rom. 3:21-22). For the New Testament writers, Christ is the focal point of the parabolic mirror of Old Testament Scripture, of which the law is a part.

The church can understand the significance of Jesus' life only when it understands the legal system established in the Torah. New Testament presentations of Jesus as the "Lamb of God, who takes away the sin of the world" (John 1:29, NIV) and Christ's body as the curtain through which people must pass to enter the Most Holy Place (Heb. 10:19-20) indicate that the church is expected to interpret at least certain details of the Mosaic cultic law as "a shadow of the good things that are coming" in Christ (Heb. 10:1, NIV). The New Testament leaves no doubt that aspects of Israelite worship were divinely intended to be representative of realities found uniquely in the person of Christ.

If contemporary Christians follow the logic of the New Testament writers, they will unapologetically read the Torah—especially the ceremonial laws—with the expectation of learning more about the purpose and ministry of Christ. Thus, a sermon about the atoning death of Christ could legitimately include a reading of Exodus 12:5-6. This passage, which directed Israel to kill an unblemished male lamb as part of the climatic event of the Passover season, can easily be seen as a Scripture which helped prepare Israel for the coming of Christ. Leading Christians to a thorough knowledge of Mosaic law actually ought to have the effect of leading them closer to Christ.

Background.—First-century Jewish society was forged under the hammer of Mosaic law. Its social structure, religious institutions, marketplace, ethical code, and calendar all bore the imprint of the Torah. Many of the New Testament narratives focus on incidents that depicted Jesus and the apostles challenging the Torah-based norms of their culture. The record of these encounters served as an essential guide to the earliest followers of Jesus, helping them to clarify the distinctives that set Christianity apart from its Jewish roots. For many in the community, these stories provided needed answers to the question, What does it mean to be a *Christian* Jew?

Direct and indirect allusions to the Torah abound also in the nonhistorical sections of the New Testament. It is evident that the minds of the New Testament writers were saturated with a knowledge of Mosaic law. It was the primary reservoir from which their illustrations were drawn and the stem supporting the flower of their ethical teachings.

In light of these facts, and because we affirm the value of a holistic approach to biblical hermeneutics, evangelical Christians are obligated to know and teach the laws of the Torah. A proper understanding of the New Testament cannot be achieved apart from the fulfillment of this responsibility. Therefore, most Bible studies or expository sermons on New Testament passages should contain at least an explanatory reference to some portion of Mosaic law. In a study of John the Baptist (Matt. 3:4; Mark 1:6), this could involve a reference to Old Testament dietary regulations (Lev. 11:22); in one of Jesus' early childhood (Luke 2:22-24), reference to purity regulations (Lev. 12:8); in one of homosexuality (1 Cor. 6:9), reference to the prohibition in the Torah (Lev. 18:22); in one of the heavenly Jerusalem (Rev. 21:12), reference to the priestly breastpiece (Ex. 28:21).

Illustrative.—Anyone who has a Bible teaching ministry needs a continual supply of good and varied illustrations. A proven source from which illustrations can be found are the Mosaic laws. Certainly the writers of the New Testament drew from this source. References to circumcision of the heart (Rom. 2:29; compare Gen. 17:10; Deut. 10:16), yeast as a corrupting agent (Matt. 16:6; compare Ex. 12:18-19), and the unequal yoking of animals (2 Cor. 6:14; compare Deut. 22:10) to illustrate truths about the Christian life suggest that the church today can do the same. Discrete and creative use of these and other images from the law can increase the interest level and liveliness of biblical exposition.

In Spiritual Warfare.—Probably the most subjective—yet certainly a valid—use of Mosaic law is as a resource in dealing with temptation. Satan regularly assaults believers' souls and usually aims his attacks at the points of greatest vulnerability. During these invisible, internal onslaughts, Christians are enticed to choose some course of action destined to degrade or ruin their life and witness. Whether the conflict involves lust, hatred, materialism, apostasy, or some other sin, the Torah can be used as a strong ally, helping the soul to withstand Satan's most determined efforts. By following Jesus' example and silently or vocally quoting the relevant commands/prohibitions found in Mosaic law (Matt. 4:4,7,10), we reinforce our commitment to do the right and shun the wrong.

For this reason, it is a good idea for Christians to memorize key moral laws in the Pentateuch. At the very least, they should be able to quote the Ten Commandments.

Summary

The legal code found in the Torah possesses no power to save the soul of an individual. Nevertheless, Mosaic law is "holy, righteous, and good" (Rom. 7:12, NIV) and should be studied diligently by Christians. In its moral requirements it teaches a value system that produces sterling character and stable social institutions. In its civil requirements it teaches compassion and responsibility in business practices, as well as sensitivity to the needs of the most easily neglected persons of the community. In its ceremonial requirements it creates a pattern of expectation that is satisfied fully in the person and ministry of Jesus Christ. The law is truly able to make us "wise for salvation" of body, soul, and society "through faith in Christ Jesus" (2 Tim. 3:15, NIV).

A Demonstration of the Use of OT Law

"Redeem the Firstborn!"
Exodus 13:11-16

God spoke the words found in this passage while Israel was still reveling in its first days of freedom from Egypt. The words were bright with hope, for they included the promise of a successful end to Israel's journey from bondage. In accordance with the oath He had made and affirmed repeatedly, Yahweh would bring His people into the land of the Canaanites.

I. Because God Demands Redemption (vv. 11-13a)

The Israelites were not to enter their promised land empty handed. They must carry with them a ritual pregnant with meaning and heavy in cost. That ritual, apparently one similar to those found in other Semitic cultures during the time of Moses, involved the shedding of a firstborn male's blood. Yahweh required the Israelites to "give over" (heᶜebir) to Him the firstborn of every living being within the households of the Israelite families.

Why did God require this? Perhaps it was to remind His people that the land into which they would enter was not their own—it was Yahweh's land. He was the possessor of Canaan; they were His subjects, residing there at His good pleasure. In handing over to Him the firstborn of all living, they were paying to Him His due as their sovereign.

The sacrifice certainly served as a confession of faith. Each time the command was fulfilled, the one making the sacrifice was in effect agreeing that God was the promise-keeping King who faithfully brought Israel into His domain.

In this way life was used to testify to God's lordship over all that is. If Yahweh could exercise dominion over the most prized and complex realities on earth—from the Israelite perspective that was male animals and children, then by extension it is clear that He was also Lord of everything else.

II. Because God Values Human Life (v. 13b)

Yahweh unhesitatingly required Israel irrevocably to hand over to Him valuable economic resources. However, a sterner demand was made. Every family of the faith must also give Him their firstborn son. The demand was not unknown in the ancient world of Canaan. Lesser deities required human sacrifice, so why should not Yahweh?

Yet Israel's God made a unique request: "Redeem every firstborn among your sons" (v. 13b, NIV). God was to retain ownership of the person; however, in an act of sovereign grace He would permit the person's life to be spared. All firstborn males were thus to be "living sacrifices, holy and pleasing to God" (Rom. 12:1, NIV).

While Yahweh would magnanimously permit the Israelites' children to live, this freedom was not without its price. A child could be redeemed only by a redeemer who would cover the ransom expense. The price could be quite steep. Originally it might have been another human being who would have to live in lifelong service to the Lord (Num. 3:45). More likely, it would be a sizable sum of money (3:46-47). In either case, the fulfillment of the command required sacrifice on the part of family and/or community. Redemption was a gift, but it was not free. God demanded life for those condemned to die under other religious systems, but life bought at a price.

As Christians, we are able to see in this law a picture of ourselves and our Redeemer Jesus Christ. All of us—male and female alike—are firstborns when it comes to the family of sin. We stand perilously in the position of deserving to be handed over to death. But the same God who provided the means for life for the Israelites so many centuries ago also sent us a Member of the human community, the God-man Jesus Christ, to pay our ransom price (Gal. 3:13; 4:5; Rev. 5:9). Through the acceptance of His gracious provision by faith, we are set free to live in the world of the redeemed.

III. Because God Wants Witnesses to His Salvation and Glory (vv. 14-16)

God intended both the slaying of the firstborn animal and the redeeming of a child to create interest and arouse curiosity among those who witnessed the spectacle. A child observing the bloody ritual slaying of a tender animal whose birth he had only recently observed, would naturally wonder at the meaning of the event. The resulting question would provide the perfect opportunity for a parent to imprint God's act of redeeming Israel on the child's impressionable soul. By retelling the story of God's salvation in answer to the child's question, the parent was simultaneously identifying with the faith and passing it on to a future generation.

Christians today likewise should use God-given opportunities to confess their faith in Christ and teach their children about God's saving grace. When a child witnesses a baptism or Lord's Supper, he or she may ask about its meaning. What a perfect occasion to help that one learn the timeless story of God's ransoming, redeeming love for humanity!

The story of God's love for the hated and freedom for the slave is glorious and meant to be shared. By sharing it with others we can also bear witness that we are part of it. The person who knows Christ as Savior can confess along with the apostle Paul, "I am not my own, I am bought with a price" (1 Cor. 6:19-20). Jesus Christ has paid my redemption. The Lord that has indeed brought me out of Egypt with a mighty hand!

Notes

1. Compare L. Koehler and W. Baumgartner, *Lexicon in Veteris Testamenti Libros*, s.v. (III *yadah*); F. Brown et al., *Hebrew and English Lexicon of the Old Testament*, s.v. (*torah*); and J. E. Hartley, *Theological Wordbook of the Old Testament*, s.v. (*torah*). The word *torah* derives from an underlying verb expressing the idea of "throwing" or "casting."

2. These portions are primarily the divine quotations found in Genesis-Numbers, as well as the Mosaic speeches in Deuteronomy.

3. Compare the Babylonian Talmud tractates Sanhedrin 56-60 and *Yad. Melakhim* 8:10; 10:12.

4. Examples of moral laws include Ex. 20:12-17 and Lev. 18:6-24.

5. Examples of civil laws include Ex. 21:2-11; 18-36; Lev. 13:1–15:33; and 19:9-10.

6. Examples of ceremonial laws include Ex. 20:24-26; 23:10-19; Lev. 1:1–7:38; 11:1–12:8; and 16:1–17:16.

7. These divisions are present in the Mishnah, and were probably based on traditions known in the time of Jesus. The Hebrew/Aramaic names of the six different orders of law are: *Zeraim* ("Seeds"), *Mo'ed* ("Festivals"), *Nashim* ("Women"), *Nezikin* ("Damages"), *Kodashim* ("Holy Things"), and *Toharoth* ("Purifications").

8. 1 Kings 15:26,34; 16:26,31; 22:52; 2 Kings 13:2,11; 14:24,29; 15:18,24,28.

9. Ezra 3:2,4; 6:18; 7:10; 9:10-14; Neh. 1:7; 5:10-11; 8:1–10:39; 13:15-28.

10. A number of fine works have been published in recent years addressing the issue of Law in the New Testament. For further treatment of the issue, the reader is urged to consult the following works: R. J. Banks, *Jesus and the Law in the Synoptic Tradition* (Cambridge: University Press, 1975); D. Daube, *The New Testament and Rabbinic Judaism* (London: Athlone, 1956); W. D. Davies, *Paul and Rabbinic Judaism* (New York: Harper & Row, 1948); J. D. Derrett, *Law and the New Testament* (London: Darton, Longman & Todd, 1970); L. Gaston, *Paul and the Torah* (Vancouver: University of British Columbia Press, 1987); B. L. Martin, *Christ and the Law in Paul* (Leiden: E. J. Brill, 1989); H. Raisanen, *Paul and the Law*, 2nd ed. (Tübingen: J. C. B. Mohr, 1987); T. Rhyne, *Faith Establishes the Law* (Chico, CA: Scholars Press, 1981); and E. P. Sanders, *Paul, the Law, and the Jewish People* (Philadelphia: Fortress, 1983).

11. Cf. Rhyne, *Faith Establishes the Law*, 8-13.

12. Ibid., 13-19.

13. Ibid., 19-23.

14. Davies, *Paul and Rabbinic Judaism*, 149.

15. For a well-defended argument supporting the claim that Jesus' claim to proclaim the fullness of the law's intent, see J. A. Broadus, *Commentary on Matthew* (Philadelphia: American Baptist Publication Society, 1886), 98-101. For an equally fine treatment supporting the contention that Jesus is claiming to be the fullness of what the Law and the Prophets were intending, see D. A. Carson, "Matthew," in *Expositor's Bible Commentary*, 1.3-599 (Grand Rapids: Zondervan, 1984), 143-44.

16. This interpretation is consistent with the opinions of other commentators. As representative interpretations, cf. H. B. Swete, *The Gospel According to St. Mark* (Grand Rapids: Eerdmans, 1956), 50; V. Taylor, *The Gospel According to St. Mark* (London: Macmillan & Co., 1957), 219; and W. L. Lane, *The Gospel According to Mark* (Grand Rapids: Eerdmans, 1974), 119.

17. This interpretation differs from traditional Christian exegesis of this passage. As representative, compare F. F. Bruce, *Commentary on the Book of Acts* (Grand Rapids: Eerdmans, 1954), 302; and J. W. Packer, *Acts of the Apostles* (Cambridge: University Press, 1973), 128. It is, however, consistent with a Jewish perspective: compare *Encyclopedia Judaica*, s.v. "Noachide Laws."

18. Commentators will typically include a discussion of exactly what Paul meant when he used the word "law" in this passage. Paul sometimes used the term (*nomos*) to indicate the entirety of the Old Testament, while at others to indicate specifically the Mosaic legislation. Commentators generally agree that in the present passage Paul is using the term in the broad sense that would certainly include Mosaic law. Compare W. Sanday, and A. C. Headlam, *A Critical and Exegetical Commentary on The Epistle to the Romans*, 5th ed. (Edinburgh: T. & T. Clark, 1902), 80; and J. Murray, *The Epistle to the Romans* (Grand Rapids: Eerdmans, 1959), 1.105.

19. Compare F. F. Bruce, *The Epistle to the Hebrews* (Grand Rapids: Eerdmans, 1964), lii; and T. Hewitt, *The Epistle to the Hebrews* (Grand Rapids: Eerdmans, 1960), 40-41.

20. Compare New Testament statements regarding the following topics: circumcision—Gal. 5:2,6; dietary restrictions—Mark 7:18-19; Rom. 14:1-6; Col. 2:16; animal sacrifices—Heb. 10:1-18; Cultic calendar—Matt. 12:1-13; Rom. 14:5-6; Col. 2:16.

21. This conclusion is in full agreement with that of W. Kaiser, Jr., "God's Promise Plan and His Gracious Law," *Journal of the Evangelical Theological Society* 33 (1990): 289-302.

22. Compare Matt. 4:4 (Deut. 8:3); Matt. 4:7 (Deut. 6:16); Matt. 4:10 (Deut. 6:13); Matt. 5:17-19; Matt. 15:4 (Ex. 20:12; Deut. 5:16); Matt. 18:16 (Deut. 19:15); Matt. 19:4,5 (Gen. 1:27; 2:24); Matt. 19:19 (Ex. 20:12-16; Deut. 5:16-20); and Matt. 23:2-3.

23. Matt. 5:22,28,32,34,39,44.

24. E. E. Ellis, *Pauline Theology* (Grand Rapids: Eerdmans, 1989), 133-34.

3

Preaching Poetry

George L. Klein

Introduction

From the very beginning we must acknowledge several problems inherent in writing a chapter such as this. For one, there is the problem of identifying what constitutes a poetic text.[1] Certainly, the familiar "poetic books" of the Old Testament: Job, Psalms, Proverbs, Ecclesiastes, and Song of Songs immediately come to mind. However, this collection does not adequately illustrate poetry in the Old Testament for two reasons. First, Ecclesiastes and Song of Songs are not the best examples of what is generally known as Old Testament poetry.[2] Second, some of the most sublime examples of biblical poetry can be found outside this restrictive list. No study of poetry could neglect Isaiah's noble poetry or Amos' majestic verse, not to mention other beautiful texts such as Exodus 15, Deuteronomy 32, Judges 5, and many others. Going far beyond the so-called "poetic books," at least one third of the Old Testament is written poetically.

A second difficulty in approaching this chapter is that scholars of Old Testament poetry are not always agreed concerning the identification of poetic texts. This uncertainty can be seen, among numerous other examples, in the identification of Malachi by some scholars as prose,[3] while others affirm the book as poetry.[4] (The line between prose and poetry is not always distinct, making it necessary to acknowledge texts which lie somewhere on the middle of the continuum, which we may call "prosy poetry" or "poetic prose."[5]

It is inevitable, then, that at times there will be a certain amount of overlap between this chapter and those dealing with the Prophets and Wisdom, in particular, since most of these genres are written poetically. The discussion about distinctive characteristics of Old Testament poetry will be transferable beyond the "poetic" books. The reader should have a basis for beginning to make decisions about the poetic character of a text for him/herself after considering matters raised in this chapter. Ideally, the reader should no longer be totally dependent upon the editors of the modern texts and translations who choose to lay out a passage as either prose or poetry.

Moreover, these same poetic books, except the Psalms, have been treated in the chapter on Preaching Wisdom. It will be necessary, then, for us to devote a significant amount of consideration to the Psalms. Thus, we will begin by considering the distinctive features of Old Testament poetry; we will survey selected salient features in the Book of Psalms; and we will conclude with a sermon from the Book of Psalms illustrating principles described in the body of this chapter.

Characteristics of Old Testament Poetry

Introduction

Since relatively soon after their composition, poetic texts in the Old Testament have not been fully recognized as poetry until the time of Bishop Robert Lowth (1710-1787) whose *De sacra poesi Hebraeorum* (1753) finally gave impetus to poetic studies. The reasons for this eclipse of poetic awareness in the Bible are numerous, but none figures larger than a theological tension. Many had a reluctance to emphasize poetry in the Bible because of their discomfort with granting human authors the responsibility of shaping the final form of the message in sacred Scripture. To this day, the faithful still feel the tension.

Figures of Speech

Figurative language is one of the distinguishing characteristics of biblical poetry. This is not to say that figurative language does not exist in prose, as a cursory examination of such diverse texts as Nathan's rebuke of David after his sin with Bathsheba (2 Sam. 12) to the parables in the New Testament demonstrate. The primary difference between figurative language in poetry and prose is density. The quantity (and often sophistication) of figures is much more pronounced in poetry.

E. W. Bullinger, whose study of figurative aspects of speech remains the definitive work on the subject in English, presents the following definition of figurative language:

> Applied to words, a figure denotes some form which a word or sentence takes, different from its ordinary and natural form. This is always for the purpose of giving additional force, more life, intensified feeling, and greater emphasis.[6]

Often Bible students see figurative language as incapable of precise and determinate interpretation. Another illustration of this mentality is the pejorative dichotomy between "literal" and "symbolic" or "figurative" interpretation. In other words, figurative language "is ignorantly spoken of as though it made less of the meaning, and deprived the words of their power and force."[7] This, we shall see, is not the case.

Before we begin to consider how to interpret a figure, we must determine whether an expression is a figure of speech. Thus, when is a text to be interpreted "literally," and when as a "figure"? Bullinger replies:

> The answer is that, whenever and wherever it is possible, the words of Scripture are to be understood *literally*, but when a statement appears to be contrary to our experience, or to known fact, or revealed truth; or seems to be at variance with the general teaching of the Scriptures, then we may reasonably expect that some figure is employed. And as it is employed only to call our attention to some specially designed emphasis, we are at once bound to diligently examine the figure for the purpose of discovering and learning the truth that is thus emphasized.[8]

In other words, the interpreter should make every attempt to interpret a text in its plain, normal sense (avoiding the freighted word, "literal"). Only when such meaning is unworkable can the interpreter move in the direction of a figure of speech.

Why, then, should a text contain figures? Figurative language has many purposes: embellishment, making a passage more easily recalled, and adding connotative or emotive meaning to the text, to name a few. Figurative language communicates with the reader on a more sophisticated level than prose normally does.

Types of Figures

In the following section we shall merely introduce the four major categories of figurative language, giving a brief explanation and illustration of a few of the more important figures, following Bullinger's categories and explanations. Every student of the Bible should utilize Bullinger as a standard reference work because of its thoroughness in treating figures in prose and poetry in both Old and New Testaments.

Figures of Comparison. This category is perhaps the most common as well as the easiest understood of all figures. With this type of figure, one thing is emphasized by likening it to another.

①   *Simile*: a comparison of one thing to another using "like" or "as." "He is like a tree planted by streams of water" (Ps. 1:3, NIV).

②   *Metaphor*: a comparison declaring that one thing is another. "The Lord is my light and my salvation" (Ps. 27:1, NIV).

③   *Allegory*: a continued comparison by an extended metaphor. "One day the trees went out to anoint a king for themselves. . . . 'If you really want to anoint me king over you, come and take refuge in my shade; but if not, then let fire come out of the thornbush and consume the cedars of Lebanon!'" (Judg. 9:8-15, NIV).

④   *Proverb*: a practical truth expressed in everyday terms. "Like a gold ring in a pig's snout is a beautiful woman who shows no discretion" (Prov. 11:22, NIV).

⑤   *Personification*: ascribing human attributes to inanimate objects or animals. "Your brother's blood cries out to me from the ground" (Gen. 4:10, NIV).

⑥   *Anthropomorphism*: describing God with human form or attributes. "Sing to the Lord a new song, for he has done marvelous things; his right hand and his holy arm have worked salvation for him" (Ps. 98:1, NIV).

⑦   *Zoomorphism*: describing God (or humans) with the form or attributes of animals. "Hide me in the shadow of your wings" (Ps. 17:8, NIV).

Figures of Addition or Amplification. The common denominator of this type of figure is some form of expansion of an idea in one line of poetry as compared to a former line.

Parallelism: this figure will be discussed in the next section at some length.

Repetition: the repetition of a word or words.

> Do and do, do and do,
> rule on rule, rule on rule,
> a little here a little there (Isa. 28:10, NIV).

Paronomasia: repetition of similar sounding words. "Now the earth was formless (*tohu*) and empty (*wabohu*)" (Gen. 1:2, NIV).

Acrostic: repetition of the same or successive letters at the beginning of successive lines of poetry. Some of the partial or complete examples of this device are found in Psalms 9; 10; 25; 34; 37; 111; 112; 119; 145; compare Lamentations.

Inclusio: a means of bracketing or setting apart a literary unit by repeating the same word or clause at the beginning and end of the unit.

> O Lord, our Lord,
> how majestic is your name in all the earth! (Ps. 8:1,9, NIV).

Chiasmus: a balanced reversal or words or clauses ranging from the simple to the very complex.

> What he opens no one can shut,
> and what he shuts no one can open (Isa. 22:22, NIV).[9]

Hyperbole: exaggeration for the purpose of emphasis.

> The voice of the Lord breaks the cedars;
> the Lord breaks in pieces the cedars of Lebanon (Ps. 29:5, NIV).

Figures of Subtraction or Omission. This category represents increasing complexity as important aspects of the poetic line is omitted.

Ellipsis: the omission of a word or words from the poetic line.

> Better is one day in your courts
> than a thousand [elsewhere] (Ps. 84:10, NIV).

Rhetorical Question: a question asked without expecting an answer for the purpose of emphasizing the poet's perspective.

> Why do the nations conspire
> and the peoples plot in vain? (Ps. 2:1, NIV).

Belittling: lessening something in order to increase someone or something else. "But I am a worm and not a man" (Ps. 22:6, NIV).

Demeaning: a lessening of something in order to increase it. "A broken and contrite heart, O God, you will not despise (that is, he will accept with pleasure)" (Ps. 51:17, NIV).

Figures of Substitution. These figures are surely the most involved and sophisticated of all figurative language. Figures of substitution often require careful thought to analyze fully the point they make.

Metonymy: a change of one noun for a related noun.

Metonymy of Cause for Effect: the cause of an action is substituted for its effect. "A gentle tongue can break a bone" (Prov. 25:15, NIV, replacing "speech" with "tongue").

Metonymy of Effect for Cause: the effect of an action is substituted for its cause. "Let me hear joy and gladness" (Ps. 51:8, NIV, replacing the intended declaration of forgiveness with the effect of "joy and gladness").

Metonymy of Subject: the subject substitutes its adjunct or some circumstance associated with the subject. "You prepare a table before me" (Ps. 23:5, NIV, replacing the food and drink at the banquet with the "table" on which the feast was placed).

Metonymy of Adjunct: the adjunct, or some circumstance associated with the subject, substitutes its subject. "May the name of the God of Jacob protect you" (Ps. 20:1, NIV, replacing the Lord God Himself with His "name").

Synecdoche: the exchange of one idea for anther related idea (metonymy deals with the replacement of nouns, while synecdoche replaces ideas).

Synecdoche of the Genus: the genus is substituted for the species (general for specific).

> The glory of the Lord shall be revealed,
> and all flesh [NIV "mankind"] will see it (Isa. 40:5, KJV).

Synecdoche of the Species: the species is substituted for the genus (specific for general).

> "I do not trust in my bow,
> my sword does not bring me victory" (Ps. 44:6, NIV, signifying   weapons in general).

Synecdoche of the Whole for the Part: the whole is substituted for the intended part. "All who see me mock me" (Ps. 22:7, NIV, implies all who wish the psalmist ill).

Synecdoche of the Part for the Whole: a part is substituted for the whole. This is often similar to "Synecdoche of the Genus." "Their feet rush into sin" (Prov. 1:16, NIV, that is, the entire evil person).

Merism: two opposite statements or extremes denote the whole. "You know when I sit and when I rise" (Ps. 139:2, NIV, indicating the entire day from beginning to end).

Hendiadys: one idea conveyed by two formally coordinated terms. "My soul will be satisfied as with fat and fatness (Ps. 63:5, author's translation; NIV 'the richest of foods')."

Apostrophe: addressing someone (inanimate objects may be personified) who may not be actually present. "Hear, O heavens! Listen, O earth!" (Isa. 1:2, NIV).

Type: a divinely ordained person, institution, or event which foreshadows something later in biblical revelation.[10]

Irony: stating an idea in such a way that the opposite of the intended meaning is expressed.

> Go to Bethel and sin;
> go to Gilgal and sin yet more (Amos 4:4, NIV).

Malediction: communicating a negative sentiment by means of an imprecation.

> Break the teeth in their mouths, O God;
> tear out, O Lord, the fangs of the lions! (Ps. 58:6, NIV).

Parallelism

Although, strictly speaking, parallelism is also a figure of speech, as we saw in the preceding section, it is such a prominent aspect of Old Testament poetry that it could be called its most important feature. Lowth introduced the term *parallelismus membrorum* ("parallelism of the clauses"), itself a geometric metaphor, to describe the interplay between lines of poetry. Indeed, the metaphor is somewhat misleading in that it implies that the two lines of poetry never intersect, while in poetry, the meaning of the poetic lines do converge in manifold ways. Although many have sought to replace Lowth's understanding of parallelism, and in particular, his classification of different types of parallelism into broad categories,[11] the resilience with which Lowth's understanding has resisted major alteration is a tribute to his insight and creativity.

Lowth's own definition of parallelism is perhaps the best definition penned to date. He writes:

> The correspondence of one verse or line with another, I call parallelism. When a proposition is delivered, and a second is subjoined to it, or drawn under it, equivalent, or contrasted with it in sense, or similar to it in the form of grammatical construction, these I call parallel lines; and the words or phrases, answering one to another in the corresponding lines, parallel terms.[12]

This often quoted definition describes the relationship between the meaning of one line and another. However, students of biblical poetry have begun to recognize even deeper levels on which parallelism can operate.

Before proceeding with our introduction to parallelism, we must distinguish between grammatical and semantic parallelism. Grammatical parallelism occurs when comparable grammatical forms are paralleled in paired lines of poetry. Grammatical parallelism is usually discernible only after a careful analysis of a text.[13] Semantic parallelism, on the other hand, is the more familiar aspect of parallelism, focusing on meanings in the respective lines of poetry, and is readily seen in most Old Testament poetry. Although Lowth was the first to give a formal analysis of semantic parallelism, the essential features of balanced lines were recognized from antiquity, with such ancient texts as the noncanonical Thanksgiving Psalms from Qumran mimicking biblical poetic style. Henceforth, we shall mean semantic parallelism when we use the term "parallelism," unless otherwise noted.

Most treatments of parallelism begin by introducing the common types of parallelism, but it would be wiser to begin by examining the building blocks of parallelism. To be sure, more than two lines can be parallel, but one naturally thinks of two parallel lines. Such is also the case with Old Testament poetry. One may encounter three parallel lines of poetry (a triplet) or even four parallel lines (a quatrain), but the vast majority of the time one finds two parallel lines (a couplet) of poetry. Within these paired lines one further realizes that the basis for the parallelism is ultimately the "word pair."

"Word pairs" are "pairs of synonymous, antonymous, or heteronymous words, whose components are found in tandem as a result of a mutual affinity; at least twice in one language."[14] The stock of word pairs in Semitic languages from which the poets could draw was vast, as the 800 page tome by Avishur attests. These word pairs were virtual cliches which "in the hands of a skilled poet ... can be transformed into an instrument of immense power and a most able vehicle for intense emotional expression."[15] Examples of common Old Testament word pairs are: "heaven/earth," "day/night," "sun/moon," "sin/ transgression," and the like. From this vast collection of word pairs the poet could shape his text in a marvelously creative way, all the while utilizing familiar themes for his hearers.

These word pairs were utilized by poets in each of the major Semitic languages, not just Hebrew. For instance, one could find the same poetic devices at work in such diverse languages as: Akkadian, Arabic, Aramaic, Hebrew, Moabite, Phoenician, and Ugaritic, to name the most prominent illustrations. Often, the same word pairs, albeit in the form of the cognate language in which they are found, can be seen in non-Hebrew texts. Of particular note to the student of poetry is the Ugaritic texts, vast collections of poetry whose word pairs, parallelism, and sometimes even entire texts (for instance, Ps. 29) are profoundly similar to that in the Bible.

Types of Parallelism

Recognizing that the smallest unit of poetry with real meaning is the line (word pairs have no real significance outside of the line in which they reside), we must survey the most common types of parallelism in the Old Testament. In each subsequent type one may discover a different relationship between the interrelated lines, each in point-counterpoint fashion. We must be cautious not to see biblical parallelism fitting within a few neat categories. In all, Lowth's categories presented below are functional, but Lowth's most vocal critic, James Kugel, warns us that:

> the ways of parallelism are numerous and varied, and the intensity of the semantic parallelism established between clauses might be said to range from "zero perceivable correspondence" to "near-zero perceivable differentiation" (just short of word-for-word repetition).[16]

Synonymous Parallelism

Synonymous parallelism states the idea of one line and then restates the same notion in successive lines of the poem. Without question, synonymous parallelism is the simplest category of parallelism and is the most recognizable.

As with the term "parallelism," so with "*synonymous* parallelism," we encounter a problem with terminology. Synonymity implies a degree of precision in the repetition or the idea in the second line (often called the "B-line") when compared to the first line (called the "A-line"). This is never the case either in poetry or in language in general where there is no such thing as absolutely synonymous words meaning exactly the same thing.[17] The key in analyzing synonymous parallelism is to avoid searching for "mathematical equality" between the respective lines. Rather, one should expect no substantial addition or deletion of ideas between the lines.

Note the relationship between the following lines (the end of each poetic line will be marked by a single diagonal, and the end of each poetic unit or caesura, usually a couplet, will be indicated with a double diagonal):

"Come, let us sing for joy to the Lord;/	A
let us shout aloud to the Rock of our salvation.//	B
Let us come before him with thanksgiving/	A
and extol him with music and song.//	B
For the Lord is the great God,/	A
the great King above all gods.//	B

In his hand are the depths of the earth,/	A
and the mountain peaks belong to him.//	B
The sea is his, for he made it,/	A
and his hands formed the dry land."//	B
(Ps. 95:1-5, NIV)	

Examining more closely the paired lines clearly indicates that precise equality or synonymity is nearer in view. If it was, the second line of poetry would be redundant and uninteresting. Rather, one line adds subtle nuances which focus the poet's thoughts more sharply for the reader as well as captivate one's interest. For example, in the first couplet "singing for joy" is very close to the idea of "shouting aloud," but not identical. Even more distinction can be drawn between "Lord" in the "A-line" and "Rock of our salvation" in the "B-line." Each word pair, when juxtaposed with its yoked word, adds *shades* of meaning which would not occur unless in the presence of its mate.

An efficient symbolic notation summarizes the relationship between the ideas within the line and the interplay between the lines. Using Psalm 95:1 above we analyze the parallelism as:

```
     a          b                  c
"Come,   let us sing for joy   to the Lord;/            A
           b′                  c′
         let us shout aloud   to the Rock of our salvation."//  B
```

or verse 2:

```
     a          b                  c
"Let us come   before him   with thanksgiving/         A
     a′          b′              c′
 and extol      him         with music and song."//    B
```

This approach to analyzing and recording the results of one's understanding of a text's parallelism should quickly prove indispensable to the student of Old Testament poetry.

It is important to note that synonymous parallelism is often "incomplete," that is, not every member of the line is paralleled by another in the paired line. For example:

```
     a        b          c            d
"Tremble,   O earth,   at the presence   of the Lord,/   A
           c              d′            e
     at the presence   of the God   of Jacob."//         B
                                   (Ps. 114:7, NIV)
```

The verb "tremble" does "double duty," serving as the implied verb for the B-line also.

Antithetical Parallelism

Antithetical parallelism, like synonymous parallelism, exhibits symmetry between the poetic lines as well as the internal elements of each line. Unlike synonymous parallelism, terms in antithetical parallelism express contrast or opposition.[18] No literature in the Old Testament is better suited to antithetical parallelism than the Wisdom literature, and the Book of Proverbs in particular. As Duane Garrett's chapter in this volume notes, Wisdom emphasizes the two paths of life open to every individual. These two courses are typically presented in the starkest contrast to one another. For instance:

	a	b	c	
	"Whoever	loves discipline	loves knowledge,/	A
	a′	-b′	-c′	
	but he who	hates correction	is stupid."//	B

(Prov. 12:1, NIV)

Note that letters with a prime mark, for example, "-b′," are used to indicate that an analogous term is used, without encountering the identical term. The negative sign, for example, "-c′," signifies that the term in the B-line opposes or contrasts with the corresponding term in the A-line. Notice another example from the "Wisdom sounding" Psalm 1:

	a	b	
	"For the Lord watches over	the way of the righteous,/	A
	-b′	-a′	
	but the way of the wicked	will perish."//	B

(Ps. 1:6, NIV)

"Watching over" clearly has the sense of "protect," completing the symmetry of the verse. One also observes the a-b-b-a pattern, the simplest form of chiasm. Like synonymous parallelism, antithetical parallelism need not have every member of the poetic lines paralleled by its analog.

Synthetic Parallelism

"Synthetic parallelism," sometimes known as "formal parallelism," is typically defined as parallelism in which the B-line (plus the C- and D-lines, if present) advanced the thought of the A-line beyond what the initial line states.

The nomenclature, "synthetic parallelism," fails to indicate the relationship of the lines so classified as do synonymous and antithetical parallelism. For this reason, the name itself has been incessantly criticized. Some would prefer a term such as "incomplete parallelism," which would be a subdivision of synonymous or antithetic parallelism.[19] Kugel even suggests the cumbersome designation "A is so, and *what's more*, B is so" in an attempt to describe the additional information conveyed by the B-line.[20]

Furthermore, the category is ill defined, leading some to object to the classification on grounds of being a "catchall."[21] In other words, any type of "parallelism" which does not neatly fit into one of the major categories such as synonymous or antithetical could fit in the synthetic category. Thus, many see synthetic parallelism as too broad to be a meaningful category. Gray writes:

> There are other examples of what Lowth called synthetic parallelism in which no term in the second line is parallel to any term in the first, but in which the second line consists entirely of what is fresh and additional to the first; and in some of these examples the two lines are not even parallel to one another by the correspondence of similar grammatical terms. Two such lines as these may certainly be called synthetic, but they are parallel to one another merely in the way that the continuation of the same straight line is parallel to its beginning; whereas synonymous and antithetic parallelisms, even of the incomplete kind, do really correspond to two separate and, strictly speaking, parallel lines.[22]

We chose to retain the term and category, "synthetic parallelism," because the two lines of couplets, the three of triplets, and the four of quatrains in "synthetic parallelism" manifest sharp breaks in thought and syntax from the preceding and succeeding lines of the poem.[23] In extended sections of verses with synthetic parallelism, the pattern of couplets, triplets, and quatrains is clearly in view. This Gottwald calls "parallelism of form," despite the fact that "parallelism of thought" is sometimes absent.[24] Notice the varied examples of synthetic parallelism:

a	b	
"I have installed	my King/	A
c	c′	
on Zion,	my holy hill."//	B
	(Ps. 2:6, NIV)	

a	b	
"The kings of the earth	take their stand/	A
a′	b′	
and the rulers	gather together//	B
c	d	
against	the Lord/	C
c′	d′	
and against	his Anointed One."//	D
	(Ps. 2:2, NIV)	

Clearly, in Psalm 2:2 the first couplet, the A- and B-lines, represent a synonymous parallelism, as does the second couplet, the C- and D-lines. However, the relationship between the first pair of the quatrain and the second is synthetic.

Minor Types of Parallelism

Emblematic Parallelism occurs when one of the lines of a poetic unit illustrates the truth of the other line with an emblem such as a simile.

> "Like arrows in the hands of a warrior/   A
>   are sons born in one's youth."//   B
>   (Ps. 127:4, NIV)

Chiastic Parallelism inverts the order of the A-line in the B-line.

> "Ephraim will not be jealous of Judah,/   A
>   nor Judah hostile toward Ephraim."//   B
>   (Isa. 11:13, NIV)

Number Parallelism likens a number such as "seven" in one line to another, like "eight," in the next line. Since numbers do not have synonyms, the pattern is n//n+1.

> "There are six things the Lord hates,/   A
>   seven that are detestable to him:"//   B
>   (Prov. 6:16, NIV)

Staircase Parallelism moves forward in steps, typically involving three or more lines.

> "Ascribe to the Lord, O mighty ones,/   A
>   ascribe to the Lord glory and strength./   B
>   ascribe to the Lord the glory due his name."//   C
>   (Ps. 29:1-2, NIV)

Many additional minor types of parallelism exist, some of which are obliterated when translated out of Hebrew, but the foregoing list affords the interpreter ample types to begin a study of Old Testament poetry.

Purposes of Poetry

We have seen that poetry is capable of evoking a deeper emotional response from the reader than the corresponding prose text, partly because of the aesthetic nature of the text and partly due to the emotional force of the figurative language. The contrast is pointedly put by Berlin who lists parallel biblical accounts, one in prose and the other in poetry to illustrate the point: "'I'm thirsty,' he said. 'Please give me some water.' She opened a skin of milk, gave him a drink, and covered him up" (Judg. 4:19, NIV) and "Water he asked, Milk she gave; In a princely bowl she offered curds."[25] The same can easily be seen by comparing the account of the exodus in Exodus 13–14 compared with 15.

In addition to the emotional force poetry possesses, poetry has a profoundly heightened sense of aesthetics. To be sure, prose does exhibit careful attention to the artistry with which its own message is presented. However, the difference between the beauty of presentation with prose and poetry is essentially one of degree.

Finally, poetry is inherently memorable. It is common experience to recall verse more easily than prose. Most have had heard a verse, perhaps set to music, once, and then realize that most of the composition can be recalled after only one hearing. This fact must not be underestimated, since the effectiveness of expressions of corporate or individual worship, aphorisms, and prophetic oracles all depend upon the hearer's ability to remember the content of the message long after hearing the work. Poetry, then, was a perfectly suited medium to the message of psalmist, sage, and prophet.

Psalm Genres

Up to this point we have considered elements of poetry which relate to biblical poetry wherever it is found. Next, we shall consider the basic psalm types which recur in the Psalter, and in some cases, can be found in poetry outside of the Book of Psalms.[26] We shall survey the following genres in the Psalter: the hymn, the individual and community lament, the individual and community narrative praise, and royal psalms.

Psalm types or genres are isolated on the basis of structure and content. To be sure, each genre shares themes with other exemplars. Thus, all hymns praise Yahweh for His goodness. Interestingly, most genres share a similar structure. In other words, community laments, for example, tend to follow the same outline. To know the genre to which an individual psalm belongs is to have a preliminary idea, not only of the themes found within the psalm, but also how it is arranged.[27]

Hymn

Although not the most common psalm type, the hymn, sometimes called "descriptive praise," is often seen as the most characteristic genre in the Book of Psalms.[28] The hymn held pride of place in the worship of ancient Israel, focusing on the praise of Yahweh. The occasion of a hymn was not any specific action God had performed on Israel's behalf like the narrative praise psalms. Rather, hymns arose almost spontaneously, celebrating the character of Israel's God and His general blessings on the people. Hymns seek nothing from God, only that He would receive the praise of His people.

The structure of hymns in the Psalter is less rigid than other types, but a general pattern will be followed. First, hymns begin with a call to praise which serves as the introduction. Often this introduction begins with the familiar "Praise the Lord!" and continues with several verses admonishing the reader to join in the praise. Second, the body of the hymn outlines the two major reasons God is to be praised: He demonstrates His lordship over His entire creation; and He faithfully preserves His people. Many hymns close with a final exhortation to "Praise the Lord!"

Psalms which should be classified as hymns are: 8; 19; 29; 33; 57; 65; 66; 89; 100; 103–05; 107; 111; 113; 117; 134–36; 139; 145–50. Some of the most prominent examples outside the Psalms include: Exodus 15; Isaiah 12; Jeremiah 10; and numerous examples in Job.

Lament

Laments in the Bible are uttered both by individuals and the community, depending upon whether the crisis is personal or corporate. Associated with the prayer of lament were fasting, covering one's head with ashes, abstinence, sacrificial purification, clothing oneself with sackcloth, weeping, and other gestures of humiliation.

Community laments begin with a brief introductory address to God, imploring His favor, serving to initiate communication with God. Next, one encounters the community's complaint. The circumstances, such as famine, imminent military conflict, or exile, are sometimes mentioned in general terms; the complaint is focused primarily upon God. Expressions like "how long will you be angry?" typify the complaint section of community laments. "Complaint" in these psalms does not have the negative connotation the word has for us today. Rather, the people express freely and honestly their concerns with God.

The third section of community laments takes an unexpected turn, considering the major examples of God's saving acts in history. This survey of God's salvation serves to motivate God to action once more, as well as to stimulate faith in the heart of the hearers as they consider God's marvelous acts in the past.

Typically, the next section of community laments is the entreaty or petition. Here the people make clear what they expect God to do. Occasionally, community laments conclude with a vow to praise God for the salvation already in process. Usually this vow is found in individual laments. Relatively few community laments are found in the Old Testament. Good examples are: Psalms 44; 60; 74; 79; 80; 83; 89; Isaiah 63; Jeremiah 14; Lamentations 1–2; 4–5; Habakkuk 1. Psalms with some community lament features include: 82; 85; 68; 90; 106; 115.

The individual lament shares many themes as well as the basic structure of the community lament. Of course, the fundamental difference is that the individual lament focuses upon the crisis experienced solely by the psalmist. The psalmist typically faces illness or some sort of false accusation by a foe.

The individual lament possesses an address, complaint, and petition, as does the community lament. However, individual laments more clearly demonstrate the psalmist's pilgrimage from distress to trust in God. Many individual laments also possess imprecations or maledictions pronounced upon their foes.[29] A final, customary characteristic of individual laments is the psalmist's concluding vow of praise and confidence in Yahweh.

Individual laments are the most frequent genre in the Psalter, and are not uncommon in other biblical books as well. A representative list would include: Psalms 3–7; 10–14; 16–17; 22–23; 25–28; 31; 35–36; 38–43; 51–59; 61–64; 69; 71; 73; 77; 86; 88; 94; 102; 109; 120; 130; Lamentations 3; Jeremiah 11; 15; 17–18; 20; and numerous texts in Job.

Narrative Praise

As with the laments, we meet both individual and community narrative praise genres. The community narrative praise is only rarely found in the Psalter. In fact, this genre is so rarely attested that it is unwise to postulate structural similarities between them. The emphasis is on the awesome acts of deliverance by God for His people, Israel. Examples of this genre, according to Westermann, are found in Exodus 15:1–21; Psalms 106; 124; and 129.[30]

Westermann wisely observes that, while the Book of Psalms contains more laments than narrative praise psalms, one must not assume that the lament "outweighs praise. . . . The narrative or confessing psalm of praise by the individual corresponds to the psalm of lament by the individual. They belong together like two acts of a drama."[31] In fact, the vow to praise concluding some individual laments is identical to the vow to praise beginning the individual narrative praise.

The individual narrative praise has one of the most consistent organizational schemes of any of the genres. These psalms usually begin with a call to praise, followed by a recitation of the complaint and how God intervened. The conclusion always focuses with renewed vigor upon God's praise, particularly in light of the recent deliverance.

Good illustrations of this genre can be found in Psalms 9; 18; 30–32; 40; 66; 92; 107; 116; 118; 138; Jonah 2; Lamentations 3:25-58; and Job 33.

Royal Psalms

Royal psalms share no structural affinity, but are related solely by the theme of the king. In some fashion, royal psalms always concern the king. Although some have hypothesized elaborate ceremonial court backgrounds to these psalms,[32] there is virtually no evidence for such claims. Furthermore, it is problematic to determine who the king was. Was he merely a human king, the divine King, or a human king who typified the divine one? A quick perusal of modern translations of the Psalms will reveal the inconsistency, both within individual translations and when compared with other translations, with which "king" is capitalized.

Most royal psalms should be seen addressing a literal human king in need of God's help in protecting and guiding God's people. A mere reference to "king" should not immediately imply messianic overtones. However, Psalms 2 and 22 in particular, seem to be clearly typological.[33] In other words, these two psalms focus upon a real human king, but because of the special circumstances the king faced and the language used to describe it, later biblical writers interpreted the text as a type of the Messiah. Psalm 110, on the other hand, should be interpreted as a prophetic, messianic psalm. The language it contains, for example "My Lord says to my Lord," if David is understood to be the author as the New Testament authors assumed, requires that the psalm be interpreted messianically as does the Book of Hebrews.

Royal psalms can be seen in Psalms 2; 18; 20–22; 45; 72; 89; 101; 110; 132; and 144.

Conclusion

We could examine numerous other subtypes of psalms, such as wisdom psalms and creation psalms, to name two. However, the genres we have treated cover virtually the entire Psalter, with additional themes being mentioned within the framework of these major types.

A Sermon from Biblical Poetry

"Fleeing From God!"
Psalm 139

I. God Knows Everything About Us (vv. 1-6).

Verse 1 begins with the psalmist's acknowledgment that God has searched him, an anthropomorphism. The next verse adds that God knows David's "sitting" and "rising." These two extremes of his day, a merism, signify that God knows everything about his life. Verse 3 also contains a merism, "the going out" and "the lying down," and everything in between are known by God. Plus, in verse 4, David reluctantly acknowledges that God knows what he will say, before a word is on the tip of his tongue.

Thus far, what we have read in this psalm could be understood positively, as most do, as an expression of praise to God for His greatness, including His all-knowing character. I do not think this approach fits the passage. Rather, it seems to me that David is dismayed, perhaps even depressed, that God has such familiarity with his life.

Perhaps no verse in this psalm is more frequently taken out of context than verse 6. Usually it is taken in its most positive light, signifying David's delight that God has such encyclopedic information about him. This idea comes from the word "wonderful," which sounds quite positive. The Hebrew word *peli'a* has a different connotation; it means "extraordinary." David used the word in its positive sense when he spoke of his love for his fallen friend Jonathan in 2 Samuel 1. On the other hand, Deuteronomy 28 speaks of God sending "wonderful" plagues on everyone who disobeys His word, which obviously means "unusual." In verse 6, only the "extraordinary fearsome" meaning fits.

II. God's Presence Always Surrounds Us (vv. 7-12).

In the previous section we observed that David was overwhelmed at God's knowledge of his life. Here, David feels God's presence like a noose around his neck, growing tighter and tighter.

In verse 7 David asks a question anticipating a negative reply. "Where can I go from the Spirit of God?" (author's translation). Nowhere! This is no abstract philosophical statement about the omnipresence of God. No, David is terrified that a holy God knows all about him, and worse—is already everywhere he might think of hiding. For example, in verse 8 David considers ascending to the height of heaven to get away from God. No escape! He next wonders if he could go down to Sheol and be free. No escape! David views the rising sun in the east as though it was a bird on the wing and asks, "Can I fly away eastward and evade God?" No escape!

In verse 10 David contemplates the right hand of God which both guides him and seizes him. Once more, David feels God's heavy hand upon him, and there is no deliverance! Finally, in verses 11-12 the psalmist asks hypothetically if the darkness, humanity's greatest ally in disguising secret, sordid acts, is capable of veiling him from God's gaze. He quickly realizes again that there is no escape!

David understands that he is powerless against God. God knows everything about him and, furthermore, is present everywhere he might try to live without God's scrutiny. This section is intensely personal for David, and it should be so for us today. David is upset that God knew him so well, because he understands that he is utterly a sinner. Remember, this is the same psalmist who pled with God saying:

> "Have mercy on me, O God, according to your unfailing love; according to your great compassion blot out my transgressions. Wash away all my iniquity and cleanse me from my sin. For I know my transgressions, and my sin is always before me" (Ps. 51:1-3, NIV).

As the second section draws to a close, the theme is that of darkness, a darkness which David hoped would be thick enough to cover his evil deeds. This theme carries into the third section, verses 13-18, which presents an all creative God, fashioning wonders in the darkness of the womb.

Certainly the pessimistic tone of the first two sections begins to change for the better here. The link between verses 7-12 and 13-18 is that of darkness. However, darkness, like several other motifs now has positive connotations whereas they were formerly negative. Darkness in verses 11-12 refers to a shadowy, murky place where man's sin could be concealed. Now, darkness is something which does not hinder God as he fashions his most spectacular creature—humanity.

III. God's Creatively and Personally Makes Us for His Purposes (vv. 13-18).

In these verses one does not encounter an abstract idea of humanity's creation by God. Rather, the psalmist makes the whole concept personal: "You created *my* inmost being; you knit *me* together in *my* mother's womb" (v. 13, NIV). It is this personal touch from God which underlies the shift from a negative view of the Lord to the positive one emerging. It is true (and sobering) to remember that God knows everything about David (or me). Furthermore, it is true (and disconcerting) to recall that God cannot be escaped no matter how hard David (or I) might try.

However, since it is true that God made David (and me), neither David nor I need dread the presence of God any longer since He is the One who created us (and everyone else) with such care. Moreover, in verse 14 the word "wonderful" or "extraordinarily fearsome" in now "delightful, tremendous, awesome." David's heart is moved from fear to praise, from flight to abiding.

IV. God's Holiness Fits Us to Do His Work (vv. 19-24).

David's present world is full of difficulties which he can now courageously face with God to guide him. His prayer in verses 19-22 is an imprecation, a malediction. The prayer here is harsh and must be understood in light of several observations. First, David served as God's anointed king; the one who opposed him in this role opposed God. We cannot say the same. Second, the statements are not to be seen as an expression of a personal vendetta. The Mosaic law forbade personal revenge (Lev. 19:18). Third, imprecations verbalize the psalmist's revulsion toward sin. Fourth, imprecations can be seen as prophetic, that is, as a prediction of the imminent judgment of evildoers by God.

Finally, verses 23-24 conclude the psalm in a fashion similar to that in which the psalm began. The same word used for "search" in verse 1 is found also in verse 23, meaning a very careful and thorough examination. Now, however, the apprehension about God searching David is gone. In fact, David even asks God to search him.

Conclusion

We have now come full circle. In the beginning, David sees God as a holy and terrifying God. In the end, David understands that God is holy; but, since He had created him, is intimately interested in his life. Truly, God is personal, merciful, and approachable. It is this circle which I think applies the most forcefully to us today.

Notes

1. For an introduction, see T. Longman, II, *Literary Approaches to Biblical Interpretation* (Grand Rapids: Zondervan, 1987), 119-34.

2. See D. Garrett, "Preaching Wisdom" in this volume.

3. W. C. Kaiser, Jr., *Malachi* (Grand Rapids: Baker, 1984), 18.

4. D. E. Sellin, *Das Zwolfprophetenbuch* (Leipzig: A. Deichertsche, 1930), 2.587.

5. G. L. Klein, "An Introduction to Malachi," *Criswell Theological Review* 2 (1987): 28-29; see Wilfred G. E. Watson, *Classical Hebrew Poetry* (Sheffield: JSOT Press, 1984), 46-60.

6. E. W. Bullinger, *Figures of Speech Used in the Bible* (Reprint ed.; Grand Rapids: Baker, 1968), v-vi.

7. Ibid.

8. Bullinger, *Figures*, xv.

9. See the involved study by J. W. Welch, ed., *Chiasmus in Antiquity* (Hildesheim: Gerstenberg, 1981).

10. See the chapter in this book by D. S. Dockery, "Typological Exegesis: Moving Beyond Abuse and Neglect."

11. J. Kugel perhaps has been the most vocal; see *The Idea of Biblical Poetry* (New Haven, CT: Yale University Press, 1981), 12.

12. R. Lowth, *Isaiah: A New Translation with a Preliminary Dissertation and Notes* (Reprinted ed., 1778; London: William Tegg, 1848), ix.

13. See S. A. Geller, *Parallelism in Early Biblical Poetry* (Missoula, MT: Scholars Press, 1979), for an example of a study of parallelism which includes grammatical parallelism.

14. Y. Avishur, *Stylistic Studies of Word-Pairs in Biblical and Ancient Semitic Literatures* (Neukirchen: Neukirchener, 1984), 1.

15. S. Gevirtz, *Patterns in the Early Poetry of Israel* (Chicago: University of Chicago Press, 1973), 9.

16. J. Kugel, *The Idea of Biblical Poetry* (New Haven, CT: Yale University Press, 1981), 7.

17. See the very helpful discussion in L. A. Schoekel, *A Manual of Hebrew Poetics* (Rome: Editrice Pontificio Istituto Biblico, 1988), 64-84.

18. See Schoekel, *A Manual of Hebrew Poetics*, 85-94.

19. G. B. Gray, *The Forms of Hebrew Poetry* (reprint ed., 1915; New York: KTAV, 1972), 49.

20. Kugel, *Idea* 8.

21. Kugel, *Idea*, 12.

22. Gray, *Forms*, 50.

23. N. K. Gottwald, "Poetry, Hebrew," in G. A. Buttrick, ed., *The Interpreter's Dictionary of the Bible*, 4 vols. (Nashville: Abingdon, 1962), 3:832.

24. Gottwald, "Poetry," 832.

25. Following the translation and discuss by A. Berlin, *The Dynamics of Biblical Parallelism* (Bloomington, IN: Indiana University Press, 1985), 12.

26. For a helpful introduction to the Psalms, see T. Longman III, *How to Read the Psalms* (Downers Grove, IL: InterVarsity, 1988); and B. W. Anderson, *Out of the Depths* (Philadelphia: Westminster, 1974).

27. See H. Gunkel, *The Psalms: A Form-Critical Introduction* (Philadelphia: Fortress, 1967); and Claus Westermann, *The Psalms: Structure, Content, and Message* (Minneapolis: Augsburg, 1980). W. Brueggemann, *The Message of the Psalms* (Minneapolis: Augsburg, 1984), presents the overall Psalm types as "Psalms of Orientation," "Psalms of Disorientation," and "Psalms of New Orientation."

28. Explanations of psalm genres vary slightly from author to author. Our approach follows that of Westermann, *Psalms*.

29. See the brief discussion of imprecations in the sermon on Psalm 139:19-22 below.

30. Westermann, *Psalms*, 48-49.

31. Ibid., 71.

32. See, for example, S. Mowinckel, *The Psalms in Israel's Worship*, 2 vols. (Nashville: Abingdon, 1962), among others.

33. See D. Dockery's article on typology within this volume.

4

Preaching the Prophets

Dan G. Kent

Philip Yancey suggested in *Christianity Today* that if you examine the Bibles of even the most committed Christians, "you may find a telltale band of white on the paper edges about halfway through. That mark of cleanness shows how seldom fingers touch the Old Testament Prophets."[1]

Is Philip Yancey right? If he is correct, how much of the blame rests on our failure to preach and teach the prophets? Surely one of the most important ways to remedy such a lamentable situation is for those of us who preach the Bible to do a better job with those vital and important figures we call "the prophets."

James Ward has insisted that "the books of the prophets are more explicit theologically than other parts of the Old Testament, so they lend themselves more directly" to preaching and teaching. Furthermore, the dominant forms of prophetic speech are closer to those of the modern preacher than most of the rest of the Bible. Thus, the oracles of the ancient prophets can serve to some extent as models for preaching, and they provide a rich resource of thematic material for proclamation.[2]

The Difficulty of the Task

There are several reasons why the prophetical books are among the most difficult sections of the Bible to handle properly.[3] Bernard Ramm has suggested that "the prophetic language itself partakes of a measure of ambiguity."[4] Think of how puzzled the Jewish people of Jesus' day were when they tried to make sense of the Old Testament predictions about His first coming.

Then there is the matter of the extent of the prophetic Scriptures.[5] Ramm writes:

> To assemble each passage, to thoroughly digest its meaning, to arrange the passages in a prophetic harmony, would involve a prodigious memory, years of exacting work, a masterful knowledge of Biblical languages, an exhaustive reading of prophetic literature, a keen exegetical sense, a thorough knowledge of the histories of many peoples and a knowledge of all relevant archaeological materials.[6]

It is not surprising, is it, that there is so much disagreement about the message of the prophets? It makes one wonder, rather, about those who claim that the prophetic Scriptures are easy to interpret.

Furthermore, Joel Green has reminded us of our "failure to read the text on its own terms."[7] We are even tempted to read what we want to read, to see what we want to see. So we isolate a verse from its setting (context) or read modern ideas back into ancient texts. The focus becomes what we want the author to say. This is sometimes phrased, "What does it mean to me?" Thus, we remake the Bible in our own image.

In the excellent book, *How to Read the Bible for All Its Worth*, Gordon Fee and Douglas Stuart suggest another reason preaching the prophets is difficult; there is so much misunderstanding about the function and form.[8]

One of the least understood things about the prophets is that their message had a meaning for the people of their own day. Our faith is a historical faith, both in its Old Testament initiation and in its New Testament fulfillment. To overlook the fact that the prophets spoke directly and clearly to their own day is to uproot our faith from its moorings in history.

The prophets meant their words for particular audiences in particular places and times. Amos spoke primarily to the 8th century B.C., and Jeremiah to the 7th and 6th. We, of course, must understand their meaning for us today in relation to those original historical settings.[9] The basic meaning of a biblical prophecy is that which the author intended the hearers or readers of his own day to understand.[10]

Our first question must always be: What did the prophet say to the people of his own time? How was the message intended then? How was it understood then? It is hard to answer such questions, but it must be done.

The prophets were not oblivious to the problems and crises of their own times. To be so would be like a modern pastor who preached regularly and extensively, but never mentioned any current need. I do not believe the Lord would have sent the prophets to speak about matters irrelevant to their own situation.

Because prophecy is so complex, we must have an attitude of humility toward interpreting it. No one has all the answers. Whoever implies that he or she does is providing certain evidence that he or she does not. We do not lose credibility if we admit that we do not understand some things; we are merely being honest. There are mysteries yet remaining in the Scriptures. The Lord still knows some things He has not yet told us.

Who Were the Prophets?

The Old Testament prophets were preachers. They were other things, but they were primarily preachers. Their "books" (better: anthologies—see below) are collections of sermons.

Unfortunately, when average people hear our English word "prophet" they think of prediction. That is what the English word has come to mean. However, the main Hebrew word, *nabi*, meant "spokesman," "speaker," "messenger."[11] The prophet was one appointed by the Lord to call out the Lord's message (the active meaning).[12]

As an example of the prophets' role, think about the matchless Moses. How many predictions did he make? Perhaps only one, in Deuteronomy 18. Yet he was the archetypical prophet. His ministry regularly presented the Lord's message to the waiting people.

These Old Testament preachers we call prophets spoke a great deal about the past. They certainly addressed their present world. They even spoke about the future. However, they did all of that in order to preach the Lord's message to the people of their day.[13] They did it in order to get the people who heard them to turn back to the Lord.[14] Douglas Stuart has called them covenant enforcement mediators,[15] calling people back to their covenant obligations.

If one studies the prophetic materials, one will find that the prediction of the future played a less important part in their messages than one might suppose.[16] After detailed study, my students over the years have concluded that the prophetic materials consist of only about 25 percent prediction of any kind, including both general (such as "an enemy will invade our land") and specific ("the Messiah will be born in Bethlehem.")

Moreover, many of the prophets' predictions concerned matters that were future to them, but now are long past. They spoke about their future, not always about our future.[17]

What Are Their "Books" Like?

If there is a single word that describes the prophetic materials, it is "diversity."[18] The prophets themselves were diverse in background, personality, approach, and ministry, and so are the collections that bear their names. One gets a sense of this diversity in the first line of the Book of Hebrews: "In the past God spoke to our forefathers through the prophets at many times and in various ways" (NIV).

But there is much misunderstanding about what the prophetic "books" are like. As we said above, a better term for them would be anthologies.[19] They are not the kind of book produced by someone who sat down at a desk, started writing, finished writing, and got up. Far from it. These "books" are collections of oracles. They are collections of sermons, snatches of sermons, and sermon notes, plus narratives, biography, history, laments, visions, sayings, and prayers.[20]

The various oracles may have been preached over a period of many years. Jeremiah, for example, dictated his messages only after two full decades of his ministry (Jer. 36:2). Today, however, those materials, originally so separated by time, appear side by side in adjoining chapters, or even in the same chapter, as the hymns do in our hymnals. These diverse materials are arranged in ways we often do not understand, frequently with no clear division between them or indication of where one section ends and another begins.[21] For example, some see seven changes of subject in Amos 5.[22]

Ramm points out that "the prophets were preachers and visionaries and not academic lecturers. Prophetic writings are not organized like lecture notes. . . . The prophets are not systematic in their presentation."[23] Needless to say, it can be confusing.

What Was Their Preaching Like?

The preaching of the prophets was poetry. They were poets.[24] They preached poetically as any modern translation indicates.

However, the most important thing about prophetic preaching was not the form but the content. There were prophets in other nations at the same time, and there were many popular or court prophets in Judah and Israel, though the Hebrew prophets added an important and distinctive element. It was a

moral element. They told who the Lord is and, because of who
He is, what He wanted the people to do. Deuteronomy 13:1-3
indicates that the content of the message was the crucial factor
in a prophet's ministry.[25]

This means that the prophetic "books," like all the Bible, are
a combination of two essential elements: the message of the Lord
and the imprint of human personality. The Bible is a divine-
human book, just as Christ is the God-man—it is the Word of the
Lord in human words.

Most of what the prophets said was delivered orally. Sometimes they may have written their message themselves. At
times, disciples who received their messages took pains to pre-
serve their teacher's words.

What About Interpretation?

The same general principles of hermeneutics that we apply
to the entire Bible we also must apply to the prophets, for example, the law of context.[26] The literary context affects the
meaning of any text. Therefore, we take into account the entire
"book" or all of the prophetic "books" as we try to understand
representative passages from them. Ward writes:

> The more we know about the origin and purpose of the books, their
> shape and component parts, the social settings in which they were
> produced, the better we may understand an individual text. Fre-
> quently we can also be helped by studying a text in relation to oth-
> ers of a similar type, in the same book or in other books.[27]

Ramm has insisted that we preachers "should take the literal meaning of a prophetic passage as [our] limiting or controlling guide. How else can [we] proceed? This is the footing
for the interpretation of any passage of Scripture."[28] LaSor has
defined "literal interpretation" as "the understanding which
any person of normal intelligence would get, without any . . .
'code' or 'key.'"[29]

A. B. Davidson, a British scholar at the beginning of the 20th
century whom we need to hear said: "This I consider the first
principle in prophetic interpretation, to assume that the literal
meaning is *his* meaning—that he is moving among realities,
not symbols, among concrete things like people, not abstrac-
tions."[30] (Professor Davidson was, of course, just as much opposed to a forced literalism.)

Having said that, we also recognize that the prophets
preached in poetic and figurative language.[31] When we interpret the prophets, we must give attention to the principles for

interpreting poetry. For example, we know that poetic figures were never intended to be taken literally. Ramm calls them "figurative literal."[32] It is wrong to interpret a literal statement figuratively, but it is also wrong to interpret a figurative statement literally. Our problem is that it is not always easy to determine whether a passage is to be understood literally or figuratively (see Amos 9:13).

A related point is that the prophets spoke the Lord's message in their own language. If the prophet was a farmer, he used the language of the farm in proclaiming the message, speaking in terms of sheep and bears, lions, droughts, famines, and pestilence. If the prophet was of royal lineage (or at least of noble birth as Isaiah apparently was), he spoke of kings, palaces, and foreign policy. Therefore, in order to understand the prophets and their messages, we have to reconstruct as much of their historical situation as possible.

Prophets often expressed their confidence in the future in the best way they knew. Future blessings were often mentioned in material terms, usually as agricultural abundance. Isaiah spoke of peace in the Messianic Age in terms of the lion and the lamb lying down together. Ramm has insisted that "insufficient attention has been paid to the idealized pictures in the Old Testament which are not properly interpreted either by a strict literalism or a vapid spiritualizing."[33]

What About Fulfillment?

There is much oversimplification regarding the fulfillment of prophecy that often leads to misunderstanding. For example, some say the test of a true prophet is whether his predictions were fulfilled or not, an oversimplification that can be abused.

As we have seen, the prediction of the future was only a part of the prophet's message. Therefore, the fulfillment of predictions could be only one element in his validation as a true prophet. Besides, when one verifies whether his words were true or not, it was usually too late; judgment had already fallen.

More important than fulfillment was the moral and religious content of the message. Did the prophet call the people back to the obligations of their covenant relationship? Deuteronomy 13:1-3 warns the people against following a prophet who can interpret dreams or perform miracles, if he leads away from the Lord instead of toward Him.

Many promises and predictions in the prophets were conditional. (Perhaps "contingent" would be a better term.) Jonah

3:4 is one of the best and clearest examples: "Forty more days and Nineveh will be overturned" (NIV). Did that prediction come true? No, it did not. Does that mean that Jonah was a false prophet? Hardly, but what does it mean?

Jonah was a true prophet because he faithfully spoke the Lord's message. He called the people to repentance and to the Lord. The fact that his prediction did not come true does not affect the validity of his message. All of this apparently means that Jonah's prediction was conditional. The condition is not stated, but it is there. It must have been something like this: "Unless you repent, in forty more days Nineveh will be destroyed."

Are there other predictions in the Old Testament that are contingent, even though the condition may not be stated? Jeremiah 18:7-10 seems to indicate that the answer is yes. That passage speaks of a prediction, either of doom or blessing which was capable of being modified or reversed depending on the response of the people or their lack of response.

Isaiah predicted the imminent death of Hezekiah. No sooner had he done so than the Lord sent him back in to tell the king that he would live. There are several other examples of conditional or contingent predictions.[34] Scott comments:

> God retains the full freedom of an active will; he cannot be tied down by any preannouncement of events or charts of dates, but his freedom is neither capricious or arbitrary. Its limitations are the requirements of his own nature—justice, mercy, and truth."[35]

In fact, many predictions were given so that they would not have to be fulfilled. The Lord's purpose all along was to get the people to turn back to him. H. L. Ellison, an outstanding interpreter of the prophets, said that "with minor but most important exceptions, prophecy is conditional."[36]

According to the New Testament, much Old Testament prophecy has been fulfilled in Christ. Not all Old Testament prophecy is about Christ—we do not find Him behind every Old Testament bush, not even every burning bush. My long-time colleague F. B. Huey has suggested that it is not profitable for us to search the messages of judgment Amos delivered on the Philistines, Edomites, Ammonites, and Moabites for hidden meaning about Christ. Amos was condemning those nations for historical sins. He was not cryptically speaking of the Messiah.[37]

But much of the Old Testament certainly is about the Messiah. If we take the Bible as a whole, Jesus Christ is central. The Old Testament does point basically and ultimately to Him.

As Christians, we have to read the Bible from front to back, as well as from back to front.

There are numerous hints, at times bright and clear beams of messianic expectation. We remember how Jesus dealt with His two troubled disciples on the Emmaus Road: "Beginning with Moses and all the Prophets, he explained to them what was said in all the Scriptures concerning himself" (Luke 24:27, NIV). Do you not wish we knew what those particular passages were?

How to Proclaim Prophecy

Consider some examples of how to deal with prophetic texts in proclamation. Isaiah 6:1-8 might well be treated under the title, "What Happens When a Person Meets the Lord?" T. B. Maston often told us that, if we truly worship the Lord, something will happen to us. What should happen, what does happen, in a true experience of worship?[38]

This is one of those wonderful passages that outlines itself.

    I. The Lord convicts the person who meets Him, 6:5.
       A. Conviction of personal sinfulness, 6:5a.
       B. Conviction of the sinfulness of the people, 6:5b.
    II. The Lord cleanses the person who meets Him, 6:6-7.
       A. The condition of uncleanness (removal of guilt).
       B. The sinful deeds (sin) are atoned.
   III. The Lord commissions the person who meets Him, 6:8a.
       A. A new capacity to hear the Lord's message.
       B. A new vision of the task.
   IV. The person who meets the Lord makes a commitment, 6:8b.
       A. An immediate response.
       B. A voluntary response.

Several elements of the message bear comment. Obviously, we need to know something about the layout of the temple and its altar of burnt offering. We need to know what "seraphim" were. We certainly need to know the historical background, such as King Uzziah's significance and why his death was significant. This historical information in 6:1 has a bearing on the message of the passage: the Lord is the true king. The king may be dead, but the true King continues to reign.

Isaiah heard the threefold cry of the heavenly beings and realized he was not fit to join in their song. In realizing his own condition, he felt a responsibility for the spiritual condition of his people.

Conviction of sin comes first, but the Lord (and only He) can remedy the situation. A word study of "iniquity" or "guilt" (*awon*) and "sin" (*het*) is in order here. The first means present uncleanness, the root of the problem. The second refers to the symptoms, the outward acts that express the inner condition. Only after the cleansing comes the call. Only then do we see the task before us and our part in it.

But the vision of the Lord does not end until there is commitment. Note how immediate Isaiah's response was. He was like the elementary school child who knows the answer, bouncing up and down in the seat, jabbing her hand into the air, saying, "Teacher, me, me, call on me!" When we see the Lord in His holiness and glory, we volunteer for service.

When Isaiah stepped from the world of self into the presence of the Lord, his life was completely and permanently altered. The same is true with us. If these things have not happened to us, there is only one explanation: It has been some time since we have met the Lord.

A completely different type of passage demands a totally distinct treatment, though once again substantial word studies are involved. For example, we need to find what was the background of the prophet's hearers? Why did they need this message? What would it have meant to them in their situation? Regardless of one's view of the date of writing of Isaiah 40–55, all will agree that the message was directed to the people of the exile.

The following approach is synthetic. The passage is more or less taken apart and put back together in a logical fashion. The outline is also considerably simpler, the kind that I have come to favor more and more over the years.

We Are His, Isaiah 43:1-7
   I. He created us, 43:1,6-7.
  II. He loves us, 43:4.
 III. He redeemed us, 43:1,3-6.
 IV. He claims us, 43:1,7.
  V. He accompanies us, 43:2,5.
 VI. He protects us, 43:2-3.

The outline is simple, but still somewhat lengthy and involved. I have found help by having it printed for the people to refer to. I have even used a chalkboard to put it before the people during a Sunday evening service.

Who are we, as the Lord's people? We are His. (Of course, we are talking as much about who *He* is as He relates to us as we are about who we are.)

There is more about creation in the last part of Isaiah than in any other part of the Bible, even more than in Genesis. The Lord is the Creator. He formed us (Isa. 43:1). He created us for His glory (43:7). There are also numerous related passages, such as 40:13-14,28. The verb (*bara*) appears in the Old Testament only with the Lord as the subject; it refers to His unique creative activity.

We are the Lord's because He loves us. The Old Testament has far, far more to say about the Lord's love than we usually think, for example in 43:4: "I love you," or even "I have loved you." Moffatt translates the verse saying we are beloved.

We are His because He has redeemed us (43:1). He is our Savior; He has ransomed us (43:3-4; see also 50:2). This prophet mentioned this truth thirteen times in twenty-seven chapters. Only one other prophet, Jeremiah, mentions it once. The idea of redeemer had its basis in the family. The nearest relative, the (*goel*), looked out for the family members in several important ways, illustrated in the story of Ruth and elsewhere.

The exodus was the great redemptive act of the Old Testament; Isaiah talked about a new exodus, greater than the old one. The Old Testament idea of redemption—deliverance and protection—is based on the exodus concept.

We are His because He claims us, in Isaiah 43:1,6-7. Claims are important in the Bible. He claims us as His special possession, His precious treasure (see Ex. 19:5-6).

Verse 2 assures us that the Lord is with us. He is with us all the time, in times difficult or bright. What a word for needy people today; we need not be alone. Finally, we are His because He cares for us (Isa. 43:2-3). He protects us. Therefore, we are safe. After such an examination of this marvelous passage, both preacher and hearer should be saying, "*I* am His."

A third passage, Jeremiah 18:1-11, is the most difficult of all. It is difficult in part because it is so familiar and because its message is deep and complex. The message is entitled, "What the Lord is Like," based on Jeremiah 18:1-11. Again, the outline is a simple one.

    I. The Lord is completely sovereign, 18:1-3,6.
    II. The Lord is often disappointed, 18:4,7-10.
    III. The Lord is always free, 18:4,7-11.
    IV. The Lord is always patient, 18:4,11.

The historical background is less important in this passage and contributes to our understanding only in a general way; Judah was sinful and would soon suffer the Lord's judgment unless she turned (returned) to Him.

Jeremiah saw something at the potter's house that showed him what the Lord is like. He learned first that the Lord is sovereign, 18:1-3,6. He is the potter; we are the clay. This is the most obvious teaching of this familiar passage. However, we must be careful to note that the passage teaches other things about what the Lord is like.

For example, the Lord is often disappointed, 18:4,7-10. Though he is completely sovereign, this does not mean His perfect will is always done. In the present scheme of things, everything that happens does not happen because He wants it to happen. Other factors are also involved, such as human choice and the presence of evil in the world.

According to 18:4, the clay vessel the potter was making was spoiled in his hands. Was this because he spoiled it, or wanted it to be spoiled? Did he intend to make a spoiled vessel? Of course not. The Lord is often disappointed.

Our passage further teaches that the Lord is always free, 18:4,7-11. He is sovereign, and that means He is free. He is free to change the way He relates to us. He is free to respond to our response to Him or our lack of response. The passage says that the Lord changes His mind, His attitude. He can change the way He works out His will. He can change the means and approaches He uses to accomplish His eternal purposes. If He is not free to do this, then He is not sovereign.

This means that prophecy is often conditional (see above). Predictions of both blessing and doom were often conditional. Verses 7-8 give the negative to the positive side of this truth, and verses 9-10 the positive to the negative side. The Lord is free to adjust to someone's change of heart.

Most important of all, the Lord is always patient (18:4,11). What did the craftsman do when the vessel was marred in His hands? He kept on working. He kept reshaping it until He had molded "it into another vessel to his liking" (NEB).

The Lord is a God of grace. He does not give up on us. He always gives us another chance. This is the gospel, the gospel of grace, right here in the Old Testament. It is the good news of forgiveness, the good news that the Lord is always patient.

Other Ways to Do Prophetic Exposition

I am fascinated by the creative possibilities of preaching the prophets. An area pastor developed a monologue based on the experience of Jonah. A recent student did the same with Job's reactions to his so-called friends. When I taught in college and preached and taught Hosea in the churches, a student developed a monologue and presented it, in full costume, during my introductory session.

Or what about a dialogue message? A dialogue between Malachi and the people he preached to would almost prepare itself. Haggai often seemed to be dialoguing with his hearers about rebuilding the temple. Or what about a dialogue between Habakkuk . . . and the Lord?

More important than how we do exposition is *that we do it.* We must regularly, faithfully, earnestly proclaim the message of the Lord's servants, the prophets.

Suggested Bibliography on the Prophets

Blenkinsopp, Joseph. *A History of Prophecy in Israel: From the Settlement in the Land to the Hellenistic Period.* (Philadelphia: Westminster, 1983).

Buber, Martin. *The Prophetic Faith.* (New York: Collier, 1949).

Heschel, Abraham Joshua. *The Prophets.* (New York: Harper & Row, 1962).

Lindblom, J. *Prophecy in Ancient Israel.* (Philadelphia: Muhlenberg, 1962).

Rad, Gerhard von. *Old Testament Theology: The Theology of Israel's Prophetic Traditions*, II. Trans. D. M. G. Stalker. (New York: Harper & Row, 1965).

Suggested Bibliography on Preaching the Prophets

Ackland, Donald F. "Preaching from Hosea to a Nation in Crisis." *Southwestern Journal of Theology* 18:1 (1975) 43-55.

Fasol, Al. "Preaching from Malachi." *Southwestern Journal of Theology* 30:1 (1987) 32-34.

Gloer, W. Hulitt. "Preaching from Malachi." *Review and Expositor* 84:3 (1987) 453-64.

Stanfield, V. L. "Preaching Values in Jeremiah." *Southwestern Journal of Theology* 4:1 (1961) 69-80.

Strange, John O. "Preaching from Amos." *Southwestern Journal of Theology* 9:1 (1966) 69-79.

Tuck, William P. "Preaching from Jeremiah." *Review and Expositor* 78:3 (1981) 381-95.

Notes

1. P. Yancey, "The Bible's 'Fusty Old Men,'" *Christianity Today*, 2 October 1987, 17.

2. J. M. Ward, *The Prophets* (Nashville: Abingdon, 1982), 10.

3. G. Fee and D. Stuart, *How to Read the Bible for All Its Worth: A Guide to Understanding the Bible* (Grand Rapids: Zondervan, 1982), 149; see also Yancey, 17.

4. B. Ramm, *Protestant Biblical Interpretation*, 3rd ed. (Grand Rapids: Baker, 1970), 244-45.

5. See Ward, 9.

6. Ramm, 245.

7. J. B. Green, *How to Read Prophecy* (Downers Grove, IL: InterVarsity, 1984), 25.

8. Fee and Stuart, 149.

9. Ward, 24-25.

10. W. S. LaSor, "Interpretation of Prophecy," in *Hermeneutics* (Grand Rapids: Baker, 1967), 98.

11. W. S. LaSor, D. A. Hubbard, and F. W. Bush, *Old Testament Survey: The Message, Form, and Background of the Old Testament* (Grand Rapids: Eerdmans, 1982), 298; J. Hastings, ed. *Dictionary of the Bible*, s.v. "Prophecy and Prophets".

12. See Ex. 4:15; 7:1.

13. "By means of warnings and encouragements regarding the *future*, all Israel was called to *present* faithfulness." Green, *How to Read Prophecy*, 59.

14. LaSor, "Interpretation of Prophecy," 94f.; W. Hulitt Gloer, "Preaching from Malachi," *Review and Expositor* 84:3 (1987): 454.

15. Fee and Stuart, 151.

16. C. E. Armerding, "Prophecy in the Old Testament," *A Guide to Biblical Prophecy*, eds. C. E. Armerding and W. W. Gasque (Peabody, MA: Hendrickson, 1989), 70.

17. Fee and Stuart, 163; Armerding, "Prophecy in the Old Testament," 70.

18. Ward, 9, 22.

19. R. K. Harrison, *Introduction to the Old Testament* (Grand Rapids: Eerdmans, 1969), 780.

20. Ward, 9.

21. Ward, 9.

22. Fee and Stuart, 158-59.

23. Ramm, 249.

24. Fee and Stuart, 161.

25. A. B. Davidson, *Old Testament Prophecy* (Edinburgh: T. & T. Clark, 1905), 153, 248.

26. LaSor, "Interpretation of Prophecy," 94-95.

27. Ward, 21.

28. Ramm, 253.

29. LaSor, "Interpretation of Prophecy," 99.

30. Davidson, *Old Testament Prophecy*, 167-68.

31. Armerding, "Prophecy in the Old Testament," 69-70.

32. Ramm, 49.

33. Ramm, 254.

34. See, for example, Amos 7:1-6; 1 Kings 21:17-29; Ezekiel 26:7-14 compared with 29:17-20; and Haggai 2:19b in light of Malachi.

35. R. B. Y. Scott, *The Relevance of the Prophets: An introduction to the Old Testament prophets and their message* rev. ed. (New York: Macmillan, 1968), 11.

36. H. L. Ellison, "Jonah" in *The Expositor's Bible Commentary* (Grand Rapids: Zondervan, 1985), 385.

37. F. B. Huey, *Yesterday's Prophets for Today's World* (Nashville: Broadman, 1980), 88.

38. Christian Ethics class, Spring, 1957.

5

Preaching Wisdom

Duane A. Garrett

Why Preach Wisdom?

Why Wisdom Is Not Preached

Many pastors may wonder if it is possible, or even desirable, to preach from biblical Wisdom Literature. Preaching from Wisdom[1] is difficult. Much of Proverbs appears to have no order whatsoever. One proverb simply follows another, and there seems to be no unity, structure, or direction in the text. One cannot preach through a chapter of Proverbs if that means preaching on as many different topics as there are verses in the chapter.

The lengthy discourses of Job are often difficult to interpret and seem gloriously irrelevant to anything the modern Christian is likely to face. More than that, the speeches that seem most plausible as sermon material come from the mouths of men who are explicitly declared to have been in the wrong—Job's three friends! One might make a meaningful sermon out of Job 8 (Bildad's speech), but what is a preacher to make of Job 19 (a complaint by Job) or for that matter of Job 38–41 (God's speeches)?

Ecclesiastes is a greater problem yet. Here is a biblical book which looks positively skeptical and pessimistic. Although some passages have potential as sermon texts (such as 5:10-17, on the folly of pursuing wealth), others appear to question the reality of afterlife (3:18-21), warn the reader against being overly righteous (7:16), and question the value of wisdom itself (1:12-18).

Song of Songs presents even greater, more obvious difficulties for the preacher. A love song is not a likely source for a Christian sermon. Indeed, not a few Christians would be embarrassed even to hear a text from the Song read aloud in a church service! The difficulty of interpreting the Song, moreover, adds to the dilemma of how to preach from the book.

Perhaps an even greater hindrance to preaching Wisdom is the suspicion many have that it contains no gospel. This is not merely because it is in the Old Testament, but because Wisdom is, more than even the Law, heavily concerned with personal ethics. To be sure, Proverbs contains many warnings against promiscuity and criminal behavior, but does it lead a person to God? It may convict a person of his or her guilt, but this is more a function of Law than of Wisdom. The frequent injunction to "get wisdom" in Proverbs is good as far as it goes, many would say, but how can this compare to the New Testament appeal to repent and believe in Christ? If the absence of gospel is apparent in Proverbs, moreover, how much more formidable is it to relate the philosophic wrestling of Job and Ecclesiastes and the poetry of the Song to the evangelical faith?

Why Wisdom Must Be Preached

To answer these questions, one must grapple with the issue of the purpose of the preaching ministry of the Christian pastor. If his only function is to draw the unbeliever to faith in Christ, then indeed there is little material for him in Wisdom. He can only use Wisdom texts as springboards for moving into evangelistic messages or claim to find the gospel message in Wisdom through allegory. If he does either of these, however, he really does not preach biblical Wisdom at all, but only uses a Wisdom passage as a pretense for a New Testament sermon.

On the other hand, if it is the function of the Christian pastor not only to call the unbeliever to repentance but also to edify his congregation through the teaching of biblical doctrine and morality, then he must preach Wisdom. The apostle Paul, moreover, both by example and pronouncement, indicates the latter to be the case. He devoted prolonged periods of his life to the teaching of the Word of God to the churches (Acts 18:11; 20:20) and exhorted Timothy to do the same (1 Tim. 4:13; 2 Tim. 3:16). His rule was not to refrain from teaching anything that might be helpful to the churches (Acts 20:20).

Wisdom is both helpful and needed in the church. It is no exaggeration to say that the current moral climate of the church is alarming. (I particularly refer to evangelical churches.) The in-

famous cases of television preachers who have fallen to the
seduction of wealth, power, and sex are merely the most conspicuous examples. Throughout North America, pastors who
would readily identify themselves as "Bible-believing" are scan-
dalizing their churches through immoral behavior of every kind.

More than that, the corruption of pastors in churches com-
prises but a fraction of the acts of folly committed by the
"laity," whose acts receive less attention in the Christian community perhaps because they are less conspicuous. Divorces
and domestic conflict, poor financial management, substance
abuse, and simple dishonesty entrap men and women who consider themselves born-again Christians. Children who grow up
in the church succumb to peer pressure and other emotional
stresses (often brought on by disillusionment with their Christian elders) and abandon the faith. In many cases, it is absurd
to contend that these young men and women have not been
sufficiently evangelized. They are not only scripturally baptized—they have heard the gospel so many times they could re-
cite a gospel sermon verbatim.

Precisely for these reasons, pastors must preach Wisdom as
part of their regular sermon schedule. In an age of seduction,
what biblical text condemns casual sex more forcefully than
Proverbs 7? What text better than Proverbs 1:10-19 addresses
the young man who is drawn by the comradeship and easy
wealth of gang life? Simply put, Wisdom helps the Christian
learn right from wrong.

It is not even enough to say that we must preach Wisdom because it teaches morals. Brevard Childs correctly observes that:

> The didactic function of biblical wisdom literature is far broader
> than that which is usually implied by the term ethics. When the
> sage challenged his pupils to pursue wisdom, it not only involved
> moral decisions regarding wrong and right behavior, but was an
> intellectual and pragmatic activity which sought to encompass
> the totality of experience. Nevertheless, it is striking that the
> pattern of human conduct which the sage sought to inculcate
> overlapped to a large extent with that set as obedient behavior
> within the Pentateuch and prescribed for the covenant people.[2]

Both John Bright[3] and Walter Kaiser[4] have also noted the correspondence between Wisdom and Law.

The point is that Wisdom does more than teach right from
wrong. It teaches moral principles *as part of the life of faith.* In
other words, the ethics taught in Wisdom show the believer
how to have a peaceful, ordered, and happy life by which he or
she may more fully glorify God. Unlike the Law, moreover,

Wisdom teaches the reader how to deal with practical, ordinary issues in life. This may include matters as mundane as not being a nuisance to others (Prov. 27:14) and as specific as a warning not to be surety on another's debt (Prov. 22:26). This advice may appear trivial, but there is nothing trivial about acquiring social skills or financial prudence. Here again, the advice in Proverbs does not come as "secular" common sense, but as guides for practical living for those who desire to please God.

In addition, Job and Ecclesiastes face questions addressed nowhere else in the Bible, and they do so with a bluntness that demands the reader's attention. The Song concerns itself with a matter too long neglected by the church, that of sexual and romantic love. For the pastor, the question is not one of whether but how he may use these texts for the edification of his church.

Principles of Interpretation in the Wisdom Sermon

Interpretation precedes proclamation. Before the preacher can draw a message from a text, he must have some idea what that text means. This brings us to the broad questions of hermeneutics, and some survey of general principles must be given here. The emphasis, however, shall be interpretive principles as they apply to Wisdom.

Allegory

A method commonly employed in the interpretation of Old Testament texts is allegorization. In this approach, biblical texts are seen as elaborate systems of symbols which stand for doctrinal and practical truth. No sustained attempt is made to relate the interpretation of the text to its historical setting or the author's intended meaning. Although many examples of allegorization can be found in the history of exegesis, it is not originally a Christian approach to the Old Testament.[5]

Nevertheless, allegorization holds a real attraction to Christians, especially preachers, since it seems both to provide an avenue for dealing with difficult or embarrassing texts and to offer a bridge between the text of the Old Testament and the truths of the New. Thus, one can contend that Psalm 137:9 is not really about smashing Edomite babies on rocks; it is a command for Christians to put little sins to death before they become big sins.[6] One might equally well take Proverbs 7 as a warning not so much against the prostitute as against the false teacher and cult leader. Or, one could preach Proverbs 20:18

which warns the reader to seek advice before going to war as a gospel sermon, "Seek the Lord before going to do battle with death and the devil."

The problem with this method, however, is obvious—the texts themselves give no indication that they mean what the allegorist claims. The authority of the allegorizing preacher is thus seriously undercut. If, after all, the real authority of the preacher is the Bible, what weight do his words carry if they do not legitimately arise from his text? The allegorist works under the *pretense* of preaching a passage in order to proclaim his own ideas. He may amaze an audience with his cleverness, but the actual meaning of the text will be lost to his listeners. Those who preach Wisdom through allegory will never bring the real messages of Wisdom to their flock.

The Topical Approach

Another possible method is to preach on selected topics from Wisdom. This approach is particularly attractive with regard to Proverbs and Ecclesiastes because it escapes the dilemma of the lack of clear arrangement in the text. It also allows the minister to address specific issues and concerns.

One could thus choose, for example, the topic of "honesty" and select a number of proverbs which address that concern. The preacher could then arrange the selected proverbs into a coherent, organized sermon outline and deliver his message accordingly. Other potential topics would include "alcohol abuse," "laziness," or "seeking advice."

A topical sermon on laziness might be something like this:

"The Path of Laziness"
 I. Laziness leads to poverty (Prov. 10:4).
 II. Laziness leads to abject humiliation (Prov. 12:24).
 III. Laziness leads to empty pride (Prov. 26:16).

In the hands of a skillful preacher, the topical sermon can be an effective way of bringing out essential points of biblical teaching on a given subject.

Several problems with the topical approach, however, are evident. First, while it may work well with Proverbs and perhaps Ecclesiastes, it is less useful for Job or the Song. Second, verses that relate to a given teaching are not always easily discovered. Texts that pertain to laziness are not all found simply by looking up "laziness" in a concordance. A topical sermon which is not thoroughly researched may give a dangerously incomplete analysis and really be no more than a pretentious word study. Third, implicit in this approach is a certain shallowness which obscures the complexities and tensions in the biblical text itself.

Fourth, and perhaps most important, the topical approach virtually concedes that Proverbs is a disorganized chaos which, as it stands, is useless for preaching and teaching. One cannot but wonder if the scriptural authors did not know better than we what they were about. In other words, there may be some very good reasons why Proverbs and Ecclesiastes are written the way they are. Instead of abandoning the search for deeper understanding, perhaps we should work a little harder before we pronounce a book, in its present form, unusable for sermons.

The Contextual Approach

The contextual[7] approach takes a single, connected passage of Scripture (usually at least several verses in length) and expounds upon the meaning of that text. It operates from the assumption that the task of the preacher is to explain the meaning of the Bible *as it is written, in its literary and historical context*, to his congregation.

The biblical writers did not write verses and sermon texts. They wrote books. The minister who claims to be an expositor of the biblical text must therefore begin at the highest level of the material, the complete book of Genesis, John, Romans, Proverbs, or Song of Songs. That is, he must understand what the book as a whole is all about before he can begin to expound on any individual text.[8] It is not too much to say that one should embark on study of the history, theology, and message of a biblical book before preaching any sermons from that book.

Having come to initial conclusions about the overall argument of a book, the expositor must examine how the book is structured. This will enable him to mark off the boundaries of individual units in the book. In Wisdom, these units are not always as easy to find as the pericope of the synoptic Gospels, but they are important nonetheless. They are the basic texts for the sermon. Normally, a sermon should cover a passage which has a clear beginning and end *in the structure of the text itself* and not simply in the mind of the preacher.

When the expositor has isolated and chosen a sermon text, he must observe both its *external* and *internal* context. The external context of a passage is the texts that come before and after it. Especially in the exposition of Job, knowledge of what precedes and follows a particular section is critical for the interpretation of that section, since it is part of a larger argument. The internal context of a passage is its structure or outline. Understanding of internal context is not only crucial for interpretation, it also often contributes materially to the sermon outline itself.

From this point, the normal steps of exegesis follow,[9] albeit the interpretation of a Wisdom text will emphasize some aspects of exegesis over others. The historical and geographical setting of a Wisdom text is not generally of major significance, but the social setting of a text (especially its intended audience) can be of great importance. The interpreter would obviously want to know if his text were prose or poetry (the latter being more common in Wisdom). The genre of a single passage will usually be determined (in the case of Wisdom) by the genre of its book, but the *form* of a single text (observational proverb, prohibition, numerical saying, extended discourse, hymn, etc.) will vary greatly in Wisdom.[10] Grammatical and lexical analyses follow; in Wisdom as in the rest of the Bible, the interpreter who does not maintain his facility in the biblical languages is seriously handicapped.

At this point, the minister will need to seek out the life issues (violence, business ethics, sexual behavior, the need for wisdom, etc.) in his text. He probably has some fairly clear ideas about the life issues of the text already (since he has some reason for choosing to preach this specific text), but careful investigation may bring him to see issues and concerns in the text that he had not seen before. Also, the preacher should generally try to emphasize the issues that the text itself emphasizes.

As he moves to the actual preparation and presentation of his sermon, the pastor will need to keep two goals in focus. First, he must preach or teach the lessons of the text itself. As described earlier in this essay, it is only in this way that he will be able to edify his members of his congregation in order that they grow into mature men and women of God. Second, as a Christian minister, he must preach Christ. Even so, the movement from the specific concerns of the text to the preaching of the evangelical faith must be legitimate and natural; if the transition is forced, it will be apparent to all and the power of the message will be lost.

The contextual approach allows the pastor to preach from a single text, use the same structure and argument as the biblical writer himself, and yet select the topics he considers most needful for his congregation by choosing his texts carefully. For these reasons, it should be the normal approach for the evangelical pastor.

The Books of Wisdom

Rather than continue in an abstract discussion on preaching from Wisdom, we must now turn to the Wisdom books themselves and then to some specific examples. For the purposes of this essay, the books of Wisdom are Proverbs, Ecclesiastes, Job, and the Song.[11] These four books are anything but alike, and statements of general principles for using them in the sermon risk obscuring major differences among them. Therefore, it is necessary to consider each book separately as a possible source of sermon texts.

Job

The immediate problem that confronts the preacher who tries to use Job is that of the overall purpose and meaning of the book. He will have scarcely completed a superficial reading of the book before he realizes that the cliché that Job deals with the problem of "why the righteous suffer" is inadequate. The reader who comes to Job looking for a simple solution to that problem is apt to be confused, if not disappointed.

Discussion of avenues toward interpreting Job is of necessity very brief here, but the following suggestions may be useful. The initial challenge that sets the whole book in motion is not the problem of suffering but Satan's question, "Does Job fear God for nothing?" (Job 1:9, NIV). In other words, the central issue here is, "Why should a person serve God?" and the implication is that the only reason people obey God is for personal safety and material gain. Through the testing of Job, the text shows the reader that the reasons for trusting God, even in the face of extraordinary suffering, are much greater than that.

Job, his three friends, and Elihu (who enters in ch. 32) all begin the book with the presupposition that piety is the safest path in life. God protects and prospers the righteous but destroys the wicked. Because of his sufferings, however, Job realizes that his theology has been facile. He knows he has not deserved what has happened to him (2:3 makes it clear that in this, he is correct), and, in his bewilderment, he challenges God to come down and explain Himself. Job's friends, meanwhile, are offended at what they hear coming from Job's mouth and vainly try to make him bow to the traditional orthodoxy.

The book lays out a clear development in the thought of Job and of his friends. The friends become more and more frenzied in their efforts to bring Job to "repentance." They move from gentle rebuke (4:1–5:27) to ferocious (and undeserved) condemnation (22:1-30). At the same time, Job becomes increasingly disgusted with the trivial and inappropriate orthodoxy into which his friends try to force him. Nevertheless, Job does not simply get angrier and angrier. He also comes to believe that God will yet give him a redeemer and that he will someday be vindicated, even if his vindication has to await the resurrection (14:13-17; 19:23-27). Job ends his speeches with a profound assertion of his innocence, and then falls into silence. There is nothing more for him to say.

God's speeches (Job 38–41) perplex many readers, but Job's response (42:1-6) indicates that they fully answer his questions. God's answers primarily focus on the smallness and weakness of Job over against God's creation and emphasize that only God can tame the monster Leviathan (41:1-34). The language is almost apocalyptic, and the message is that, in the conquest of evil, *God knows what he is doing.* Job, while in the middle of his sufferings, cannot see that God is in the process of righting all wrongs.

The answer to Satan's challenge, "Does Job serve God for nothing?" is apparent. Job's reward, as Job himself has learned, is not his safety and prosperity, but is God Himself. He knows God, and that is reason enough to serve God. He realizes, moreover, that he can trust God to do right. Any present injustice is only apparent or temporary.[12]

For the modern preacher, the task is to bring these lessons home to his congregation. He probably will not preach all the way through Job, which would be a difficult and time-consuming task in any case, but he could preach a series on passages in Job which bring out the essentials of the message of the book. Major themes in Job would include the dangers of pharisaical orthodoxy (Job 22), the value of knowing God for His own sake (Job 1:9), the need for compassion on the suffering and oppressed (Job 24), and the greatness of God's power (Job 38). These are only a few of the themes of the book; moreover, the necessity of an advocate before God (16:19) and the elusiveness of true wisdom (Job 28) are also major themes. Job 31 is perhaps the clearest statement of the ethical life in the Bible. With Job, the pastor can bring his congregation to a new depth of appreciation for what it means to know God.

Proverbs

The individual proverbs are for the most part straightforward and do not present major problems in interpretation.[13] Here, the more serious dilemma is organizational. It is difficult to make a coherent sermon of a passage that appears to be little more than a random collection of proverbs. In much of the book, however, this problem does not exist. In Proverbs 1–9 we have a series of lengthy discourses on such subjects as the value of wisdom (Prov. 4), the danger of adultery (Prov. 7), and the folly of laziness (6:6-11). Chapters at the end of the book are also organized into fairly obvious segments, such as the poem in praise of the good woman (31:10-31). Still, many pastors will be driven away by the seeming confusion in the heart of the book (especially Prov. 10:1–22:16).

This confusion is only apparent. The proverbs of 10:1ff are not dropped into the text at random but are, for the most part, carefully arranged in accordance with the standards of ancient literature. Parallelism, chiasmus, merismus, and other such devices abound. In particular, many proverbs are grouped into small collections according to the standards of ancient rhetorical technique.[14] When the pastor or preacher learns to recognize these collections, he will find himself better able to develop sermons on Proverbs that cohere to the actual structure of the text itself.

As examples of proverb grouping, some of the texts of Proverbs 11 illustrate well the way the book is organized. Proverbs 11:1-21 are grouped together by the inclusio formed by of "abomination of the Lord" (*tocabat Yahweh*) and "his delight" (*resono*) in verses 1 and 20 (vv. 20 and 21 are bound together as a couplet). Several smaller collections appear within this inclusio; three are noted here.

Verses 1-4 are the first collection. It is chiastic (ABB'A') in structure: verse 1 describes God's hatred of fraud, and verse 4 answers it with the warning that wrongfully gained wealth does a person no good on the day of judgment. Between these two verses, verses 2-3 teach that humility and integrity rather than arrogance and duplicity are the best guides to life. A pun (a favorite device of the Hebrews) links 1b and 2a. God delights in accurate weights (weights that are as heavy as they ought to be—1b), but the fate of the arrogant is disgrace (*qaton*, literally "lightness"). Behind this pun is the concept of the root (*kbd*) "to be heavy" or "honored." The idea is that "weight" is something that both the humble[15] man and the accurate measure have in common and something that the proud man and the fraudulent weight both lack.

A shorter couplet, also bound together by an inclusio, is 11:7-8. The inclusio is formed by the word "wicked" (*rsc*) at the beginning of verse 7 and end of verse 8.[16] The text asserts both the hopelessness of the wicked in the face of death and misery and irritation of their lives as they see the troubles that the righteous avoid falling on their own heads. By implication, it holds out the hope of eternal life to those who fear God in that they, unlike the godless, have hope in the face of death.

A somewhat more complex unit is that found in 11:9-13. It is a chiasmus (vv. 9-12) with an afterword (v. 13). The center of the chiasmus, vv. 10-11, is an obvious parallel couplet. These verses deal with the blessing that comes to a city when the righteous prosper and the wicked are destroyed and speak of how the upright and wicked respectively build up or tear down a town with their mouths. The outer verses of the chiasmus, 9 and 12, also parallel one another in that both concern the destruction of a neighbor through slander. In addition, vv. 9-12 all begin with the letter (*b*). Verse 13 stands outside the chiasmus but appears to relate to it; the reader needs to find trustworthy friends who can maintain a confidence. The point is that nothing is so harmful to a community as a gossip, and this theme links together the two ideas of the chiasmus.

Similar collections and patterns are found throughout Proverbs. Many of the collections, moreover, are much easier to discover. Proverbs 22:17–24:22, for example, is a collection of thirty sayings (22:20) modeled on the sayings of Amenemope,[17] and the thirty sayings are easily identified in the text. The various collections of Proverbs 25–31 are also fairly self-evident.

For the preacher who desires to bring the message of Proverbs home to his congregation, awareness of these collections is essential. They not only mark off the intended limits of individual texts, they also form the basic structure of the Proverbs sermon.

Ecclesiastes

One might say that Ecclesiastes combines the difficulties of both Job and Proverbs. That is, it is both difficult to interpret because it appears excessively pessimistic, and it seems loosely organized at best.

Both problems, in fact, must be examined in light of the *genre* and *intended audience* of Ecclesiastes. The book was not written for the ordinary Israelite. To the contrary, members of its original audience had access to the king (8:3), devoted themselves to the pursuit of wisdom (1:12-18), and either had or were in pursuit of wealth (5:10-17).[18] In short, the first readers were members of the aristocracy. This implies that Ecclesiastes must be read in light of other wisdom literature which addressed the ruling or educated classes, especially the literature from Egypt.

When Ecclesiastes is compared to Egyptian instructional literature, at least two parallels are immediately evident. First, both move somewhat at random from subject to subject. When analyzing the structure of Ecclesiastes, therefore, one should not seek a modern, hierarchical outline. Second, both deal with the matter of how a person in a position of prominence should behave,[19] and in particular, speak against the oppression of commoners and the poor.[20] This does not mean that Ecclesiastes is in all points like its Egyptian counterparts. It certainly is not, but these parallels should aid in the task of interpretation.

Because Ecclesiastes does not adhere to a modern type of structure the reader must be prepared for fairly abrupt changes as the book moves about among its topics. These topics include the quest for wisdom, the value of wealth, the value of fame, the use of political power, and the power of death as the nullifier of human achievement. The modern preacher who seeks to use Ecclesiastes will find his task easier if he learns to identify the sudden transitions in the book and selects passages that adhere to the book's own structure.[21]

The apparent pessimism of the book, moreover, is a result of its genre and intended audience. Those who first received the book were apparently well educated in not only Israelite, but international wisdom as well. They were not children who needed to be taught the first principles of wisdom, as the readers of Proverbs apparently were.[22] On the other hand, they may have been inclined to seek happiness through intellectual achievements, wealth and all that goes with it, political power, or some other form of success. Ecclesiastes warns precisely these readers that all their achievements will mean nothing when they go to the grave and that any effort to find happiness in accomplishments leads only to futility.

In addition, Ecclesiastes both answers objections the readers may raise and contradicts the notions of security to which they cling. The apparent challenge to the concept of afterlife (3:18-21) is a case in point. When carefully examined, the text does not deny the very possibility of afterlife, but it does question the common notion that the human is immortal *apart from the work of God*. This idea is as old as ancient Egyptian and Greek religion and as recent as "New Age" concepts of immortality or reincarnation. Ecclesiastes attacks the common view that one need not regard death as an enemy and a dreadful force because humans are immortal anyway. In this, Ecclesiastes is wholly in agreement with the New Testament doctrine that death is an enemy (overcome by Christ) and that the real hope of eternal life is the *resurrection*. Simply put, Ecclesiastes rejects pagan or "New Age" notions of eternal life and drives the reader to seek eternal life not in himself, but in the power of God, specifically (in light of later revelation) in the power that raised Jesus from the dead.

Far from being a problem book, Ecclesiastes should be regarded as the most evangelical book of all of Wisdom. It strips away the ideologies and false hopes by which men and women live and loosens the grip that the quest for wealth, power, and education hold over people. In so doing, Ecclesiastes eloquently turns the reader toward God, the only hope of eternal meaning and life.

Song of Songs

Christian interpretations of the Song generally fall into three categories: the allegorical, the historical/dramatic, and the poetic.[23] The allegorical approach is in fact by no means unique to Christians; many Jewish interpreters have taken the Song as an allegory of the love between Israel and the Lord. Most Christian allegorists have seen it as a song of the love between Christ and the church, but the enormous variety of Christian allegories on the Song goes far beyond that.

A few examples of allegorical interpretations of the Song are as follows:

(1) The mare of 1:9 refers to the church or to the Christian soul as she hastens after Christ or as she draws the chariot of the gospel to all nations.[24]

(2) "The king was on his couch" in 1:12 (RSV)[25] refers to the gestation period of Christ in the womb of Mary.[26]

(3) The bundle of myrrh that hangs between the breasts of the woman (1:13) refers to Christ in the soul of the believer, who lies between the great commands to love God and one's neighbor.[27]

(4) The reference to the lover feeding among the lilies (2:16) suggests that the Christian must be masticated by Christ with suffering and trials.[28]

(5) The triple address for the bride to come from Lebanon (4:8) is a call for the Christian to come away from the devil, the world, and the self, or alternatively, to be consecrated in thought, word, and deed. Or, it refers to the Assumption of the Virgin.[29]

The list of similar allegories on the Song could go on indefinitely, and in fact several different allegories could be listed for almost any verse of the book. It goes without saying that these interpretations are arbitrary and indeed altogether implausible as the actual meaning of the texts. Nevertheless, the enticement of allegory is such that many pastors cannot resist it. Before succumbing, however, the preacher should ask two questions: (1) Is it reasonable to think that this is what the author really means? (2) Will an allegorical sermon enhance my congregation's understanding of the Bible? Honest answers to these questions should keep the preacher off of the path of allegory.

Many Christians, disgusted at the bizarre nature of allegorical interpretations, have seen the Song as a kind of historical drama. Two principal interpretations of this type persist. These are the "two character" drama (in which the Song describes Solomon's joy in his one true love, the Shulammite woman) and the "three character" drama (in which Solomon tries to seduce the Shulammite woman, but she remains faithful to her "shepherd lover"[30]).

Neither interpretation is possible. First, there is no evidence that the drama, least of all the historical drama, existed in ancient Israel. Second, both interpretations are highly forced at points and must rely on reading a great deal into the text. This is especially true of the "three character" drama.[31] Third, the language of the Song is highly poetic and symbolic, and efforts to read the text as a kind of narrative history is not only contrary to the genre of the book but often produces strange results.[32]

The most reasonable interpretation is that the Song is neither history nor allegory but exactly what it appears to be: love poetry.[33] The term "love poetry" can of course embrace a wide variety of potential interpretations, and a full exegesis is not possible here. Nevertheless, the reader should look upon this text as a song in celebration of love between a man and woman. The man is variously described as a shepherd, Solomon, a stag, and an apple tree, and the woman is described as a shepherdess, a doe, a garden, and a princess.[34] These descriptions should not be taken literally or as indications that the characters are actual historical persons. Instead, the language serves to show that a man and woman in love are regal, graceful, powerful, and inviting to one another.

The Song does not tell a story as such. It has no plot. On the other hand, the Song does revolve around the consummation of love between a man and a woman on their wedding night.[35] The structural center of the Song is 5:16–6:1,[36] which euphemistically tells of the sexual union between the couple. The book describes the excitement, joy, fear, and love that fill this event.

Seen in this light, it has profound messages for the Christian. It is not, as some have tried to take it, a kind of 10th century B.C. sex manual, but it does have important lessons in these areas. Some specific lessons of Song of Songs, to which a pastor may look for sermon themes, are as follows:

Sexual love is not by nature immoral, but is beautiful in its proper place. Christianity has a long tradition of looking upon sexuality as degraded, lustful, and of value for procreation only. Protestants have not shaken off this bias, and it can be quite destructive to a healthy marriage. The Song gives no support to ascetic or squeamish tendencies.

Sexual love is a matter of the mind and heart, and not just of the body. At the other extreme, many regard sexual affection as the fundamental expression of love in marriage. In fact, the love that is expressed between the hearts of a couple is far more important. The many *words* of love expressed in the Song demonstrate that verbal expressions of love must come first.

Sexual enjoyment should be reserved for marriage. This is not the major theme of the Song, and it would be a mistake to over-moralize here. Nevertheless, the woman is the man's bride (4:8, etc.). The kind of exuberant expectation and fulfillment the Song describes is not to be found in a casual attitude toward sexual love.

The desires as well as the fears and anxiety that precede marriage are normal, and should be expected. The Song expresses a fair amount of tension, especially in the woman's part, as well as longing. This is part of the excitement and joy of love.

The grace of God overcomes human sin. Behind all the allegorical and ascetic interpretations of the Song is the belief that human sin is so strong and sex is so dangerous that physical love must be rigidly controlled and never openly affirmed. Sexuality does indeed pose dangers, as many biblical texts assert. Nevertheless, the attempts to smother the fires of love by harsh proscription or embarrassed silence are not only contrary to creation but in the final analysis are doomed to fail. The grace of God affirms the sexual aspect of our nature even though we are in a fallen state. We do not sin that grace may abound, but even here, we live by grace and not by law.[37]

A final question is whether the Song should be preached (as in sermons) or taught (as in Bible studies). Probably the pastor will find it more appropriate to teach the Song in a Sunday night or week night series instead of preaching it on Sunday morning. Even so, the line between preaching and teaching should not be too rigidly drawn; each should include a fair amount of the other.

The sermon is a very individual form of expression. This is true not only because each preacher is different from another, but because every preacher must hone his sermon to the needs of his church. Thus, practical applications drawn and illustrations used in a text will vary significantly. At the same time, although each minister will bring his own *interpretation* to the text, one can reasonably assume that the main bounds of interpretation will remain relatively constant. Therefore, the following example of a Wisdom sermon has a minimal amount of illustrative material after the introduction; the focus here is on interpretation. Also, the example below does give special attention to the introductory material. This is to suggest how the preacher might begin a sermon from Wisdom. Proverbs 11:9-13, a text discussed above, is the sample text.

An Example of a Wisdom Sermon

"Something Rotten in Denmark"
Proverbs 11:9-13

Introduction to the Sermon

We have a saying that "There is something rotten in Denmark." The saying means that there is something wrong in a community, be it a neighborhood, a workplace, or a church. Usually, when we use it, we mean that some *person* is causing a problem. The people in that community may not know exactly what is wrong, but they know that somebody is making trouble.

Introduction to the Text

We can tell that the author means for us to take verses 9 to 12 together because he has presented them to us as a "chiasmus." This means that verse 9 and verse 12 both deal with the same idea, namely, slander. Also, verses 10 and 11 both deal with what the righteous and the wicked each do to a city. This gives the text an A-B-B-A pattern, which we call chiasmus. In addition, all four verses begin with the Hebrew letter *beth*.

Verse 13 stands outside of verses 9 to 12 and is a kind of conclusion and commentary. It tells us that gossips betray confidence but that trustworthy people can maintain it. Do you see the connection? Do you see how the idea of verse 13 binds together the message of verses 9 to 12? The point is that gossip and slander can destroy a community. The man or woman who goes around town spreading rumors is the something rotten in Denmark. For us, in the community of this church, anyone who slanders other members and carries about tales is a source of misery and pain.

Proposition

Gossip can destroy a church.

Main Body

   I. What the wicked do:
      A. Destroy others (v. 9a):
         1. Ruin reputations
         2. Hurt feelings
         3. Ruin someone's ability to serve God
      B. Speak thoughtlessly (v. 12a):
         1. Without finding out the truth
         2. Without first speaking to the person himself or herself
         3. Without consideration for consequences
  II. What the righteous do:
      A. Escape the trap laid by the gossip (v. 9b):
         1. Through maintaining integrity
         2. Through confronting the gossip directly
         3. Through God's help
      B. Control his or her tongue (v. 12b):
         1. Because he or she does not seek attention
         2. Because of concern for the well-being of others
         3. Because of concern for the life of the church
 III. What the church does:
      A. It grows and prospers where slander is absent, but begins to die where it is present (v. 11)
      B. It approves of those who build up the church with their words (v. 10a)
      C. It is glad to be rid of tale bearers (v. 10b)
 IV. What you should do (v. 13):
      A. Do not slander and gossip
      B. Be discerning and avoid the conversation of those who do such things

Conclusion

If you want to kill the church, start a rumor; if you want to build up the church, stop a rumor.

The above sermon is but a simple example of how Wisdom can contribute to Christian life by calling believing men and women to a life that is worthy of their calling.

Notes

1. In this essay, capitalized "Wisdom" refers to the wisdom literature of the Bible. Lower case "wisdom" refers to wisdom as an abstract concept. Similarly, "the Song" refers to Song of Songs.

2. B. Childs, *Old Testament Theology in a Canonical Context* (Philadelphia: Fortress, 1985), 211-12.

3. J. Bright, *The Authority of the Old Testament* (Grand Rapids: Baker, 1975), 136.

4. W. C. Kaiser, Jr., *Toward Rediscovering the Old Testament* (Grand Rapids: Zondervan, 1987), 178-79.

5. Prior to the Christian era, there were four types of allegorization. These included: (1) pagan Greek allegorization, which sought to discover philosophic truths embedded in the myths of Homer and Hesiod; (2) Palestinian rabbinical allegorization of the Old Testament for religious and moral lessons; (3) the allegorization by Philo, who sought to show that Moses had anticipated the philosophic insights of the Greeks; and (4) the allegorization by the Qumran community, who wanted to demonstrate that they were the fulfillment of Old Testament eschatological predictions. See W. A. Shotwell, *The Biblical Exegesis of Justin Martyr* (London: SPCK, 1965), 38-42; K. J. Woollcombe, "The Biblical Origins and Patristic Development of Typology," in *Essays on Typology*, by G. W. H. Lampe and K. J. Woollcombe (London: SCM, 1957), 50-51; and R. P. C. Hanson, "Biblical Exegesis in the Early Church," in *The Cambridge History of the Bible*, vol. 1: *From the Beginnings to Jerome*, ed. P. R. Ackroyd and C. F. Evans (Cambridge: Cambridge University Press, 1970), 429, for discussions of pre-Christian allegorization. Christian allegorization began as early as Justin Martyr and came to full flower in the Alexandrian school, especially in the writings of Origen.

6. This interpretation is held by no less a scholar than C. S. Lewis, *Reflections on the Psalms* (New York: Harcourt, Brace, Jovanovich, 1958), 136, cited in M. Silva, *Has the Church Misread the Bible?* (Grand Rapids: Zondervan, 1987), 65-66.

7. I here use the term "contextual" in reference to the written context of a given passage of Scripture, not in reference to the context of the reader. Some recent hermeneutical theories use the term "contextual" in the latter sense.

8. One could argue that in fact one must begin at a higher level yet, on the canonical level, but this issue goes beyond the limits of this essay.

9. For a good presentation of steps in exegesis, see D. Stuart, *Old Testament Exegesis: A Primer for Students and Pastors* (Philadelphia: Westminster, 1984).

10. A discussion of the forms of Wisdom will be found in my section on Poetic and Wisdom Literature in the *Holman Bible Handbook*, ed. David S. Dockery (Nashville: Holman, 1992). A much more extended presentation of this and

related issues will appear in my forthcoming commentary on Proverbs, Ecclesiastes, and Song of Songs.

11. One could argue that the narrative of Joseph in Genesis or the book of Ruth or even Daniel might be classified as Wisdom, but the question of preaching from these books is better addressed in the other essays of this book. Apocryphal books such as Wisdom of Solomon and Sirach are non-canonical and thus not suitable for use as sermon texts.

12. I present my interpretation of Job and of the development of its themes in greater detail in my essay in the *Holman Bible Handbook*.

13. On the other hand, the preacher should not allow the apparent simplicity of some of the proverbs *as they appear in translation* to obscure some profound difficulties and potentials for rich interpretation that exist in the original text.

14. I will attempt to demonstrate this thesis in detail, as well as demonstrate what are the actual collections of proverbs in the book, in my commentary on Proverbs, Ecclesiastes, and Song of Songs in *The New American Commentary* (Nashville: Broadman, forthcoming, 1993).

15. The term (*sanyac*) here refers to intellectual reticence, that is, avoidance of self-assured arrogance about one's own opinions. See W. McKane, *Proverbs* (Philadelphia: Westminster, 1977), 428.

16. Some have suggested that the text be emended to read, "When the *righteous* man dies, his hope does *not* perish, but the expectation *of fools* perishes." See the LXX and BHS notes. But the text makes sense as it stands and is supported by the inclusio pattern.

17. The question of the relationship between Amenemope and Proverbs 22:17–24:22 is highly complex, and opinions vary. It still appears best to assert that Amenemope is prior to Proverbs. But the dependence of Proverbs on Amenemope is by no means slavish, as McKane, *Proverbs*, 371 demonstrates.

18. It is unlikely that Ecclesiastes would have addressed these issues so thoroughly if the audience were not engaged in similar pursuits.

19. See, for example, *The Instructions of Vizier Ptah-Hotep*, in J. B. Pritchard, ed., *Ancient Near Eastern Texts*, 2nd ed. (Princeton: Princeton University Press, 1955), 412-14.

20. See D. A. Garrett, "Qoheleth on the Use and Abuse of Political Power," *Trinity Journal* NS 8 (1987): 159-77.

21. I set forth my understanding of the outline of Ecclesiastes both in the *Holman Bible Handbook* and in my forthcoming commentary on Ecclesiastes (Broadman).

22. Note the many times Proverbs addresses its reader as "my son," implying that its first audience was young men growing up and soon to face major decisions of life.

23. There are, of course, a great variety of interpretations of the Song. The threefold typology described here is offered for the sake of simplicity. Also, methods of interpretation which the evangelical pastor is unlikely to embrace are not covered here.

24. M. Pope, *Song of Songs* (Garden City, NY: Doubleday, 1977), 342.

25. An alternative translation is, "The king is at his table."

26. Attributed to Philip Harveng. Cited in Pope, *Song*, 349.

27. Cited in Pope, *Song*, 352. Alternative allegories are that it refers to God enthroned between the cherubim on the ark or Jesus crucified between the two thieves.

28. Attributed to St. Bernard. Cited in Pope, *Song*, 407.

29. Cf. Pope, *Song*, 478.

30. The three character dramatic approach is thus sometimes called the "shepherd hypothesis."

31. For example, C. H. Bullock, *An Introduction to the Old Testament Poetic Books* (Chicago: Moody, 1982), 247. He argues that the crown Solomon wears in 3:11 is a wedding crown and that "the maiden is very close to being married to the king against her wishes."

32. For example, 4:16-5:1 is read in this method as if it were an actual visit to a garden. To the contrary, the text clearly describes the sexual union of the man and woman. Attempts to interpret 5:2-8 as literal narrative (or even as a dream narrative) are also unsatisfactory in their results.

33. The poetry of Song of Songs closely resembles the love poetry of Egypt of the late second millennium. Especially instructive parallels are found in the *Papyrus Chester Beatty I*. For a good collection of Egyptian love poetry, see Miriam Lichtheim, *Ancient Egyptian Literature* (Berkeley: University of California Press, 1976), II:181-93.

34. The term "Shulammite" (6:13) may be a feminine version of the name Solomon and thus refer to a woman who is a female version of Solomon (that is, regal, beautiful, etc.).

35. The couple are evidently marrying one another, as "my sister, my bride" (4:9,10,11,12; 5:1) implies. The term "sister" is frequently used in Egyptian love poetry as a term of endearment, but "bride" appears to be meant literally.

36. The Song is structured as a chiasmus, and this text is the center.

37. I present my interpretation of the Song in greater detail in my forthcoming commentary on Proverbs, Ecclesiastes, and Song of Songs (Broadman).

PART 2

Moving from Old Testament to New Testament Truth

6

The New Testament Use of the Old Testament

Robert B. Sloan

Introduction

Though too bookishly put, it has been argued that New Testament Christianity is a distinctive way of reading the Old Testament. Such a description may sound dull to the modern church goer, but there is some merit in it. The Christian church was born on the day of Pentecost already possessing sacred Scriptures (the Old Testament) and having, at least among its leaders, a good, if not settled, idea as to how those Scriptures ought to be interpreted. The historical and theological implications of the fact that the earliest generation of Christians existed as, among other things, Scripture-reading bodies of worshipers, long before they possessed their own explicitly Christian documents, should serve to focus our attention upon the gravity of both interpretive method and theological result in the reading of Scripture in the early church.

What Christians now call the "Old Testament"[1] did not receive that name until there was a comparable body of Christian literature to place alongside it, which was called the "New Testament," so named for the new covenant to which it bore witness. The first Christian Scriptures, however, were in fact the Jewish Scriptures: the Law, the Prophets, and the Writings. The earliest Christians were Jews, and thus it was never a matter of debate for them that their Scriptures were the literary foundation of their confession of trust in the crucified and risen Messiah Jesus. Though there was much to dispute between those messianic Jews, who ultimately came to be called "Christians" (Acts 11:26), and those Jews who rejected the messianic claims being made about Jesus, there was never any debate between these two groups as to the text, inspiration, and authority of the sacred Scriptures. Because of the widespread Christian use of the Septuagint, the Greek Old Testament, there came to be in later years something of a suspicion on the part of many Jews regarding the Septuagint—they regarded it as "the Christian Bible." Nonetheless, in the earliest days of the church, and for many decades thereafter, Jews and Christians shared a common body of sacred writings, the Scriptures.

The real difference therefore between these two groups lay elsewhere. Jewish Christians were convinced that one Jesus of Nazareth, a controversial preacher, teacher, and miracle worker, recently crucified by Roman authority with the complicity of Jewish leaders in Jerusalem, had in fact been raised from the dead and was now installed at the right hand of the Ancient of Days as reigning Messiah, Son of God, and Lord. Non-Christian Jews vehemently denied these assertions, and thus the debate was on. Much of this internal Jewish debate centered upon the proper reading of the Scriptures. Non-Christian Jews denied that the crucified Nazarene, doubtless a sorcerer and blasphemer,[2] could have been the fulfillment of Jewish messianic hope. There was, they claimed, no expectation of a crucified Messiah to be found in the sacred texts,[3] and thus the Christian assertions were totally without scriptural warrant. Christians responded by declaring that the ancient texts did indeed predict a crucified Messiah.

It is therefore not surprising that Isaiah 52:13–53:12, a prophetic passage about a mysterious, suffering servant of the Lord, found extensive play in the New Testament documents.[4] Philip's encounter with the Ethiopian eunuch (Acts 8:26-40) is probably best understood as reflecting the controversy in Jerusalem over this significant Isaianic text. The Ethiopian, we learn, has just returned from Jerusalem and, we may surmise, has heard the internal debate between those Jews who declare that Jesus is the long-awaited Messiah and those who deny this claim. Christian Jews argued that the Isaianic text was an anticipation of a suffering Messiah. Non-Christian Jews argued that the prophet was merely referring to himself. When Philip joins the Ethiopian, this court official of Queen Candace is struggling with this significant text, and the central question upon the eunuch's mind reflects precisely the kind of debate that we may assume was raging in Jerusalem: "Tell me, of whom does the prophet say this? Of himself, or of someone else?" (8:34, NASB). There was no doubt in Philip's mind as to the correct interpretation of that sacred text: "Beginning from this Scripture, he preached Jesus to him" (8:34, NASB).

Thus, battle lines were being drawn, especially with regard to the reading of the Scriptures. The Christian interpretation of the death of Jesus as a fulfillment of sacred Scripture continued to be offensive to many Jews. Paul would later refer to "the word of the cross" (NASB) as "a stumbling block to Jews" (NIV; 1 Cor. 1:18-25). But, however much their message was rejected and they themselves were ostracized and persecuted, there was never any thought among these earliest Christians of giving up their sacred Scriptures. Indeed, it was these very Scriptures which provided them, so they believed, with the basis of their faith.[5] Thus, inextricably tied up with their traditional commitment to the authority of the sacred Scriptures was the new prophetic insight regarding the most recently accomplished divine acts of salvation. They were overwhelmingly convinced that Jesus was in fact the long-awaited Messiah. His resurrection was widely attested by credible eyewitnesses, and the descent of the Spirit, accompanied by the ongoing presence of "signs and wonders" in the lives of the apostles, the closest followers of Jesus, constituted compelling evidence for their newfound faith. Jesus Himself had made extensive use of the Scriptures, and His life, even His suffering and resurrection, had a surprisingly scriptural cast about them. Given the certainty of their beliefs about Jesus, who was Himself a teacher of the sacred writings, and given their own traditional commitment to the Jewish Scriptures, it was only natural that the earliest Christians should fight their way through to a vigorous re-reading of the ancient texts, a kind of theological re-reading which would not only substantiate their beliefs about Jesus, but show themselves to be the (true) people of God, whose faith in the Lord Jesus was scripturally vindicated. The Christian reading of Scripture would often be dramatically different from the interpretive traditions proposed throughout their Jewish heritage, but early Christian leaders were convinced, led not only by their own experience of the Spirit (Eph. 3:5), but also by the theologically suggestive ways of reading the Scriptures already given to them by Jesus,[6] that their new readings were coherent, and though mysterious, consistent with the divine

purposes of God accomplished in the history of Israel as revealed in the sacred texts.

In view of the scripturally oriented struggles of the earliest
Christian communities, an examination of the use of the Old
Testament by the writers of the New Testament is highly suggestive for our understanding of New Testament theology.
Those matters that were uppermost in Christian theology and
experience became the focal point for religious debate, scriptural analysis, and a new theological reading of the ancient
texts. The kinds of texts assembled, the way those texts were
read, the kinds of theological assumptions operative in the
minds of the New Testament authors as they cited and interpreted those texts, and the pattern (if any) of conclusions they
derived from their chosen texts are clues to the central theological impulses that drove the writers of the New Testament.
Therefore, by examining the New Testament use of the Old
Testament we may gain insight into the earliest, primary levels of theologizing among the leaders of the new movement. We
may learn more of the real "New Testament theology"—that is,
the theology that lies behind the New Testament and thus, in
connection with and in response to the various questions and
problems in the earliest Christian assemblies, actually produced the individual documents.

Furthermore, how do we read the Old Testament? Can we
read the Old Testament Scriptures as the New Testament writers read them? The answer to such a question may usefully be
divided into two sub-categories, one a theological matter and
the second an exegetical and literary one. That is, if we ask the
question, "Can we read the Old Testament as the New Testament writers read it?" the answer is presumably yes if we are
referring to the theological conclusions either taken to or drawn
from those texts, in which and by which New Testament writers
argue that Jesus is the Christ and that those who follow Him
are the people of God. If, however, we ask that same question in
terms of the interpretive methods whereby they read those ancient texts, the answer is a much more difficult one (a discussion of the "literary phenomena," that is, the kinds of exegetical
maneuvers executed by the New Testament writers when dealing with Old Testament texts, will be offered below). If it should
turn out that we see in the writers of the New Testament certain exegetical moves that we ourselves—because of our commitment to certain commonly accepted historical methods of
interpretation, methods constrained by attention to context,
grammar, and literary genre—do not feel comfortable in mak-

ing as modern Christian readers of the Old Testament, can we continue to accept their theological conclusions without adopting their methods of reading the Old Testament? Or are their theological commitments so intimately tied to a way of reading the Scriptures that depends to such an extent on certain eccentric, exegetical maneuvers that interpretive method and theological conclusion cannot be finally separated? Or is there in fact no real problem at all; that is, is it perhaps the case that the writers of the New Testament strictly follow the same rules of context, grammar, and literary genre that we follow, in which case there is no difficulty with our use not only of their theological conclusions but also their exegetical methods? Or finally, if our methods are different, have we been unnecessarily self-limiting; that is, is it possible that we as modern readers may boldly assert ourselves to be in an analogous hermeneutical situation to that of the New Testament writers, with the result that, however odd their reading techniques may have been, we too may feel free to employ the same interpretive methods in our reading of the Old Testament?

The discussion that follows will, first of all, attempt to survey certain literary phenomena which occur in the various New Testament readings of the Old Testament; will, secondly, survey briefly two major theological uses of Scripture found in the New Testament; and, thirdly, will endeavor to draw some conclusions in terms of how we, as Christian readers of the Old Testament, may continue to use those same sacred texts as a quarry for mining the foundation stones of our faith.

Literary Phenomena

It is sometimes surprising to note the varied and oftentimes odd ways in which the New Testament writers employ the Old Testament. Though there have been many attempts to categorize the patterns of New Testament exegesis of the Old Testament,[7] it is difficult to construct a precise list of exegetical and/ or interpretive methodologies. What follows is an attempt rather to describe, not exhaustively but illustratively, some of the phenomena of scriptural use and interpretation found in the New Testament. What will be observed is a rather great variety of textual, literary, verbal, syntactical, historical, and metaphorical applications and appropriations of Scripture by the New Testament writers. Therefore, without attempting to systematize strictly the various kinds of scriptural phenomena found in the New Testament, the following discussion offers a descriptive survey of some of the phenomena to be found. In the end, it will be suggested by this study that, within the constraints of certain Christian assumptions about the nature of Scripture, a coherent pattern is to be found not so much at the level of exegetical method as at the point of extrinsic theological—especially Christocentric and ecclesiocentric—control.

Before looking at some of the phenomena themselves, some preliminary discussion is in order. The New Testament use of the Old Testament is known in modern theological and literary studies as intertextuality. The term "intertextuality" is used to refer to the literary process whereby an author incorporates, whether at the level of a phrase, a verbal or conceptual parallel, and/or a direct quote, material from a prior text into a current composition.[8] In the case of the New Testament use of the Old Testament, we are dealing with the appropriation of a certain body of religious literature, the Jewish Scriptures (known to Christians as the Old Testament), within historically more recent religious texts, namely, the New Testament.

Though obvious, it is necessary to note that the phenomenon of intertextuality depends upon one clear-cut assumption; that is, that there is a correspondence, at some level, between the two texts in question. The nature of the correspondence, the focus of the correspondence, the level of the correspondence, and the ultimate point of the correspondence are all matters worthy of discussion, but the presupposition of any of these questions is the fact of some kind of correspondence between a given text and its historical predecessor. Whether the correspondence takes place, in the case of the New Testament use of the Old Testament, along the lines of prophecy-fulfillment, thematic correlation, or analogy between the situation of the writer/readers and the ancient text, the fact remains that some kind and level of correspondence have occurred whereby, in the mind of the author/readers an imaginative connection (conscious or unconscious), a correspondence, takes place between two bodies of literature with the result that the historically prior material is in some way incorporated into the historically more recent text.

Explicit Citations

Probably the most obvious type of intertextual relationship between Old and New Testaments occurs when a New Testament writer explicitly cites an Old Testament text and also elaborates the nature of the correspondence.[9] This kind of phenomenon takes place frequently in Matthew (see below), where we read that certain events in the life of Jesus must be understood as fulfillments of the words of the prophets. In such cases the given scriptural proof text is cited and the correspondence, usually at the level of event, is theologically interpreted as a prophetic promise (in the older text) now fulfilled in the life of Jesus and/or events related to the rise of the Christian faith (1:22-23; 2:5-6,15,17-18,23; 3:3; 4:14-16; 8:14-17; 13:34-35; 21:4-5; 27:3-10). Similarly, in the Petrine sermon of Acts 2:14-40, the death, resurrection, and enthronement of Jesus, coupled with His subsequent outpouring of the Spirit upon His followers, are related as fulfillments of, among other texts, the explicitly cited texts in Joel 2:28-32; Psalms 16:8-11; 110. Though not as numerous as the more inconspicuously incorporated occurrences of "allusion" (see below), explicit citations of Old Testament texts are fairly commonplace within the New Testament.

Typology

Typology may be considered a method of interpretation whereby a larger level of correspondence is established between persons and events.[10] Matthew 12:1-8, for example, establishes this sort of larger level of correspondence between David and his companions, on the one hand, and Jesus and His followers, on the other. In fact, another point of typological correspondence is found in the same story when, according to Jesus, the action of His disciples in picking the heads of grain on the sabbath and eating them may be likened to the legal breaking of the sabbath done every sabbath day when the priests work in the temple and yet are innocent. Similarly, in Matthew 12:40, a kind of typological correspondence between Jesus and Jonah is established so that it may then be argued that "just as Jonah was three days and three nights in the belly of the sea monster, so shall the Son of Man be three days and three nights in the heart of the earth" (NASB). A typological correspondence for Paul between Adam and Christ may be observed in two well-known texts, Romans 5:12-21 and 1 Corinthians 15:21-22,45-49. Indeed, in the Romans passage we are explicitly told that "Adam . . . is a type [*tupos*] of Him who was to come" (5:14, NASB).

Correspondence at the level of event and/or people also occurs in 1 Corinthians 10:6 when we read regarding Israel's sins that "these things happened as examples [*tupoi*] for us, that we should not crave evil things, as they also craved" (NASB). First Peter 3:20-21 likewise correlates Old Testament events with

Christian experience when it compares the rescue of eight persons in Noah's family to the divine rescue which takes place "through the resurrection of Jesus Christ" (NASB) in the experience of baptismal confession: "Eight persons were brought safely through the water. And corresponding [*antitupon*] to that, baptism now saves you" (3:20-21, NASB). Other examples of this kind of typological correspondence could be adduced (see 1 Cor. 5:6-8; 9:8-10; Gal. 4:21-31), but we will content ourselves with a final illustration found in Hebrews. There, the argument/exhortation of the epistle is significantly advanced by the author's stated (typological) correspondence between the temple of old and Jesus' enthronement at the right hand of God: "for Christ did not enter a holy place made with hands, a mere copy (*antitupa*) of the true one, but into heaven itself, now to appear in the presence of God" (9:24, NASB).[11]

Phrases, Allusions, and Echoes[12]

This particular intertextual phenomenon is exceedingly difficult to analyze or describe because it involves the use of smaller units of verbal correspondence which may either be employed as specific—though not necessarily verbatim—citations of biblical material for the purpose of apologetic proof texting, or it may simply involve the allusive (and elusive!) use of biblical language in such a way that it is not completely clear to what extent the original context of the older material is important for understanding the point being made in the later text. It is the existence of this "phrase level" kind of correspondence that is often referred to as "allusion" or "echo." Such labels are usually our testimony to the fact that while we are confident Scripture is being used, we may be uncertain as to the actual textual predecessor of the given allusion, the significance of the prior (Old Testament) context for understanding the more recent (New Testament) text, or the importance of authorial intention.

Where the larger context is relevant for understanding an interwoven scriptural phrase, we may have what is sometimes referred to as metalepsis, where certain transumed (covered up or suppressed) material in the earlier text is presumed as a kind of literary preunderstanding necessary for the readers' fuller appreciation of the author's intent.[13] This kind of intertextual phenomenon, in which the larger context lying behind an appropriated text is necessary to appreciate the fuller significance of the author's (in this case Paul's) meaning, is found in 2 Corinthians 8:15.[14] There, Paul, in the larger context of encouraging the Corinthians regarding the offering that he would take to Jerusalem, appealed to Exodus 16:18, where it is written, "He who gathered much did not have too much, and he who gathered little did not have too little" (NIV).

Commentators differ significantly in their reading of Paul's intent in his appeal to that text. That is, why should the Exodus story of God's equal provision for His people, whereby He provided manna in the wilderness, be used by Paul to enjoin material equality between Gentile Christians in Corinth and Jewish Christians in Jerusalem? The provision in the case of the Exodus story is by supernatural intervention. In the case of Paul's appeal to the Corinthians, the exhortation is to share from congregation to congregation. As Hays notes, "One might use the same story to argue a position diametrically opposed to Paul's. Why worry about sharing goods if God will provide miraculously for those in need?" But, as Hays goes on to point out, what Paul's text requires is greater, not less, attention to the text of Exodus. The story of Exodus 16 is the account of God's provision for His people in the wilderness. Implicit in the story of the quail and the manna is the exhortation to live in dependence upon God's provision (compare the Deuteronomic interpretation of the Exodus experience, especially the provision of manna, as a series of lessons for Israel to learn that one "does not live by bread alone, but . . . by everything that proceeds out of the mouth of the Lord"—Deut. 8:3, NASB). The children of Israel must trust Him. They are not to take more than each person can eat, nor are they, failing to trust in God's provision, to attempt to hoard any of the manna. Each one should gather only enough for the given day, and on the sixth day collect enough both for that day and the sabbath, on which no work would be done. When more than enough was gathered and hoarded, "it bred worms and became foul; and Moses was angry with them" (Ex. 16:20, NASB). Surprisingly, however, the two-day provision gathered on the sixth day did not become foul, even though a portion was left over for the sabbath, thereby indicating both the necessity of hallowing the sabbath and again the fact of divine provision.

When these implied exhortations are taken back to the Pauline text, the point of the correspondence lies in a similar warning to the Corinthians not to hoard, a practice which would demonstrate their lack of trust in God, who is still capable of providing their needs (exactly the point that Paul developed in 2 Cor. 9:8-12). Rather, they are to regard their present abundance as a divine provision intended to promote generosity (compare again 2 Cor. 9:8-11, where Paul explicitly argues that

God's grace to the Corinthians in the form of material blessing is for the purpose of sharing).[15] The set of correspondences thus invoked by Paul between the Corinthian situation and the story of the manna in the wilderness requires our larger reading of Exodus 16 (and the Deuteronomic interpretation of the story as well) to discover the implied (and explicitly stated in Deuteronomy 8) exhortation against hoarding. Indeed, even another set of correspondences may be set off when we interpret the Corinthian act of sharing with the Jerusalem Christians, in the light of Exodus 16, as a form of "hallowing the sabbath." In that way we may also hear a kind of theological resonance between the Pauline theology herein implied and that of Jesus (known to Paul perhaps by oral tradition) in which the Lord Himself declared the hallowing of the sabbath to consist in the "doing of good."[16]

Other instances of biblical allusion, or echo, however, may simply be an appropriation of biblical language that does not require any larger contextual appeal. In this regard it is instructive to consider the highly allusive use of Job 13:16 (LXX) in Philippians 1:19: "this shall turn out for my deliverance" (NASB).[17] It is unlikely that the level of correspondence between Job and Paul is to be understood as a kind of typological correspondence, that is, where Paul projects himself and his life on the model of the innocent Job who is used as a kind of heavenly courtroom test case. On the other hand, it may well be that Paul's invocation of the Job text is, consciously or unconsciously, induced by the analogous situation of finding himself both beleaguered and in the presence of false friends (compare Phil. 1:15-18 with Job's "comforters"). As Hays suggests in his analysis of this intertextual echo, there is a point at which the Pauline echo of Job finally vanishes and we are ultimately incapable of assessing the extent and/or level at which intended correspondence(s) take place.

Indeed, even more illustrative of this often frustrating level of analysis is the *oida gar hoti* of Philippians 1:19, the phrase which introduces in rather elevated language the previously cited words of allusion. The phrase "for I know," surprisingly enough, shows up in only three places in the Greek Old Testament, but all of them are in the Book of Job (9:28; 19:25; 30:23). An examination of those contexts is initially of some interest to us when our search uncovers the well known text, "for I know that my redeemer liveth" (19:25, KJV), and leads us to suspect that some note of vindication may be in the air. The other two instances, however, are not so promising: "I know that thou wilt not hold me innocent" (9:28, KJV), and "I know that thou wilt bring me to death" (30:23, KJV). Thus, it may well be that there is not a specific contextual association for the phrase "for I know" that is relevant in Paul's use of it. It could be a mere coincidence of language. On the other hand, it may well be that the point of correspondence, though not lying at the level of any one theological context in Job, does lie in the broader common function which the "for I know" phrase serves in all three of the Job occurrences; namely, the introduction of a religiously solemn remark of either hope or despair regarding one's personal vindication in the face of death. Certainly we would not be surprised to learn that Paul, confronted with the prospect of death in the cause of Christ, out of familiarity with the ancient text and its invocation of the "for I know" phrase to introduce Job's remarks of solemn and sober hope/fear about an impending future, should, in an analogous situation, likewise introduce his remarks with the same solemn and elevated expression. Indeed, the Philippians context itself (1:19-30) repeatedly suggests a kind of "confident ambiguity."[18] On the other hand, however, it is hard to know at what point we have discovered an authentic correspondence and at what point we are ourselves engineering elaborate, but artificial bridges of similarity between two texts which coincidentally share a turn of phrase or, at best, merely reflect in the later text a certain habit of speech drawn unreflectively from the pool of the tradition.

The point to be made here, in summary, is that the nature of and/or the level or point at which the correspondence takes place is not always obvious. The modern reader of the New Testament, with patience and historical sensitivity, will simply have to examine historical contexts, literary styles, and, with an artistic as well as objective assessment of probabilities, attempt to understand the significance, at various possible levels, of a given New Testament use of an Old Testament text. Thus, in many instances, it is clear that the context of the Old Testament text is utterly critical for understanding the significance of a New Testament allusion, whereas in other instances the correspondence takes place more at the level of the words themselves, though, it must again be asserted, one must never fail to pay close attention to the function of those words in both contexts before reaching any conclusions.

Words

It is of course virtually impossible to separate words from the sentences and larger contexts in which they occur. In referring to "words" as illustrating a particular category of literary phenomena, we are not intending to suggest that any given word has meaning apart from its context, nor even that the use of a given Old Testament text is limited in its significance to the isolation of one particular word. Nonetheless, it is the case that Old Testament texts are often chosen by New Testament writers because of the occurrence of certain "catchwords" (a phenomenon called *gezerah shawah* in rabbinic exegetical studies). Indeed, the gathering together of certain Old Testament texts to be used together in a single New Testament context often occurs by virtue of the recurrence in each of those texts of a single "catchword." Such is the case, for example, in the repeated association in the New Testament of various "stone" passages from the Old Testament.[19] Another illustration of this kind of "catchword" phenomenon may be seen as well in the Luke 4:18-19 citation of Isaiah 61:1-2a; 58:6d.[20] Though it was not customary for one to scroll backwards in the reading of the text, Jesus' reading in the Nazareth synagogue of the prophetic text included not only Isaiah 61:1-2a (an abrupt place to stop the reading!), but also included within the reading of 61:1-2a a single phrase from Isaiah 58:6. There may be little doubt that the inclusion of 58:6d is based upon the occurrence in that phrase of the word "release." Such an act of cross referencing was highly appropriate since Jesus' announcement of the "Favorable Year of the Lord" was based upon Old Testament notions of the sabbath and/or Jubilee Year, also known as the Year of Release. Thus, we have an example in the preaching of Jesus (in Luke) of this very phenomenon of linking texts together on the basis of a "catchword," in this case a word (*aphesis*) related to "forgiveness" and "release."

A similar kind of "catchword" linkage may be seen in the Old Testament exegesis that occurs in Hebrews 3–4 with regard to the scriptural word "rest." There is, first of all, a presumption by the author of a knowledge on the part of the audience of the story of Moses and the children of Israel in the wilderness who, because they sinned, did not enter the "rest" of God, that is, the promised land (compare Deut. 3:20; 12:10; 25:19). Second, drawing upon the importance of the term in Joshua (1:13,15; 21:44), coupled with its subsequent use in Psalm 95:11 as an illustrative theological reflection upon the failures of the wilderness generation, the author of Hebrews deduces that even Joshua did not give "rest" to the people of God, since David, long after Joshua, addresses his audience, with regard to the (apparently still available) possibility of entering God's rest, with the word "today" (Ps. 95:7). Thus, third, since we know—and here the author of Hebrews draws upon yet a third "rest" passage (Gen. 2:2)—that there is a "rest" of God that may be entered, and since we know furthermore that neither Moses nor Joshua were able to give the people "rest," then obviously the "rest" of God about which the Holy Spirit continues to speak—since the Spirit in Scripture uses the word "today" long after the time of Joshua—must pertain to a still unentered rest that the Christian readership of Hebrews may enter. Thus, diligence must be maintained "lest, while a promise remains of entering His rest, any one of you should seem to have come short of it" (Heb. 4:1, NASB).

Other instances of focus upon a single word are likewise quite prevalent in the New Testament use of the Old Testament. That is, apart from the above illustrations of the use of a single word as the basis for holding together a collection of Old Testament texts, there are also instances whereby a single word in a given Old Testament text is the centerpiece of the interpretive maneuver made by the author. Paul, for example, in Galatians 3:15-29, made a great deal of the fact that the Greek texts of Genesis 13:15 and 17:8 do not refer to "seeds" plural, but to a singular "seed." Paul interpreted the singular here to mean "Christ." Romans 10:11 and the use therein of Isaiah 28:16 is another instance of the significance of a citation turning on a single word, in this case "whoever." The same phenomenon is also attested in Romans 10:13 when Joel 2:32 is cited to the same purpose, "whoever will call upon the name of the Lord will be saved" (NASB).

Paul's foundational story of the promise of God to Abraham, a promise which involved the divine declaration of Abraham's righteousness prior to Abraham's being circumcised, is the basis in Romans 4 of Paul's argument, asserted in 3:31, that his gospel does not "nullify the law." On the contrary, he argued, "we establish the law" (NASB). Paul's scriptural argumentation, based upon the order of events in the Abraham story as alluded to in Genesis 15:6 (Rom. 4:3), is that Abraham is declared righteous while he was still uncircumcised, and therefore he is "the father of all who believe without being circumcised . . . and the father of circumcision to those who not only are of the circumcision, but who also follow in the steps of the faith of our father Abraham which he had while uncircumcised" (Rom. 4:11-12, NASB). Paul's argument from historical sequence in terms of the timing of the divine reckoning of righteousness to Abraham is actually introduced in Romans 4:7-8 with a citation from Psalm 32:1-2 to the effect that there is a blessing upon "the one whose sin the Lord will not reckon" (author's translation). The word "reckon" is the key word from Genesis 15:6 which led Paul to Psalm 32:2. David's blessing, then, upon the one whose sin is "not reckoned" is then applied both retrospectively to the righteous, but uncircumcised, Abraham (Rom. 4:9-10) and also prospectively upon all who "follow in the steps of the faith of our father Abraham" (4:11-12, NASB). The Davidic blessing and the righteousness of the uncircumcised Abraham are thus theologically connected by Paul through the word "reckoned."[21]

General Appeals to Scripture Without the Use of Texts

There are a number of instances in the New Testament use of the Old Testament which do not involve specific texts. That is, there are passages in which the Scriptures are appealed to where there is no indication that any specific text, word, story, or event is in mind. The New Testament author appeals to the general witness of the Scriptures as supplying authority for whatever theological assertions are being made. This kind of appeal has perhaps its best modern analogy in the preacher's habit of saying "the Bible says" without actually supplying a given text to support the intended homiletical assertion. This kind of rather broad appeal to Scripture is frequently in evidence in the New Testament. In Matthew 26:24, without our receiving the benefit of any specific text in the mind of Matthew/Jesus, we read: "the Son of Man is to go, just as it is written of Him" (NASB). Then, a few verses later, we hear Jesus addressing the multitudes: "Have you come out with swords and clubs to arrest Me as against a robber? Everyday I used to sit in the temple teaching and you did not seize Me. But all this has taken place that the Scriptures of the prophets may be fulfilled" (Matt. 26:55-56, NASB). We find, similarly, in Luke 21:22 the assertion: "these are days of vengeance to fulfill all that is written." Likewise, John 5:39 contains this sort of broad appeal to Scripture when Jesus, in dispute with the Jews, declares, "you search the Scriptures, because you think that in them you have eternal life; and it is these that bear witness of Me" (NASB). Acts 3:18, arguing for the messianic status of the recently crucified Jesus, shows Peter sermonically maintaining that "the things which God announced beforehand by the mouth of all the prophets, that His Christ should suffer, He has thus fulfilled" (NASB). Paul too is capable of this kind of general scriptural appeal, as evidenced by the traditional assertion of 1 Corinthians 15:3-4 "that Christ died for our sins according to the Scriptures, and that He was buried, and that He was raised on the third day according to the Scriptures" (NASB).

It is possible of course that a specific text can be in the mind of a writer even when no verbal clues are given as to the location of that text. Indeed, the use of Scripture in supporting the kinds of claims maintained above was so commonplace among early Christians so as not always to require explicit citations of specific texts (let the reader understand), even when a specific text is apparently in mind. Nonetheless, it is also the case that some of these larger appeals are best understood as appeals to the cumulative effect or witness of Scripture and/or to larger patterns (such as the fact that Jewish prophets typically suffered and therefore it should not be surprising that the Messiah should suffer; compare Matt. 23:29-37; Luke 13:33).

Surprising Shifts

The discussion contained under this rubric is difficult to place in a study of this sort. The fact that it is given here as a separate sub-category should not be taken to imply that what has been discussed heretofore represents very normal patterns of exegesis, patterns which contain for us no element of the unusual. The contrary is true. What we are here referring to as "surprising shifts" could be attested and catalogued among any of the types of phenomena discussed above. Whether one refers to typologies, phrases, or exegetical maneuvers that function more specifically at the level of a single word, the New Testament writers are capable of rather sudden and surprising shifts of significance in their use of Old Testament materials. Indeed, some of the illustrations given above of the various phenomena could also be repeated here as indicative of the innovative theological maneuvers of the New Testament writers.

What stands, for example, in Hosea 13:14 as a summons to Death to come forward and do its worst, because of the disobedience of God's people, is dramatically transformed in the context of 1 Corinthians 15 into a triumphal crowing on the part of Paul against the powers of death and the grave. In view of the resurrection of Jesus, which has begun the glorious processes which will finally culminate in the resurrection of "the rest" and is the basis upon which "this perishable will have put on the imperishable and this mortal will have put on immortality" (15:54), Paul could taunt the powers of the grave (15:55), as if to say, "Oh death, where now is your victory? Oh death, where now is your sting?" (author's translation).

Another innovative, interpretive twist is found when Paul applied to Gentile Christians Old Testament texts which refer to Israel. There is, of course, an interpretive logic to this kind of shift inasmuch as Paul regarded all (whether Jews or Gentiles) who believe in Jesus as the true heirs of the promise made to Abraham. That is, Jesus is the true seed of Abraham, the ultimate child of the promise, and all who are "in Christ" (whether Jew or Gentile) are ipso facto children of Abraham (Gal. 3:15-29). Thus, it is commonplace in Paul (and elsewhere in the New Testament as well) to find Israel's Scriptures applied to Gentiles. It is, nonetheless, surprising to find, for example, Paul's use of Psalm 44:22 in Romans 8:36, wherein what was originally in the psalm a reference to the persecution of Israel by Gentiles is being at least partially understood by Paul as a reference to the persecution of Christians—absent any Roman/governmental persecution of Christians at the time of the writing of Romans—by Jews.

An even more surprising shift of referent which involves the juxtaposition of Jews and Gentiles occurs in Romans 9:25-26, Paul's rather free paraphrase of Hosea 2:23; 1:9-10. The original setting of Hosea suggests the prophet's anticipation of the mercy of God upon the Northern Kingdom. Though Israel has fallen to such an extent that it may be said to them, "you are not my people," the day will come when those who are called "not my people," will hear the comforting words, "you are my people!" The startling feature of Paul's use of this text from Hosea in Romans 9:25-26 is found in the interpretive explanation with which he introduced, in 9:23-24, the proof text: " . . . that He might make known the riches of His glory upon vessels of mercy, which He prepared beforehand for glory, even us, whom he also called, not from among Jews only, but also from among Gentiles" (NASB). What clearly refers to the Northern Kingdom of Israel in the text of Hosea is treated by Paul as a prophetic anticipation of God's inclusion of Gentiles. It is not enough for us to say that the basis of Paul's appropriation of the text from Hosea is to extract a general point about the mercy of God upon sinners, so that Gentiles as sinners may be drawn under the thus stated umbrella of mercy.

Rather, it must be noted that Paul's interpretation of the text of Hosea applies to the specific point of God's mercy upon Gentiles. What was originally in Hosea a promise regarding the mysterious mercy of God that will, out of God's covenant faithfulness, overcome stubborn Israel's recalcitrance, so that Israel will be brought into covenant righteousness again, is applied to the remarkable and unexpected inclusion of Gentiles into the number of the people of God. This remarkable shift must therefore be accounted for not in terms of general appeals to the analogy of grace (God saved the Jews by grace and therefore can also save the Gentiles by grace), but by the more central Pauline assumption that Gentiles are in fact the people of God, for it is they who have been grafted in because of the kindness of God (see Rom. 11:11-24). Certainly Paul believed that his kinsmen according to the flesh will ultimately—if they do not continue in their unbelief—be grafted in again (11:23-32); but, it is nonetheless—in the mysterious outworkings of the purposes of God in the dynamic of alternately Jewish, then Gentile, salvation history—the Gentiles who currently "abide in his kindness" (11:22, author's translation). Thus, if it is now predominantly the Gentile mission that represents the fulfill-ment of Israel's history, then it is, however, surprising it may be, fully within Paul's theological warrants to read the text of Hosea, with its reference to the redemption of the covenant people of God, as fulfilled in the salvation of Gentiles.[22]

Illustrations of this sort abound in New Testament literature. What must be noted especially, however, is that the warrant for such shifts lies not so much, or at least not completely, within the normal constraints of historical-critical, contextual analysis. It is rather more often the theological givens—especially the gos-pel commitments of the early Christian kerygma—which opened up the ancient texts of Scripture for such innovative readings. Such innovative readings are often mistakenly referred to as "spiritualizing" or "allegorizing." Neither word does justice to what is rather a question of hermeneutical direction (that is, from Christian theology to scriptural reading), or starting point. In the case of our last illustration, the Pauline use of Hosea 1:9-10; 2:23 in Romans 9:25-26, it is the Pauline missionary experi-ence of seeing the blessing of God upon the Gentiles (nor may we exclude the implications of the divine commissioning on the Da-mascus Road, whereby Paul is explicitly commanded by the risen Lord to go to the Gentiles), that drove Paul to the conclusion that Gentiles are now, in Jesus, the Israel of God and thus propels his thereby historically and theologically warranted rereading of the sacred Scriptures of Israel.

The Septuagint and Textual Variations

With almost no exceptions, the writers of the New Testament use the Greek Old Testament, the Septuagint (LXX) as their Bible.[23] It must be said from the outset that any discussion of the use of the Septuagint in the New Testament is fraught with difficulty. The textual criticism of the Septuagint is leagues behind the textual criticism of the New Testament. What septuagintal texts were being used at the time of the composition of various New Testament writings is a problem which opens up a whole range of questions which remain largely unanswered.[24] The modern scholar's assertions about how this or that New Testament writer may have altered the text of the Septuagint in order to amplify or highlight a given theological point must be qualified by the reminder that we are only able to compare a New Testament writer's use of Greek Old Testament texts with our editions of the Septuagint.[25] However, with these qualifications, it is still important to note the kinds of textual variation that, as far as we know, occurred between what we may presume to have been the Greek Old Testament texts available to the various New Testament authors and the actual citations, allusions, and/or readings which they render within the New Testament itself. Before progressing to a couple of illustrations of the significance of textual variations for interpreting Old Testament texts in the New Testament, it is well to remember that the phenomenon of textual variation, just as we argued earlier with regard to "surprising shifts," may occur with any of the literary phenomena of scriptural citation, allusion, or echo.

In pointing to the significance of the use of the Septuagint and related textual variations, we are actually referring to at least two distinct areas of consideration. First, we are referring to the fact that there are certain theological points scored by the New Testament writers which seem to depend more upon the text of the Septuagint than the underlying Hebrew (here we must presume upon the Masoretic) text, when the Septuagint and the Hebrew differ from one another. For example, the Jewish and Christian belief, evidenced in various places in the New Testament (Acts 7:38-53; Gal. 3:19; Heb. 2:2), that the law was given through angels is rather more evident in the Septuagint's rendering of the Hebrew text of Deuteronomy 33:2 than in the Hebrew text itself.[26] That is not to say, in this case at least, that the Septuagint's translators have not correctly understood the Hebrew text; but it is to argue that the Jewish and Christian belief in the mediation of the law to Moses on Mount Sinai via angels is more obviously reflected, if not grounded, in the Septuagint than in any Hebrew text with which we are familiar.

Another interesting illustration of this kind of phenomenon is found in Paul's citation of Habakkuk 2:4 in Romans 1:17 and

Galatians 3:11.[27] Most English versions of Habakkuk 2:4 leave ambiguous what is also somewhat ambiguous in the Hebrew text, namely, about whose faithfulness (that is, God's or the righteous one's) the prophet speaks when he says, "the righteous one shall live by his faith" (author's translation; probably most scholars lean toward the faithfulness of God as the primary meaning, though one cannot be certain). Most Septuagint manuscripts clearly suggest, by the use and placement of "my" (instead of "his"), that the faithfulness in question is that of God: "the righteous one shall live by my faithfulness." Hebrews 10:38, on the other hand, seems to adopt the reading of a couple of Septuagint versions[28] where the "my" is strategically placed so as to produce "my righteous one shall live by faith" (RSV). Romans 1:17 and Galatians 3:11, however, by the use of no possessive pronoun, seem to opt for an ambiguity that chooses between neither the (already somewhat ambiguous) Hebrew text nor the Septuagint. Is this a deliberate ambiguity on the part of Paul? May we assume that Paul intended us to understand "faith" in Romans 1:17 to include both the faithfulness of God and human trust in the faithful God? Certainly the introductory phrase of 1:17, the very phrase which is being interpreted by the citation of Habakkuk 2:4 in 1:17b, lends itself to just such a dual meaning: that is, "the righteousness of God is revealed from the faithfulness (of God) to faith (human trust)."

Second, there are problems of textual variation which are constituted by the New Testament writer's deviation from any known septuagintal (or Hebrew) text. An interesting Pauline variation of this type is attested in a passage already considered (although we did not note the textual problem with it), namely, the use of Isaiah 28:16 in Romans 10:11: "whoever believes in Him will not be disappointed" (NASB). Paul's argument in Romans 10:9-13 is, among other things, that Jew and Gentile are alike saved in the same way, through belief in the risen One and the confession of Him as Lord (10:9). This word of promised salvation is for all, Paul argued, whether Jew or Greek, "for the same Lord is Lord of all, abounding in riches for all who call upon Him" (10:12, NASB).

This same point is then reinforced with another well-known text for early Christians, Joel 2:32 (LXX 3:5). Paul's point in citing both the Joel text and the text from Isaiah 28:16 is, as noted in our earlier discussion, surely focused on the word "whoever" or, in Greek, the small word (*pas*). What must be noted now, however, is that neither the Septuagint nor the Hebrew text of Isaiah 28:16 has any word or grammatical form which lends itself to the universalizing/indefinitizing meaning which Paul understood and thus highlights in his rendering of the text with the addition of *pas*. We can easily understand (and even sympathize with theologically) Paul's inclusion of the quote from Isaiah 28:16 as an adaptation naturally influenced by the closely associated septuagintal text of Joel 3:5, cited in Romans 10:13, where the word in fact occurs. Nonetheless, it is still not a little surprising to note that the key term in Paul's proof text from Isaiah 28:16, that is, the term which most clearly focuses the universal nature of the gospel invitation for Jew and Gentile (that is, *pas* ["whoever"]), is in fact not supported by any known Hebrew or Greek versions of the ancient text. It seems that Paul's reading of the text is a distinctively Christian one. That is, Paul's already received sense of the gospel as a mystery which may now be revealed to the Gentiles, who are in that act of revelation now included among those who experience the blessings of salvation as found in Jesus Christ (see Eph. 2:11–3:10), has influenced his reading of the text of Isaiah. This is of course not to say that Paul's commitment to Gentile inclusion is not otherwise scripturally warranted. Romans 15 is a Pauline collection of Old Testament texts which pointedly celebrate the divinely intended inclusion of Gentiles now revealed in the gospel of God. Thus, we may theologically appreciate Paul's rendering (and reading) of Isaiah 28:16 in a way that is similar to his reading of other Old Testament texts. Nonetheless, Paul's version of the text of Isaiah 28:16 in Romans 10:11 must be understood for what it is: a theologically nuanced and amplified reading of an ancient text, a reading which for Paul is consistent with what he believes on other grounds (perhaps such things as personal experiences, other texts, or Christian tradition) to be God's gracious intention to include the Gentiles in His saving purpose.

One final illustration, this one from a non-Pauline text, is appropriate. The Petrine sermon of Acts 2:14-40 also illustrates the early Christian capacity for theologically reading and nuancing the ancient text. Luke's/Peter's inclusion of "signs" in 2:19 as a parallel to the word "wonders" has no basis in either the Hebrew or Greek texts of Joel 2:28-32 (LXX 3:1-5). Nonetheless, the addition of "signs" is of central significance for the Petrine sermon inasmuch as it becomes, in the exposition of the Joel text which follows (Acts 2:22-40), the scriptural basis for the argument by Peter that Jesus was divinely attested with "wonders and signs" (2:22, NASB). Indeed, these "wonders and signs" anticipated by the text of Joel—as theologically amplified by Peter/Luke are perpetuated in the ministries of the apostles, as God continues to bear witness through them to His saving work in connection with the coming of Jesus (Acts 2:43).[29] Thus, the inclusion of "signs" as parallel to "wonders" in the Joel text becomes a clue to the interpretation of the divine "wonders and signs" in Lukan theology; namely, beginning with the miracle ministry of Jesus and continuing in the lives of the apostles, the "wonders and signs" of the last days, prophesied by the prophet Joel, have been revealed. In view of these heavenly and earthly portents, we must call upon the name of the Lord Jesus to be saved (Acts 2:21,38).

Theological Use of Scripture

Christocentric

To remark the Christocentric nature of the New Testament use of the Old Testament is commonplace among scholars.[30] Though we would contend (see below) that there is also a significantly ecclesiocentric ("church centered") use of Scripture in the New Testament, surely none may dispute the Christological emphasis to be found in the New Testament writers' use of the Old Testament. The Gospels and Acts especially represent such a decidedly Christocentric appropriation of the Old Testament.[31] Examples abound. At least ten events in the life of Jesus are supported by explicitly introduced Old Testament citations in Matthew: the announcement of the angel to Joseph (1:22-23); the designation of Bethlehem as the scripturally indicated place of Messiah's birth (2:5-6); the return of the holy family from Egypt (2:15); the slaughter of the innocents by Herod (2:17-18); the residence of the holy family in Nazareth (2:23);[32] the preaching of John the Baptist (3:3); the residence of Jesus in Capernaum (4:14-16); Jesus' healing ministry (8:14-17); the fact of Jesus' teaching ministry by way of parables (13:34-35); the triumphal entry of Jesus into Jerusalem (21:4-5); and the betrayal of Jesus at the hands of Judas (27:3-10). Coupled with the fact of these explicitly introduced scriptural citations is the presence of a number of explicit Scripture proofs which, though not introduced by a fulfillment formula such as "this happened in order that the words of the prophet might be fulfilled," nonetheless are clearly intended to point to given fulfillments of Scripture through the life and ministry of Jesus (see 10:34-36; 11:2-5; 27:34-35,43).

The same kind of thing may be attested in Luke, though certainly not to the same extent as may be found in Matthew. In

Luke 4:18-19, the reference to Isaiah 61:1-2a is clearly understood by Luke (and Jesus) as having its fulfillment in the ministry of Jesus. Indeed, the rejection of Jesus in Nazareth pericope in Luke 4:16-30 serves as the programmatic passage in the Third Gospel with respect to the presentation of Jesus that follows therein. With regard to Old Testament Scripture, there is little doubt that Isaiah 61:1-2a; 58:6d is normative for Luke for the story of Jesus.[33] Jesus as the anointed preacher of the gospel and herald of the favorable year of the Lord, the long-awaited Year of Release/Jubilee, is foundational for the Lukan presentation of Jesus as the One who preaches the kingdom of God, brings forgiveness to sinners, and is the Messiah for Jew and Gentile alike.

The Gospel of John likewise evidences a profoundly Christocentric use of Scripture. In 2:17, following the cleansing of the temple, we are told that His disciples later remembered that the Scriptures had already declared, "zeal for your house will consume me" (NRSV). Though not done in the more formal, explicit fashion of Matthew, the Johannine representation of Jesus repeatedly draws upon scriptural themes and motifs. He is the Bread of heaven. He is, in fulfillment of the scriptural festivals of Judaism, the Water of life (7:37-38) and the Light of the world (8:12). He is the one about whose rejection Isaiah spoke when the prophet declared, "Lord, who has believed our report? And to whom has the arm of the Lord been revealed?" (Isa. 53:1 in John 12:38, NASB). In anticipation of His own betrayal, Jesus declared that the Scriptures are fulfilled when "He who eats My bread has lifted up his heel against Me" (13:18, NASB). His crucifixion too was a fulfillment of Scripture, as He cried, "I thirst" (19:28); and when, though His body was pierced, "not a bone . . . [was] broken" (19:31-37, NASB).

Acts also employs a kind of Christocentricity in its use of the Scriptures. The earliest sermons especially draw upon Old Testament texts for affirmation of the early Christian preaching. He is the Lord of Joel 2:32, upon whose name one must call to be saved (Acts 2:21). He is likewise the mysterious Lord who ascended into heaven at the right hand of God, about whom David spoke in Psalm 110 (Acts 2:34-35). He is the holy servant of God against whom the Gentiles raged and the peoples devised futile things, just as David (Ps. 2:1) had predicted (Acts 4:23-28). Such examples could easily be multiplied throughout the New Testament and require no further elaboration here. The Christocentric nature of the early Christian use of the Old Testament is patent.

Ecclesiocentric

What is not as frequently noticed as the Christocentricity of the New Testament appropriation of Scripture is the strikingly ecclesiocentric nature of many Old Testament citations in the New Testament.[34] The writings of Paul are a particularly rich resource for such evidences. Certainly Paul does on occasion allude to Christ as the fulfillment of Scripture (Rom. 1:1-3; 1 Cor. 10:1-4; 15:3-4), but it is more often the case that Paul's use of Scripture has to do with matters related to the relationship of Jew and Gentile, that is, participation in the church and life among the people of God. Romans, which is the most concentrated Pauline piece with respect to the use of Scripture, abundantly illustrates this phenomenon of ecclesiocentricity. It is the relationship of Jew and Gentile and the question of the Jewish law with respect to participation in the salvation of God that occupies Paul's attention as he reads the ancient texts. For example, the collection of texts in Romans 3:10-18 is brought forth by Paul to indicate the unanimous witness of Scripture in proving that both "Jews and Greeks are all under sin" (3:9, NASB). Likewise, the words of David invoked in 4:6-8 are for the purpose of insisting upon righteousness as a gift of God for Jew and Gentile alike. Romans 9–11 repeatedly invokes the Scriptures of Israel, but not with regard to the messiahship of Jesus; rather, Paul's intent is to define the covenantal "children of the promise," so as to demonstrate the scriptural validity of Gentile inclusion among the people of God (9:25-26), to assert Israel's culpability for her rejection of Christ (10:16-21), and to declare the divine plan for Israel's re-inclusion among the number of those who experience saving grace through Jesus Christ (chap. 11). Finally (with regard to Romans), the concentrated use of Old Testament texts in chapter 15 again relates to the joint participation of Jew and Gentile in the mercies of God. The fact that the Gentiles may experience God's mercy was all along, Paul contended, the divine intention, as the cited texts of 15:9-12 demonstrate.

The story is the same when we turn to Galatians. Paul's application there of various Old Testament texts was for the purpose of arguing that the Gentiles too belong under the umbrella of God's mercy. The Scripture had all along "foreseen" that the Gentiles would be justified by faith (3:8) and that the law would not be the basis of salvation (3:11). Indeed, the law brings only a curse (3:10). Following these arguments, Paul's extensive, typological application of the stories of Hagar and

Sarah, the mothers respectively of Ishmael and Isaac, continued the inclusive goal of his scriptural ecclesiocentricity; it is
those who are of the promise who are the children of God and
not the children of the flesh (4:21-31).

Thus, when it comes to the theological uses of Scripture in
the New Testament, questions of Christology and ecclesiology
seem to have influenced the basic hermeneutical choices (of
both text and method) for the New Testament writers. That
Jesus, the crucified and risen one, is the fulfillment of scriptural
promise was the burden of much of New Testament preaching,
debate, and proclamation. Furthermore, that Jews and Gentiles, apart from Jewish ethnocentricity and as those who believe in Jesus, are the true heirs of the scriptural promises and
together constitute the people of God, is likewise a significant
burden of scriptural appropriation in the New Testament.
Surely, if we are in any way to read the Old Testament with the
same kind of theological focus represented by the New Testament writers' use of it, we too must read the ancient Scriptures
with a view to both their Christocentric and ecclesiocentric
functions. We must learn to read the fulfillment of Scripture, as
seen by the New Testament writers, in the person of Jesus and
in the fellowship of all people who come to God through the crucified and risen Lord.

Conclusion

The constraints of space, to say nothing of the complexity of
the material, will allow us only a few conclusions. First of all,
it is clear from our study that the use of the Old Testament in
the New Testament is governed by certain extrinsic controls. It
is not always what we would call the "original intent" of a passage that determines the meaning a New Testament writer derived from it. The New Testament writers did not use what we
would call "historical-critical methods" for interpreting the Old
Testament. Nonetheless, before passing judgment (rather
anachronistically) on the standards of exegesis employed by
the New Testament writers, it is incumbent upon New Testament readers to understand the hermeneutical controls which
have influenced the interpretive maneuvers executed by the
New Testament writers when applying their Scriptures.

1. What seems to have been a primary given for the New
Testament writers is the gospel, the message of and/or the
central events related to, the death, burial, and exaltation of
Jesus.

2. It must be noted that the writers of the New Testament sense themselves to be in continuity with the scriptural people of God. Thus, the church, the company of those who believe in the crucified and risen One, is the Israel of God.

Furthermore, these two primary extrinsic controls, when coupled with certain other apparently given assumptions about the nature of the Scripture (see below), serve to open up a wide range of interpretive possibilities for the writers of the New Testament as they read the ancient Scriptures of Israel. As to these assumptions, the evidence leads us to say that, for them:

1. The Scriptures of Israel are the living Word of the living God. The Scriptures do not possess a merely historic and/or historical value. They continue to convey the Word of God to God's people. There is, thus, because of this ongoing applicability, a certain elasticity to the Scriptures which allows for their creative reapplication in history. This phenomenon is, of course, especially evidenced in the creative reappropriation of Israel's Scriptures by the early church with respect to the life, death, and resurrection of Jesus of Nazareth and the inclusion of Gentiles in the company of God's people.

2. The Scriptures of Israel have a certain eschatological/prophetic character. Even in passages which are not prophetic according to literary type or genre, there is to be found again, even in historical/narrative texts the possibility of hidden meanings which prophetically anticipate the saving acts of God at the end of history. Thus, for example, Hosea's historical allusion to God's deliverance of Israel from Egyptian slavery (Hos. 11:1) becomes in Matthew—given the evangelist's Christian conclusion, legitimated no doubt for Matthew by the gospel events, that Jesus is the fulfillment of Israel's history and that therefore Israel's history is a prefiguring of Jesus' history—a messianic prophecy (Matt. 2:15).

The fact that the New Testament writers are guided by such primary, extrinsic controls (the truth of the gospel and the conviction that the church is the Israel of God) does not, however, imply a final solipsism on their part. Put another way, to say that the New Testament writers have certain precommitments—overwhelmed as they were by the perceived historical fact of the resurrection—regarding the truthfulness of the gospel and the sense that they were the people of God in no way argues that the New Testament writers are guilty of a final subjectivism in their reading of the Old Testament. Indeed, certainly both Jesus, that is, what He thought, and that for which He lived and died, and the rise of the church are in no small way also the result of the generative force of Israel's Scriptures in the matrix of first century A.D. Judaism. The extrinsic controls of Christianity's gospel Christology and its new, not exclusively Jewish, ecclesiology are in a large measure reflective of the central features of Old Testament theology. Thus, while the New Testament writers certainly represent one very distinctive and historically particularized version of what we would call "Old Testament theology," they are neither historically isolated from their religious forebears nor are they theologically eccentric. They are themselves, in light of the things recently accomplished among them, dialoguing with and giving answer to the rebounding sound of a rather harmonious chorus of scriptural witnesses—witnesses to the historical (and thus potentially eschatological), communal (and thus potentially ecclesiological), and largely monarchical (and thus potentially Christological) religion of Israel. Therefore, the extrinsic controls operative upon the New Testament writers (what we have called the gospel and/or Christocentricity on the one hand and ecclesiocentricity on the other), though reflective certainly of certain historical particularities that were divinely effected about A.D. 33, are nonetheless themselves an apt, and thus legitimate, reflection of the original scriptural vision. It does not seem to us arbitrary to argue that what we have called the extrinsic controls of Christology and ecclesiology, whereby the New Testament writers read, shape, amplify, and nuance the various texts of the Old Testament which they press into their missionary, apologetic, and ministerial services, are themselves appropriate and legitimate conclusions to certain trajectories already begun within the theology and history of the Old Testament itself. Seen in this way, the two-sided (Christocentric and ecclesiocentric) goal of Israel's Scripture—that is, Jesus and the church—has become as well the vantage point from which the (Old Testament) origins themselves may be better understood, origins which in turn will continue to shed new light on the goal.

We must, therefore, think of the New Testament writers' use of the Old Testament as having gone "beyond intentionality." That is, it is historically necessary for us to think of the New Testament writers as having interpreted the Old Testament in ways unanticipated by the original authors. The intention of the Old Testament writer, therefore, while still very important, and while still a necessary canon of interpretation for establishing certain moorings for our texts, cannot in the end be the last word as to meaning and/or final application(s). It seems clear that the New Testament writers go beyond the intentions of the Old Testament writers (if by "intention" we mean to refer to "consciously anticipated applications") in their use of Old Testament texts. On the other hand, it does still seem appropriate to speak of what I would call "aptness" or "fitness." That is, though we must understand the New Testament writers to have gone beyond intentionality, in the sense defined above, we must, unless we are to be left with canons of reading which finally deny all value to the historically given significations of a particular text, still think in terms of an acceptable range of interpretive options. Texts do not have complete elasticity. Some interpretations "fit" and others do not. The fitness of a given text, it seems to me, depends thus upon both its original intention and its adaptability to, via the medium of a creative mind, the constraints of the given, historically affirmed (and likewise scripturally generated) truths of the Christian faith.

The authors of the New Testament had a body of sacred texts. These texts, they believed, were divinely given, prophetic in character, and susceptible of interpretive (and inspired) reinterpretation. These early Christian leaders were furthermore utterly convinced that God had powerfully acted through the crucified, risen, and exalted Jesus to establish them (and all his followers) as the continuation of the Israel of God, through whom he would no doubt continue to act to accomplish His purposes. These convictions led them to see in their sacred texts prophetic anticipations of the aforesaid mighty acts of God accomplished through Jesus.

Given the creativity, not to mention inspiration, with which they read their Old Testament Scriptures, can we today still use their methods? It would be audacious to try, but the answer to that question depends in large measure upon one's view of the uniqueness of the role of the apostles and early Christian prophets. If, as I am strongly inclined to argue, those offices have closed, it may well be that the prophetic insights reflected in the New Testament use of the Old Testament represent a historically particularized set of interpretive acts which, in salvation-history, are as unique as the gospel events themselves (see Eph. 1:8; 3:4-5)—in which case we may perhaps pronounce (though humbly, please) upon their historical-critical status as exegetical maneuvers, but are in no position to replicate them. But here we would embark upon historical and theological matters related to inspiration, authority, and canonicity, and space will not permit.[35]

Certainly if we are even to attempt to read the Old Testament as the New Testament writers read it, we must at the very least be prepared to press the limits of disciplined study, spiritual experience, and participation in the authentic life of a living community of faith, under the full persuasion of the truths of the gospel. On the other hand, it is hardly necessary, and historically impossible, to place ourselves in the place of the earliest writers of the New Testament, as they read their inspired Scriptures. We are the beneficiaries of their readings. We may (and do) live in their light. Whatever hermeneutical maneuvers they have performed, we can certainly, as sympathetic readers willing to engage them via the disciplined enterprises of historical and literary studies, appreciate the theological conclusions and assumptions which energized, reflected, and even resulted from their labors. But our readings of the Old Testament, if we are to live with any sense of historical humility, that is, any acknowledgment at all of the Christian traditions which we have received, must be, and in fact already are, focused in the light of the New Testament writers' readings of the Old Testament. Who are the people of God? What is the temple of God? Need we continue to practice the cultic exercises of the ancient Hebrews? Who is the mysterious figure of (say) Isaiah 53 and 61? Answers to these questions, or at least the general outlines from which we may take specific answers for our generation, have been given us already by the writers of the New Testament. To attempt to read the Old Testament as if the New Testament had not been written is not only historically naive, but also is virtually as audacious as the attempt to add to the New Testament itself. Indeed, to read the Old Testament as Paul (and other New Testament writers) read it is impossible, for we have already read Paul. You cannot "unread" a story. You can only read it again. And if we cannot read as Paul read, then for the same and other reasons we can never write as he wrote. The canon is closed. Though we may not read or write as Paul, we may, by the power of the Spirit, in the fellowship of the people of God, under the persuasion of the gospel truths, and with the aid of the writings of the great apostle himself, begin to understand what Paul himself wrote. Therefore, through the prism of the apostolic literature itself, we may come to appreciate more fully the glorious Light of God which first shone in the Scriptures of the ancient Hebrews, later burst forth into the world of humankind, and is even now (though oftentimes too faintly) still reflected in the life and worship of the church. It is that Light which must be preached and which in the very act of preaching can still itself bring illumination.

Notes

1. "While some of the earliest Christians thought in terms of an Old and New Covenant (2 Cor. 3:14; Heb. 8:7), it was the church fathers Tertullian (about A.D. 160-230) and Origen (A.D. 185-254) who first used the term 'Old Testament' for the pre-Christian Scriptures as a whole." See "Old Testament," in *Harper's Bible Dictionary*, ed. P. J. Achtemeier (San Francisco: Harper & Row, 1985), 719.

2. See Talmudic tractate *Sanhedrin* (43a): "Jesus was hanged on Passover Eve. Four days previously the herald had cried, 'He is being led out for stoning, because he has practiced sorcery and led Israel astray and enticed them into apostasy. Whosoever has anything to say in his defense, let him come, and declare it.' As nothing was brought forward in his defense, he was hanged on Passover Eve."

3. For a discussion of the question of Jewish expectations with regard to a suffering servant/crucified Messiah, see R. N. Longenecker, *The Christology of Early Jewish Christianity* (London: SCM, 1970), 104f. Longenecker asserts, "There is no explicit evidence that this general attitude towards suffering was ever consciously carried over to ideas regarding the Messiah, God's servant par excellence."

4. Isaiah 52:13–53:12 is utilized, according to Shires, by quotation and reference more than any other Old Testament passage of similar length. Ten New Testament books reflect the use of it directly in approximately fifty-eight verses (see for example Matt. 8:17; John 12:38; Luke 22:37; Acts 8:32-33; Rom. 10:15; 1 Pet. 2:22). See H. M. Shires, *Finding the Old Testament in the New* (Philadelphia: The Westminster Press, 1974), 43.

5. Early Christian preaching largely took place, whenever possible, in synagogues. It was often there that the new, particularly Christian way of reading Scripture was presented and debated. For examples of such "synagogue debating" see Acts 13:1-47; 14:1-6; 17:10-15.

6. See Matthew 22:41-45; Mark 11:15-18; 12:1-12; Luke 24:25-27,32,44-47.

7. For Example, W. C. Kaiser, Jr., *The Uses of the Old Testament in the New* (Chicago: Moody, 1985); J. Weir, "Analogous Fulfillment: The Use of the Old Testament in the New Testament," *Perspectives in Religious Studies* 9 (1982): 65-76; I. H. Marshall, "An Assessment of Recent Developments," *It is Written*, ed. D. A. Carson and H. G. M. Williamson (Cambridge: Cambridge University Press, 1988), 1-24; E. E. Ellis, *Prophecy and Hermeneutic in Early Christianity* (Grand Rapids: Eerdmans, 1978).

8. Among some literary critics "intertextuality" is defined so broadly as to include the larger appropriation of a prior culture into the writing of the text. For our purposes, however, we will limit the term to "how writers cite and allude to specifically identifiable precursors," Hays, *Echoes of Scripture in the Letters of Paul* (New Haven: Yale University Press, 1989), 14-16.

9. Various counts of the number of explicit citations can be found. C. H. Toy found 613 Old Testament quotations and allusions in the New Testament, *Quotations in the New Testament* (New York: Scribner's, 1884); Shires found 239 formal quotations in the New Testament drawn from 185 different Old Testament passages. He also noted 198 unacknowledged quotations taken from 147 Old Testament texts, *Finding the Old Testament in the New*, 15. Kaiser writes, "it is safe to conclude that there are approximately 300 formal citations in the New Testament from the Old Testament in addition to an almost incalculable influence on language, modes of expression, and thought in the New Testament," *The Use of the Old Testament in the New*, 3. According to Shires, "A rough count of

the references in Nestle's Greek Testament yields about 950 quotations and allusions, and the United Bible Society's Greek text lists over 2,500 New Testament passages from nearly 1,800 Old Testament passages," *Ibid.*, 2.

10. Two works have greatly assisted my study of typology in regard to the New Testament use of Old Testament passages. See E. E. Ellis, *Paul's Use of the Old Testament* (Grand Rapids: Eerdmans, 1957), 126-35; and D. E. Aune, "Early Christian Biblical Interpretation," *The Evangelical Quarterly* 41 (1969), 96. The distinction between "typology" and "allegory" is a modern one and should not be pressed when examining the biblical material.

11. For a more detailed study of typology see D. S. Dockery's chapter elsewhere in this volume.

12. The use of the word "echo" is borrowed from R. Hays. Hays writes, "The concept of allusion depends both on the notion of authorial intention and on the assumption that the reader will share with the author the requisite 'portable library' to recognize the source of the allusion; the notion of echo, however, finesses such questions: 'echo is a metaphor of, and for, alluding, and does not depend on conscious intention.'" See *Echoes of Scripture*, 29. Hays himself, in turn, depends on John Hollander, *The Figure of Echo: A Mode of Allusion in Milton and After* (Berkeley: University of California Press, 1981), 64.

13. Ibid., 18-24.

14. Ibid., 88-91. I am beholden to Hays for the following discussion regarding 2 Corinthians 8:15.

15. It is a shame that the logic of the Pauline exhortation of 2 Corinthians 9:8-11 is so routinely twisted from its plain sense of "God has given to you so that you may give," to "give, so that you may get."

16. Mark 3:1-6; compare parallels Matthew 12:9-14; Luke 6:6-11.

17. For an extended discussion of this particular intertextual echo see Hays, *Echoes of Scripture*, 21-24.

18. Though I have greatly used Hays's material in the analysis of this phrase, I have gone beyond Hays's conclusion in my interpretation of the "for I know" phrase. Whereas Hays seems finally skeptical of hearing any echoes of correspondence between the texts of Job and Philippians in the "for I know" phrase, I have suggested above that one may well be found.

19. Mark 12:10; Luke 20:18; Romans 9:33; 1 Peter 2:6; Ephesians 2:20. The possible topical selection and collection of Old Testament passages by early Christians is a process which has intrigued scholars. J. R. Harris proposed that a "Book of Testimonies" existed from which New Testament writers drew material for their quotations. C. H. Dodd, however, challenged the existence of such a testimonial collection. See R. Longenecker, *Biblical Exegesis in the Apostolic Period* (Grand Rapids: Eerdmans, 1975), 89-90.

20. R. Sloan, *The Favorable Year of the Lord*, (Austin: Schola, 1977), 115-21.

21. See the discussion of this passage in Hays, *Echoes of Scripture*, 54-57.

22. Ibid., 65-68.

23. There are of course some possible exceptions. See Sloan, *The Favorable Year of the Lord,* 31. It is clear that Luke 4:18-19 uses a tradition which reflects the MT (Masoretic Text) and not the LXX when quoting Isaiah 61:1-2a and 58:6. More specifically, in Luke 4:19, a quotation of Isaiah 61:2a, Luke has rendered the MT (*liqro'*) with (*keruxai*) instead of the LXX (*kalesai*). For further discussion see R. T. France, *Jesus and the Old Testament* (London: Tyndale, 1971), 241, 243, 248, 252f.

24. A helpful volume on LXX study is S. Jellicoe's *The Septuagint and Modern Study* (Ann Arbor, MI: Eisenbrauns, 1978). For a specific study on Paul's use of the LXX see Ellis, *Paul's Use of the Old Testament*, 12-20.

25. The LXX edition relied upon by most scholars is that of A. Rahlfs, *Septuaginta* (Stuttgart: Wurttembergische Bibelanstalt, 1935).

26. B. Reicke, "The Law and this World According to Paul," *Journal of Biblical Literature* 70 (1951): 262.

27. For a discussion of various interpretive possibilities associated with these texts see R. B. Hays, *The Faith of Jesus Christ* (Chico, CA: Scholars, 1983), 150-57.

28. LXX, a, c.

29. R. B. Sloan, "Signs and Wonders: A Rhetorical Clue to the Pentecost Discourse," *Evangelical Quarterly*, forthcoming.

30. S. E. Balentine, "The Interpretation of the Old Testament in the New Testament," *Southwestern Journal of Theology* 23 (1981): 50.

31. Shires, *Finding the Old Testament in the New*, 46.

32. Though the expression "he shall be called a Nazarene" is problematic when it comes to finding a specific Old Testament text to which Matthew refers, it is nonetheless clear that the residence of the family of Jesus in Nazareth was regarded, either generally or specifically, as a fulfillment of Scripture. For a discussion of the passage, see R. H. Gundry, *The Use of the Old Testament in St. Matthew's Gospel* (SNT 18. Leiden: Brill, 1967), 97-104.

33. Sloan, *The Favorable Year of the Lord*, 28ff., 115ff.

34. Hays, *Echoes of Scripture*, 84-87. Hays concludes: "What Paul finds in Scripture, above all else, is a prefiguration of the church as the people of God. . . . In short, Paul operates with an ecclesiocentric hermeneutic," 86.

35. See my article, "Unity in Diversity: A Clue to the Emergence of the New Testament as Sacred Literature," a chapter in *New Testament Criticism and Interpretation*, edited by D. A. Black and D. S. Dockery (Grand Rapids: Zondervan, 1991).

7

Typological Exegesis:
Moving Beyond Abuse and Neglect

David S. Dockery

Like many others, I began my studies in seminary hoping to discover the right formula for interpreting the Bible. In my first semester, I enrolled in a class that I hoped would accomplish this purpose. This course was called hermeneutics. I was not sure what "hermeneutics" meant, but I was told it involved the "how to's" for understanding the right principles used in interpreting Scripture. This sounded great to me; just what I was looking for. Yet, in this class we were introduced to a variety of ways that people had interpreted the Bible in the history of the church which was perhaps more unsettling than what I had hoped.

By the end of the semester, we had been told that the best way to interpret Scripture was to interpret it literally, grammatically, and historically. This basically eliminated all symbolic approaches such as the allegorical or typological. The abandonment of the allegorical method was consistent with Reformation practices. Yet, I believe the dismissal of typological practices was a reaction to abuses in popular preaching and dispensational-oriented study Bibles. This, coupled with the outlandish typological schemes in post-Reformation times provided a sensible foundation for this seeming overreaction.

On the other hand, twentieth-century New Testament scholars have avoided typological approaches because of the paradigm established by Rudolf Bultmann. Bultmann's radical disjuncture between the Old Testament and the New created a virtual neglect of a synthesizing, typological approach to interpretation.

In this chapter we shall aim to steer a middle course between the extremes of abuse and neglect. Following the suggestions of D. L. Baker in *Two Testaments: One Bible*, we believe that a typological reading of Scripture is in line with the pattern of Jesus and the apostles, thus providing an overarching unity to the Bible's story. Also we think that this approach can help bring about a rapprochement between the different wings of the evangelical world. A balanced and sane approach to typological exegesis can bring together those in the dispensational and covenant theology communities. While this chapter is much more descriptive than prescriptive, we trust the historical analysis will prove useful and beneficial.

From the beginning of the Christian movement, the early believers shared the Holy Scriptures of the Jews. Following the example of Jesus, Scriptures were for these believers first and foremost the authoritative religious writings. Indeed, not only did the earliest church inherit its Scriptures from the Jews, it also inherited from them various methods of interpretation, as well as actual interpretations. The interpretation of the Jewish Scriptures by the earliest church, however, took on a new factor which stamped a new meaning on the Scriptures: the life, death, and resurrection of Jesus. In this essay our attention will focus on the typological interpretation of the Old Testament by Jesus and the early church.

Jesus and Christological Hermeneutics

Jesus and the Old Testament

In the New Testament account of the ministry of Jesus, it is maintained that Jesus Himself was responsible for instructing His followers that His life and ministry was a "fulfillment" of the Scriptures.[1] While it is true that Jesus interpreted the Scriptures in a manner similar to His contemporary Jewish exegetes, it is also true that there was novelty in His method and message.

This new method was a Christological reading which means that Jesus read the Old Testament in light of Himself. For example, in John 5:39-40, it is reported that Jesus said, "You diligently study the Scriptures because you think that by them you possess eternal life. These are the *Scriptures that testify about me*" (NIV, italics mine). And in John 5:46: "If you believed Moses, you would believe me, for *he wrote about me"* (NIV, italics mine). Also on the Emmaus road with His disciples following the resurrection, Jesus said:

> "How slow of heart [you are] to believe all that the prophets have spoken: Did not the Christ have to suffer these things and then enter his glory?" And beginning with Moses and all the prophets, he explained to them was was said in all the Scriptures concerning himself (Luke 24:26-27, NIV).

Jesus understood the Old Testament Christologically and it is to Him that we owe the identification of Himself, in some way, with Israel. In the temptation narratives (Matt. 4:1-11; Luke 4:1-13), where we find Jesus' own estimation of His status and calling, His answers were taken from Deuteronomy 6–8. In this passage Moses, following the forty years of wandering in the wilderness, exhorted Israel toward wholehearted obedience and continued faith in the divine provision for them. It was a time of hunger and testing, preparatory to a special task, in which God disciplined His nation Israel (Deut. 8:5), to teach them to worship the true God. Jesus, at the end of the forty days, accepted afresh His messianic mission and His status as Son of God, seeing Himself succeeding where Israel had failed.[2] His belief in His forthcoming resurrection seemed to be motivated both by the promises of Israel's resurrection (Hos. 6:2) and by seeing Himself in light of the Jonah story (Jonah 1:17, Matt. 12:40). He observed His own experiences prefigured in the psalms of vindication and suffering that were used both by individual Israelites and corporate Israel as well (Pss. 22; 41; 42; 43; 118).[3]

R. T. France sums up the evidence of the synoptic gospels in these words:

> He uses persons in the Old Testament as types of himself (David, Solomon, Elijah, Isaiah, Jonah) or of John the Baptist (Elijah); he refers to Old Testament institutions as types of himself and his work (the priesthood and the covenant); he sees in the experiences of Israel foreshadowings of his own; he finds the hopes of Israel fulfilled in himself and his disciples, and sees his disciples as assuming the status of Israel; in deliverance by God he sees a type of the gathering of men into his church, while the disasters of Israel are foreshadowings of the imminent punishment of those who reject him, whose unbelief is prefigured in that of the wicked in Israel and even, in two instances, in the arrogance of the Gentile nations.[4]

In all these aspects of the Old Testament people of God, Jesus saw foreshadowings of Himself and His work. This resulted in the opposition and consequent rejection of the majority of the Jews, while the true Israel was now to be found in the new Christian community. The history of Israel had reached its decisive point in the coming of Jesus. The whole of the Old Testament was summed up in Him. He embodied in Himself the redemptive destiny of Israel, and in the community of those who belong to Him that status and destiny are to be fulfilled.

It is because Jesus is the representative of Israel that words originally spoken of the nation can rightly be applied to Him, and it is because Jesus is the representative of humankind that words spoken originally by the psalmist can be fulfilled by Him (John 13:18; 15:25; 19:28). Jesus was the key to understanding the Old Testament for everything pointed to Himself. The New Testament writers, following the pattern of Jesus, interpreted the Old Testament as a whole and in its parts as a witness to Christ.[5]

It would be surprising if the new and radical way in which the earliest Christians interpreted the Jewish Scriptures was entirely their invention and owed nothing to Jesus Himself. The gospel tradition indicates that Jesus both understood His mission in a way that ran counter to the assumptions and expectations of His closest followers as well as His opponents and also saw His mission as a fulfillment of the Scriptures. We can content ourselves with C. K. Barrett's words:

> The gospel story as a whole differs so markedly from current (i.e., first century) interpretation of the Old Testament that it is impossible to believe that it originated simply in meditations of prophecy; it originated in the career of Jesus of Nazareth.[6]

It is not surprising that in providing different pictures of Jesus' life, the biblical writers saw that at almost every point, His life had fulfilled the Old Testament. His birth had been foretold (Isa. 7:14 = Matt. 1:23; Mic. 5:2 = Matt. 2:6); as had the flight to Egypt (Hos. 11:1 = Matt. 2:15); the slaughter of the innocent children by Herod (Jer. 31:15 = Matt. 2:18); and His upbringing in Nazareth (in a prophecy not identified in Matt. 2:23). The overall impact of His ministry had been described (Isa. 42:1-4 = Matt. 12:17-21) as well as His use of parables in His teaching (Isa. 6:9-10; Ps. 78:2 = Matt. 13:14-15,35). The message of Jesus' passion is filled with allusions to the Old Testament including accounts of the triumphal entry into Jerusalem (Zech. 9:9 = Matt. 21:5); the cleansing of the temple (Isa. 56:7; Ps. 69:9 = Matt. 21:13) as well as Old Testament pictures behind the events surrounding the cross (John 19:24,28,36-37).

The question that faces us for the purposes of our study is "How did Jesus interpret the Old Testament so that this Christological hermeneutic developed?" The answer to this question requires us to look carefully at the Jewish approaches to biblical interpretation before and at the time of Jesus' life.

Jewish Approaches to Biblical Interpretation

Jewish interpreters, no matter how diverse their hermeneutical methods, found agreement on several common points. First, they held a common belief in the divine inspiration of Scripture. Second, they affirmed that the Torah contained the entire truth of God for the guidance of humanity. The texts, for the Jew of the first century, were extremely rich in content and pregnant with plural meanings. R. N. Longenecker illustrates this with quotations from the rabbis:

> From the school of R. Ishmael (second-generation Tannaim, c. A.D. 90-130) we have the maxim: "Just as the rock is split into many splinters, so also may one biblical verse convey many teachings" (b. Sanhedrin 34a). Bemidbar Rasbbah, the most recent of the pentateuchal Midrashim, dating no earlier than the eleventh or twelfth century A.D. in its codified form, expands this to insist, based on the numerical value of *dgl* ("standard") in Cant. 2:4, that the "Torah can be expounded in forty-nine different ways" (Num. R. 2.3) and based on the value of *yayin* (wine), that "there are seventy modes of expounding the Torah" (Num. R. 14.15f).[7]

Third, Jewish exegetes, because of the view that the text contained many meanings, considered their task to involve dealing with both the plain or literal meaning and the implied meanings as well. Finally, they maintained the purpose of all interpretation was to translate the words of God into life, thus making it relevant for people in their own particular situations.

Traditionally, five hermeneutical methods have been considered the primary alternatives for studying the exegetical practices behind the New Testament writers. These include the typological along with literal, allegorical, pesher, and midrash.[8]

It is helpful to be reminded that these classifications may not have always been consciously considered categories for early Jewish interpreters. R. Loewe rightly notes that in dealing with a system that thinks more holistically, functionally and practically than it does analytically, stressing precedent more than logic in defense of its ways, any attempt at classification inevitably goes beyond that system's explicit statements as to its own principles.[9] Nevertheless, as others have suggested, the Jewish treatment of Scripture falls rather easily into one or the other of these five categories.

Typological exegesis seeks to discover a correspondence between people and events of the past and of the future or present.[10] The correspondence with the past is not necessarily discovered within the written text, but within the historical event. This approach can be distinguished both from predictive prophecy, where the text functions only, or primarily, as a prediction of the future, and from allegorical hermeneutics, where the correspondence is found in the hidden meaning of the text and not in the history it presents. Typological exegesis does not ignore the historical meaning of a text, but begins with the historical meaning.[11] Typological exegesis then is based on the conviction that certain events in the history of Israel prefigure a future time when God's purposes will be revealed in their fullness.[12]

Jesus is recorded as pointing out typological correspondences between earlier events in redemptive history and circumstances connected with His person and ministry. Longenecker suggests three examples where Jesus invoked this correspondence theme: (1) Matthew 12:40, where Jesus paralleled the experience of Jonah and His own approaching death and entombment; (2) Matthew 24:37; where the relationship was drawn between the days of Noah and the days of "the coming Son of Man"; and (3) John 3:14, which connected the evaluation of the serpent in the wilderness to Jesus' own approaching crucifixion.[13] In each case, "Jesus viewed these Old Testament events as typological, pointing to their fulfillment in his person and ministry—not just analogies that could be drawn for the purpose of illustration."[14]

Summary

Jesus employed the literal usage of the Old Testament for moral injunctions, but primarily the Old Testament was interpreted by Jesus as having an obvious Christological reference. No one single image or pattern, no one motif or theme can adequately express this concept, yet what is emphasized throughout the New Testament is that numerous themes, images, and motifs of revelation and response were fulfilled in Jesus Christ. The note of Philip's jubilant words, "we have found him" (John 1:45, KJV) was echoed by the gospel writers as the way to interpret the Old Testament events, pictures, and ideas. It was not so much one fulfillment idea, but a harmony of notes presented in a variety of ways by different hermeneutical methods.[15] The teaching of Jesus and His hermeneutical practices became the direct source for much of the early church's understanding of the Old Testament. The church appears to have taken Jesus' own interpretation of Scripture and its themes as a paradigm for their continued exegetical endeavor. We must now direct our attention to the apostles' hermeneutical practices.

The Apostles and Typological Exegesis

In the record of the missionary preaching of the apostles in Acts, the apostles' eyewitness testimony concerning the mighty acts of God was always accompanied by a word of Scripture that shed light on the age (Acts 1:21ff.; 2:32; 3:15; 5:32; 10:41; 13:31). From the very beginning, the apostolic witness of the New Testament was linked to the prophetic witness of the Old Testament in order to evoke faith through the witness of the Spirit (Acts 2:33; 5:32). The central point in the church's preaching was the heavenly lordship of Jesus Christ. He had been put to death as Messiah and was also raised as Messiah (1 Cor. 15:3-4), ready at God's right hand to be the agent of His kingdom (Heb. 1:1-3). Thus the renewal of the preaching of Jesus after His crucifixion carried with it a statement concerning His own person and mission; and reception of the message involved acknowledgment of Jesus as the exalted Lord and allegiance to Him. This greatly influenced their reading of the church's Scriptures, the Old Testament, and had literary consequences for the development of the New Testament. By reading the Old Testament in this fashion, the church preserved the Christological-typological approach that it learned from Jesus. In this section we shall examine the usage of Scripture by four writers of the New Testament: Luke, Paul, Peter, and the author of Hebrews.

Luke

We have considered the gospel writers' understanding of the Old Testament as it was presented through the voice of Jesus Himself. Now we must consider the early church's message in Luke's work known as the Acts of the Apostles. Luke's work is not only a history of the early church, but is an apologetic for its existence based on the revelation of God in the Old Testament. Behind both Jesus and the Scriptures stood the witness of the Spirit. It was the Spirit who continued to direct the early church in its Christological-typological interpretation of the Old Testament.[16] To account for the beginning of this most original and fruitful process of rethinking the Old Testament,

C. H. Dodd suggests the church needed a creative mind: "The gospels offer us one (Jesus). Are we compelled to reject the offer?"[17]

One obvious factor is that the Old Testament passages in Acts are set entirely within Jewish contexts, with the one exception of Paul and Barnabas at Lystra (Acts 14:15). The dominant portion of the quotations and allusions occur in chapters 1–15. This indicates that it was only among Jews that such a direct appeal to the Old Testament would have been appreciated or understood.[18]

Literalistic and midrashic modes of exegesis are present in Acts (Acts 3:25 = Gen. 12:3; Acts 2:25-28 = Ps. 16:8-11/Ps. 110:1), but what appears to be most characteristic are pesher and typological approaches.[19] These approaches coupled with concepts of corporate solidarity and correspondences in history provide a way to understand the biblical message and history from a Christocentric or Christological perspective.

In Stephen's defense at the expansion of Christianity, given prior to his martyrdom at the hands of the Jewish authorities, he took what Jesus said about the prophets serving as types of his own ministry and suffering and reshaped them into a finished typology by giving them special application to Moses (Acts 7:17-43). The Mosaic period served as a model for the new age since Moses referred to himself as a type of the future deliverer (Acts 7:37 = Deut. 18:15). In the new age, the fulfillment of the promises made to the nation of Israel was inaugurated. Moses' actions, like those of Jesus (Acts 2:22) and the apostles (Acts 4:30) were accompanied by signs and wonders (Acts 7:36). Like Jesus, Moses became "a man powerful in speech and action" (Acts 7:22 = Luke 24:19; author's translation) and likewise was rejected by his people (Acts 7:27), though God gave him the honor of being a deliverer of his people. The description offered of Moses led L. Goppelt to offer the following conclusion: "By crucifying Jesus the present generation has completed what their fathers did to Moses, the prototype of the redeemer, and to all the prophets who predicted the coming of Christ" (Acts 7:51f.).[20]

Further examples could be offered, but this one chapter (Acts 7) illustrates how the early church preserved the typological and pesher approaches that Jesus taught and modeled for them, thus shaping their interpretation of the Old Testament as the basis for their preaching of salvation. For the earliest believers, this meant that the living presence of Jesus, through His Spirit, was to be considered a determining factor in all their biblical exegesis and also that the Old Testament was to be interpreted Christologically.[21] W. D. Davies has noted that there existed the expectation that the coming of the Messiah would make plain the enigmatic and obscure in the Torah.[22] Such an expectation seems to have developed into a basic conviction among the earliest believers, as evidenced by their hermeneutical approaches. We shall find the same thing in the other groups of New Testament Scriptures.

Paul

As the church grew and the missionary practices went further afield, there was bound to be a need to continue contact and consultation with the new churches. These practical concerns were handled by sending letters, and so the internal life of the church included written correspondence. The fact of apostolic instruction by letter has produced a type of writing for which there are not ancient parallels. The letter of Christian instruction was in fact almost as distinctive a Christian contribution to literary types as the written gospel.[23] The idea of collecting these letters and preserving them for posterity developed after the letters had been written. When Paul wrote his letters, there were no Christian books. His library was the Old Testament and his interpretation of those Scriptures must now be considered.

The way Paul used Scripture was not exactly identical with the way it was used in the Gospels. Yet, Paul generally shared the current exegetical presuppositions and attitudes toward Scripture.[24] His own personal experience and background would lead us to expect this. We can see a commonality among Paul and the rest of the New Testament writers in their use of the Old Testament.

The general consensus among Pauline scholars recognizes that Paul read the Old Testament Christologically and that he worked from two primary presuppositions: (1) the messiahship and lordship of Jesus, as validated by the resurrection and as witnessed to by the Spirit: and (2) the revelation of God in the Scriptures of the Old Testament.[25] Paul's starting point was the scriptural text in its context. Longenecker has insightfully observed:

> While the early Christian leaders at Jerusalem characteristically began with Jesus as the Messiah and moved on to an understanding of the Old Testament from this Christocentric perspective, Paul usually started with the text itself and sought by means of a midrashic explication to demonstrate Christological significance.[26]

This is not to suggest an extreme dichotomy between Paul and Jesus nor to elevate one approach as superior to another,[27] but only to point out that the Pauline approach to the Old Testament varied to some degree from that practiced by Jesus and the earliest Jewish Christians. Most likely, the variety can be traced to differences in training, ideological environment confronted in the missionary enterprise, and personal spiritual experiences. Recognizing these variations, let us look at some examples from the writings of the apostle.

Paul manifested such a wide range of the various uses of the Old Testament that we cannot give special treatment to his particularities. It is significant to note that for Paul, the Old Testament was credible as it was believed to be the Word of God, whose authority must be reverenced (Rom. 3:1-2; 7:12,14; Gal. 3:17).[28] The large majority of Paul's Old Testament quotations and allusions are found in the four major books of Galatians, Romans, 1 and 2 Corinthians, and the *Hauptbriefe*; half of these occur in Romans.[29]

At times it is difficult to discern exact allusions and conflated ideas from the Old Testament. Biblical language is found throughout the Pauline corpus. The Old Testament, notes Ellis, "was for Paul not only the Word of God but also his mode of thought and speech" and thus parallels of language are inevitable.[30] Like the usage in Acts, the dominant usage by Paul in the four major books can be traced to the hypothesis that, in one way or another, these communities primarily had Jewish audiences or were affected by some Jewish teaching. While he primarily read Scripture from his rabbinic heritage, Paul also employed Scripture typologically (Rom. 5:12-21; 1 Cor. 15:20-22; Gal. 3:10-12; 1 Cor. 10:1-11).[31] In Romans 5:14, this concept produced a tension which basically broke through the typological method.[32] Paul's point in this exposition was that the world and history of the first Adam stand over against those of the last and have been overcome by the latter.[33] Adam is designated a type of the one to come.[34]

The most obvious usage of typological exegesis found in Paul's writings is 1 Corinthians 10:1-11. Paul used the typology concept to interpret the events in the Corinthian church in the light of Israel's experiences in the wilderness. The punishment of God's ancient people which followed their disgraceful practices was seen as a prefiguration of judgment on those who abused the Lord's Supper.[35] The typological method was employed to expound the analogous relationship of concrete historical Old Testament events, in the sense of the past prefiguring present or future eschatological happenings.

Contrary to Davidson, who understands typology in a cause-and-effect relationship, Paul was using the typological pattern to mean that after the fact one saw a correspondence between earlier biblical events and the current situation.[36] Paul did not understand the events surrounding the exodus as prophetic of the Corinthian situation, rather they were to be understood as divinely given instruction. Granted they prefigured, but they did not demand further fulfillment.[37]

The question regarding Paul's usage of allegorical interpretation has brought many diverse responses. Some, such as James D. G. Dunn and R. N. Longenecker, see 1 Corinthians 9:9-10; Galatians 4:22-31; and 2 Corinthians 3:7-18 as a form of allegorical interpretation.[38] Others, such as A. T. Hanson, reject any idea that Paul used allegorical interpretation.[39] The issue at stake is the important distinction between allegory and allegorical. The concept of allegory differs from the allegorical method of interpretation. Allegory is a continuous metaphor which already includes in itself the intention of having more than one point. Allegorical interpretation, on the other hand, is an attempt to find hidden meaning quite different from the intended or historical one. Like Jesus, Paul used allegory to communicate his story, but did not seem to adopt outright an allegorical methodology.[40] The most debated of the Pauline messages is Galatians 4:22-31. It will be helpful for us briefly to focus on this passage. The verb (*allegoreo*) (to say an allegory) occurs in Galatians 4:24 in a participle form, translated "which things are figurative." Paul is comparing Hagar to Sarah, the old covenant with the new.

The two women represented the two covenants. One was from Mt. Sinai, bearing children for slavery; she was Hagar. Paul then compared Mt. Sinai with the present Jerusalem symbolizing bondage to the law, which was contrasted with the Jerusalem which is above, which is free, and is our mother (Gal. 4:26). We believe that Longenecker is correct in his observation that Paul is adopting a rabbinic methodology to "counteract in particular the Judaizers' application of this Jewish motif which argued in effect that Paul's teaching is the elemental while theirs is the developed."[41] The context was obviously triggered by polemical debate and was strongly circumstantial. Therefore, like Jesus, Paul adopted an approach similar to the allegorical method for both apologetical and polemical purposes.

Yet, in this instance, allegory was really an elaborate piece of typology. Paul's use of (*allegoreo*) should not be interpreted in light of third century Alexandrian exegesis which was bound up with philosophical ideas alien to Paul.

Paul's apostolic qualifications were unique and therefore his understanding of the Old Testament could not be directly related to the teaching and example of the historical Jesus. He was, however, well-schooled in the rabbinic tradition of Old Testament interpretation; yet he had been confronted by the exalted Lord Himself which brought about a change in his view of the Old Testament. Now he viewed the Scriptures from the pattern of redemptive history grounded in the life, death, and resurrection of Jesus of Nazareth.

Peter

The writings of the apostle Peter are not as voluminous as Paul's or Luke's, yet his importance in the early church is unquestioned. Peter abundantly used a typological approach to the Old Testament, serving as an excellent means of assuring the believers of their salvation. His basic statement about the Old Testament can be found in 1 Peter 1:10. In it a point of view is expressed that is distinctively typological.[42] The usage of the Old Testament by the apostle Peter was in continuity with early Christian interpretation and mirrored a distinctly apostolic treatment. There are a number of parallels between its teaching and those attributed to Peter in the Book of Acts.[43] Peter's typological approach paralleled Paul's as evidenced in 1 Peter 3:21. Noah's deliverance through the waters of the flood was seen as a prefiguration and type of the saving event of baptism, which thus became the antitype. The typological material that was appropriate for the purpose of the epistle was not only Christ's life and death, but the church's corporate salvation in relation to the exalted Jesus.

First Peter, broadly speaking, can be considered an exposition of Isaiah 53. The author employed phrases from his prophecy to describe the sufferings of Christ (1 Pet. 2:22-25). The comparison of Jesus with a lamb (1 Pet. 1:19) finds its basis in Isaiah 53:7. Likewise the price of redemption (1 Pet. 1:18) is grounded in Isaiah 52–53. The epistle presents a typological comparison that communicates that Jesus' death was effective because "when he offered his blood, Jesus acted as a lamb suitable for sacrifice."[44] Even in this brief analysis we can see that Peter interpreted the Old Testament in a truly typological fashion. Within the brief scope of 1 Peter there is exemplified a comprehensive typological approach that appears to conflate the patterns of Jesus, the early church in Jerusalem, and a Pauline influence.

Hebrews

The author of Hebrews is unknown to us, but what is known is that the author was thoroughly immersed in the Old Testament. To our author, the Old Testament was a divine oracle from first to last. As F. F. Bruce has indicated:

> It is a divine oracle . . . not only passages which in their original setting are the direct utterance of God (such as Psalm 110:4, . . .) but others are treated as spoken by God—like the words of Moses in Deuteronomy 32:43 (Hebrews 1:6) and the words of psalmists concerning the messengers of God (Psalm 104:4, quoted in Hebrews 1:7), addressed to a royal bridegroom (Psalm 45:6f. quoted in Hebrews 1:8f.), or addressed to God (Psalm 10:25-27, quoted in Hebrews 1:10-12). Chapter 3:7 introduces a quotation from Psalm 95:7-11 with the words "even as the Holy Spirit saith"—words which apply not only to the divine utterance quoted in Psalm 95:8ff., but the psalmist's cry which precedes them: "O that you would hear his voice today!" (Psalm 95:7b). In the details of the Old Testament sanctuary the Holy Spirit signifies spiritual truths for the present time (Hebrews 9:8). The psalmist's words of consecration and obedience in Psalm 40:6-8 are spoken by the Messiah "when he cometh into the world" (Hebrews 10:5-7).[45]

From this brief overview, we can see the dominance of the Old Testament as a foundation for the Epistle to the Hebrews. Yet, the letter cannot be classified as a typical representative of biblical interpretation in the apostolic period. It was generally assumed by many interpreters in the early part of this century that the author of Hebrews was influenced by Philo and the Alexandrian philosophy. With the work, however, of C. Spicq, this approach has been reversed. The explanations given in the epistle combine elements of rabbinic interpretation seeing the Old Testament as a mystery that awaits explanation and a form of messianic typology. Spicq observes, "we never find in our author the least trace of that allegorical exegesis which was to remain, alas, the specialty of the Alexandrian school."[46]

The author of Hebrews builds his argument around: (1) Psalm 2; 2 Samuel 7; and Deuteronomy 32; (2) Psalm 8:4-6; (3) Psalm 95:7-11; (4) Psalm 110:4; (5) Jeremiah 31:31-34. While these verses may have carried some messianic nuances in certain quarters of pre-Christian Judaism, the author seems to have given these passages a new Christological meaning that had possibly developed within the church.[47] How he brought these passages together is unknown. He may have adopted some particular collection of messianically relevant texts known to his readers. Or it may have been his own original contribution to the church's Christology. To this point in the study of Hebrews, there is no consensus on this matter.

What can be suggested is that these Old Testament passages were interpreted to point to the coming of the Messiah. They were used to underscore the incompleteness of the old economy under Moses and looked forward to a forthcoming consummation. Basically the author was dependent on a typological approach that combined the ideas of the corporate solidarity of the people of God with historical correspondence. This can be summarized in one statement, as Longenecker observes: The author of Hebrews approaches the Old Testament with a straightforward question, "What do the Scriptures mean viewed from a Christocentric perspective?"[48] While there is originality in his approach, he still was in continuity with the Christological-typological hermeneutic that had preceded him.

Summary and Conclusion

We have observed the approach that Jesus and the apostles employed when interpreting the Old Testament. We have seen that they were dependent on hermeneutical practices established in later Judaism, but yet they were adapted to the church with the addition of a Christological focus. The early church, probably unconsciously rather than intentionally, practiced the exegetical procedures of later Judaism. But the Jewish context in which the New Testament was born was not the primary paradigm for the formation of Christian hermeneutics. As C. F. D. Moule maintains, "At the heart of their biblical interpretation is a Christology and Christocentric perspective."[49]

Jesus became the direct and primary source for the church's understanding of the Old Testament. The new paradigm developed because the prior paradigm lacked the Christological focus. What was needed was a hermeneutical perspective that could transform the Torah into the messianic Torah. Thus it was through such a typological pattern that Jesus served as the ongoing source of the early church's hermeneutical approach to the Scriptures. The Christological perspective of the earliest Christians, therefore, enabled them to adopt Jesus' own usage of the Scriptures as normative and look to him for guidance in their hermeneutical task. This pattern continued among the church fathers and must be the pattern of the contemporary church as well if we are to read the Old Testament as the church's book with the same power and authority it provided for Jesus and the apostolic church.

We can emphasize the literal and historical meaning of the Old Testament as we attempt to discover the intended meaning of the biblical author. Yet, while rejecting fanciful allegorical interpretation, we must, nevertheless, be sensitive to figures of speech in Scripture. Sensitivity to the types of biblical literature generally will help us to avoid a wooden literalism. We must be cautious that no figurative expression in the Bible is misunderstood either from a too literal or too fanciful interpretation.

Theology and biblical interpretation are not theoretical exercises, but are basically practical and pastoral. We believe the biblical message makes changes in people's lives and prepares people for good works.

In continuity with earlier practices, the contemporary church must read and preach Scripture Christologically. This is accomplished through typological exegesis similar to that of Jesus and the apostles. We have noted that their typological usage emphasized the historicity of the parallel event.

Typological exegesis in the following centuries was greatly abused, especially in post-Reformation times. Thus, in recent days there has been a neglect of a typological approach to avoid such abuse. Also, the rise of the historical-critical method has limited the use of typological approaches. Yet, we have seen that typological exegesis was a positive theological construct for Jesus, the apostles, and the early church. The unity of the two testaments is most clearly seen through the window of typological exegesis. It therefore seems appropriate to move beyond abuse and neglect and once again reconsider the values of careful typological approaches in order to see the historical correspondence between the two testaments of Holy Scripture.

Notes

1. J. Rogerson, C. Rowland, and B. Lindars, *The Study and Use of the Bible* (Grand Rapids: Eerdmans, 1988), 3-5; D. Guthrie, *New Testament Theology* (Downers Grove, IL: InterVarsity, 1981), 955-57.

2. J. W. Wenham, *Christ and the Bible* (Downers Grove, IL: InterVarsity, 1973), 106-08.

3. Compare Matthew 21:42; 23:39; 26:38; 27:46; Mark 12:10; 14:18,34; Luke 13:35; 20:17.

4. R. T. France, *Jesus and the Old Testament* (London: Tyndale, 1971), 75.

5. The literature on the way the New Testament writers use the Old Testament is numerous and varied in its approach, but the overall Christological emphasis is generally accepted. For instance, D. L. Baker, *Two Testaments, One Bible* (Downers Grove, IL: InterVarsity, 1926); E. E. Ellis "How the New Testament Uses the Old" *New Testament Interpretation*, ed. I. H. Marshall (Grand Rapids: Eerdmans, 1976), 199-219; D. L. Bock, "Evangelicals and the Use of the Old Testament: Parts 1,2" *Bibliotheca Sacra* 142 (1985): 209-23; 306-19.

6. C. K. Barrett, "The Old Testament in the New" *Cambridge History of the Bible* 1 (1970): 405.

7. R. N. Longenecker, *Biblical Exegesis in the Apostolic Period* (Grand Rapids: Eerdmans, 1975), 19.

8. B. R. Sang, "The New Testament Hermeneutical Milieu: The Inheritance and the Heir" (Ph.D. dissertation, Drew University, 1983), 1-38.

The following definitions can help us understand the differences between these five approaches:

Allegorical Interpretation—that kind of interpretation that assumes that the text to be interpreted says or intends to say something other than its literal working suggests. It seeks to draw out the deeper, mystical sense not derivable from the words themselves.

Literal Interpretation—an attempt to understand Scripture in its plain and ordinary sense without seeing a deeper or spiritual meaning.

Midrashic Interpretation—an interpretation that offers a commentary on the biblical passage in order to contemporize Scripture for current and practical situations.

Pesher Interpretation—an approach to commenting on Scripture, particularly the Old Testament prophets, by the Qumran community who believed itself to be living in the last days. Pesher is a divinely illuminated interpretation of the divine mysteries of Scripture, relating such texts to the last days.

Typological Interpretation—From the Greek work *typos*, meaning pattern or archetype. It is an approach to biblical interpretation in which persons, events or things of the Old Testament are interpreted as being foreshadowings or prototypes of persons, events, or things in the New Testament. Typological interpretation differs from allegorical in that the latter sees the hidden, spiritual meaning of a text whereas the former understands a revelatory connection between two historically distinct but religiously significant persons or events. Specifically, in this chapter, we are speaking of typological interpretation with a Christological focus, which means the Old Testament is to read in light of the belief that Jesus of Nazareth is the Messiah/Christ and the fulfillment of the Old Testament promises and prophecies.

9. R. Loewe, "The 'Plain' Meaning of Scripture" *Papers of the Institute of Jewish Studies, London*, ed. J. G. Weiss (Jerusalem: Hebrew University Press, 1964), 140-85.

10. Because typological approaches have been abused by post-Reformation exegetes, many people tend to ignore the typological method. When it is carefully defined and distinguished from allegorical exegesis, however, it can be and should be considered a separate exegetical category for both Jewish and Christian interpreters of the first century. The most complete work on the subject to date is R. M. Davidson, *Typology in Scripture: A Study of Hermeneutical Typos Structures* (Berrien Springs, MI: Andrews University Press, 1981).

11. D. S. Russell, *The Method and Message of Jewish Apocalyptic* (London: SCM, 1961), 283-84, offers the following examples of typological events within the Old Testament that find correspondence in the New Testament: (1) para-

dise (Isa. 11:6-8); (2) the exodus and the wilderness wanderings (Isa. 43:16-21); (3) David (Isa. 11:1); and (4) Moses (Deut. 18:15-18).

12. Cf. L. Goppelt, *Typos: The Typological Interpretation of the Old Testament in the New*, trans. D. H. Madvig (Grand Rapids: Eerdmans, 1982), 61-208.

13. Longenecker, *Biblical Exegesis*, 74.

14. Ibid.

15. F. F. Bruce, *New Testament Development of Old Testament Themes* (Grand Rapids: Eerdmans, 1968), 20-21.

16. Longenecker, *Biblical Exegesis*, 79.

17. C. H. Dodd, *According to the Scriptures* (London: Nisbet, 1952), 110.

18. W. Barclay, "A Comparison of Paul's Missionary Preaching and Preaching to the Church," *Apostolic History and the Gospel*, ed. W. Gasque and R. P. Martin (Grand Rapids: Eerdmans, 1970), 165-75.

19. Behind these approaches are the hermeneutical presuppositions of: (1) corporate solidarity, (2) correspondences in history, (3) eschatological fulfillment, and (4) messianic presence. Cf. Ellis "How the New Testament Uses the Old," 212-14.

20. Goppelt, *Typos*, 122.

21. Bruce, *Biblical Exegesis*, 77.

22. W. D. Davies, *Torah in the Messianic Age and/or the Age to Come* (Cambridge: Cambridge University Press, 1952), 84-94.

23. This statement is true in the strict sense of letters composed for a didactic purpose. The format and style of Paul's letters, however, follow conventional patterns known to us from methods of letter-writing in the Hellenistic world. There were four parties involved: the author, the secretary, the messenger, and the recipient.

24. Cf. E. E. Ellis, *Paul's Use of the Old Testament* (Grand Rapids: Eerdmans, 1957).

25. Cf. E. E. Ellis, *Prophecy and Hermeneutic* (Grand Rapids: Eerdmans, 1978), 3-22; Longenecker, *Biblical Exegesis*, 104-07.

26. Dodd, *According to the Scriptures*, 23; Longenecker, *Biblical Exegesis*, 105.

27. Cf. M. Hengel, "Zwischen Jesus und Paulus" *Zeitschrift für Katholische Theologie* 72 (1975): 151-206; H. M. Ridderbos, *Paul and Jesus* (Philadelphia: Presbyterian and Reformed, 1958).

28. Cf. Barrett, "Interpretation of the Old Testament in the New," 393-94, 407-08; G. E. Ladd, *A Theology of the New Testament* (Grand Rapids: Eerdmans, 1974), 376-95.

29. See the introductory comments in C. E. B. Cranfield, *A Critical and Exegetical Commentary on the Epistle to the Romans*, 2 vols. (ICC; Edinburgh; T & T Clark, 1975-79), 1:24-27.

30. Ellis, *Paul's Use of the Old Testament*, 10.

31. See the extensive discussion in Goppelt, *Typos*, 127-52.

32. H. Muller, "Type" *The New International Dictionary of New Testament Theology* 3 (1978), 906.

33. E. Käsemann, *Commentary on Romans*, trans. G. W. Bromiley (Grand Rapids: Eerdmans, 1980), 142-43. Käsemann correctly notes "typology fundamentally presupposes history."

34. Cf. M. Black, "The Pauline Doctrine of the Second Adam" *Scottish Journal of Theology* 7 (1954): 170-79; W. Barclay, "Romans v. 12-21" *The Expository Times* 70 (1958-59): 132-35.

35. C. K. Barrett, *First Epistle to the Corinthians* (HNTC; New York; Harper and Row, 1968), 218-27. It is quite possible that Paul was quoting an

existing Exodus midrash, though with some modification (see Barrett's discussion, 220-21); also see W. A. Meeks, "And Rose Up to Play: Midrash and Parenesis in 1 Cor. 10:1-22" *Journal for the Study of the New Testament* 16 (1982), 67-68.

36. Cf. Davidson, *Typology in Scripture*. For a contrasting view see L. Goppelt "Typos" *Theological Dictionary of the New Testament* 9 (1972): 246-59.

37. G. Beasley-Murray, *Baptism in the New Testament* (Grand Rapids: Eerdmans, 1973), 181-85; J. D. G. Dunn, *Baptism in the Holy Spirit* (Philadelphia: Westminster, 1977), 125-26.

38. J. D. G. Dunn, *Unity and Diversity in the New Testament* (Philadelphia: Westminster, 1977), 90-91; Longenecker, *Biblical Exegesis*, 126-29.

39. A. T. Hanson, *Studies in Paul's Technique* (London: SPCK, 1964), 159-66; 169-200.

40. C. Brown, "Parable" *The New International Dictionary of New Testament Theology* 2 (1976): 751-56.

41. Longenecker, *Biblical Exegesis*, 128.

42. Goppelt, *Typos*, 152-54.

43. L. Goppelt, *Theology of the New Testament*, 2 vols., trans. J. Alsup (Grand Rapids: Eerdmans, 1982), 2:186-89.

44. A. Schlatter, *Petrus und Paulus nach dem Ersten Petrusbrief* (Stuttgart: Calwer, 1937).

45. F. F. Bruce, *The Epistle to the Hebrews* (NIC; Grand Rapids: Eerdmans, 1964), X1IX-1.

46. C. Spicq, *L'Epitre aux Hebreux*, 2 vols. (Paris: Gabalda, 1952-53), 1:61. Others have strengthened Spicq's position such as C. K. Barrett, "The Eschatology of the Epistle to the Hebrews," *The Background of the New Testament and its Eschatology*, ed. W. D. Davies and D. Daube (Cambridge: Cambridge University Press, 1954), 363-93.

47. Longenecker, *Biblical Exegesis*, 185.

48. Ibid.

49. C. F. D. Moule, *Birth of the New Testament* (New York: Harper and Row, 1966), 58.

8

The Kingdom of God in the Old and New Testaments

G. R. Beasley-Murray

Introduction

A constant cause of misunderstanding the biblical teaching on the kingdom of God through the centuries has been the failure to grasp and apply the fundamental meaning of the term "kingdom." Yet, curiously, there is complete unanimity among the scholars concerning this. The terms used in the languages of the Bible—Hebrew, Aramaic, and Greek—all have the same meaning, as the dictionaries show. Brown, Driver, and Briggs in their lexicon define the Hebrew (*malkuth*) as "royalty, royal power, reign, kingdom (chiefly late)," and the Aramaic (*malku*, emphatic *malkutha*) as virtually the same: "royalty, reign, kingdom." Bauer in his lexicon of New Testament Greek uses precisely the same terminology for the meaning of (*basileia*): "royalty, reign, kingdom." It appears to be little known that the English word "kingdom" has the same basic significance. The unabridged Oxford English Dictionary gives three chief meanings for kingdom. First, "kingly function, authority or power; sovereignty, supreme rule; the position or rank of a king, kingship." A citation from Hobbes in 1681 illustrates this: "Monarchy ... which Government if he limit it by Law, is called Kingdom; if by his own will, Tyranny," a striking example of the fundamentally dynamic or active meaning of kingdom. Secondly, the term is defined as, "An organized community having a king as its head; a monarchical state or government"; the name "The United Kingdom" is cited as an example of this, since it denotes, not the territory of Great Britain, but the people of the countries constituting Britain, united under an act of Union made in 1800. Finally, the word "kingdom" signifies *the territory or country subject to a king; the area over which a king's rule extends; a realm.* This last meaning is not very frequent in the Bible. It occurs in the temptation narrative of Matthew 4:8, where the devil shows Jesus "all the kingdoms of the world and their glory" (NASB).

The dominant use of the term, particularly in relation to God, is the first, the dynamic significance. It represents God putting forth His almighty royal power to judge and to save, especially the latter. That is the emphasis in the expression "the kingdom of God" above all in our Lord's teaching, where it is virtually a synonym for salvation. One has but to reflect on the meaning of the first three petitions of the Lord's Prayer to see the significance of this: "Hallowed be your name, Your kingdom come, Your will be done, as in heaven, so on earth" (Matt. 6:9-10, NIV; see ASV on final phrase). The three petitions are strictly parallel, and relate to the action of God, not that of human beings. Note also the use of the term "kingdom" in the song of Revelation 12:10: "Now the salvation, and the power, and the kingdom of our God and the authority of His Christ have come" (NASB). In that context "the kingdom of our God" virtually means God's salvation and power and the authority of His Christ; certainly the four terms are closely linked in meaning. For which reason the term "kingdom" when used in such contexts is often represented by the word "sovereignty," and the expression "kingdom of God" is often replaced by "the saving sovereignty of God." Either phrase is acceptable, so long as their significance as representing God's action in the world in fulfillment of His saving purpose is borne in mind.

The Kingdom of God in the Old Testament

1. It is an odd fact that "kingdom of God" does not occur in the Old Testament, for it is transparently clear that the reality is present throughout its length. The declaration of the royal psalms, "The Lord reigns" (Ps. 93:1; 96:10; 97:1; 99:1) is fundamental to the Old Testament. It should not be maintained that the idea first entered the people's consciousness when Israel

had its own king. "The application of the term (*melek*) "king" to the Godhead is common to all the ancient Orient," said von Rad.[1] Martin Buber was strongly of the opinion that this held good in Israel from the nation's earliest days, not however with a formal definition of kingship in mind, but in the sense of God as Israel's lord and leader; in those early years, when Israel was a nomadic people, they looked to Him to guide them to good pastures and to care for them.[2]

2. The most crucial revelation of the kingship of God in the Old Testament took place in the exodus. It was initiated in the revelation of the name of the Lord to Moses at the burning bush and God's commission to him on that occasion. The name "I am who I am" manifestly conveys more than the mere idea that God exists; it suggests that God is and will be with His people and that He acts and will act for them. "God's name is his being," wrote H. D. Preuss, "but his being is his working."[3] And so in the events of the exodus, the Lord showed that His "working" is royal and powerful in judgment and salvation. He manifested His judgment in a series of calamities upon the obdurate Pharaoh and his people and in the deliverance of Israel. The whole succession of events at the exodus was seen as the coming of God to rescue Israel from their slavery, to make them His covenant people at Sinai, to lead them through the perilous wilderness to the promised land, and there to subdue the nations and establish Israel as the free people of God in a land now their own.

3. This history of deliverance, celebrated through the generations in Israel's festivals, came to be understood as the pattern of God's way of salvation. Indeed, it led to the prophetic hope of a second exodus, when God would deliver His people from tyranny and tragedy and would give them a far greater inheritance in a kingdom of salvation.

One sees a sustained application of this expectation in Isaiah 51–52. The old cartoon of the conquest of the monster of the sea by the God of heaven is applied to the Lord's subjugation of Egypt ("Rahab") and Israel's deliverance through the waters of the Red Sea. It is affirmed that the like is to happen again.

> The ransomed of the Lord will return.
> They will enter Zion with singing;
> everlasting joy will crown their heads.
> Gladness and joy will overtake them,
> and sorrow and sighing will flee away (51:11, NIV).

In 52:3 it is stated: "You were sold for nothing,/and without money you will be redeemed" (NIV). The passage that follows elaborates on the theme of the coming "redemption." Israel will then truly know "Your God reigns!" In the day when "The Lord will lay bare his holy arm . . . and all the ends of the earth will see the salvation of our God," then, unlike what happened at the first exodus, "You will not leave in haste or go in flight," for an even greater deliverance will take place! Significantly there follows at once the description of the saving intervention of the Servant of the Lord, who will be exalted as Savior and Lord of all peoples by virtue of His redeeming death and resurrection on behalf of all (52:13–53:12).

In accord with this hope, Hosea told of God's dealing with Israel in a manner reminiscent of His leading of Israel in the wilderness after the deliverance from Egypt:

> I am now going to allure her;
>> I will lead her into the desert
>> and speak tenderly to her. . . .
> There she will sing as in the days of her youth,
>> as in the day she came up out of Egypt (2:14-15, NIV).

The passage goes on to describe in moving language the betrothal of Israel to the Lord forever and their becoming the people of God in a manner beyond anything known in their history, for the kingdom of God will come in that day (Hos. 2:14-23). Not surprisingly, Jeremiah links with this expectation the making of a new covenant with the Lord's people, "not like the covenant I made with their forefathers when I took them by the hand to lead them out of Egypt." This covenant will be accompanied by a spiritual renewal of the newly redeemed people of God, which will enable them all truly to know the Lord and to do His will from the heart (Jer. 31:31-34, NIV).

4. It is wholly in accord with the concept of the kingdom resulting from a new exodus that God's redeeming action is described in terms of His "coming," and that the ancient language of theophany is employed to set it forth.

The earliest example of such language is in the Song of Deborah, in which the victory over Sisera through the help of the Lord is celebrated (Judg. 5:4-5):

> O Lord, when you went out from Seir,
>> when you marched from the land of Edom,
> the earth shook, the heavens poured,
>> the clouds poured down water.
> The mountains quaked before the Lord, the One of Sinai,
>> before the Lord, the God of Israel (NIV).

Here two basic thoughts are expressed: the Lord comes forth to intervene in the affairs of this world, and the elements of nature tremble in fear before the almighty God of creation. That is characteristic of descriptions of theophany.

A more elaborate account of the coming of God is described in the poem of Habakkuk 3. The prophet had heard of the great deeds of God, above all those that took place at the exodus, and he prayed that God would do the like again (v. 2). There follows a description of how God went forth to intervene for His people Israel:

> He stood, and shook the earth;
>> he looked, and made the nations tremble.
> The ancient mountains crumbled
>> and the age-old hills collapsed....
> You split the earth with rivers;
>> the mountains saw you and writhed....
> You came out to deliver your people,
>> to save your anointed one....
> I will wait patiently for the day of calamity
>> to come upon the nation invading us (Hab. 3:6-16, NIV).

First exodus and second exodus are here presented side by side: judgment on Egypt and deliverance of Israel, Day of the Lord on a contemporary oppressor and deliverance of Israel again awaited. The pictorial language is extraordinarily vivid. It is the poetry of faith that celebrates the coming of the Lord, before whom every power in heaven and earth shrinks in terror. Needless to say, one could never write the story of the exodus on the basis of Habakkuk 3, nor project from it an advance narrative of the end of the age.

5. In the Old Testament the constant precedent of God's coming to establish His kingdom in power is the Day of the Lord, that is, His judgment upon rebellious peoples. The terminology reflects Israel's experiences of deliverance from their foes, hence reference is made to "the Day of Midian" (Isa. 9:4), in recollection of an overwhelming defeat of Midian who had severely oppressed the Hebrews (compare Judg. 7–8). For this reason descriptions of the Day of the Lord are dominated by the picture language of warfare. Not infrequently these descriptions relate to impending judgments upon nations about Israel, as in Isaiah 21:13-17. Other prophecies of the Day of the Lord clearly have in view events that immediately precede the establishment of the kingdom of God (compare for instance Isa. 24:17-23; followed by 25:1-8, the feast of the kingdom; 26:19, the resurrection; 26:20–27:1, the Day of Wrath; 27:12-13, the gathering of Israel for the kingdom of God).

Since the concept of the Day of the Lord is linked with the coming of God, similar pictorial language is characteristic of these descriptions, often telling of cosmic phenomena which appear to denote the collapse of the universe (compare Isa. 34:4). Examination of such passages, however, will show that they are no more to be taken literally than those which recount the "writhing" of the mountains in fear before the coming of the Lord. Isaiah 34 is a prophecy of judgment upon Edom, but in representing it as the Day of the Lord upon Israel's neighbor all the hyperbolic descriptions of the final Day of the Lord are used, including the falling of the stars of heaven and the rolling up of the sky like a scroll, and the wrath of God on the nations. Even when the last Day is in mind the hyperbole must be observed. The Book of Zephaniah begins with a statement that the Lord is to sweep the earth clear of man and beast, birds of the air and fish of the sea and all humanity will be wiped out (1:2-3). The same affirmation is made in 3:8: "The whole world will be consumed by the fire of my jealous anger" (NIV); but that is immediately followed by the promise, "Then will I purify the lips of the peoples,/ that all of them may call on the name of the Lord,/ and serve him shoulder to shoulder!" (v. 9, NIV). All of which shows that the prophets are more concerned to drive home their message than adhere to prosaic descriptions of the end.

6. The character of the kingdom of God is variously described, and, as one would expect, is more fully developed in the later books of the Old Testament.

A Kingdom for Humanity in This World

The kingdom of God is consistently represented as *a kingdom for humanity in this world*. God comes to this earth to deliver and save His people, the Day of the Lord is declared to fall upon specific nations about Israel, and in the kingdom the people of Israel are established in their land, and Jerusalem becomes the center of the world. This is clear in the well-known descriptions of the kingdom in Isaiah 2:1-4 and of the Messiah in Isaiah 9:1-10. It is especially plain in the description of God's gathering of Israel as a shepherd gathers his sheep in Ezekiel 34:22-31 and the detailed description of the new temple and the apportionment of the land among Israel's tribes in Ezekiel 40–48. This holds good even in the description of the new heavens and earth in Isaiah 65:17-25, for therein life is still completely earthly, only exceedingly better than formerly, and with greater longevity ("he who dies at a hundred/ will be thought a mere youth,/ he who fails to reach a hundred will be considered accursed/. . . . For as the days of a tree,/ so will be the days of my people," vv. 20-22, NIV). It is evident that the prophet is describing a renewed world, not one that replaces the old world.[4]

The Kingdom of God Is Essentially Universal

The kingdom of God is for all nations, not that this is always explicitly stated. The prophets addressed Israel and were primarily concerned to call the nation to repentance and to console them with God's promises of redemption (for instance, Amos and Hosea). Nahum and Habakkuk were so taken up with the Day of the Lord on Israel's oppressors they did not even mention the kingdom of God. Others stressed the foremost place that Israel as the covenant people of God would have among the nations in the kingdom of God (for instance, Isa. 60:10-12; 61:5-6; 66:18-21), but characteristically the blessings of the kingdom are portrayed as for all nations (compare Isa. 2:1-4; 19:18-25; 42:1-4,20-25; 51:4-5; 52:10; Jer. 3:17; Zeph. 3:8-10; Zech. 2:11; 8:20-21).

Righteousness Will Prevail in God's Kingdom

This is linked at times with the descriptions of the Messiah's righteousness (for instance, Isa. 11:3-5; Jer. 23:5-6), at other times with that of the people (Isa. 26:2; 28:5-6), but more commonly with God's action in cleansing and renewal of His people (Isa. 1:25-26; 4:3-4; 32:15-16; Jer. 31:31-34; Ezek. 36:25-26; 37:23-24).

Peace

Peace is so integral to the kingdom of God, it became among the Jews the most inclusive term for the salvation of the kingdom. Naturally peace immediately brings to mind the thought of absence of war, as in Isaiah 2:1-4; 9:5-6 and Zechariah 9:9-10, but peace between man and the animal kingdom also is explicitly included (Isa. 11:6-7; 35:9). This latter feature suggests a return of the paradisal age, a thought which is developed at length in the final vision of the Book of Revelation. Most importantly, the peace of the kingdom extends to humanity in its relations to God (so Isa. 12:17-24; 33:17,20-24; Jer. 31:1-14; Hos. 2:14-15; 14:4-5; Zeph. 3:14-20).

With peace, *joy* is the great characteristic of the kingdom. It is vividly portrayed in Isaiah 25:6-9, a favorite description of the kingdom among later Jews, and is particularly mentioned in Isaiah 30:18-19; 35:10; 56:6-7; 65:17-18; and Ezekiel 34:22-31.

7. *The Place of the Messiah in the Kingdom of God* is curiously ambivalent. The Royal Psalms celebrate the rule of God alone,

for instance, Psalm 97:1, "The Lord is king, let the earth be glad" (NEB). "Salvation is of the Lord" (Ps. 3:8, author's translation) is a foundational affirmation. In accordance with that Isaiah 33:22 asserts: "The Lord is our judge,/the Lord is our lawgiver,/the Lord is our king,/it is he who will save us" (NIV). Even more strongly it is affirmed in Zechariah 14:9: "The Lord shall become king over all the whole earth. On that day the Lord shall be one Lord, and his name the only name" (author's translation). That appears to admit of no other sovereignty in the kingdom than that of the Lord. Yet we know well that the Messiah features in a number of passages of the Old Testament, such as Isaiah 9:6-7; 11:1-10; Micah 5:2-5a. R. H. Charles considered that the concept of the Messiah was comparatively late in Israel's development of eschatological thought, and he categorically stated, "The Messiah formed no organic part of the conception (of the kingdom of God)."[5] This view was common in the earlier part of the twentieth century, but it is surely mistaken. The principle of representation is deeply embedded in the faith and institutions of Israel, applying alike to priests and prophets and kings. It should occasion no surprise that these figures and institutions should find their peak in the Messiah, who is depicted as the representative of God in His kingdom, in whom God is uniquely present and through whom He acts. It is significant to compare Isaiah 40:10, "See, the Sovereign Lord comes with power . . . ," (NIV) and Zechariah 9:9, "See, your king comes to you . . . " (NIV); both employ the "herald's call," proclaiming a king who comes for salvation, but the former relates to God, the latter to the Messiah. There is accordingly ground for the belief of H. H. Wolff that the Messiah is "the form of the appearance of Yahweh the Lord."[6] What he meant by that is explained in the following statement:

> As in the pillar of fire, as in the Angel, as in the prophetic word, so the Lord appears in the Messiah; not in such a fashion as to be restricted thereby, but rather that he himself, and none other than he, appears to men as one who has fellowship with them and deals with them, and that in a manner in which he cannot normally be with them if they are not to perish from the sight of his full appearance.[7]

On this basis the Messiah essentially belongs to the kingdom of God. But it is important to observe that in the Old Testament *God* is typically set forth as the Deliverer; He comes for judgment and salvation, and so establishes the kingdom, then with the kingdom He gives the Messiah to be Ruler and Representative for Him (compare especially Isa. 9 and 11; Jer. 23:5-6; Ezek. 34:11-13,22-24; Mic. 5:2-5).

There is a clear exception to this in the Servant Songs of Isaiah 42; 49; 50:4ff; 52:13–53:12, wherein the supreme service of the Servant of the Lord is to be God's instrument in the establishment of His kingdom. The first of these songs makes this clear:

> Here is my servant, whom I uphold,
>   my chosen one in whom I delight;
> I will put my Spirit on him,
>   and he will bring justice to the nations. . . .
> He will not falter or be discouraged
>   till he establishes justice on earth.
>   In his law the islands will put their hope (Isa. 42:1,4, NIV).

The same way conceivably applies to the vision of "one like a son of man" in Daniel 7. Just as the four beasts that emerge from the ocean are said to be four "kings" who will arise and represent their respective empires, so the "one like a son of man" represents the people of the saints of the Most High, and in all likelihood receives the rule of this world from God because He has overcome the antigod ruler (Dan. 7:11-14). Certainly this understanding of the Servant of the Lord and the Son of Man emerges plainly in the New Testament; it is noteworthy that it was adumbrated in the Old Testament.

The Kingdom of God
in the Intertestamental Literature

Before we review the teaching of the New Testament on the kingdom of God it is desirable briefly to consider views on this theme in the so-called apocalyptic literature, most of which appeared in the period from the second century B.C. to the end of the first century A.D. The great theme of these works was the coming of the kingdom of God. One feature they had in common was an increasing emphasis on the transcendental element in God's works. They represent God as coming from above to bring wickedness on earth to an end and to introduce the new age of righteousness and life. But their application of this conviction to the kingdom of God had considerable variations.

1. There were those who maintained the prophetic view of the coming of God and the Day of the Lord, which is to issue in the overthrow of the evil powers and the establishment of the

kingdom of God in this world. This appears to be set forth in the Book of Daniel, for although the judgment scene in Daniel 7:9-10 is described in transcendental terms, it relates to the judgment of an earthly tyrant and his empire and the kingdom which replaces it is on this earth (Dan. 7:16-18,23-27). The same understanding is set forth in 1 Enoch 6–36 and 83–90, the Psalms of Solomon, and possibly the Testaments of the Twelve Patriarchs.

2. With the precedent of the prophecy of Isaiah 65–66 concerning new heavens and earth, and the emphasis on the transcendent nature of God's future intervention, the belief was all but inevitable that the coming of God will issue in a judgment of all generations of mankind, followed by a kingdom of God in a transformed creation. This appears most plainly in the section of 1 Enoch known as the Similitudes or Parables of Enoch (chs. 37–71). In these the Son of Man is closely associated with the "Head of Days" in the judgment, and he is appointed to carry it out. The universe is transformed to be a worthy setting of the kingdom of God. So in 1 Enoch 45:4-5 we read:

> I will transform the heaven and will make it an eternal blessing
>   and light;
> And I will transform the earth and make it a blessing.
> And I will cause mine elect ones to dwell upon it;
> but the sinners and evil-doers shall not set foot thereon.

3. The representation in the Old Testament of the kingdom of God on earth, yet also in a renewed creation, was bound to lead to an attempt to combine both elements of hope. So we find the belief in a kingdom of the messiah within this world which gives place to a final judgment and the kingdom of God set in a new creation. The most notable expositions of this view are in two works composed towards the end of the first century of our era, namely Fourth Ezra (2 Esdras in the Apocrypha) and 2 Baruch. The former teaches that the messiah will be revealed in the kingdom of God, and after four hundred years will die, along with "all in whom is human breath," then the world will return to primeval silence as at the beginning; the resurrection for judgment will follow, and the furnace of Gehenna and the paradise of delight will be revealed. On this view the messianic kingdom is reckoned as falling within this age, the final kingdom within the age to come. Second Baruch distinguishes itself from this representation by a more exalted understanding of the messiah: "His principate will stand forever, until the world of corruption is at an end" (40:3); then,

"When the time of the advent of the Messiah is fulfilled he shall return in glory," that is, to heaven (30:1-2).

It would appear that the interpretation of the kingdom of God and of the messiah are correlated in these writings, though other factors also played their part in shaping the understanding of the kingdom of God. An expectation of a purely earthly kingdom with Israelite domination over the nations encourages the idea of a purely earthly messiah-king of the order of David, such as we find in the Psalms of Solomon (chs. 17– 19). The concept of a kingdom of God within a new creation would call for a messiah with attributes beyond those of humanity in this world, which is what most scholars find in the Son of Man in the Similitudes of Enoch. A view that combines a temporary kingdom in this world with a kingdom that will follow in the new creation makes quite varied concepts of the messiah possible, which is why we find such differences in the portrayals of the messiah in 4 Ezra and 2 Baruch. It should be added, however, that the notion of a transcendent messiah, such as the Son of Man enthroned in heaven, does not appear to have been an element of Jewish expectation in the period prior to Jesus. The Similitudes of Enoch, in which that concept appears, can hardly have been written before the time of our Lord's ministry, and may well have come later.[8]

The writings of the Qumran community are of unusual interest, in that they reveal the belief that not one, but two messiahs will be raised up by God, the one a priest and the other a king, the former superior to the latter. The Manual of Discipline lays down judgments in accordance with the community's regulations "until the coming of a prophet and the Messiahs from Aaron and Israel" (1QS 9:10-11). This view is reflected extensively in the Testaments of the Twelve Patriarchs, but it appears to be rejected in the Zadokite Document in the statement: "These shall escape during the period of visitation, but the rest shall be handed over to the sword when the Messiah comes from Aaron and Israel" (9:10). This difference of views is explained by D. C. Duling thus:

> Palaeographical analysis indicates that the two messiahs' doctrine was central to the community at least until the invasion of Pompey (63 B.C.), and that the messiah of the line of David became more prominent, especially in the first century of the Christian era.[9]

It is evident that quite varied views concerning the kingdom of God and the messiah existed among the Jews in the period of Jesus and the early church. This variety requires to be taken into account in considering the teaching of our Lord and the rest of the New Testament concerning the kingdom of God and the messiah.

The Kingdom of God in the New Testament

The Proclamation of Jesus

The earliest statement of *the proclamation of Jesus* concerning the kingdom of God occurs at the conclusion of Mark's introduction to his Gospel (Mark 1:14-15), "After John was put in prison, Jesus went into Galilee, proclaiming the good news of God. 'The time has come,' he said. 'The kingdom of God is near. Repent and believe the good news'" (NIV).

On reflection it is clear that Jesus did not go about Galilee constantly repeating these words. They are *a summary* of his preaching. Who was responsible for the summary? Mark could have written it up on the basis of the teaching of Jesus he had assembled. It is the belief of many scholars that it went back to the earliest days of the church and was part of the instruction given to converts as to the words and the works of Jesus (the "catechesis," as it is often called). Mark included it because he saw that it was the sum and substance of the word of God brought by Jesus to His people.

What is the meaning of this digest of the message of Jesus? Attention has been focused on the sentence, "The kingdom of God is near." Earlier scholars assumed that the meaning is self-evident: the kingdom of God is *near*, and so *not yet here*. Albert Schweitzer saw in this the key to the message of Jesus: He proclaimed that the kingdom of God was to appear shortly, in the immediately impending future.[10] By contrast C. H. Dodd held that Mark 1:15 means, "The kingdom of God has come," on the basis that both Mark's word (*engiken*), and Matthew's (*ephthasen*, 12:28) render the Aramaic term (*meta*), which means "to reach, come to, arrive." Matthew 12:28 thus shows how Mark 1:15 should be understood.[11] A battle royal has taken place on this issue through two generations. The difficulty is that the very idea of "near" is ambiguous. How near is "near"? In Daniel 4:11 (MT=4:8) the tree in Nebuchadnezzar's dream (*yimte lismayya*); the Septuagint translates *meta* by (*engizen*), the tree "neared heaven," but Theodotian's version has (*ephthasen*), it "reached heaven" (so KJV, NEB, NIV). Similarly in Daniel 7:13 we read that one like a Son of Man was "coming with the clouds of heaven." Then "he came into (*meta*) the Ancient of Days and was brought (*haqrebuhi*) before him." (The rendering of the NIV, "he approached the Ancient of Days and was led into his presence" is paraphrastic). Is this what Jesus was teaching in Mark 1:15—"the kingdom of God has *come unto you*"?

I frankly confess that for years I was uncertain about this, until I realized that this summary of Jesus' teaching contains not one clause but two:

The time has come;

The kingdom of God has come near.

If the time has "come," the time of waiting for the promised kingdom is over—the kingdom has *arrived!* A. M. Ambrozic expressed this conclusion soundly and convincingly:

> The first clause enunciates clearly that the divinely decreed time of waiting has come to an end. The decisive manifestation of the saving God, promised in the prophecies quoted in vv. 2-3, must therefore be taking place. The second member of the parallel can be seen as interpreting the first; it states the same truth. The only difference between the members: the first looks backward, while the second looks to the present and the future; the first announces the end of the old era, the second proclaims the beginning of the new.[12]

As Ambrozic suggests, it is the *beginning* of the saving kingdom that is in view in Mark 1:15. Jesus is proclaiming not an end but a beginning—the initiation of the kingdom of God that is to end in a transformed universe. The saving sovereignty of God has begun because, in Jesus, God has "come" to achieve His saving work.

This interpretation is in harmony with a number of the key sayings of Jesus. We have already alluded to Matthew 12:28, part of Jesus' answer to the allegation that He was in league with the devil. "If I drive out demons by the Spirit of God," said Jesus (that is, by God's Spirit and not the devil's aid) "then the kingdom of God has come upon you" (NIV). The kingdom of salvation is here!

Luke does not reproduce Mark's summary of Jesus' preaching but recounts instead His visit to Nazareth. There Jesus reads Isaiah 61, a passage which tells of the coming of the kingdom of God in terms of an inbreaking of the year of Jubilee, described in Leviticus 25. In the fiftieth year liberty was to be proclaimed to all, family lands sold were to be returned, people sold as slaves were to be freed, debts were to be remitted. It was "the year of the Lord's favor." Luke summarized Jesus' sermon on this passage in one short sentence: "Today this scripture has been fulfilled in your hearing" (4:21, NRSV). As George Caird commented: Jesus turned this Scripture into a royal proclamation of release.[13] The Kingdom-Jubilee had begun!

When John the Baptist in Herod's prison sent disciples to Jesus to ask if He really were "the Coming One," Jesus sent a gracious answer (Matt. 11:5-6) which combined words from Isaiah 35 and 61:

> Go back and report to John what you hear and see: The blind receive sight, the lame walk, those who have leprosy are cured, the deaf hear, the dead are raised, and the good news is preached to the poor. Blessed is the man who does not fall away on account of me (NIV).

Isaiah 34 is one of those fearful descriptions in the Old Testament of the Day of the Lord on the wicked—portraying the kind of action that John the Baptist was waiting for Jesus to carry out. It is followed in chapter 35 by a beautiful picture of the transformation of creation and of the human situation when God comes for His people's salvation. That is what the disciples of John saw taking place as they heard and watched Jesus: through Him the promised deliverance and the blessings of the kingdom of God were happening. And *that* answered John's question!

When John's messengers had departed, Jesus paid a great tribute to John, in the midst of which He made the following statement (Matt. 11:12, NIV): "From the days of John the Baptist until now, the kingdom of heaven has been forcefully advancing, and forceful men lay hold of it." It is possible that the last clause of this saying should be rendered: "and forceful men are making a forceful assault on it," expressing violent opposition to the kingdom rather than enthusiastic adherence to it (note that John is in prison for his preaching, and Jesus is being strongly resisted by various factions in Israel). Whichever interpretation is adopted, the statement assumes the presence of the kingdom of God in the ministry of Jesus, and Jesus links the work of John with His own in the initiation of the kingdom of God.

In Luke 17:20 it is reported that Pharisees asked Jesus when the kingdom of God would come. Calculating the time of the coming of the kingdom by means of the Old Testament held a fascination for many Pharisees. Jesus replied, "The kingdom of God does not come with your careful observation, nor will people say, 'Here it is,' or 'There it is,' because the kingdom of

God is within you" (vv. 20-21, NIV). The expression "with your careful observation" relates to the observation of signs and symptoms that precedes deduction, and among Jews especially the observation of the heavenly bodies through which seasons and festivals were dated. Jesus rejected this kind of calculation of the coming of the kingdom, but what did He mean by saying, "The kingdom of God is within you"? The difficulty of this interpretation is: (a) Jesus was addressing Pharisees; was the kingdom within them? and (b) in the Bible the kingdom of God is not a purely interior phenomenon, it affects the totality of existence (compare Isa. 11:6-9!). For this reason NIV margin reads "among you." That would make good sense: the kingdom of God is among the Jews because the King was among them. That meaning of (*entos*), however, is rare. Evidence has been mounting of late for translating the term "within your reach (or grasp)"[14]; that would indicate that it is within the power of the hearers of Jesus to enter the kingdom and receive its blessings, if they would but renounce their opposition to Him and receive the word of God which He brought.

Many of the parables of Jesus reinforce the truth and the challenge of the presence of the kingdom of God in His ministry, such as the Strong Man Bound (Mark 3:27, and parallels), the Sower (Mark 4:1-9, par.), the Seed Growing Secretly (Mark 4:26-29), the Mustard Seed and Leaven (Mark 4:30-32, par.; Matt. 13:33), the Treasure and the Pearl (Matt. 13:44-46), the Laborers in the Vineyard (Matt. 20:1-16). But did Jesus not also teach about the future of the kingdom of God? Most certainly, yes. We have already cited the Lord's Prayer (Matt. 6:9-13), the first half of which is prayer for the coming of the kingdom "as in heaven, so on earth." The Beatitudes, recounted in Matthew 5:3-12, all relate to the future kingdom; the second half of each provides an aspect of the kingdom to be given (author's translation):

> Theirs is the kingdom of heaven.
> They shall be comforted.
> They shall inherit the earth.
> They shall be satisfied.
> They shall obtain mercy.
> They shall see God.
> They shall be called sons of God.
> Great is their reward with God.

There are sayings relating to entry into the kingdom of God which clearly have in view entering the kingdom of the future.

In those of Mark 9:43-48, for example, entering into the kingdom of God, or into life, is set over against going off to Gehenna; the like applies to Matthew 7:21-23, which immediately precedes the parable of the two houses (Matt. 7:24-27) and so makes plain that the latter is a parable of judgment. And, of course, there are numerous parables relating to the future coming of the kingdom, such as the Judge and the Widow (Luke 18:1-8), the Unjust Steward (Luke 16:1-8), the Burglar (Matt. 24:43-44, par.), and the three parables of Matthew 25, the Virgins, the Talents, and the Sheep and the Goats. The intention of most of these is to emphasize the necessity for readiness for the coming of the kingdom in the future.

The link between the present and the future of the kingdom of God is given in the mediatorial work of Jesus, the Son of Man, in His death and resurrection on the one hand and His coming in power and glory on the other to complete the salvation of the kingdom of God initiated in His ministry.

There are three so-called "predictions of the Passion" in the Synoptic Gospels in which Jesus spoke of His impending rejection by the Jewish leaders, His death, and His resurrection. In Mark they are found in 8:31; 9:31; 10:32. The first one occurs immediately after Peter's confession that Jesus is the Messiah (8:27-29), indicating that this is the way He has to fulfill His messianic calling. In this connection we note that in these prophecies it is *the Son of Man* who is to be rejected, suffer, die, and rise; the Son of Man is the representative of the kingdom of God (so Dan. 7:13), hence it is a fitting title for Him whose ministry showed Him to be the Mediator of the kingdom of God. That mediatorial work for the kingdom of God in His earthly ministry is to find its climax in His suffering, death, and resurrection. Thereby Jesus will fulfill various prophetic strains of the path appointed for Him through whom redemption comes. They are the sufferings of *the Righteous Man*, opposed by the unrighteous, but who is vindicated by God; *the Servant of the Lord*, who suffers as the innocent on behalf of the guilty and is exalted by God; *the Prophet* whose message of the kingdom is rejected by His contemporaries, but who is honored by God; and *the Martyr for God's truth*, whose death is seen as a sacrifice, and who is exalted by the Lord in His kingdom.

The first two of these "types" belong together, inasmuch as they are exemplified in the Psalms of the Righteous Sufferer (above all Pss. 22 and 69), and they come to supreme expression in the final Servant Song, Isaiah 52:13–53:12, concerning Him who bears the iniquity of all humanity. The Jews were notorious for their rejection of the prophets, as they themselves admitted (Matt. 23:29-31), and Jesus recognized that their fate would reach its apex in His own death (compare Luke 13:33; Matt. 23:37). The suffering and vindication of the martyrs for God's truth is reflected in the Book of Daniel, and forms the theme of various contemporary Jewish writings (above all 2 and 4 Maccabees). In all these instances stress is laid on the obedience of the man of God, rejection by his contemporaries, and vindication by God. These emphases are embodied in our Lord's prophecies of His destiny, and are exemplified by His words and actions at the Last Supper: "This is my body . . . this is my blood of the covenant, shed for many" (Mark 14:22,24, author's translation), words accompanied by actions which show that His death is to be a sacrifice for the sin of the world. But Luke 22:29-30a indicates the goal of the sacrifice: "I confer on you a kingdom, just as my Father conferred one on me, so that you may eat and drink at my table in my kingdom" (NIV). The word "confer" is the verb normally used of making of a covenant, and should be rendered here, "I covenant with you a kingdom." The context of the saying applies primarily to the apostles, but its essence is valid for all Christians. The intent of the New Covenant made in the body and blood of our Lord is salvation in the kingdom of God, mediated by His total redeeming activity as the Son of Man. And that includes His coming in power and glory.

Perhaps the most significant saying of our Lord relating to His coming at the end of the age is His reply to the High Priest at His trial (Mark 14:62). The latter had asked, "'Are you the Christ, the Son of the Blessed One?' 'I am,' said Jesus, 'And you will see the Son of Man sitting at the right hand of the Mighty One and coming on the clouds of heaven'" (NIV). This is the sole occasion when Jesus publicly stated that He was the Messiah, and He proceeded to define it in a way no member of the Jewish Sanhedrin would have done: they are to see Him as the Lord exalted to God's right hand, in fulfillment of Psalm 110:1 (they being beneath His feet!), and coming on the clouds of heaven, as in Daniel 7:13 the Lord of the kingdom is revealed. For declaring that answer He knows that He must die; but He also knows that all things are in the Father's hands, and that through them He will achieve His kingdom purpose and so enable His Son to carry through the vocation of the Son of Man through resurrection, exaltation, and sending in glory.

The like applies to Mark 13:24-27. It should be observed that the "Olivet Discourse" sets out from a prophecy of Jesus of the destruction of the temple in Jerusalem (vv. 1-2); it brings together statements of our Lord relating to the future which elucidate the implications of the prophecy. "Not one stone here will be left on another" relates to the building Jesus *at that moment* was leaving. There is not question of His speaking of a temple to be built later. He has in view the judgment of God on His own generation, which was "finishing off what their fathers began" in rejecting the Messiah (Matt. 23:32, author's translation). Jesus, like the prophets before Him, spoke of the Day of the Lord on Jerusalem and its people, and to that even verse 30 refers: "This generation will certainly not pass away until all these things have happened" (compare Matt. 23:34-36; Luke 11:49-51; author's translation). By contrast Mark 13:32 has in view the coming of the Son of Man; that day the Father alone knows, because He alone determines the time of the coming of the kingdom of God. Jesus was content to leave that day in His Father's hands and not know the time. If His followers through succeeding centuries had shared the humility of their Lord, the church would have been spared fearful anxieties and disappointments through the ages.

The Kingdom of God in the Teaching of Paul

The gospel that Paul preached was fundamentally the same as that of the apostles of Jesus, namely the redemptive death and resurrection of the Christ "according to the scriptures" (1 Cor. 15:1-11, NIV). That last phrase relates the redemptive event not alone to isolated passages of the Old Testament, but to the saving purpose of God made known in the Old Testament: through Christ's death and resurrection judgment was enacted and the kingdom of God was inaugurated for all humanity.[15] This teaching is bound up with Paul's doctrine of the believer's participation in Christ's death and resurrection, which is the presupposition of his teaching on justification and life in the new creation (2 Cor. 5:14-19), of baptism (Rom. 6:3-13), and the Lord's Supper (1 Cor. 10:14-16) and is expressed in the affirmation, "He (God) has rescued us from the dominion of darkness and brought us into the kingdom of the Son he loves" (Col. 1:13, NIV).

The relation of all this to the consummation of the ages through Christ is concisely expounded in 1 Corinthians 15:20-28. The decisive points in the redemptive history are here declared to be the resurrection of Christ, His parousia (coming), and "the end ... when he hands over the kingdom to God the Father"

(v. 24, NIV). Whether Paul here interposes a period of time between the coming of Christ and "the end," just as between the resurrection of Christ and the coming, thereby assuming a kingdom of Christ after the parousia, is hotly contested; it is a possible interpretation (I would say probable) but uncertain. In any case the ultimate end is "that God may be all in all" (v. 28, NIV), which is the ultimate hope of the eschatology of the Bible.

Special attention was given by Paul in the Thessalonian letters to the parousia, the coming of Christ. Paul knew that the church was grieving, in a manner that does not comport with Christian faith, for some of their number who had died (1 Thess. 4:13). He encouraged them, first by adducing the significance of the resurrection of Jesus (v. 14) and then by that of Christ's coming (vv. 15-17). This latter he did "according to the Lord's own word"; such language by Paul usually relates to a statement of Jesus in His ministry, as, for instance, in 1 Corinthians 7:10,12; 9:14; compare 11:23-25; Romans 14:14. There is no saying in the Gospels that states that living Christians will not precede deceased believers in the resurrection; verse 15, however, may plausibly be viewed as a deduction "in accord with" verses 16-17, a statement which reproduces the Lord's word about the parousia in Mark 13:24-27, and its parallel in Matthew 24:29-31. Every feature of verses 16-17 occurs in the latter passage. There is, accordingly, no ground for believing that Paul was stating something unheard of in verses 16-17.

Paul's instruction in his first letter evidently encouraged some enthusiasts to believe that "the day of the Lord has already come" (2 Thess. 2:2, NIV; the language is closely parallel to Mark 13:5). This Paul countered by declaring that before that happens "the rebellion" must occur, and "the man of lawlessness" be revealed, who "sets himself up in God's temple, proclaiming himself to be God" (NIV, compare Dan. 9:26-27; 11:31; 12:11; the language originally related to the Jerusalem temple, but is here probably figurative, as in Mark 13:14). Paul had formerly told the Thessalonians all about this and what was "holding back" the "lawless one" and who continued to do so "till he is taken out of the way" (vv. 6-8, NIV). Unfortunately Paul has not told *us*, and left no record of it in his writings; we have to admit that we do not know what and whom he had in mind. The most common interpretation through the ages has been that the restraining power was the law and order of the Roman empire and the restraining person its ruler, the emperor; since that time "the secular power in any form (when it) continues to discharge its divinely ordained commission" fulfills that function, and so restrains evil and prevents anarchy.[16] Whatever the truth of the matter, Paul seems clearly to have anticipated the appearance of an Antichrist prior to the coming of the Lord.

The Kingdom of God in the Book of Revelation

This book describes itself as "the revelation of Jesus Christ, which God gave him" (1:1, NIV), otherwise expressed as "the word of God and the testimony of Jesus Christ" (1:2, NIV; note the statement in 19:10, "The testimony of Jesus is [the burden of] the spirit of prophecy"). Despite the apocalyptic imagery of the work, the doctrine of the kingdom of God in the Book of Revelation shows essential unity with the teaching in the Gospels. The theme of the central vision in the book, that of the Lamb in chapter 5, indicates that the turn of the ages happened when the Lamb was slain and lived again, so that He was able to take the scroll from God, which symbolized the covenant to give the kingdom to redeemed humanity and put it into effect. The same is set forth in the highly apocalyptic vision of chapter 12; the victory over the dragon by the archangel Michael is symbolic of the victory of the "male child" exalted to heaven, for the victors "overcame him by the blood of the Lamb/and by the word of their testimony" (12:11, NIV): they overcame because the sacrifice of the Lamb gave no room for the Accuser to accuse "our brothers," hence Satan was "hurled to the earth" precisely as in the related John 12:31-32. The victory of the Lamb brought about "the salvation and the power and the kingdom of our God/and the authority of his Christ" (12:10, NIV), hence the final victory of "the kingdom of our Lord and of his Christ" is assured (11:15, NIV). That is the situation of faith in which the original readers of the Revelation stood, and where the modern believers also stand.

The description of the three series of woes in Revelation 6–8, 8–11, 15–16, constitute an elaboration of the Day of the Lord on rebellious humanity. They appear not to be consecutive but (at least in measure) parallel, for each series ends at the same point, namely the coming of Christ for the kingdom (see especially 11:15-19; 16:17-21, hence the same applies to 8:1-5; compare 6:12-17). After the description of the fall of "Babylon," the antigod kingdom, 19:11–21:8 provides a consecutive portrayal of the events of the end. The description of the defeat of the enemies of Christ as His parousia in 19:19–20:3 clearly shows that the kingdom described in 20:4-6 is subsequent to the Lord's coming, not prior to it. That is, it is the kingdom inaugurated through the death and resurrection of Christ now brought to victory at the coming of Christ. The vision of the City of God, the "Bride of the Lamb," is an addendum, forming a contrast picture to the city of Antichrist, the "Mother of Harlots" in chapter 17 (also an addendum to chapter 16). It is likely that we are meant to understand that the City of God, the New Jerusalem, forms the context of life in "the kingdom of our Lord and of his Christ," alike in the millennial age and in the new creation.[17] Every feature in the description of the City of God in 21:9–22:5 is as applicable to the City in this world as it is in the new creation; that is not surprising, since Christians are citizens already of that City (Heb. 12:22-24). In it heaven and earth are united (21:16), as in it God and the Lamb have their throne (22:12-2). Thus the new Jerusalem, not the old, is forever the center of the kingdom.

Conclusion

From the foregoing it should be evident that whoever would preach the gospel of Christ must preach the kingdom of God, at least if he is to follow in the footsteps of Jesus and His apostles. Doubtless, that demands recognition of the breadth and length and height and depth of the biblical teaching on the kingdom of God. Eschatology, the doctrine of "the last things," belongs to the first things, as well as the last things of the Bible. That is inevitable, since it concerns Him who is alpha and omega, the first and the last, the beginning and the end. As Origen saw long ago, Jesus Himself is the kingdom. That is where the pastor who would preach the kingdom of God in the Jesus way must begin. Whoever focuses on *His* teaching on the kingdom of God and moves out from that center will find himself occupied with the Lord, not with Gog of the land of Magog. Moreover our people need this instruction on the first and last things, for it is on their ignorance that sects like Jehovah's Witnesses, Mormons, Christadelphians, and the like flourish; most of their converts are members of mainline churches.

If the kingdom of God is theological, revealing God's purpose for the world and for the individual, for history and for eternity, it also of necessity has fundamental ethical consequences. The first word that followed Jesus' preaching of the kingdom was, "Repent!" He bade His hearers to seek first the kingdom of God; first, that they should not miss it, and then in order to serve it and thereby be released from the anxieties of this age (see Matt. 6:33 in context). It is well to bear in mind that the Sermon on the

Mount is an exposition of life in the kingdom of God. It conveys both great consolation and enormous challenge.

Finally, it is needful to acknowledge the severe limits to our knowledge in these matters. The coming of God, the Day of the Lord, the kingdom of God are sure and certain matters of Christian hope, for they are rooted in the character of God in Christ. But the very nature of these elements of God's promise is such as to defy the ability of our minds or even imagination to grasp them. The revelation of the Lord in His power and glory, the City of God which is the context of the existence of God's people in His kingdom, the new creation and its relation to this creation, the resurrection body and its relation to space and time, the mode of our existence as individuals in that new existence, and the judgment of the world of all time are matters which exceed our understanding, for they go beyond anything which can be experienced in this mode of life. This is not said to deter from speaking of them; on the contrary, we may do so in the confidence that, precisely because the reality of those things which God has prepared exceeds our powers of thought, they will prove to be the more wonderful. This should, however, inculcate in us a sense of humility with regard to our knowledge and a recognition that there are elements of the revelation which we may not have rightly understood. Charity accordingly is in place, as well as humility.

In this respect the apostle who was granted to see the risen Lord in His glory, and ardently looked forward to its revelation in yet greater measure, provided us with a moving example:

> Love will never come to an end. Prophecies will cease; tongues of ecstasy will fall silent; knowledge will vanish. For our knowledge and our prophecy alike are partial, and the partial vanishes when wholeness comes. . . . At present we see only puzzling reflections in a mirror, but one day we shall see face to face. My knowledge now is partial; then it will be whole, like God's knowledge of me. There are three things that last for ever: faith, hope, and love; and the greatest of the three is love (1 Cor 13:8-13, REB).

Notes

1. Gerhard von Rad, *Theological Dictionary of the New Testament I*, 568. Similarly O. Eissfeldt in "Jahwe as Konig," *Zeitschrift für die alttestamentliche Wissenschaft* 5 (1928): 81-105.

2. Martin Buber, *The Kingship of God*, trans. by R. Sheimann (New York: Harper & Row, 1967), 2-23, 95, 99-100.

3. H. D. Piouss, *Jahweglaube und Zukunftserwartung* (Stuttgart: Kohlhammer, 1968), 16.

4. So C. Westermann, *Das Buch Jesaja, Kapitel 40-66*, Das Alte Testament Deutsch (Göttingen: Vandenhoeck u. Ruprecht, 1966), 324.

5. R. H. Charles, *A Critical History of the Doctrine of a Future Life*, 2nd ed. (London: A. & C. Black, 1913), 85.

6. H. H. Wolff, "Herrschaft Jahwes und Messiasgestalt im Alten Testament" *Zeitschrift für die alttestamentliche Wissenschaft* 13 (1936): 181-82.

7. Ibid., 193.

8. For a discussion on the differing views of the date of the Similitudes of Enoch, see the present writer's excursus and the literature there cited in *Jesus and the Kingdom of God* (Grand Rapids: Eerdmans, 1986), 63-68.

9. D. C. Duling, "The Promises to David and their Entrance into Christianity" *New Testament Studies* 19 (1973-74): 64.

10. Schweitzer believed that Jesus expected the kingdom of God to come during the mission on which He sent His disciples to preach this message. See *The Mystery of the Kingdom of God*, trans. by W. Lowrie (London: A. & C. Black, 1914), 87-93, and his better known *Quest of the Historical Jesus*, trans. by W. Montgomery (2nd ed.; London: A. & C. Black, 1910), 328-95.

11. C. H. Dodd, *The Parables of the Kingdom* (London: Nisbet, 1936), 44, and in greater detail "The Kingdom of God has come," *Expository Times* 48 (1936-37): 138-40.

12. A. M. Ambrozic, *The Hidden Kingdom. A Redaction-Critical Study of References to the Kingdom of God in Mark's Gospel*, CBQ Monograph Series II, Washington, D.C. (1972): 21-22.

13. G. Caird, *St. Luke*, Pelican Gospel Commentaries (London: Penguin, 1963), 86.

14. See C. H. Roberts, "The Kingdom of Heaven (Luke XVII:21)" *Harvard Theological Review* 41 (1948): 1-8, and A. Kustow, "*ENTOS GMŌN ESTIN*: Zur Deutung von Lukas 17:20-21," *Zeitschrift für die Neutestamentliche Wissenschaft* 51 (1960): 197-224.

15. So C. H. Dodd, *The Apostolic Preaching and its Developments*, 2nd ed. (London: Hodder & Stoughton, 1944), 11-13; also his exposition of this theme in *According to the Scriptures. The Sub-Structure of New Testament Theology* (London: Nisbet, 1952).

16. F. F. Bruce, *1 & 2 Thessalonians*, vol. 45 in *Word Biblical Commentary* (Waco, TX: Word, 1982), 171, 182. For a review of other interpretations of the passage, see E. Best, *A Commentary on the First and Second Epistles to the Thessalonians*, Harper's New Testament Commentaries (New York: Harper & Row, 1972), 295-301.

17. So R. H. Charles, *The Revelation of St. John*, ICC (2 vols.; Edinburgh: T. & T. Clark, 1920), 2:154-61.

9

The Renewal of the Promise of Rest:

A Canonical Reading of Hebrews 3:7–4:13

David E. Garland

Introduction

The canonical approach to Scripture emphasizes the final form of the text as the authoritative word for the church rather than probing behind the text to investigate various stages in its composition. It recognizes that a text, as sacred Scripture of a community of faith, may acquire a meaning other than the one intended by the original author and asks about what the text has said to the living community of faith in the past and what it says to the community of faith in the present. Brevard Childs, a major proponent of the canonical approach, writes, "the canon of sacred Scripture was a living vehicle through which the Lord of the church continued to address his people. It was not moored in the past, but was a word from the ever-present Saviour."[1] The meaning of a text may therefore eclipse what may have been intended for the original addresses as it speaks afresh to a new audience.

The canonical approach also takes seriously the fact that a text is included within a canon and that it should be heard within its canonical context. Consequently, determining the historical context of a passage is not as essential for letting the text speak to a community of faith in the present as viewing it in that canonical context. A text should be read in light of what other books in the canon say. Most of the time, however, the Old Testament is ignored by those interpreting the New Testament. This neglect is primarily due to a misguided assumption that the Old Testament has been superseded by the New. This attitude overlooks the fact that the early Christians accepted the Hebrew Scripture (and Greek Septuagint) as its Bible and used it as its reference plan for relating the gospel of Jesus Christ. When one interprets the New Testament, one cannot disregard what is said in the Old since it provided the data and the imagery for reflection on the gospel and its implications for the first Christians.[2]

One of the best examples for demonstrating this truth is found in the exegesis of the Old Testament in Hebrews. This author, whoever he may have been, was clearly steeped in the Old Testament. George B. Caird contended, " . . . Hebrews is one of the earliest and most successful attempts to define the relation between the Old and the New Testaments. . . . "[3] To state things less anachronistically, Brevard Childs maintains that the epistle addresses the theological problem of the relation between the two dispensations. According to Childs, the author seeks to answer the question, "What is the relation of life under the old covenant with life under the new?"[4] I will attempt to show how this statement is true in an analysis of Hebrews 3:7–4:13 as well as reflect on how the author uses the Old Testament for proclaiming God's Word for the "today" of His readers and how it has impacted on our "today."

The Context of Hebrews 3:7–4:13

The tenor of the argument in the whole of Hebrews indicates that the author addressed Christians who are afflicted with a kind of spiritual anemia. They were losing their zest for living the Christian life and were growing dangerously lazy in their commitment (6:11-12). They were losing the confidence, the certainty of things unseen (11:1), that had enabled them to stand their ground in the face of persecution (10:32-35). They were losing heart and growing faint in the struggle against sin (12:3-4). They had left the starting blocks in an endurance race, but they had slackened their pace to a crawl as their strength waned (12:1). Now they were shrinking back in the face of adversity (10:39) and were in grave danger of being swept off course as they pined for former ways that seemed to them to provide a more secure refuge than their Christian faith. Perhaps they were tempted to retreat into the cocoon of the Jewish traditions of their past, but they were definitely in danger of falling away. The preacher cited Psalm 95 in 3:7-11 as a word of God that spoke directly to that circumstance. It was a warning shot fired across their bow that harks back to the spiritual collapse of the wilderness generation who also suffered from a loss of courage and confidence. They had witnessed firsthand the mighty works of God, but they refused to believe and died in the wilderness after forty years of aimless wandering.

This portion of the author's intricate argument drew an analogy between the church called out by Jesus and the people of Israel called out into the wilderness by Moses. The church was likened to a pilgrim people on the march. They were advancing in the last days, having been called out on a new exodus under a greater Joshua who brings them to a divine rest. What leads our author to make this comparison was his conviction that a "divine purpose is running through the ages and that parallels can be discerned between the various stages in the fulfillment of this divine purpose."[5] What governs the author's exegesis of the Old Testament was the conviction that Scripture is directly relevant to his generation. As Markus Barth states it, for Hebrews, "What *has* been said is also *being* said."[6] The author does not treat the Scripture as an object to be analyzed and annotated but as the voice of God that needs to "be heard and honored, trusted and done."[7]

This conviction is reflected in the introduction to the citation of Psalm 95 (94) from the Septuagint in 3:7.[8] It is not repeated as the words of the psalmist; it is the Holy Spirit who speaks. Or, in 4:7, it is God who speaks "in David" (see also 1:6,7,13; 9:8; 10:15). It follows that Hebrews assumes that God spoke through David to David's generation and that God still speaks through David to every new generation. Caird writes of our author: "The Old Testament retained is validity for him because in it God had spoken to the fathers, so that those who read it could hear in it the living and abiding Word of God."[9] It is not a book of Bible stories recounting tales of long dead heroes and sinners. One can find in the Old Testament both anticipations of the gospel and the same call to live by a faith that looks to what is to come in the latter days (11:13). But Hebrews demonstrates exegetically that "the Old Testament provides aspirations to which only Christ furnishes the answers."[10] In that sense, the Old Testament is in a dialectical relationship with the New.[11] This dialectical relationship is particularly apparent in Hebrews' reading of

Psalm 95. The psalm is interpreted as God's Word that is still applicable to the people of God, but its fulfillment is possible only now through what Christ has accomplished. Augustine's adage: "The New Testament lies hidden in the Old, and the Old is made plain in the New," still bears repeating.

The Context of Psalm 95

Old Testament scholars have offered a variety of opinions about the original life setting of Psalm 95. I would concur with those who contend that the psalm was used in the preparation of the people for their worship and their entry into the sanctuary.[12] The opening verses (95:1-7a) comprise a call to worship that possibly was recited as the people solemnly moved "in procession into the area of God's presence."[13] The concluding section (95:7b-11) poses a warning from God that was pronounced as the people prostrated themselves before the Lord prior to the sacrifice. The psalm became a significant element of Israel's worship in the times of covenant renewal with the Lord. The warning draws upon Exodus 17:1-7, an account of Israel's crisis and rebellion at Rephidim.

In the Exodus account, Israel was on the move from the wilderness of Sin to Mount Sinai when they bickered with Moses over the scarcity of water and questioned whether the Lord was with them. The deadly combination of belligerence, doubt, and ingratitude caused them to forfeit the promise of rest in the land of Canaan. According to Exodus 17:7, Moses memorialized the people's faithlessness with a play on words, calling the place where they tested God and wrangled with Moses, Massah, which means "testing" or "proof," and Meribah, which means "quarreling" or "contention" (see the parallel account in Num. 20:13). In the Septuagint version of Psalm 95 (LXX 94), these place names are not transliterated but translated into Greek as "testing" and "rebellion."[14] The fate of the rebellious, wilderness generation becomes a warning to those who are hard hearted and who would desire to enter into God's rest. It is this warning that the author of Hebrews seizes to caution his readers.

The Desert Generation As a Cautionary Example

The iniquity of the twelve tribes at Massah and Meribah, a historical event, became, in the canon, a grim reminder of the potential for spiritual disaster that could befall even the people of God. The generation led out of Egypt by Moses became renowned for their stubbornness and disobedience and for their grumbling and murmuring. Any who might exhibit the same spirit as that generation, therefore, should take to heart their disastrous end. We find an example of the desert generation being used as a cautionary lesson in Psalm 78:12-22 which recounts God's miracles and Israel's unbelief:

> He did miracles in the sight of their fathers
> in the land of Egypt, in the region of Zoan.
> He divided the sea and led them through;
> he made water stand firm like a wall.
> He guided them with the cloud by day
> and with the light from the fire all night.
> He split the rocks in the desert
> and gave them water as abundant as the seas;
> he brought streams out of a rocky crag
> and made water flow down like rivers.
> But they continued to sin against him,
> rebelling in the desert against the Most High.
> They willfully put God to the test
> by demanding the food they craved.
> They spoke against God, saying,
> "Can God spread a table in the desert?
> When he struck the rock, water gushed out,
> and streams flowed abundantly.
> But can he also give us food?
> Can he supply meat for His people?"
> When the Lord heard them, he was very angry;
> his fire broke out against Jacob,
> and his wrath rose against Israel,
> for they did not believe in God
> or trust in His deliverance (NIV).

Because they "kept on sinning," refused to believe, and put God to the test again and again, they ended their days in futility and terror (Ps. 78:32-33,40-41). Similarly, in Psalm 106, the wilderness generation is condemned because: "Then they despised the pleasant land; they did not believe his promise. They grumbled in their tents and did not obey the Lord. So he swore to them with uplifted hand that he would make them fall in the desert" (vv. 24-26, NIV).

In the New Testament, Stephen labeled his antagonists a stiff-necked people who betrayed and murdered God's Righteous One and who had always resisted the Holy Spirit. He likened them to the wilderness congregation who refused to obey Moses and turned back to Egypt in their hearts (Acts 7:35-53). Paul also held up the wilderness generation as a warning to the brazen Corinthians (1 Cor. 10:1-12). In his typological interpretation of the exodus events, he argued that those who passed through the sea were baptized into Moses in the cloud and in the sea. They also partook of supernatural manna and supernatural drink; but, in spite of these experiences, they died in the wasteland. Paul underscores the fact that those who were overthrown in the wilderness now serve as "warnings for us, not to desire evil as they did" (1 Cor. 10:6, RSV). He concludes his discussion of the exodus generation with the assertion that these things "were written down for our instruction, upon whom the end of the ages has come" (1 Cor. 10:11, RSV). The story of that generation is interpreted as a forewarning to any who might boast that they stand and ignore the possibility that they might fall (1 Cor. 10:12). Jude also appeals to the lesson of the wilderness generation by reminding his readers that the one "who saved a people out of the land of Egypt, afterward destroyed those who did not believe" (v. 5, RSV).

The Failures of the Desert Generation

Hebrews presents an extended exhortation based on the failures of the wilderness generation that is comparable to Paul's exhortation in 1 Corinthians. While the primary text is Psalm 95, the author of Hebrews does not limit himself to that psalm alone. He interprets the passage in terms of Numbers 13–14, which gives an account of the people's failure to act decisively in taking the land. The events at Kadesh in the Desert of Paran are as much a part of the backdrop for the exhortation as those at Massah and Meribah. Lane contends that in Hebrews 3:16-18 a question is raised about the meaning of a phrase in Psalm 95 and answered with a reference from Numbers 14.[15] In 3:16, the preacher asked, "Who were they that heard and yet were rebellious?" (RSV; see also 3:8). The answer basically comes from Numbers 14:2-3, "all those who left Egypt under the leadership of Moses" (RSV). In 3:17, the question arises from the statement in 3:10, "with whom was he provoked forty years?" (RSV). The answer comes from Numbers 14:28-35, "those who sinned and whose bodies fell in the wilderness" (RSV). The final question in 3:18 (RSV) asks, "to whom did he swear an oath that they shall never enter this rest?" and recalls 3:11. This last question also echoes Numbers 14:22-23 where God swore, "None of the men who have seen my glory and my signs which I wrought in the land of Egypt and in the wilderness, and yet have put me to the proof these ten times and have not hearkened to my voice, shall see the land which I swore to give to their fathers; and none of those who despised me shall see it" (RSV). In Numbers 14:29, God swore that their dead bodies would fall in the wilderness.

The fusion of Psalm 95 and Numbers 13–14 in Hebrews' interpretation means that the errors of the wilderness generation that are held up as a warning are to be found from both passages. Hebrews solemnly warns the readers not to repeat the same grievous mistakes. What precisely were the transgressions of the wilderness generation that are to be avoided?

The Demand for Proof of God's Presence

The psalm denounces the fathers for putting God to the test and provoking God's wrath (3:9).[16] The psalmist had in mind Exodus 17:7: "they put the Lord to the proof by saying: 'Is the Lord among us or not?'" (RSV; see Deut. 6:16). The psalm therefore not only warns the hearers against being contentious as their fathers were about the waters of Meribah but warns that they should not "question the presence of God here today, as your fathers questioned it at Massah."[17]

The author of Hebrews slightly modifies the significance of the reference to the forty years with the addition of "wherefore" (*dio*) to his quotation from the psalm in 3:10. The forty years do not refer simply to the duration of God's wrath against that generation,[18] but to the length of time that they witnessed God's works, that is, God's miraculous deliverance and gracious provision. As Psalm 78 recounts, that generation had been spared the plagues, saved by the angel of death, and miraculously delivered through the divided sea. They were led by a cloud by day and a fire by night (Ex. 13:21), given water to drink and manna, the bread of angels, to eat (Ex. 16:4-5); but they still insisted that God provide them with certified proof that God was indeed with them. They demanded further verification of God's power and God's presence among them (see Deut. 29:2-6). In Numbers 14:11 (RSV), we read of God's exasperation, "And the Lord said to Moses, 'How long will this people despise me? And how long will they not believe in me, in spite of all the signs which I have wrought among them?'"

Hebrews picks up on the theme that God gave the wilderness bunch forty years of proof, but it was not enough (3:9). When they were on probation and God was putting them to the test, they tried to turn the tables and for forty years put God to the test. Seesemann states that to test or tempt God basically means that one fails to acknowledge His power or take seriously His will to save.[19] To test God is to impugn God's power and faithfulness to fulfill His promises. The word, (*dokimasia*), "testing," that appears in the Hebrews text, can imply a skeptical scrutiny that finds God wanting.[20] They wanted incontestable proof that God would do all that He had promised before they would budge. Because of their skepticism, they were disobedient (3:18); and their disobedience led to their demise.[21] But the testing of God also entails trying to force God's hand to serve our own interests. They wanted God to serve them, rather than vice versa. The question they kept asking God was, "What have you done for us lately?"

The Refusal to Believe

The wilderness generation is also characterized as having hardened their hearts (3:8), of always going astray in their hearts (3:10), and of having an evil, unbelieving heart (literally, "a wicked heart of unfaithfulness," 3:12). They were hardened by the deceitfulness of sin (3:13) that caused them to fall away from the living God. The adjective "hardened" comes from a stem that means "to dry up," and one could say that their time in the wasteland caused their hearts to shrivel into a husk. Hardening implies a stubborn disobedience. They are accused of failing to know God's ways (3:10), but the truth is that they did not want to know God's ways. They wanted God to follow their way.

The unbelieving heart of the wilderness generation was expressed concretely in the fact that they became more concerned with the assurance offered by temporal, physical realities than with security provided by the spiritual presence of God in their midst. The rancorous dispute over water and food (see Num. 11:4-6; 20:2-5) was only symptomatic of the people's hankering for other gods (Ex. 32:1-6). Even when God miraculously met their need, it met with sulking protests. They complained: "If only we had meat to eat! We remember the fish we ate in Egypt at no cost—also the cucumbers, melons, leeks, onions, and garlic. But now we have lost our appetite; we never see anything but this manna!" (Num. 11:4-6, NIV).

The Failure to Heed God's Voice Today

The people started out well. They left Egypt under the leadership of Moses (3:16) and witnessed the works of God for forty years (3:9). They had the gospel to them (4:2,6). The NIV has good grounds for translating it, "they had the gospel preached" (from the verb *euangelizein*), but hearing the promise is no guarantee that the promise will be received. Hearing in the past is fine, but the key is whether one hears today and obeys. The message for the Hebrews is clear: hearing the gospel is not a token of salvation if it meets only with token faith.

The word "today" is a refrain throughout the passage in Hebrews (3:7,15; 4:7). Attention to the account in Numbers 13 helps elucidate the urgency of responding "today." According to Numbers, the promised land was in sight, and the people were poised for its conquest (Num. 13:1-2). They sent out a detachment of spies to prepare for their onslaught, and they returned to report that all that God had promised was true—it was indeed a land flowing with milk and honey (Num. 13:23-24,27). But they also informed the people that the land was inhabited by forbidding enemies, and they became frantic with fear (Num. 13:28-29). Caleb dismissed their apprehension and urged, "Let us go up at once and occupy it; for we are well able to overcome it" (Num. 13:30). But the majority blanched at the prospect of confronting such a fearsome foe and protested, "We are not able to go up; they are stronger than we." "The land devours its inhabitants"; "compared to them we are grasshoppers" (Num. 13:31-33, author's translation). They forgot or did not trust God's promise that He would enable them to take the land. Again, they lamented, "Would that we had died in the land of Egypt. Would that we had died in this wilderness. Why does the Lord bring us up into this land, to fall by the sword?" (Num. 14:2-3, author's translation). It is only later, after Moses divulged God's resolve to exclude this wicked congregation from the land forever, that they had second thoughts and decided that they might be ready to attack (Num. 14:39-40). But later was too late (compare Heb 12:16-17);[22] they were quickly dispatched by the enemy when they tried to take the land without Moses and the ark of the covenant (Num. 14:44-45).

We can see from this story that one of the elements of the disobedience of the wilderness generation was their hesitation and cowardice when God called them in their "today." They preferred to mark time in the wilderness or they longed for the good old days of bondage back in the brick factory in Egypt (see Ex. 14:10-12). The climax of Hebrews' analysis of the failure of the desert generation is God's oath that they shall never enter into His rest (3:19; see 3:11; 4:3; Deut. 1:34-36). Because of their hesitation, they were doomed to know only un-rest and to wander aimlessly in the desert.

The Promise of Rest Unfulfilled

The word "rest" recurs throughout the passage (3:11,18; 4:1,3,5,10-11) and is a key concern. In Hebrew, the noun (*nuah*) means "quietness," "quiet attitude," "tranquil."[23] In the Old Testament, "rest" is used particularly to refer to the final conquest of the promised land. Lombard observes, "This 'coming to rest' of a tired and beleaguered people played a decisive role in the religious and theological thought of Israel."[24]

Rest in the Old Testament

God promised Moses: "My Presence will go with you, and I will give you rest" (Ex. 33:14, NIV). Moses warned the people that they cannot do as they see fit. "For you have not as yet come to the rest and to the inheritance which the Lord your God gives you" (Deut. 12:9, RSV). In Deuteronomy 25:19, the promise of rest is recalled with the added feature that God will give the people rest in the land from all their enemies round about (see Deut. 3:20). In these passages, rest is related to God's works on behalf of His people that will bring them victory.

The emphasis on rest appears throughout Joshua with the promise that the Lord will give them rest in the land beyond the Jordan (Josh. 1:15) and the fulfillment of the promise when the land was conquered and had rest from war (Josh. 11:23; 21:43-44; 22:4; 23:1). In 2 Samuel 7:1, we find the report that David dwelt in his house and had been given rest from all his enemies round about and the people are assured that they also will dwell in their own place and be disturbed no more and have rest from their enemies (7:10-11). In 1 Kings 5:4, Solomon affirmed that the Lord had given him "rest on every side; and there is no adversary or disaster" (NIV). Therefore, Solomon resolved to build a house for the Lord. In 1 Kings 8:56, Solomon stood before the assembly and said, "Praise be to the Lord, who has given rest to his people Israel just as he promised. Not one word has failed of all the good promises he gave through his servant Moses" (NIV). In 1 Chronicles 22:9, Solomon himself is identified as a man of rest, who, like David, will have rest from all his enemies round about.

In these various passages, "rest" basically refers to a secure dwelling place, freedom from war, and relief from drudgery and affliction. It means refuge and tranquility on this earth. After the conquest of the land, it seems that the promise had been fulfilled (see 1 Chron. 22:18; 23:25; 2 Chron. 14:6-7; 15:15; 20:30);

but when one looks at things historically, one knows that God's promise of rest was not fulfilled by the possession of the land. Israel did not have permanent rest, and it would not be long before the enemies round about would be gathering ominously on the horizon. Israel will be exiled. Later, the prophet Isaiah foresaw Israel's return from exile as another time of rest. The Lord would give them rest from their pain and turmoil (Isa. 14:3; see 28:12). But Hebrews stresses the fact that the promise of rest was not realized by the settlement (or resettlement) of an earthly Canaan. When one looks at things canonically, one sees that a rest still remains for the people of God (Heb. 4:8-10).

Rest in Psalm 95

The meaning of "rest" is slightly modified in Psalm 95. The people of Israel had entered the land and had conquered it. David was established as king, but the psalm still holds out the promise of rest and a warning that some may fail to attain it. How was it that the promise of rest could be renewed for the people? How was it that some might be excluded? The answer to these questions may be found in the fact that the sanctuary had become associated with God's resting place (see Ps. 132:7-8,13-14; 2 Chron. 6:41; Isa. 66:1, cited in Acts 7:49). In the liturgical context of Psalm 95, it was possible to understand the approach into the sanctuary as an entering into God's rest.[25] The fate of the wilderness generation served as a grave warning to anyone who might aspire to enter into God's resting place, the sanctuary, with a hard heart. But within the psalm are the seeds for an even greater understanding of what it means to enter into God's rest.

Rest in Hebrews

The basic premise in Hebrews' reading of the psalm and the Old Testament is that God's promise of rest was not ultimately fulfilled when the people finally made it to the promised land. The true fulfillment of God's promise was not simply the historical fulfillment of settlement in a land. His argument is this: Those who first received the good news did not enter the rest because of their disobedience (4:6). If they had entered that rest, then God through David would not have needed to plead with His listeners to heed His call "today," long after Canaan had been occupied. If Joshua had given them rest, why does David still look to rest as something yet to be attained (4:7-8)?

The conclusion is that God is still offering His promise today, another today, and that the warning of the Holy Spirit in the psalm is still applicable. As Moses testified to things that were to be spoken later (3:5), so the rest that God has in mind for God's people points beyond what Joshua did.

The concept of "rest" was also associated in the Old Testament with the rest of the seventh day. This aspect of rest is taken up in Hebrews 4:4,10 with a reference to Genesis 2:2: "God . . . rested on the seventh day" (NASB). Sabbath rest is more than ceasing from work on the sabbath. The rest is identified in the psalm as "my rest" (3:11; see 3:18, "his rest"; and 4:5, "my rest"). This phrase opens the way for Hebrews to understand "rest" in a new and different dimension as belonging to God. The rest that God promises His people is one that corresponds to God's sacred rest that God entered into at creation. The preacher appealed to Genesis 2:2 to demonstrate that rest points beyond Joshua (4:8) and David (4:7) to something that resides in the realm of God.[26] It is not simply a place of rest but a divine condition of rest.[27]

The concept of rest therefore takes on a quite different meaning in Hebrews than it has in much of the Old Testament, although that meaning has been gleaned from the Old Testament itself.[28] Here we see the dialectical relationship between the two testaments. The term *rest* is initially ambiguous (Heb. 3:7-19). Rest seems to refer to that which the exodus generation failed to attain in the land of Canaan. But the preacher clarified exactly what he meant by rest and what they really failed to enter in 4:1-11. Rest refers to a heavenly reality that God entered after the creation.[29] This rest is quite unrelated to an earthly geography or calendar.

The history of the people in the land revealed that they did not have perpetual rest from famine, enemies, and disease. But Hebrews does not make its case from the disappointments of historical events. The argument is based only on the Scripture as it is interpreted in light of Christ by whom God has spoken to us in these last days. The preacher affirmed in 11:40, "God had foreseen something better for us" (RSV). God wants us to share the joy of His own rest, and the offer is renewed in Christ (compare Matt. 11:28). The land of rest that God has in store for us is not encircled by enemies because it has no boundaries. It is not something temporal but eternal. Humans have pursued it, but it has eluded them because one can never be completely at rest in this world and because rest can only be realized through Christ.

H. Attridge comments that, for Hebrews, "the Christians' 'entry into rest' parallels Christ's entry into the divine presence" (see 4:14; 9:12,24-25).[30] Christ has already passed through the wilderness temptations (2:18), and has entered in God's rest which is illustrated by His sitting down (1:3; 8:1; 10:12; 12:2). The entry of Christians into the presence of God is made possible only by Christ's turning the key and opening the doors for us to follow (4:8; 6:20; 10:19-21). Attridge concludes:

> Thus the imagery of rest is best understood as a complex symbol for the whole soteriological process that Hebrews never fully articulates, but which involves both the personal and corporate dimensions. It is the process of entry into God's presence, kingdom (12:28), begun at baptism (10:22) and consummated as a whole eschatologically.[31]

One can only fully receive this rest after this life, but it is made available now through the work of God's Son. The people of God are still called to enter that rest, to go on pilgrimage with Jesus, to go outside the camp to Him (13:13) in order to reach the rest, their ultimate salvation.[32]

The Parallels Between the Church and the Wilderness Generation

A. B. Davidson wrote years ago, "Israel stood at the farther end of a road, the hither end of which leads to the true Rest of God. They refused to enter upon it."[33] Hebrews conceives the history of Israel in the wilderness as a urgent warning for his readers. The phrase "that generation" in Psalm 95 (94):10 is changed to "this generation" in Hebrews' citation in 3:10, possibly to help the reader to spot the connection between the generation in the days of Moses and the current generation.[34] Several parallels between the desert generation and the church are apparent. "Good news" came to them as it has to us (4:2,6). The Word of God made the same kind of demand for faith and obedience upon them as it does upon us. As Israel was delivered from captivity, so Christians have been delivered from an even worse captivity, the captivity of sin and death (2:15). As Israel was delivered by Moses, a servant in the house of God (3:5), Christians are saved by Christ, the Son of God who is over the house (3:6). The promise of rest was held out to them, and that promise has been renewed for us in Christ. As Israel was led to the land of Canaan by the first Jesus (the name for Joshua and Jesus in the Greek text is identical [Iesous]), the church is on the move under the leadership of a new Jesus and also heads for a divine goal. As Israel faced the dangers of temptation in the wilderness, the span between initial deliverance and final attainment of the goal, so does the church. The church must hear the warning lest they too should be tempted to "turn away" (3:12) by the same sort of disobedience (4:11).[35]

The generation of the wilderness failed to enter the rest because of a failure of faith even though they witnessed God's great provision for them for forty years (3:18). The message of good news which they heard (see, for example, Ex. 19:3-6) did not benefit them because it did not meet with a trust that led to a resolute commitment. As a result, they were excluded. Christians have witnessed a far greater work of God than anything performed in the wilderness because they have encountered firsthand the salvation that God offers in Christ.[36] They have tasted "the heavenly gift," "the goodness of the word of God and the powers of the coming age" (6:4-6, NIV). This work of Christ can be ignored only with the direst of consequences (2:3). But as God called Israel in their today, God calls us today. Hebrews pictures the church, like Israel, in the wilderness, primed and ready for their entrance into God's rest. Christians cannot allow themselves to be hobbled by doubts. The author of Hebrews sounds the alert for his readers who are in the process of entering the rest of God (4:3) so that they may not fall by the wayside because of the same sort of iniquity that caused Israel to flounder and die in the barren wilderness (4:11).

Striving to Enter God's Rest

Hebrews exhorts the reader to strive to enter God's rest (4:11). One enters God's rest by faith, but that faith can be sapped by persecution and suffering. It can also be crippled by fear that causes us to recoil rather than respond when God calls us into the unknown.

In Hebrews, the people of God have been mobilized for a heavenward journey (3:1) to a heavenly country (11:16) and a heavenly Jerusalem (12:22). The call to venture forth may seem fraught with dangers. When we leave our "Egypt," temptations still abound, the same temptations that caused Israel to succumb in the wilderness. We are still subject to "the deceitfulness of sin" (3:13). Luther comments that sin is beguiling, "because it deceives under the appearance of good."[37] One of the ways that sin entices is to hold out the lure of earthly security. It charms us to want to settle down in this world before we have reached the true goal. Because the rest resides in God's sabbath, however, it can only be promise on earth and we can have no lasting city here (13:13). Even the heavens will be rolled up like an old garment (1:10-12). Therefore, we must live by the promises of God and place our trust in invisible realities which are the only realities that are ultimately sure and true. The rest is attained by faith, which, according to Hebrews 11:1, is what gives substance[38] to our hopes and convinces us of the things that are unseen. The readers are exhorted to hold fast to that confidence which they had at first (3:14) because when one does not trust in the invisible presence of God, one will inevitably fall away. And God has no use for those who would shrink back (John 6:66), who would bury their talents (Matt. 25:14-30), or who would postpone commitment to go back to bury their dead (Matt. 8:21-22). God calls us today to leave all and follow.

The people of God who have responded to God's call therefore may not shift into neutral and coast into God's rest. They must continue to strive and will receive that rest only after persevering to the end of their sojourn. But they are not called to go it alone. They follow One who has already entered into that rest and who helps those who are on the way now (2:18). They also travel together with fellow pilgrims who are to exhort one another *daily*. They are to recall for one another the words of God, both warning and comfort, to spur one another on (3:13; see 10:25; 13:22). They need not fear the unknown frontier where God leads them, for Christ has gone before them and the voice of God rings throughout the canon, "Fear not" (Gen. 15:1; Ex. 14:13; 20:20; Josh. 8:1; Matt. 14:27; 28:5,10; Acts 18:9; Rev. 1:17). They need only fear that they might fail to heed God's call (Heb. 4:1).

Hearing God's Voice Today

The word "today" that reverberates through the passage emphasizes that God's call is ever present and ever urgent. It is even more so now that God has now spoken through His Son (1:1-2). One may not evade or dispute God's commands; one must be obedient. Therefore, one must be ready to let go and go the moment one hears God's call. It is not enough simply to leave Egypt; one must be attuned to God's call each step of the journey. The fear and trepidation Israel experienced during their wilderness journey are typical of the experiences of the people of God (see Mark 4:41; 10:32; 16:8; Matt. 28:17; John

20:19). Many hesitate to give themselves in complete obedience
to God's call that leads them out into a new frontier. Many are
tempted to turn their hearts back to Egypt to what seems to be
a place of greater security. Their apprehension may be compared to the panic of one who might venture for the first time
to swing from a trapeze. The first temptation is never to risk
climbing up to the platform at all. The second is never to jump
off. But if one should take the plunge and go hurtling through
the air, one might then be tempted to hold on to the bar for
dear life and never let go to reach out for the next trapeze that
carries one safely to the next support. But to reach that goal
the trapeze artist must let go of the trapeze at just the right
moment and, as Paul Tournier writes, "hover for a moment in
the void before catching hold of the other trapeze."[39] It means
that one has to pass through "the anxiety of the middle of the
way," the time when one has let go of the first support and has
not yet seized the second. That anxiety of the middle way is not
unlike Israel's anxiety when they left Egypt and had not yet
entered into God's rest, nor unlike that of the first readers of
Hebrews who had left Judaism but had not yet entered into
God's eternal rest at the end of time. It is not unlike the anxiety of those of us who today still live in the interim between
Christ's first advent and the parousia.

The people of God have been called out by Christ and live in
the anxiety zone between the safety of the maternal bosom and
the bosom of Abraham. They will not be spared the desert and
must undergo testing as the wilderness generation did. Droop-
ing hands, weak knees, faint hearts, and flimsy faith are an
ever present peril to those on pilgrimage in a hostile and dete-
riorating world. But, like the trapeze artist, once we leave the
platform, we are committed; there is no turning back. Tournier
observes, "We cannot live without support, but we must always
be letting go of our support under pain of being left behind by
the current of life." If we fail to let go at just the right moment
and reach out for the next trapeze when God says, "Now!" we
are doomed to be left hanging in the air. As the arc gets ever
smaller, our strength will finally give out; and we shall plum-
met to the earth.

It is our response today that readies us for tomorrow. Scroggie writes, "The only proof that we shall be equal to tomorrow's
test is that we are meeting today's test believingly and courageously. The only evidence that we shall be willing for God's
will tomorrow is that we are subject to His will today."[40] Today
is the time of decision, because God's call always requires a re-

sponse, and it has a time limit. The solemn lesson of the wilderness generation is that God does not extend the time of grace and opportunity indefinitely. Today can be lost. Opportunity can be squandered. God does get provoked (3:10,17) and angry with the disobedient (3:11,18). God can and will exclude those who refuse to listen (3:11,18). God's oath in Psalm 95:11, "As I swore in my wrath, if they shall enter my rest" (author's translation), is cited in 3:11 and four times thereafter (3:18; 4:3,5) to underscore the danger of disobedience. God is confessed as a "living God" (3:12), and it is a fearful thing to fall into the hands of the living God (10:31) who is also a consuming fire (12:29).

The exhortation concludes in 4:12-13 with the affirmation that the Word of God is also alive. It is not a dead letter to a long ancient people. Even when it has been spoken long ago, it remains active and calls us to give an account of ourselves today (see John 12:48). It is powerful. It can probe and diagnose. It can penetrate our existence, and its sharp, double-edged blade is able to separate even what we find inseparable, soul and spirit. Therefore, God's word must be obeyed as long as we have today.

Notes

1. B. S. Childs, *The New Testament as Canon: An Introduction* (Philadelphia: Fortress, 1985), 29. For a critique of this approach from a conservative evangelical perspective, see D. A. Brueggemann, "Brevard Childs' Canon Criticism: An Example of Post-Critical Naiveté," *Journal of the Evangelical Theological Society* 32 (1989): 311-26; from a liberal perspective, see J. Barr, "Childs' *Introduction to the Old Testament as Scripture*," *Journal of the Study of the Old Testament* 16 (1980): 12-23. This issue of *JSOT* contains six other reactions to Childs' *Introduction to the Old Testament as Scripture* and a response from Childs.

2. See D. Juel, *Messianic Exegesis: Christological Interpretation of the Old Testament in Early Christianity* (Philadelphia: Fortress, 1988), 140.

3. G. B. Caird, "The Exegetical Method of the Epistle to the Hebrews," *Canadian Journal of Theology* 5 (1959): 45.

4. Childs, *The New Testament as Canon*, 415.

5. Markus Barth, "The Old Testament in Hebrews: An Essay in Biblical Hermeneutics," in *Current Issues in New Testament Interpretation: Essays in Honor of O. A. Piper*, ed. W. Klassen and G. F. Snyder (New York: Harper & Row, 1962), 65.

6. Ibid., 60-61.

7. Ibid., 71.

8. The quotation varies only slightly from the Septuagint text we have. A commentary on the psalm follows in 3:12-19 that is set off by an inclusio, a literary device whereby similar words or phrases appear at the beginning and at the end of a section to frame it as a unit. In 3:12-19, the words that bind the

unit are "see" and "unbelief." The next section divides into two segments. The first, 4:1-5, is set off by the words "entering his/my rest" and contains a citation from Psalm 95 in the middle. The second segment, 4:6-11 is framed by the words "entering the rest" and "disobedience" and contains another quote from the psalm in the middle of the section.

9. Caird, "Exegetical Method," 46.

10. Ibid., 51.

11. B. S. Childs, *Old Testament Theology in a Canonical Context* (Philadelphia: Fortress, 1985), 9.

12. G. Henton Davies, "Psalm 95," *Zeitschrift für die alttestamentliche Wissenschaft* 85 (1973): 183-95. For a summary of the exegesis of Psalm 95 in Jewish literature, see O. Michel, *Der Brief an der Hebrer* (KEK: 12 ed; Göttingen: Vandenhoeck u. Ruprecht, 1966), 183-86.

13. H.J. Kraus, *Psalms 60-150* (Minneapolis: Augsburg, 1989), 246.

14. Hebrews 3:8 follows the Septuagint with the phrases "in the rebellion" and "on the day of testing."

15. W. L. Lane, *Hebrews* (Peabody: Hendrickson, 1988), 65. See also O. Hofius, *Katapausis: Die Vorstellung vom endzeitlichen Ruheort im Hebraerbrief* (Tübingen: J. C. B. Mohr [Paul Siebeck], 1970), 127-31.

16. The LXX of Psalm 94:9 simply has your fathers "tested" (*epeirasan*); some texts of Hebrews 3:9 have your fathers "tested me" (*epeirasan me*).

17. Davies, "Psalm 95," 194.

18. According to Num. 14:33-34, they were on the receiving end of forty years of God's wrath. Hebrews picks up on this theme in 3:17.

19. H. Seesemann, "*peira* . . . ," *Theological Dictionary of the New Testament* 6:27.

20. The LXX has the verb form (*dokimazein*) in Psalm 94:9. Compare Romans 1:28 where the verb occurs with a play on words: "they did not see fit to have God in their knowledge, so God gave them up to an unfit mind."

21. The verb (*apeithein*), translated "disobey," can also mean to fail to be persuaded.

22. The basic meaning of the verb (*hysterein*) in 4:1 is "to come too late." It could be translated, "be careful that none of you be found to have come too late" and be excluded from the promise as a consequence.

23. Francis Brown, S. R. Driver, and Charles A. Briggs, *A Hebrew and English Lexicon of the Old Testament* (reprinted: Oxford: Clarendon, 1953), 629.

24. H. A. Lombard, "*Katapausis* in the Letter to the Hebrews," *Neotestamentica* 5 (1971): 68.

25. A. T. Lincoln, "Sabbath, Rest, and Eschatology in the New Testament," *From Sabbath to Lord's Day: Biblical, Historical, and Theological Investigation*, ed D. A. Carson (Grand Rapids: Zondervan, 1982), 208.

26. O. Bauernfeind, "(*katapauo, katapausis*)," *Theological Dictionary of the New Testament* 3:628.

27. In Exodus 35:2, *katapausis* is used of sabbath rest (see also 2 Macc. 15:1). Sabbath is also an image used for the world to come in *Gen. Rab.* 17:12.

28. For a tradition history approach to the motif of rest, compare the discussions in E. Käsemann, *The Wandering People of God: An Investigation of the Letter to the Hebrews* (Minneapolis: Augsburg, 1984), 67-96; and O. Hofius, *Katapausis. Die Vorstellung vom endzeitlichen Ruheort Aim Hebraerbrief* (WUNT 11; Tübingen: J. C. B. Mohr [Paul Siebeck], 1970). This approach does not ask the question about what the message of revelation is for today in light of the history of salvation as revealed in the canon.

29. H. W. Attridge, *Hebrews* (Hermeneia; Philadelphia: Fortress, 1989), 123.

30. Ibid., 128.

31. Ibid. See 10:25,37-38; 12:26-29.

32. Compare Rev. 14:13.

33. A. B. Davidson, *The Epistle to the Hebrews* (Edinburgh: T. & T. Clark, 1882), 100.

34. C. Spicq, *L'Epitre aux Hebreux* (EtBib; Paris: Gabalda, 1952), 2:74.

35. H. Montefiore, *The Epistle to the Hebrews* (London: Adam & Charles Black, 1964), 87, comments on 4:11: "The warning is not about falling into disobedience, but falling, like the rejected Israelites, *through* disobedience."

36. F. F. Bruce, *The Epistle to the Hebrews* (NIC; Grand Rapids: Eerdmans, 1964), 65, suggests that if the epistle were written before A.D. 70, it would have been nearly forty years since the death of Jesus. This fact might explain the urgency of the author as he saw the end of the forty year probationary period rapidly approaching.

37. Cited by P. E. Hughes, *A Commentary on the Epistle to the Hebrews* (Grand Rapids: Eerdmans, 1977), 148.

38. The word "confidence" (*hypostasis*) appears in 1:3; 3:14; and 11:1, and it sounds like the words which are used as its antonyms in Hebrews, (*apostasia*), "apostasy," and (*apistia*), "unbelief."

39. P. Tournier, *A Place for You* (New York: Harper & Row, 1968), 162-63.

40. Scroggie, *Land of Life and Rest*, 14-15.

PART 3

Bringing It All Together

10

Preaching in the Present Tense:
Coming Alive to the Old Testament

Al Fasol

The Bible is a living book. Obviously, this statement includes the Old Testament as well as the New Testament. The Old Testament is alive with action, and it either gives life to or quickens the lives of its readers. The Old Testament creates, indicts, suffers, judges, marches, floods, restores, redeems, condemns, exiles, resurrects, as well as promises, predicts, prophesies, jolts, awakes, strives, yearns, groans, and seeks. Frequently, preachers are heard to ask, "How do I make the Old Testament come alive for my congregation?" Such a question represents a gross misunderstanding of the Old Testament! The Old Testament is a living collection of books that unapologetically addresses humanity all the way from biological urges and needs to spiritual needs and longings. Each Old Testament book deals realistically with the sinful nature of humankind. Each Old Testament book frankly acknowledges the sovereignty of God. The preacher's question is not how to make the Old Testament come alive. The preacher's question is how do I get myself out of the way in order that this pulsating life form that we call the Old Testament can move in all its power.

The first step in "getting out of the way" involves selection of a text. Selecting a biblical text is a critical decision when preaching from the Old Testament (or from the New Testament). Once proper text selection is accomplished, the sermon is on a correct course.

The word "text" is taken from the Latin word *textus*—a "web." The verb is *texere*—"to weave." A biblical text, therefore, is the fabric from which the sermon is woven. The length of the text may vary from a portion of a verse of Scripture to a chapter of Scripture or more. Whether short or long, the text should consist of only enough verses to form a complete literary unit of thought.

We are fortunate that the biblical writers were inspired to use various literary devices to alert us when a complete literary unit of thought begins and ends. These rhetorical devices were used because the Bible was written in aural style; that is, it was written primarily to be heard. One of the common rhetorical devices is the use of a key word, as in Genesis 1. When the key word "good" no longer appears or another key word takes its place, we realize that we have moved from one literary unit to another. Other rhetorical signals we should watch for include: brief introductions to a new unit (Jer. 11:1); summary statements (Amos 5:21-24); notations as to changes in time (2 Sam. 11:1), or place (Num. 10:11-12), or occasion (for instance, Jer. 30:1). Most of the time we can tell when a story is finished, or when a point has been made. Modern translations of the Bible such as the NIV, guide us by dividing the writings into paragraphs. From these observations we should be able to select a proper biblical text.

The next step is to interpret the text. The historical context and the linguistic nature of the text will be important in interpretation. Previous chapters in this book which dealt with the hermeneutical challenges of different literary forms should be applied here. Since the preacher's task is one of proclaiming a message from the Bible which was written centuries ago (*then*) to a contemporary congregation (*now*), we will limit our discussion of interpretation to the drawing of theological conclusions about the individual text. This movement from then to now must always occur if preaching is to occur. We can neither omit the then (the Bible), or the now (a contemporary congregation) and still have preaching occur.

We can best deal with the *then* of Scripture by summarizing the text in a brief, interpretative, past tense statement.[1] To avoid rambling, the sentence should be no longer than 15-18 words. This sentence should reflect the direct, Eternal Truth of the Text (E.T.T.). For example, we might express the eternal truth of Amos 5:21-24 in this way: "God demanded worship that was backed by just and righteous living." This brief declarative sentence interprets what the text meant at the time it was written (then).

We can deal with the now of Scripture by writing a present tense sentence application of the text. This sentence we call the Truth for Today (T.T.). The T.T. for Amos 5:21-24 might be written this way:

True worship of God must be backed by just and righteous living.

Again, this sentence should be limited to 15-18 words to avoid rambling.

The E.T.T. and the T.T. serve to guide the preacher throughout sermon development. The E.T.T. and the T.T. are like runway lights on a foggy night. They blink at us through the clouds until we can see clearly where it is we are to land. (Occasionally, the preacher may feel led of God to preach a secondary idea in the text instead of the direct eternal truth of the text. In such instances the preacher should still write an E.T.T. The E.T.T. and secondary idea must have a strong, clear relationship. Without the E.T.T., the preacher will be tempted to ramble or, worse, to impose a false interpretation upon the text.)

When the interpretive process is at least tentatively completed, the process of sermon preparation can begin. The E.T.T. and T.T. should at least suggest, if not indeed provide, a title for the sermon. The E.T.T. and T.T. for Amos 5:21-24 provides this title:

"Pleasing God in Our Worship"

If the preacher plans to outline the text, there should be a strong, clear relationship between the title and the outline. A possible outline for Amos 5:21-24 could be:

I. We do not please God with empty, hollow expressions of worship (Amos 5:21-23).
II. We do please God when our worship is backed by just and righteous living (Amos 5:24).

Notice that each point has a textual basis. Notice also that the key concepts of true worship of God that appear in the E.T.T. and T.T. also appear in the title and the outline. Notice finally that there is a strong, clear relationship between the points and title, between the title and the T.T., between the T.T. and the E.T.T., and between the E.T.T. and the text. Imagine how reassuring it is for the preacher to know that every point, every paragraph, every sentence of the sermon can be traced directly back to the text! Imagine how reassuring it is to the preacher to stand before a congregation knowing that he has a solid message from the Word of God! That is a feeling no preacher should be without, and no preacher who follows sound exegetical, hermeneutical, and homiletical practices needs ever to be without that feeling. These are the necessary preliminary steps for preaching in the present tense. Next, we need to see how these principles help to develop sermons from various Old Testament texts.

Give consideration to preaching a survey of the Old Testament. One effective approach would begin with the garden of Eden (Gen. 2:8) and conclude in the garden of Gethsemane (Matt. 26:36). In the garden of Eden, Adam told God, "Not your will, but my will be done," and sin was introduced to the world. In the garden of Gethsemane Jesus said, "Not my will, but your will be done," and salvation that eradicates the power of sin was introduced to the world.

Preaching from the garden of Eden to the garden of Gethsemane is a highly ambitious project. This immense amount of biblical material can be surveyed, however, by the citing of historical highlights, concise summaries of biblical books, and key verses. Such a survey is extremely helpful to the congregation. Much of the congregation has studied the Bible only in fragments. A survey such as we are suggesting puts the Old Testament into a perspective that will feed the congregation forevermore to a deeper understanding of the Old Testament. How does this survey work? Consider these suggestions:

Text: Gen. 2:8; Matt. 26:36
E.T.T.: God patiently worked out His plan of salvation.
T.T.: God's plan of salvation continues in effect for us today.
Title: "The Sovereignty of God from Eden to Gethsemane"

Begin the sermon by reading Genesis 2:8. Indicate that by Genesis 3, Eve and Adam had already sinned. Cite the fact that God can have no fellowship with sin, and therefore the garden of Eden was abolished. God continued to deal in judgment with sin. In Genesis 4 God emphasized that blood is precious and the shedding of blood always grieves Him. God dealt with sin by flooding the world, by confusing the language of the people, and by choosing to reveal His grace through Abraham and his ancestry. This ancestry can be briefly traced to the point that the Israelites settle in the land of Goshen.

Exodus 1:8 is a historical turning point. The contents of the Book of Exodus can be summarized by a quick review of chapters

3, 12, and 20. Leviticus can be summarized by citing 19:18b. Numbers can be summarized by a review of the faithlessness of the people. Deuteronomy contains three sermons by Moses that urge the people to obey God and be blessed, with the warning that to disobey God is to be cursed. The key idea of Joshua is the conquest of the land. Key verses include 1:6-9 and 23:6-8. Because the children of Israel did not obey 23:8, the time of the Judges is a dark age in the history of Israel. Judges 3 and especially Judges 19–20 show how low humanity can go when humanity rejects God's standards of morality. Judges 21:25 is a key verse for understanding the times of the Judges.

Samuel was the last judge. First Samuel 8:7 is a key verse for understanding why God permitted a monarchy in Israel. Saul was a weak king, but David was a man after God's own heart (1 Sam. 13:14). David was a military king. David shed much blood and because of this God would not let David build His temple (1 Chron. 22:8). David's son, Solomon, reigned during the Golden Era of Israel, a time of peace and prosperity. However, wise Solomon made a foolish mistake and worshiped idols (1 Kings 11:3). When Solomon died, the kingdom was divided (1 Kings 11:41f.).

God sent prophets to redeem His people. Hosea and Amos were sent to the Northern Kingdom (Israel). Their prophecies were rejected, and in 722 B.C. God sent the Assyrian empire to conquer and exile the Northern Kingdom and to subjugate the Southern Kingdom (Judah). God sent Isaiah, Micah, and Jeremiah as prophets to Judah. Again the prophets were rejected. Again God sent His judgment in the form of the Babylonian Empire. In 586 B.C. Jerusalem was destroyed and the inhabitants exiled to Babylon.

Daniel and Ezekiel were God's prophets during the exile. The Persian Empire conquered the Babylonian Empire. God used the Persian king to begin the restoration of Jerusalem (2 Chron. 36:22-23). Ezra and Nehemiah were the spiritual and physical rebuilders. Haggai later urged the people to commit themselves to finishing the temple. Malachi brought six indictments of the people from God. Then God called no more prophets for more than 400 years until John the Baptist.

Jesus then lived His sinless life, conquering both sin and death. In the garden of Gethsemane, Jesus reversed the sin of Eden by praying, "Not my will, but your will be done," and God's patient plan of salvation was culminated.

A sermonic survey of the Old Testament allows many opportunities for specific applications along the way. Application can be made regarding sin in Genesis; obedience to God in any of the books; the judgment of God, especially from the prophets. Since the story ends with Jesus, an evangelistic invitation is highly appropriate. In preparing a survey sermon, the preacher can choose historical highlights, key verses, and pertinent applications for a particular congregation at a particular time. Survey sermons allow for flexibility in content without departing from the main theme of the sovereignty of God.

A homiletical overview of the Old Testament could be the pilot sermon for a series on the Old Testament books. One book of the Old Testament could be preached every Sunday. In some instances, the minor prophets for example, more than one book could be covered in the Sunday services. Since the books of Kings and Chronicles overlap, they could be preached in less than four Sundays. Psalms and Proverbs perhaps could be more effectively shared on Wednesday nights during Bible study. Each book could be preached in the same way that the Old Testament was surveyed: historical highlights, key verses, and pertinent applications. For example, Genesis 1–11 could be preached in the morning service. Genesis 1:1 would be an appropriate text. The sovereignty of God as Creator and as Lord of His people could be emphasized. There will be a little more time to accentuate humanity's rebellion in Genesis 3; God's agony on the shedding of blood (Gen. 4:10); the story of Noah; the story of Babel. The evening service could cover Genesis 12–50. A focal point could be God's covenant with Abram (Gen. 15) and the history of Abram's offspring could be summarized. Application could be made on our covenant with God through His Son Jesus, (parallel with Gen. 15:6).

The next Sunday, the Book of Exodus could be preached. The morning service would cover chapters 1–11. Particular attention could be paid to 1:8, the historical turning point, and on 3:13-14 where God identifies Himself as a verb. Egypt had plenty of *noun* gods—god of the sun, god of the moon, god of the river, god of the heavens—but Israel has a *verb* God. God's name Yahweh is taken from the verb "to be" (*hayah*). God is a living being, active in history. Neither Egypt's gods, nor any god can be active, because they are not living. Yahweh is an active verb, describing only the living God. The Sunday evening service could focus on Exodus 12 and 20.

Each book will present a unique challenge to the preacher. No two books are likely to be divided or preached in the same way. The Book of Ruth, for instance, is a story written in a circle. Note the progression of events: Naomi has no husband, no family, no food, no country. Ruth decides to stay with Naomi and to become a worshiper of the living God. Naomi and Ruth travel to Bethlehem where Ruth finds food, a husband, a family, and a country, and much more.

The preacher may also decide to preach a series of sermons on an individual book of the Old Testament. This is certainly a time tested as well as biblically viable approach. A series of sermons on a book of the Old Testament has the advantage of giving the congregation a grasp of a particular book. Sermons in such a book series usually develop chronologically by dividing the books into texts. The division of a book into texts is facilitated by outlines of biblical books that appear in most study Bibles. These outlines can be subdivided into shorter texts. Remember, each text should be a complete literary unit of thought.

A series of sermons in the Old Testament could be built on specific doctrines or themes as well as on specific books. Beside the sovereignty of God, the Old Testament provides rich preaching material on God's covenants. God covenanted with Adam (Gen. 2:8-9,15-17). God's provisions for Adam and Eve were complete. However, Eve and then Adam rebelled against God and decided to taste the fruit of the tree of the knowledge of good and evil even though God had commanded them not to do so. As a result, Adam and Eve broke God's covenant and suffered because of it. The Noahic covenant (Gen. 6:18-22; 9:12-17) also calls for obedience to God's command. The Abrahamic covenant (Gen. 15) was built on Abram's belief in God (15:6) and promised that a great nation would be built. Abram was to continue his faithful obedience to God. When Abram lacked faith (for example, Abram's siring Ishmael), dire consequences were the result. The Mosaic covenant (Ex. 34:27-28) called for God's blessings on the nation Israel. The nation, in return, was to obey God's commands. This understanding of the covenant serves as the basis for Moses' sermons in Deuteronomy: obey God and be blessed; disobey God and be cursed (Deut. 31:16-18). The Davidic covenant (2 Sam. 7:12-17, esp. v. 16) is the first covenant that gives rise to messianic expectations. Again, when David sinned, the covenant suffered. God's grace, however, sustained the Davidic covenant to its fulfillment in the birth of Jesus. The new covenant (Jer. 31:31-34) would be a wonderful way to conclude a series of sermons on God's covenants with His people. As an example of a sermon on one of God's covenants, let us look at Genesis 2:8-9,15-17; 3:1-24:

E.T.T.: God blessed His creation so long as they obeyed His covenant.

T.T.: God blesses us, but expects us to obey His covenant.

Title: "The Blessing of God's Gracious Covenant"

Intro: Years ago, almost every Baptist church prominently displayed a church covenant. Sometimes the covenant was printed in large letters, framed and hung on a wall where everyone who attended the church could read it. At other times the covenant was posted on the inside cover of the *Baptist Hymnal*. Congregational readings of the covenant or portions of it were almost as much a part of the worship service as were responsive readings. New members of Baptist churches often were given an opportunity to read the covenant and then to indicate that they would or would not support all or parts of the church covenant. The church covenant served a similar purpose to our Baptist Faith and Message statement. That is, the covenant was not a test of one's salvation, but was a statement of generally agreed principles for the Christian life.

The idea for a church covenant came from the Bible itself. God established covenants with His people. Covenants are similar to contracts. For us, contracts are legal documents. When we sign a contract, we agree to abide by its conditions. A covenant is a contract dictated by God. We can agree or disagree to the conditions of God's covenant, but we cannot negotiate them. God dictates the conditions of His covenant for our good. If we agree with God's covenant, we shall be blessed; if we disagree, we shall be judged.

God's first covenant was established with Adam. Note the blessings of God's covenant are for our good (Gen. 2:8-9,15-16), the conditions of God's covenant involves obedience (v. 17), and the consequences of breaking God's covenant is the loss of fellowship with God (ch. 3).

The conclusion of the sermon would be an excellent time to share how God has restored fellowship with humanity through Jesus, His Son and our Savior.

Other sermon series possibilities include: the revivals of the Old Testament, or key experiences in the life of Israel in which the people recommitted themselves to serving God (Josh. 24:14-25; 1 Kings 18; 2 Chron. 34:14-33; and Neh. 8:1-12 among others are key passages for preaching on various times of renewal in Israel). For messianic passages in the Old Testament see, for instance, Isaiah 7; 9; Psalm 22.

To preach a survey or a series of sermons effectively, the preacher should observe these additional guidelines:

(1) Make a list of the absolutely essential verses, events, persons, and doctrines that must be included in the survey;

(2) From this list, find a unifying theme (such as the sovereignty of God) that will bring cohesiveness to the survey or series;

(3) Make each sermon in the series a sermon unto itself; and

(4) Do not preach everything you know about every text. Stick with the absolutely essential verses, events, persons, and doctrines.

Biographical sermons on various Old Testament characters are another wonderful way to combine biblical preaching and human interest. A word of warning is appropriate here. Any sermon built on a Bible character most often will be less than a direct biblical sermon. The Bible rarely provides a full character study. Isaac, Jacob, Esau, and Jacob's sons and daughter, Moses, and Samuel are among the few whom we meet in the Old Testament at their birth. Abraham is introduced to us as a mature adult. We first meet David when he is in his adolescence. The prophets are presented after they are established spokesmen for God. This lack of full characterization should not discourage us from preaching sermons on Bible characters. Our task is to use accurately the material that is available in preparing our sermons on Bible characters. For example we know little of Gideon, but a sermon (or a sermon series) on Gideon based on Judges 6:11f. can be built around the theme of knowing and proving the will of God. A particular sermon on Gideon might be developed like this:

Subject: Gideon
Title: Proving the will of God
    I. By living in fellowship with God (Judg. 6:34).
    II. By praying to know God's will (Judg. 6:36-39).
    III. By waiting upon God to reveal His will (Judg. 6:36-40).

The Book of Hosea, for example, cries out to be preached biographically. The book has two major sections: chapters 1–3 are autobiographical; chapters 4–13 are a collection of sermons by Hosea. The combination of autobiography and preaching in Hosea gives us a rare glimpse of what forgiveness looks like from God's point of view. Hosea compared the heartbreak of his wife's physical adultery to the grief of God for the spiritual adultery of Israel. The sermon can be developed by telling

Hosea's story as a story rather than dividing the story into outline points.

Text: Hosea 3

E.T.T.: God stood ready to forgive Israel of their spiritual adultery.

T.T.: God stands ready to forgive us of our spiritual adulteries.

Title: "How to Heal God's Broken Heart"

Intro: About 800 years before Christ was born, an elderly man felt the inspiration of God to tell the story of his special ministry. Hosea's life moved from the bright hope of youth, to the dregs of unrequited love, to the burdens of forgiveness, and finally to a lifetime of preaching of how God turns the tragedy of sin into the victory of redemptive forgiveness.

Body: Hosea married an adulteress (3:1). The joy of his special love for Gomer was smashed by her turning to Assyrian religious fertility cults. Hosea's wife essentially became a temple prostitute. There is no doubting Hosea's heartbreak. The deeper the love, the deeper the hurt. The deeper the hurt, the heavier the burden. The heavier the burden, the more costly the forgiveness.

A time came when Gomer was no longer desired by other men. The consequence for Gomer was to be sold into slavery. The young girl who was once the flower of Hosea's heart, is now a woman who has literally been all used up.

Hosea heard of Gomer's fate, and for a second time Hosea felt led of God to go and claim Gomer as his wife. The auctioneer must have been stunned by the high price Hosea was willing to pay for Gomer (3:2). When the purchase was finalized, Hosea put his arm around Gomer's waist and said, "It's all over now, honey. Let's go home." (3:3).

Hosea then preached from this experience. Just as Hosea forgave and forgot the physical adultery of Gomer, he proclaimed that God would forgive Israel for spiritual adultery if only Israel would repent.

Conclusion: Gomer on the slave-block is representative of all of us. We were the slaves of sin. God did not pay silver and barley for our redemption. God paid the precious blood of Jesus to redeem us. When we were ransomed from our sin, God forgave and forgot our sin and welcomed us back as His child again.

To preach a biographical sermon effectively, the preacher should observe these additional guidelines:

(1) Study the historical/cultural background of the text thoroughly. Biblical encyclopedias and dictionaries will be of help; and

(2) Do not sanctify or assassinate the biblical character. The Old Testament is straightforward with its compliments as well as its complaints about specific biblical characters. Be thou likewise.

Preaching from an individual biblical text goes back at least as far as Nehemiah 8:8: "They read from the Book of the Law of God, making it clear and giving the meaning so that the people could understand what was being read." (NIV). We do not know exactly how this understanding of the reading was accomplished. Possibly, a verse-by-verse exposition was used. Possibly, key ideas were elaborated. Possibly (but unlikely), the text was divided into sections and the preaching of each section began with what we have come to call "points" of the sermon. However the "understanding of the reading" was achieved then, we suggest now that the form of the text should strongly influence the form of the sermon. We will look now at a few specific texts to see how this might be achieved now.

Text: Genesis 22:1-14

E.T.T.: Abraham faithfully demonstrated his full trust in God's will.

T.T.: God is worthy of our faithful trust in His will.

Title: "Faith Never Fails"

Intro: (This sermon is best developed by retelling and applying the story.) For Abraham, each test of faith had helped him grow in his understanding. This final testing of Abraham's faith was the most difficult by far. How could God possibly ask Abraham to sacrifice Isaac. That Isaac was alive was a miracle. That Isaac was the son of God's promise was a fact.

Body: (Recreate the story from Gen 22:1-14, then make application).

Conclusion: The Bible is full of testimony to the fact that only in the painful, agonizing struggles of life do we grow in grace. Every Christian's struggle carries God's timetable for victory. Every God-given victory provides the strength and confidence to face life with new determination and confidence. Every God-given victory re-teaches us that faith never fails.

To preach a story sermon effectively, the preacher should observe these additional guidelines:

(1) Be thoroughly familiar with the historical context of a text. A biblical atlas, encyclopedia, a critical commentary, or a technical study of Hebrew history is vital. Without these resources, the preacher will impose subjective interpretations into the historical context and the text;

(2) Avoid overuse of words. A story must move. The preacher must mentally envision the events of the text. The hearers must mentally envision the events. This mental imagery cannot be achieved if the story is drowned in words; and

(3) Always relate the story to a significant biblical doctrine. In this case we have related the story to the veracity of faith.

An exposition of the text is another way to preach in the present tense. The expository sermon usually moves verse-by-verse, and sometimes virtually word-by-word through the text. An expository sermon on Psalm 23 can help us come alive to the Old Testament.

Text: Psalm 23
E.T.T.: Like a good shepherd, God lovingly cares for His children.
T.T.: God lovingly cares for His children.
Title: "The Heavenly Shepherd"
Intro: Psalm 23, like John 3:16 of the New Testament, is the best known passage in the Old Testament. The message of Psalm 23 is timeless and universal in its appeal. The message of Psalm 23 applies to the residents of large cities as much as it does to people who work in the fields. Psalm 23 is a love sonnet from God to His cherished children.

Body: Verse 1 "The Lord" is the name above every name. "The Lord" is the great "I Am that I Am" of Exodus 3:14. "Is my shepherd" personalizes the psalm for each of us. "I shall not be in want" (NIV) is literally, "I shall have no lack," and summarizes the entire psalm. Every other verse of this psalm will expand the thought, "I shall have no lack."

Verse 2 "He makes me lie down in green pastures" (NIV) signals an abundance of food. "He leads me beside quiet waters" (NIV) signals a safe abundant supply of another of the basic necessities of life. Verse 2 is a predecessor of Revelation 22:1-2 which symbolically describes the provisions of heaven.

To preach an expository sermon effectively, the preacher should observe these additional guidelines:

(1) Find and stay with the main theme of the text. Using the E.T.T. approach is vital here; and

(2) Steep yourself in the language of the text to catch the nuances of meaning. Word study books are especially helpful.

Notice also the expository approach in the following outlines:

Text: 1 Chronicles 21:22
Title: "The Altar of the Awakened Conscience"[2]

I. It was an altar prompted by a sense of divine goodness. ("Give me . . . this threshing floor")
II. It was an altar built to meet the rights of God. ("An Altar unto the Lord")
III. It was an altar that called for self-sacrifice. ("Grant it to me for full price")
IV. It was an altar that was to bestow a blessing. ("that the plague may be stopped")

Text: Isaiah 6:2, NIV
Title: "Life at Its Best"[3]

I. The first mark of life at its best is the spirit of reverence. ("With two wings they covered their faces")
II. The second mark of life at its best is the spirit of humility. ("With two they covered their feet")
III. The third mark of life at its best is the spirit of service. ("With two they were flying")

Finally, consider an expository homily:

Text: Psalm 119:11, NIV
Title: "The Blessing of God's Word"

I. "Your Word"
II. "I have hidden in my heart"
III. "That I might not sin against you."

How do we make the Old Testament come alive in our preaching? *We* do not. The Old Testament is already alive! To make our preaching, ourselves, and our congregations come alive to the Old Testament, we need to follow the same, basic procedures that we use when preaching from any text:

(1) Let the text dictate the development of the sermon. Whether the text is narrative, poetry, wisdom, or prophecy, each genre of literature will have its own specific requirements for interpretation. Once the passage has been interpreted, we will have all the guidelines we need for sermon preparation;

(2) Whichever sermon form is used, be certain that a textual basis exists for each point, or each movement or division of the sermon; and

(3) Apply the text to a specific contemporary congregation, using the best communicative principles available.

Notes

1. This interpretative task calls for the preacher to study the background of the book of the Bible from which the text is taken. Background study includes

RECLAIMING THE PROPHETIC MANTLE

(for example) information pertaining to the purpose, date, authorship of the book. The interpretative task also calls for the preacher prayerfully to read the text several times, calling all the while for the Holy Spirit to guide the interpretation process. Finally, the interpretative task calls for the preacher to do an exegetical study of the passage which incorporates historical, linguistic, grammatical and lexical studies. This study is done from the Bible itself as well as from commentaries, dictionaries, encyclopedias, and word study books.

2. E. T. Evans, *The Vision of Victory.* Quoted by Ian MacPherson in *Sermon Outlines from Sermon Masters: Old Testament* (Nashville: Abingdon, 1962), 92-93.

3. Hugh T. Kerr, *The Highway of Life.* Quoted by MacPherson, *Sermon Outlines from Sermon Masters: Old Testament* (Nashville: Abingdon, 1962), 165.

11

Changing the Church with Words from God:
Applying the Old Testament

C. Richard Wells

Introduction

The history of Christendom confirms Ruth Tucker's paradoxical remark about "the benefit of cults."[1] Recurring threats to orthodoxy, both ancient and modern, have forced Christians to refine, to clarify, to reevaluate; in short, to grapple with both the affirmations and the implications of orthodoxy and faith in the real world.

Nothing illustrates this fact better than the Marcionite heresy of the second century. Marcion grew up in Pontus, but made his way to Rome about A.D. 140. His acceptance by the church in Rome quickly evaporated, however, when it became known that he held views about the Old Testament (or, more precisely, the God of the Old Testament) wildly at variance with orthodox faith. In brief, Marcion regarded the God of the Old Testament as a subordinate, inferior *god*—a demiirge—who created and ruled the material world, but who lacked the qualities of love and grace which characterized the God of the New Testament.[2]

The Marcionite heresy waned over the course of two centuries, eventually dying out altogether, but the threat coming when and how it did, forced the church to respond. Most notably, the church responded by stating its "position regarding the canon [of scripture] more clearly."[3]

This action was essential because Marcion had produced his own "canon" which, predictably, omitted the entire Old Testament and the "Jewish" portions of the New Testament as well. Tertullian, Irenaeus, and the church as a whole quite properly repudiated Marcion's teaching and his canon. They thereby affirmed not only the legitimacy of the Old Testament but the unity of the whole Bible. We should remember, however, that Marcion's views sprang from what seemed to him an obvious disparity between the testaments. More than that, Marcion seems to have rejected the allegorical method of interpretation by which (it should be noted) some early writers tried, most inappropriately, to "Christianize" the Old Testament.[4] Simply stated, Marcion was a heretic; but, like many heresies, his was tinged with a certain reasonableness. Marcion thrust upon the early church a challenge that seems to resist every attempt at resolution, to connect the Old Testament meaningfully with New Testament faith. The Old Testament belongs to New Testament faith, but *how* it belongs is not so easy to decide. Not surprisingly, the problem we meet in this essay is Marcion's ancient threat revisited on those who strive both for relevance and for accuracy: How can we preach the Old Testament so as to contribute meaningfully to the life and ministry of the (New Testament) church without violating the integrity of the Old Testament itself?

The Problem of the Old Testament for New Testament Preaching

The problematic character of the Old Testament for those who affirm the "new" covenant of Christian faith stands in stark contrast to the robust affirmation of the Old Testament by the earliest believers. Following the Lord Himself (Matt. 5:17-18), these believers regarded the Old Testament as authoritative Scripture, the veritable Word of God.[5] At the same time, of course, they reflected the heritage of Judaism they had gained in the synagogue. Only as the New Testament canon began to take shape did the Old Testament become problematic. Even so, the *authority* of the Old Testament was never at issue, only its *applicability*.

Modern biblical scholarship, however, gives the contemporary church reason to question both authority and applicability. Any discussion, therefore, of the Old Testament as a "problem" for

New Testament faith must grapple on the one hand with the pre-suppositional question of authority and, on the other hand, with the more pragmatic question of applicability.

The Problem of Authority

We might well be tempted to dispense with the problem of authority as a simple matter of affirming or denying that the Old Testament is the "Word of God." Alas, the matter is not so simple. In the first place, "authority" admits of several inter-pretations. Moreover, the question of authority conceals a number of related questions about the use of critical methods. "Authority" is not merely a philosophical issue which, once de-cided, provides the foundation for all subsequent work. Author-ity is also what we might call "contextual," or "paradigmatic"; that is, authority forms part of the personal and cultural equipment which preachers bring to the Old Testament. We shall examine both of these qualifications.

The meaning of "authority."—Virtually all evangelicals would agree that the Bible in general and the Old Testament in particular, are "authoritative." But in what sense? The most straightforward sense is that the Bible possesses authority *in-trinsically* because it has God for its author. The history of canonization reminds us that both Jewish and Christian commu-nities considered a document authoritative only upon evidence that it sprang "from God."[6] Yet this plain sense of authority leaves untouched two vital issues. First, in what sense does au-thority extend to all of Scripture? Second, what exactly does authority imply?

As to the first of these issues, evangelicals increasingly dis-tinguish between soteriological and "matters of fact" authority. Charles Talbert, for example, argues for the superiority of what he calls a "developing human personality" model over compet-ing models of biblical authority: (1) The "Platonic," which "seems to lie behind most conservative thought about the Bible," and views the Bible as "a compendium of unchanging dogma, as a timeless ethical system, or as an unalterable pat-tern of church polity"; (2) The "evolutionary," which relegates older material to non-normative status in favor of "later devel-opments"; and (3) The "Heideggerian *Dasein*" model which lim-its authority to a small "kerygmatic" kernel. By contrast, the "personality" model integrates the "developing awareness of childhood" (Old Testament) and responsible "adult life" (New Testament) around the "adult value decisions that constitute the self's personal center (Jesus)."[7] For Talbert, therefore, the

Bible serves as "a recognized specialist in Christian life and faith."[8] Misstatements about "matters of fact" do nothing to obviate its role, which is to guide persons to Christ.

Historical-critical methods which cast aspersion on certain portions of the Bible illustrate the problem of extensiveness even more explicitly. Thomas Oden, for example, has written of a higher-critical "decanonization" of the Pastorals and most General Epistles, producing "systematic neglect" of this material in the churches.[9] Clearly, questions of the extent of biblical authority affect our use of the Old Testament more than of the New Testament.

Whether we chart the extent of authority in theological terms (salvific vs. "matter of fact") or in critical terms (authentic vs. inauthentic), we are left as preachers of the Old Testament with the same basic dilemma: "In what sense is the Old Testament authoritative?" The question proves much easier to ask than to answer; however, an article by O. M. T. O'Donovan helps bring it into focus.

According to O'Donovan,[10] "authority" is a question of *right*, that is, the "right to command belief and/or action."[11] Biblical authority, then, may be said to depend on divine origin. Without such legitimacy, any talk of authority is vacuous. But "claims" are another matter. Claims specify a command, an injunction, a prohibition, or a task. They do not ask whether a person or a document has a legitimate right to demand and expect obedience, but whether a person or document does, in fact, demand and expect obedience from me, now.

Preachers of the Old Testament, then, encounter the authority issue in two ways. First, does the Old Testament possess authority? If we answer "yes" on the ground of divine origin we establish at least the possibility for preaching the Old Testament. If the God of the New Testament is also the God of the Old, we have reason to expect some continuity between the testaments which we can comprehend and communicate. Second, does the Old Testament make claims on us? Surely it does; and, if it does, surely we can discover principles by which to discern its normative elements.

Authority and biblical criticism.—Let us return for a moment to the problems posed for biblical authority by modern criticism. "What happens," asks Elizabeth Achtemeier, "when the community-forming word of the Bible is approached, no longer as the word of God . . . but solely as a historical document from the past to be studied by scientific, rational methods?"[12] What happens, she replies, is a multiform emptying of the Bible's power. The Bible becomes the exclusive province of the critically trained scholar. The truth of the Bible comes to be linked with some attestable shred of history (past or present). The Bible is divided into ever-smaller pieces separate from the whole. The average preacher finds himself intimidated by the "growing array of scholarly sciences." Again, the net result is a Bible stripped of its power,[13] a loss that is felt in two different ways.

On the one hand, biblical criticism has so fragmented our knowledge of the Old Testament that we no longer retain a sense of its place in the sweep of revelation and redemption. The result is a failure to appreciate the Old Testament as the setting for the New—as formulation of the cosmology presupposed in the New, or as the "gospel God promised beforehand" (Rom. 1:2). The Old Testament thus suffers at the hand of proof texters or special interest groups; or, is ignored altogether: "The Old Testament is largely a lost book in many parts of the American church."[14]

On the other hand, methodological skepticism in Old Testament scholarship has encouraged doubt in Old Testament preaching. Writing in the "Guides to Biblical Scholarship" Series, Maxwell Miller concluded that:

> The historian of Old Testament times is constantly engaged in a "lover's quarrel" with the ancient written sources. He is dependent upon them and must listen carefully to their testimonies even when they seem to conflict. Yet he *must be ever suspicious* of their claims, and never jump to conclusions without thoroughly analyzing them with the best critical tools available.[15]

This kind of methodological skepticism suggests an operative assumption about the authority of the text itself. Princeton's William Green exposed it a few years after publication of the Wellhausen hypothesis in 1876. "The development of critical hypotheses," he declared is in reality "subordinated to the end of neutralizing the supernatural."[16]

Whatever may be said therefore to the praise of historical study (and there is much to praise), the presuppositional skepticism so characteristic of the discipline has tended over the years to create a milieu of doubt which plagues the modern preacher. John Stott has written specifically about its impact on the *ability* of preachers to preach.[17] The problem is especially acute for those who preach the Old Testament. How are preachers to apply "prophecies" (such as Isa. 44:28) claimed to be after the fact? What are they to make of narratives supposed to lack genuine historicity? In short, how can preachers of the Old Testament patch the shreds of biblical material left over from the critic's shears into an authentic and relevant message?

We must, therefore, reclaim the authority of the Old Testament. We must reclaim it as the church's book, as relevant, as applicable, as "living and active" (Heb. 4:12). We must begin with a commitment to the veracity and authority of the Old Testament, then prepare ourselves to proclaim it. We must preach the whole of God's counsel so that God may transform His people.

The Problem of Applicability

The problem of authority is mainly presuppositional and theoretical. The problem of applicability is not. The distinction we drew earlier between "authority" and "claims" can help us sort this out. Applicability involves "claims"; that is, specific injunctions, commands, or tasks the Scriptures enjoin for someone in a given set of circumstances. The problem of applicability concerns the degree to which, and the way in which, such claims are voiced. And it is a problem with which the entire history of interpretation has occupied itself.

The church early and unanimously included the Old Testament in its canon of Scripture. Thus, from its most formative period, the church had to interpret the Old Testament not as a Jewish book, but as a Christian book in the full light of Jesus Christ. At the same time, the church itself did not appear *ex nihilo* or *de novo*. It rather evolved from the world of the Old Testament, expressed in first century Judaism.

For its part, Jewish exegesis followed two principal lines of development, one rabbinical, the other Greek. The rabbis strove to develop the fullest possible application from every strand and segment of the law both for doctrinal (*haggada*) and practical (*halaka*) formulations. The *haggadic* expositions ranged over the whole of the Old Testament, while the *halakic* drew only on the Law. But they held in common an assumption about the text; that, as the Word of God, it insinuated truth in textual details, extending even to numerical values and shapes of letters.[18] The rabbis did not set aside the literal sense of the Old Testament. Indeed, they presupposed it in most instances. They even adduced principles of exegesis still regarded as valid today.[19] The rabbis rather devalued the literal sense, esteeming more highly complicated interpretive processes[20] which supposedly yielded profounder insights at deeper levels of meaning.

The second major stream of hermeneutical influence in Judaism was Greek allegorism. Philo of Alexandria (about 20 B.C.–A.D. 50) represents, or rather embodies, this influence better than any other figure. Philo had imbibed the nectar of Greek Neoplatonic philosophy which predisposed him to value the mystical experience of the Good, which to him as a Jew was God. In the service of that desire, Philo made use of the prevailing Greek hermeneutics, allegorizing, by which the venerable documents were being reclaimed for the modern Greek mind.[21] Thus, through Philo, Greek allegorism entered Judaism, transforming Old Testament interpretation.

When we recall the need of the early church to make the Old Testament its own, to make it "Christian," it should not surprise us to learn that both streams of Jewish interpretation found their way into early Christian exegesis (although allegorism finally won the day). Without denying the historical factuality of the Old Testament accounts, both "letterism" and (especially) allegorism allowed the Old Testament a wider and more explicitly New Testament application than simple grammatical and historical methods seemed to permit. In the words of Bernard Ramm, an "allegorist might find something far richer about Jesus Christ and salvation in Genesis than in Luke."[22] We have already mentioned the possibility that Marcion's heresy arose in part as a repudiation of such inappropriate "Christianizing" efforts. In any event, there is no question that from the time of Origen (A.D. 185-254), himself from Philo's city of Alexandria, the allegorical interpretation of the Old Testament gained a supremacy in the church it retained until the Reformation. Allegorical and rabbinical hermeneutics succeeded because they managed to apply the Old Testament to the life of the church. In the process, however, they sacrificed the grammatical-historical sense of the text.

At first glance, therefore, the problem for us seems straightforward and easily corrected. It turns out to be neither. On the one hand, the distinctions between "application" and "allegorizing" (and the related "spiritualizing") are somewhat blurred. On the other hand, even when we achieve some precision in making the distinctions, we struggle to do legitimate application without recourse to tempting, or easy, alternatives.

Origen himself can help us with the problem of distinctions. Most seminary students learn at some point that Origen differentiated between "the flesh of Scripture" (its literal obvious meaning), the "soul" of Scripture (its moral force), and finally the "spiritual law."[23] The value for edification of these levels corresponded to the maturity of the reader/hearer. For obvious reasons, then, Origen placed the highest value on spiritual exegesis.

We must not accuse Origen of playing fast and loose with Scripture, however. Moises Silva suggests that Origen found himself between a hermeneutical rock and a hard place. Many Greeks whose culture he shared, and whom he attempted to persuade, regarded allegorical interpretation as evidence of divine inspiration. But others regarded the allegorizing of Christian texts as an expedient for avoiding the embarrassment of contradictions. Thus, at times Origen downplayed allegory and emphasized the moral superiority of literal biblical teaching over the spiritualized pagan myths. At other times,[24] he justified the allegorical method with fervor.[25] Beyond that, and more significantly for us, Origen embraced allegorism because he believed that the New Testament itself affirmed such a model. In support, he cited cases of allegorical interpretation in the New Testament (for instance, 1 Cor. 9:9-10; Gal. 4:21-24), as well as indications of approval (for instance, 1 Cor. 10:4; Col. 2:16-17; Heb. 8:5).[26] Nor did Origen detach his allegorical interpretation from the full historicity of the Bible.

Origen seems in fact to have thought better than he practiced. Partly on that account we must be careful to distinguish between allegorical application and allegorizing. What sometimes passes for allegory, on closer inspection, might better be described as a form of application. The thrust of a passage simply receives its full significance by extended comparison. Allegorizing, by contrast, is de-historicized interpretation, connecting elements in a (historical) text, more or less arbitrarily, with "spiritual" elements drawn from other sources than the text.[27]

The problem then becomes how to apply, without recourse to a historical artifice of allegory. By way of an answer, we may summarize that allegorizing commits two basic kinds of errors. First, it distorts in some way the historical content of the text. We include here (especially) any failure to make the theological truth-intention of the passage central to the sermon. Second, it imports elements of the allegory from another source, theology, psychology, even other biblical passages. However, even otherwise legitimate interpretation and application can be guilty of allegorizing if the allegorical elements *bypass prior applications*. What might, under such circumstances, serve as a mechanism for application, collapses when it has no supportive structure. It simply cannot survive too great a distance between the original context of application and the present context.

Consider the following example. Clarence Jordan, well known for his *Cotton Patch Gospel*, preached a sermon on Daniel 3 (the story of Shadrach, Meshach, and Abednego) entitled "The Adventures of Three Students in a Fiery Furnace."[28] In keeping with the "Cotton Patch" motif, the sermon is largely allegorical. The three Hebrews are students from South Georgia. Nebuchadnezzar and his regime stand for the "establishment." The "plain of Dura" (v. 1) is "where the peasants work:" (p. 92), where live the marginalized whose labors make the image possible. The herald is "the Baptist preacher who opened the meeting with an invitation" (p. 92). The "astrologers" (v. 8) are the "ancient 'John Besmirch Society'" (p. 93). The act demanded by Nebuchadnezzar is a "loyalty oath" (p. 94). And the disobedience of the Hebrew youths is "civil disobedience"; their way of saying; "You know, if we've got to take our choice between living in a country where men are slaves or dying in a furnace where men are free, we choose the furnace" (p. 95).

Is this sermon guilty of allegorizing; or has Jordan simply woven his application creatively through the details of the account? We should add that Jordan concluded with explicit propositions drawn from the narrative and here he gives away his hand. He rightly asserts (1) that "God's call to obedience can be heard above the tumult, above the bands, and above the flag-waving," and (2) that "God alone is ultimately the Lord of history, . . . greater than kings and their furnaces" (p. 96). The book is "saying to us," he claims: (1) "that human institutions . . . are capable of gross error," and (2) "that extreme attempts are made to produce that conformity to the error (p. 96)." Without belaboring fine points of exegesis, we can say that Jordan is right on all four counts. However, the first two claims are universal theological propositions which the text *intends*. The other two are *applications* which the text may *support*. By conflating the two, Jordan has produced an allegorized sermon.

As it stands, this sermon gives the impression that God encourages civil disobedience. His political agenda intensifies that impression. Yet even apart from that, Jordan has telescoped the necessary distance between the original and present contexts so as to dissolve the distinction between what E. D. Hirsch called the "meaning" of a text and its "significance."[29]

Could Jordan have made this application differently, using the novel allegorical elements, but without allegorizing? While in most cases the possible confusion of meaning and significance hardly seems worth the risk, one might imagine appropriate settings for such an approach if the preacher covers the distance between meaning and significance before introducing allegorical features for application. For this sermon Jordan might have begun (rather than ended) with the assertion of God's claim to absolute priority in the lives of His people. He might then have moved to Daniel 3 as a classic kind of situation which forces a choice on that claim. He might have observed something of the range and character of such situations implied in this one. Finally, he might tell the story much as he did, weaving the allegorical details through.

This is only a possible approach. There are others. But any of them must guard against the danger of allegorizing.

The Theological Problem

Most evangelicals would agree with Walter Kaiser that historical, grammatical exegesis is the only solid basis for Old Testament interpretation and preaching.[30] Unfortunately, exegetical commitments do not entirely eliminate the eisegetical possibilities, for as Willi Marxsen once observed, "an appeal to the Old or New Testament is meaningless, since I can prove from the Bible whatever I want if I am allowed to choose how I am going to interpret it."[31] While evangelicals maintain that solid exegesis "saves the process of interpretation from the quagmire of cognitive relativism,"[32] they must not suppose that it delivers them from every potential danger.

These dangers are due largely to differing *theological* perspectives, especially dispensational and nondispensational, which complicate application of the Old Testament. Dispensationalists traditionally differentiate between Israel and the church and find different rules of life during the respective epochs of God's work in history. Nondispensationalists, by contrast, see the church as the new Israel and tend to de-emphasize distinctions between law and grace in God's economy. Obviously, the ramifications for carting these systems back into the Old Testament text are enormous.

Robert Saucy may help us here. He contends that: (1) the traditional disagreements between dispensational and nondispensational approaches are being reconciled; (2) the problem is not *a priori* exegetical bias; (3) the only real issue is "God's *purpose* and plan for biblical history"; and (4) most importantly, it is possible to mediate the two positions by recourse to the concept of God's *kingdom*.[33] This last point is decisive for us, for the "kingdom which is the theme of Biblical history is that program through which God effects His Lordship on the earth in a comprehensive salvation within history."[34] In the words of John Bright, "The concept of the kingdom of God involves, in a real sense, the total message of the Bible."[35] If indeed the kingdom concept undergirds the total message of the Bible, we can employ it to apply the Old Testament meaningfully without importing foreign ideas that fail to do the text full justice.[36]

The Limitations of Application

In addition to the methodological prejudices *we* bring to applying the Old Testament, the text presents problems of application in and of itself. In his *Outline of Old Testament Theology*,[37] Th. C. Vriezen explores some of these problems under the rubric of "Limitations" in his discussion of Old Testament ethics. Vriezen suggests that five "unfilled elements" hamper contemporary efforts to apply Old Testament ethical emphases and specifics.

First, the "Old Testament is *historically limited*" (p. 398), in that certain practices in the Old Testament "reflect the life and ideas of the time when it came into being" even though "it bears witness to the living revelation of God" (p. 398). Vriezen cites as instances polygamy and slavery, practices allowed and regulated despite the dissonance created for them by such theological ideas as the institution of marriage (Gen. 2) and the image of God (Gen. 1, 9). How can preachers of the Old Testament apply such historically limited materials? One answer is suggested by the methodology of Jesus Himself in handling the issue of divorce. Moses permitted the practice, Jesus declared, "because your hearts were hard. But it was not this way from the beginning" (Matt. 19:8). Jesus appealed, in other words, to a theological principle governing non-normative elements. On this reading, the application of non-normative elements takes its cue from the governing principle.

Second, according to Vriezen, "there are *national* limitations," in that a preponderance of regulatory material concerns Israel, not the nations (p. 399). At times, he writes, Israel even *appeared* to lag behind other nations in idealism; but, in truth she simply reflected the integration of religion and ethics that characterized her life so (p. 401).

These first two "limitations" will often fuse, if not in every sermon, at least in the exegetical framework which enables us to apply many Old Testament passages. A sermon on Leviticus 25:35-55, for example, might stress that slavery regulation: (1) brings the doctrine of *Imago Dei* to bear on the real world (by demanding humaneness); (2) distinguishes God's covenant people in His redemptive purpose (with differential regulations for Israelites and non-Israelites); and (3) consequently, points to the ultimate restoration of human identity in Christ.

Third, according to Vriezen, the commands of the Old Testament lend themselves to legalism, by the nature of law (pp. 402-3). We are reminded, however, not only that law-keeping does not constitute the way of salvation, but that the gospel, even when preaching the Torah, forms the center of preaching. As Lewis Smedes observes, the "commands" which form the core of the Law (the Decalogue), *are the way of life in Christ* in that they imply both justice and love.[38]

Fourth, because law regulated *acts*, it invited casuistry rather than spiritual religion (p. 403). A dictionary definition of "casuistry" is simply the application of the general rules and principles of religion and morality to specific case instances. Most definitions would also include a pejorative note, however, implying either misuse of the principles, or over-regulation of behavior, or both.[39]

Finally, the Old Testament bears some evidence of *eudaemonism*, especially in Wisdom (pp. 403-4).[40] "Eudaemonism" is belief in material reward for right religion, or, in well-being for well-doing. But as H. H. Rowley pointed out years ago, Israel never divorced the "good life" (*eudaimonia*)—from "harmony with God's will," "communion with God," or "worship and praise."[41]

These final three limitations, like the first two, often fuse in preaching, in this case by "moralizing." "Moralizing" means that the central or exclusive focus of a sermon is a behavior, an attitude, or a psychological state—a "moral."[42] Because such preaching lends itself to contemporary categories, language, and experience, it can seize control of the preacher's preoccupation with relevance.

Moralizing, however, is not application. Leander Keck calls it a "deadly" practice and argues that it distorts authentic biblical preaching in at least four ways. First it "transforms the Bible into an assortment of moral precepts." Second, it "idealizes the past," as if, for example, every act of every early Christian (or prophet, or "good" king) were praiseworthy. Moralizing also obscures "the proper relation of law and gospel." Finally, "moralizing assumes that the fundamental task of the sermon is to tell people what to do."[43] This particular temptation has such power that it deserves a more careful analysis.

Study the following example: Job 19:28 records Job's account of the accusation against him that "the root of the trouble lies in him" (NIV). One preacher creates out of that text a sermon thesis we might state as follows: "True humanness ('human-hood') depends on directing myself ('the forces of the ego') toward the ideal of the common good."[44] This sermon rests on faulty exegesis. It completely ignores the context of judgment which governs the passage. Job is warning those who accuse him of fault that judgment is imminent for them (v. 29). Aside from that *faux pas*, however, the sermon moralizes. Its central, indeed exclusive, concern is psychological commitment to a moral ideal. The preacher rightly rejects the escapism of Freudian psychology. We cannot evade responsibility for ourselves by retreat to the unconscious. But in doing so, he has simply substituted one psychological system for another; and worst of all, he has made the text a servant of that system.

Consider another example. A sermon drawn on Psalm 137 extols the value of actualizing legitimate anger against identifiable wrongs, in this case, war.[45] Again, there is faulty exegesis. The author does not express anger over the fact of war. Rather, he expresses his anger with a wish for war! Aside from that, however, the sermon moralizes. The issue for the psalmist is neither a psychological state (anger), nor a problem in ethics (war). It is rather zeal for God (compare "songs of the Lord"), "longing for the revelation of divine righteousness."[46] Doubtless, Psalm 137, like many others, models a way of handling anger. But Psalm 137 is not intended in the first place to help persons handle anger. It is intended to highlight the eternal purposes of God through Israel—purposes which the exile tempted His people to forget (compare v. 5).

Consider one final example. In Jonah 4:3, the distraught prophet prays for death (also 4:8). A death wish is surely fertile ground for sermons on suicide or psychological disorder—the causes and prevention of same. Such sermons, however, are misguided. Even if a sermon stressed that Jonah's lament grew out of his failure to grasp the character of God's grace, it would amount to moralizing and thus would fail.[47] The concern of the text is not with suicide, or even suicide resulting from despair, in turn resulting from misappropriation of God's grace. The concern is with God's grace! A thesis such as "despair results from failure to understand God's grace" is thus essentially moralistic. Its primary thrust is human despair, which, while a legitimate concern, even in preaching, transforms "the theocentric focus of the Bible" into an anthropocentric lesson.[48] A better homiletic approach might look something like "God's grace overturns human values."

What we are saying here is that while application may, within the body of a sermon, suggest moral, psychological, or behavior principles, the thrust of the sermon must be "God's cause and work in the world and in history."[49] Anything less fails as preaching however well it may succeed as ethics. Indeed, we must draw the lines more finely still. We must distinguish not only between moralizing and application, but between ethics and application (and, by extension between ethics and moralizing). We shall turn to these latter distinctions a bit later.

The Nature of the Old Testament and New Testament Preaching

The Provost at Samford University, William Hull, some years ago wrote that the "use of the Bible must be determined by the nature of the Bible."[50] Thus, we come to the very heart of our discussion. If the use of the Old Testament depends on its nature, then we are forced to deal with two questions. First, what is this *use* (preaching) to which we are putting the Old Testament? Second, what is the Old Testament?

The Nature of Preaching

As to the first of these questions we follow Sidney Greidanus who defines preaching simply as explication and application integrated in such a way that the "whole sermon comes across a relevant communication."[51] But that duality is easily lost, especially in preaching the Old Testament, and the loss is almost always in favor of explication. Yet without application there is no real preaching, for, as Broadus said long ago, "Application . . . is the main thing to be done."[52] It is also the most difficult thing to be done. It drives us from the comfortable armchair of theory into a noisy street of practice. It threatens our own sense of security; or, because it also threatens others, it may find its way back to us through less-than-enthusiastic response. As if all of this were not sufficient to immobilize us, application is just plain hard work.[53]

Our assignment here does not include a full-scale analysis of application in preaching. For that the reader should consult the literature, which is adequate though hardly impressive.[54] Our task is rather to describe the peculiarities of applying the Old Testament in the life of the church and to suggest methods for dealing with them. Still, we must be certain we have a clear sense of what it means to "apply."

John Broadus' classic formula of application distinguished between: "(1) application proper, in which we show the hearer how the truths of the sermon apply to him; (2) practical suggestions as to the best mode and means of performing the duty urged; and (3) persuasion in the sense of moral and spiritual appeal for right response." The first of these tasks involved "focalizing the claims of truth," showing "what practical demands [the subject] makes upon the persons addressed."[55]

Application is simply discovering the theological teaching of a passage and "setting it to use" in a contemporary setting. Thus, application differs from a number of related, but not equivalent activities. It is not illustration, for example, because illustration is merely a helpful (but not essential) medium for doing application. It is not relevance because relevance only takes into account the intelligibility of the subject matter or the degree to which it interests the hearers. "Relevance" suggests that a sermon topic will strike a chord with the audience. "Application" (or applicability) denotes the specific way that topic will or should impact the lives people are living.

Nor is application restatement of a theological truth in contemporary language. We might determine, for example, that the theological teaching of Jonah's experience with the vine (Jonah 4:9-11) is something akin to: "A proper understanding of God's grace is essential to missionary outreach." We might rephrase that truth something like this: "We cannot reach our world until we see it the way God sees it." Application has not yet occurred. It cannot occur until the hearers are led to grasp the implications of that truth for their lives and are called to respond to it in some way: "that means you no longer dismiss your next-door neighbors as pleasure-loving pagans but as . . . " or "What can you do to change your way of thinking about them?"

What Broadus describes as application comes very close to moralizing and certainly could support moralizing if it were misused. Greidanus helps us to avoid that error by suggesting four stages in the development of meaningful application. First, "concentrate on the original message" (p. 166). This spares preachers of the Old Testament the embarrassment of founding assertions on textual elements that are only semantically related (for instance, Joseph's pit as a "pit of despair").

Second, "recognize the discontinuity" (pp. 167-69), that is, the kinds of changes over time which affect the interpretation of a text. Preachers of the Old Testament should pay close attention to such changes, since they are so pronounced as one moves from the Old Testament to the New. Greidanus lists three kinds of change: (1) Progressive revelation (compare the law of the sabbath in Ex. 20:8-11 and Rom. 14:5); (2) Stages of kingdom history (compare Israel in Egypt and Christ in Gethsemane); and (3) Cultural changes (as in the "signet ring" of Hag. 2:23).

Third, Greidanus encourages preachers to "recognize the overarching continuity" (pp. 169-73), the continuity inherent in the "one faithful God" and in the "one covenant people." Finally, and significantly, Greidanus urges preachers to "focus on the goal of the text" (pp. 173-75).

Douglas Stuart of Gordon-Conwell, from whom Greidanus borrows at this point, considers this last step foundational in the delicate and critical process of application. He calls it "comparing life issues."[56] In order to apply a passage the exegete must "try to decide what its central issues are and what issues in it are only secondary." Then the exegete "must decide how such issues are or are not still active in the lives of persons or groups today. What do 'I' or 'we' encounter today that is similar or at least closely related to what the passage deals with?"[57]

To see how these principles might operate, consider a sermon from Leviticus 11:1-46, a catalog of clean and unclean animals. The intent of the passage is to prescribe for Israel what they may and may not consume as the people of God. Not only does that text itself affirm this intention (v. 45), the New Testament writers confirm it when, for example, Peter accepts his mission to Gentiles on the basis of a vision abrogating this ancient law (Acts 10:13; compare Acts 15:12-19). Thus the original message concerns the Israelites' identity as the people of God.

Discontinuity arises at several levels in the passage. In terms of progressive revelation, its commands are, as we have observed, superseded. At the cultural level, a number of scientific points could be made. For example, in precise scientific terms, the camel might be said to "have a split hoof."[58] Likewise, the rabbit does not actually ruminate ("chews the cud," v. 6), but only appears to do so. Thus, we encounter the familiar "discontinuity" created by popular versus technical language. Another scientific point can be made, however, about the basis for classifying the animals in the first place. Our own familiarity with modern hygienic practice might lead us to assume that health was the criterion. It is certainly possible, of course, that God took account of such realities here; but, (and this is important) we are not informed that He did so.[59] We must therefore resist the temptation to read modern notions of health back into the text.

The *continuity* between the passage and ourselves draws on the "people of God" motif, as well as the "one faithful God" motif. The whole set of commands rests upon a pervasive Old Testament and New Testament ascription that God is holy and, therefore, calls His people to holiness (compare 1 Pet. 1:15-16).

What, then, are the life issues in this passage? Clearly, one must be food, and its relation to a consecrated (that is, "holy") life-style. "Comparable" issues might include any of the whole range of food-related behaviors that impact one's relationship with God. We recall that one of the seven deadly sins was gluttony, and that many of the fathers defined it broadly to include undue attention to food *for its own sake*.[60] Food is for the body, to be sure; but, "the body is . . . for the Lord" (1 Cor. 6:13, NIV).

Yet another "comparable issue" might be drawn from the categories of "clean" and "unclean." We have established that hygiene was not the criterion for distinguishing between the animals. Rather "clean" and "unclean" constituted religious categories. Uncleanness, whatever its source, is "a concrete and dangerous reality, indicating the presence of something fundamentally wrong."[61] It is worth noting that the uncleanness here is associated with the dark side of life—carnivores, scavengers, underground, diseased, or destructive creatures. Perhaps the prohibitions in this text intend to display something of God's character and purpose—light and life, which stand in opposition to the realms of darkness and death.

The following sermon plan[62] reflects the life issues we have identified:

1. [Introduction] There are a host of things, like eating, we do without even thinking ("grab a bite," "eat on the run").

2. But God declares that even the food we eat matters [initial explication of text]. It is a matter of holiness (v. 47).

3. "Holy" means devoted to God, displaying the character of God [compare the kinds of animals perhaps reflecting God's character; but, in any case, reflecting God's demand].

4. "Holy" also means devoted to God, not to things or others [use of good distinguishes God's people; food does not exist for its own sake, but for the Lord's sake].

5. So eating, like every other part of our lives, belongs to the Lord.

6. [Conclusion] How we relate to the Lord depends on how we relate the parts of our lives to the Lord ("do not defile yourselves," v. 43, also 24, 44).

The Nature of the Old Testament

In the article mentioned earlier, Hull argued that the "reality of the Bible may be subsumed" under the rubrics of history, literature, and theology, each implying a different aspect of that reality, and each requiring a different interpretive key for full disclosure. As *history*, the Bible displays its appropriateness to the multiformity of culture. The interpretive key is "intentionality," therefore, so that the message of Scripture for today corresponds to its intended message in its *Sitz im leben* ("situation in life"). As *literature*, the Bible fixes the Word of God so that it becomes capable of transmission across cultures and eras. The interpretive key is "potentiality," the authentic "remembrance" of revelation (John 14:26) within the unfolding experience of each new generation. But the Bible is also *theology*. It is proclamation intended to engender living faith. The interpretive criterion is "centrality," locating within the diversity of the biblical library the integrating core.

In his recent work on diversity and unity in the Old Testament, John Goldingay has made use of these same formal categories of history, literature, and theology.[63] Goldingay believes, despite the prevailing skepticism of fashionable scholarship, that it is "appropriate to look for theological coherence in the Old Testament" (p. 25). The fact of canonization implies a coherence embraced by both the Jewish and early Christian communities. And the real existence of coherence implies that diversity has value for Christian theology and life today (p. 26). In this section, we will explore the homiletical implications of this tri-part nature of the Old Testament.

The Old Testament as history.—The historical rootage of the Old Testament brings to us both promise and peril. Its promise lies in the multiformity of its contexts. As evangelicals who sustain a high view of biblical authority, we have good reason to expect biblical multiformity to issue in wide ranges of application. Its peril lies, however, in the two-pronged hook of cultural remoteness. On the one hand, the Near Eastern culture we meet in the Old Testament world is strange to us. What do nomads have in common with suburbanites, shepherds with corporate vice presidents, or with technicians who repair multiport, fuel-injected engines? On the other hand, our own culture contains realities totally unknown to the world of the Old Testament. What, for example, can Psalm 8 possibly teach medical researchers who are experimenting with polymer chain reactions to DNA? The first prong denotes the culture gap that plagues any effort at relating one culture to another. The second prong denotes the even more troubling possibility that there might not be anything there to relate. The first denotes unintelligibility. The second denotes irrelevance.

Over the years, preachers have faced these dangers in a variety of inappropriate ways. We noted earlier that many of the first Christian preachers resorted to allegory, and not a few modern preachers fall into the same trap. Countless sermons on evangelism, for example, have depended on an allegorical interpretation of Psalm 126:6, "He who goes out weeping, carrying seed to sow will return with songs of joy, carrying sheaves with him" (NIV). The allegorical elements will be obvious—"seed" is the gospel, "sowing" is witnessing, "sheaves" are converts. But the passage is tied historically to the return of the exiles, and their hope in the ultimate purposes of God for them and their land. It has no immediate connection at all with evangelism.

More frequently preachers *spiritualize*, that is, make some physical reality analogous to a "spiritual" reality. For example, the four references in Genesis to Lot's affliction with Sodom are sometimes offered as a picture of the dynamics of temptation and sin: "Lot looked up and saw" (Gen. 13:10, NIV); "Lot ... pitched his tent near Sodom" (Gen. 13:12, NIV); "he was living in Sodom" (Gen. 14:12, NIV); and he was "sitting in the gateway of the city" (Gen. 19:1, NIV). Of course, these references indicate no such thing. Not only does Genesis give no warrant to the underlying assumption that Lot was predisposed to the allurements of Sodom, the New Testament explicitly declares that he was "tormented in his righteous soul by the lawless deeds he saw and heard" (2 Pet. 2:8, NIV).

These forms of misapplication are ultimately reducible to one—the de-emphasis or denial of the historical groundedness of the Old Testament text. But the question remains how to mesh historical peculiarity with the task of Old Testament application. Goldingay suggests the paradigm of "starting point," since "the OT material often has more the character of raw material for a portrayal of some aspect of belief" (p. 36). Methodologically such an approach would seem to guide our preparation for preaching in the following ways. First, it would require the concept of God's kingdom history to govern our interpretation of any particular history. Second, it would demand accurate and precise identification of the teaching of the passage, in light of the kingdom of God concept, in its own concept. Third, it would require correlation of the Old Testament context and our own cultural context sufficiently thorough to yield principles that are "genuinely comparable."[64] Only on these terms will our application be genuine, fully respecting the historical factuality of the text.

The Old Testament as literature.—It is no part of our task here to delve into the peculiar problems of preaching the assorted genres of Old Testament literature. The authors of Part I undertake that assignment. Our interest is rather the literary character of the Old Testament and the implications of that character for application in preaching.

Let us begin by specifying what we mean by "literary character." The literary character of the Old Testament (as of the New) embodies two distinct elements. First, the Old Testament is literature; and, like all literature, it exists as literature at several different levels: (1) the genres, or types of literature it contains; (2) the grammar and syntax of a given passage; and (3) words, the verbal dimension of language. Second, the literature of the Old Testament is *medium* not *message*. Our interest in preaching does not rest in the Old Testament as literature, but in the Old Testament as theological literature.

Both of these elements indicate the diversity of the Old Testament, as well as the critical importance to the preacher of grasping the nuances of different literary strands and traditions. It goes without saying that effective preaching presupposes thorough exegesis, concerned largely with the literary tasks of word study, grammatical and syntactical analysis, and the interpretation of genre. Exegesis is crucial as a method for determining what a text actually says, and what it means in its context.

Beyond that, how does the literary character of the Old Testament affect its application to the church in preaching? We have already mentioned the diversity reflected in the literature of the Old Testament; but, what, if anything, does that imply about applicability? More to the point, what, if anything, does that imply about application in preaching?

We might turn for help to the thesis of David Bartlett, a pastor and New Testament scholar, that different types of biblical literature assert their authority in distinctive ways.[65] Bartlett regards biblical authority as a function of the material itself, rather than of a structure or program extrinsic to the text. Inspiration (or better, a doctrine of inspiration), for example, cannot establish the authority of a passage because, in Bartlett's view, it lies outside the text of Scripture itself.

Drawing on Paul Ricoeur,[66] Bartlett examines the distinctive authority claims of four biblical genres: prophetic, narrative, wisdom, and witness (that is, confessional and testimonial literature). Prophetic authority rests on *words*, validated by three criteria. First, they are self-authenticating; that is, they appeal to no external authority whatever. They call for obedient response as the oracles of God.[67] Second, they are authenticated by fulfillment. Third, they separate the false prophet from the true by the forms their prophecies take. Thus, Jeremiah exposes Hananiah as a false prophet because he proclaims "peace" rather than "judgment" as "the prophets who preceded you and me have prophesied" (Jer. 28:8, NIV). Bartlett argues that prophetic authority has the peculiar function of causing "us to reformulate our questions and shift our presuppositions" (p. 37). It is confrontational, a "now hear this" kind of claim.

The authority of narrative rests on *deeds*. Bartlett points out that biblical narrative differs from ordinary biographical narrative in three ways: (1) the *goal* of biblical narrative is theological, not historical; (2) the *technique* of biblical narrative is persuasive not descriptive; and (3) the *sources* of information about the events in biblical narrative are themselves largely biblical, not "secular" and not "verifiable" (pp. 44-47). Thus, Old Testament narrative functions interpretively. It establishes patterns which recur both in later Old Testament sections and in the New Testament. It formulates the context within which we must understand both the unfolding history of salvation and our own milieu.

Bartlett suggests several ways that narrative claims authority. It enables readers to *identify* with varied perspectives and thus "feel" the relevance of the theological claim. It opens up a wider world of awareness for readers by providing nuances for and fresh descriptions of familiar experiences. Narratives also have power to question readers either explicitly, as in the questioning of Job (38:1-4), or implicitly, as in Nathan's parable to David (2 Sam. 12:1-5). Narratives may also transform understandings, and they bring the experiences they describe into present experience.

The authority of wisdom, according to Bartlett, rests on human insight. Wisdom begins with the data of experience, with the "order of experience," with "common sense," with a sense of the "inscrutable" (pp. 85-88). Unlike prophecy, wisdom issues its claim implicitly. It does not demand. It promulgates realities empirically verifiable. Unlike narrative, its claims are not straightforwardly theological. In effect, wisdom presents two sets of claims, one reality-based (as when we are warned about adultery on the basis of consequences, Prov. 5:1-6), the other theologically based (as in the guiding dictum of Proverbs: "The fear of Lord is the beginning of wisdom," 9:10, NIV). The first kind of claim warns us to limit application to general principles and promises. The second kind reminds us to interpret both the principles and promises, and the human conditions they address, in light of God's sovereignty.

Witness literature, the fourth of Bartlett's genres, appears less frequently than the other types, and it "represents an aspect of various and diverse biblical works" (p. 113). Such literature presents its claim much as legal proceedings present claims to a jury.

Bartlett summarizes by asserting that the different genres elicit different responses (p. 128). Prophecy calls for "faithful hearing." Narrative calls for "discernment" (of God's activity) and/or "identification" (with the figure[s] of the story). Wisdom elicits a learning and sharing of godly ways of living. Witness evokes "truth," both in the witness who testifies and in the validation of our own experience.

Bartlett's categories are much more focused on the *dynamics* of authoritative claim than on the *content*. Bartlett does not tell us, for instance, what exactly Haggai's demand to "build a house (temple)" in 520 B.C. requires of business people in Atlanta, or their church. He does give us some hints about how, once we have established theological intent, we might press the claims in a way that is consonant with the prophetic outlook.

The Old Testament as theology.—Preaching involves both the theological task of determining what a given text authoritatively says to a contemporary congregation and the homiletical task of forming that authoritative word according to the shape of the text itself. At this point, however, we must return to the notion of theological claim by exploring our second assertion about the "literary character" of the Old Testament, that the Old Testament literature is medium not message. We do not mean to imply by what we have just said that the content of application and what we might call the "form" of application have nothing to do with each other. We do mean to imply that application involves two rather clearly distinguished tasks, one theological, the other homiletical. We have suggested that the literary character of the Old Testament offers us powerful resources for the homiletical task, but the theological task is more complicated and more critical.

We do well to remind ourselves that while application does not end with theological teaching, it does begin there. Indeed, that may not go far enough. Preaching is, after all, not merely *theological*, but an expressed form of *biblical* theology.[68] As such, preaching must serve the centrality of the theological truth (doctrine, the gospel) in a given passage.[69]

Earlier we referred to moralizing as an inappropriate attempt to Christianize the Old Testament. It proves far easier, however, to warn than to correct, especially in preaching the Old Testament. For one thing, since the days of Immanuel Kant and Adolf von Harnack, the moral force of all Scripture has tended to insinuate itself in biblical studies. In his *Religion within the Limits of Reason Alone*, Kant reduced the totality of Christian religion to "the moral improvement of men."[70] For his part Harnack taught that the gospel leads to eternal life in that it "teaches us how to live our lives aright."[71]

For another thing, the Old Testament lends itself to moralistic interpretation. Scholars often make the point that Judaism stressed orthopraxy more than orthodoxy, made *haggadah* (doctrinal and devotional teaching) subservient to *halakah* (moral and practical teaching), and in general, regulated behavior more stringently than belief. Again, the nature of the Old Testament could be said to dispose the Jewish community in that way by the preponderance of its ethical material. Yet, it cannot be said in fairness that Judaism radically juxtaposed faith and morals. Dobschutz argues in fact that the criterion which settled questions of Old Testament canonicity was doctrine, not devotion, edification, or ethics.[72] Further, mainstream rabbinical Judaism did not reflect the balance of theology and pragmatism one finds in the Old Testament itself. Certainly it did not reflect the rejuvenated theological vision of the Old Testament one finds in the New Testament. Thus one cannot say that the Old Testament itself required a religion dominated by ethical prescription. Nevertheless, the Old Testament material is preponderately ethical as compared to that of the New Testament.

The distinction between homiletics and ethics has special significance. Preaching publicly declared moral injunctions do not constitute real preaching. Again, that is "moralizing," and while the ethical dynamics of the Old Testament may tempt us to moralize, we must keep our wits about us and maintain the uniqueness of preaching.

What, then, is that uniqueness in terms of applying the Old Testament? Of course, biblical ethics and biblical preaching that does a good job of application have much in common. Certainly they share a basic methodology. A good illustration comes from John Frame's "meta-ethic" ("general method for approaching ethical problems").[73] Frame argues that the "Word of God" (somewhat broader than, but not autonomous in relation to Scripture [p. 34]) always enters the context of human life mediately; that is, through *events* (nature and history, miracle, etc.), *words* (divine voice, prophets/apostles, etc.), and *persons* (human constitution, theophany, etc.) Yet, none of these media is exclusive of the others, so that the resolution of any ethical problem must comprehend all these: (1) evaluating human nature, and the present, (specific) as well as universal, human condition; (2) studying and analyzing the "world," that is, the relevant cultural context; and (3) the normative teaching of Scripture itself. Good application in preaching will, of course, follow the same basic pattern.[74]

Still, preaching differs from ethics at critical points. First, ethics distills a biblical teaching to its exact applicability as an answer to a carefully defined ethical problem. For example, the oft-cited allowance for divorce in Deuteronomy 24:1-4 (which is more properly a regulation of same spouse remarriage) has significance only within the narrow confines of divorce/remarriage morality. As such, it has no relevance whatever to persons never-married (except as warning) or to widows/widowers (except as information). But as a preaching text, the passage has relevance across the spectrum. It is bound up in a broad theological framework which includes at least the following features: (1) the hardness of the human heart which requires God's merciful regulation (compare Matt. 19:8); (2) God's total concern for womanhood (compare Deut. 21:10-14; 21:15-17; 22:13-29) and the stability of family life (compare Deut. 5:18; 22:22-27); and (3) the identity of the people of God, especially as opposed to the cultural milieu in which they live as God's people (4:37-38; 7:6-8; 9:4-5; 24:4).

Second, preaching, unlike ethics, endeavors to apply a theological truth-claim rather than a behavioral-claim. Put otherwise, the focal point of ethics is an act or deed, or possibly an attitude; but, the focal point of preaching is the nature and work of God. In the passage cited above, a preaching focus will thus highlight the theological framework. Divorce regulation becomes a specific instance of a theological concern which permits wider application. If, as seems likely, the regulation served to close a loophole in custom (writing a certificate of divorce as a legal seal of marital dissolution), the intent would be to prevent divorce from becoming "a 'legal' form of committing adultery."[75] The overarching concern is with the sanctity of sexual relationships (an issue that has virtually universal applicability in any congregation with members older than thirteen!). But the overriding theological concern is expressed in the words "detestable in the eyes of the Lord," and sin upon the land the Lord your God is giving you" (v. 4, NIV). Taken in connection with the military exemption of a bridegroom in v. 5,[76] this passage yields the two-sided notion that God not only commands certain marital relationships and responsibilities; but, that the relationships of God's people to him hinge on faithfulness in these relationships. Such teaching accords with New Testament emphases (compare 1 Cor. 6:18-19 and 1 Thess. 4:3-8).

Third, while ethics calls for behavioral response, preaching calls for response to the gospel.[77] Here is the clearest of all distinctions between ethics and preaching. Preaching can never rest content with explications of duties or desirable traits, nor even with careful grounding of such duties and traits in the nature of God. Preaching is preaching the good news.[78] Obviously, no sermon will be exclusively taken up with explicit gospel. But gospel should inform every sermon, guide every sermon, and serve as the terminus toward which every sermon finally moves. With Paul we must all say, "Woe to me if I do not preach the gospel!" (1 Cor. 9:16, NIV).

Notes

1. Ruth A. Tucker, *Another Gospel: Alternative Religions and The New Age Movement* (Grand Rapids: Zondervan, 1989), 30.

2. See further, E. C. Blackman, *Marcion and His Influence* (London: SPCK, 1948).

3. F. F. Bruce, *The Books and the Parchments* (Rev. ed.; Old Tappan, NJ: Revell, 1963), 109.

4. David Ewert, *From Ancient Tablets to Modern Translations* (Grand Rapids: Zondervan, 1983), 24.

5. Compare in this volume the essay by Robert Sloan, "The New Testament Use of the Old Testament."

6. R. Laird Harris, *The Inspiration and Canonicity of the Bible* (Contemporary Evangelical Perspectives; Grand Rapids: Zondervan, 1969), 175, 234.

7. Charles H. Talbert, "The Bible as Spiritual Friend" *Perspectives in Religious Studies* 13 (1986): 55-56.

8. Ibid., 57.

9. Thomas C. Oden, *After Modernity . . . What? Agenda for Orthodoxy* (Grand Rapids: Zondervan, 1990), 139 ff.

10. O. M. T. O'Donovan, "Towards an Interpretation of Biblical Ethics," *Tyndale Bulletin* 27 (1976), 58.

11. Millard J. Erikson, *Christian Theology*, 3 vols. (Grand Rapids: Baker, 1983-1985), 1:242.

12. Elizabeth Achtemeier, *Preaching from the Old Testament* (Louisville: Westminster/John Knox, 1989), 29.

13. Ibid., 31.

14. Ibid., 21.

15. J.Maxwell Miller, *The Old Testament and the Historian* (Guides to Biblical Scholarship; Philadelphia: Fortress, 1976), 39.

16. William H. Green, *The Higher Criticism of the Pentateuch* (Reprinted; Grand Rapids: Baker, reprint 1928 [1895]), 177.

17. John R. W. Stott, *Preaching: Reviving the Art in the 21st Century* (Grand Rapids: Eerdmans, 1982), 50-89.

18. See Milton S. Terry, *Biblical Hermeneutics* (Grand Rapids: Zondervan, reprint 1974), 606-10.

19. The highly-respected Hillel [about 60 B.C.–A.D. 20] formulated seven such rules, later expanded to thirteen by Ishmael, and the thirty-two Eliezar.

20. On the forms of these procedures, compare Richard Longenecker, *Biblical Exegesis in the Apostolic Period* (Grand Rapids: Eerdmans, 1975), 28-50; and Bernard Ramm, *Protestant Biblical Interpretation* (Grand Rapids: Baker, 1970), 45-48.

21. See Karlfried Froehlich, ed., *Biblical Interpretation in the Early Church* (Philadelphia: Fortress, 1984), 19.

22. Ramm, *Interpretation*, 50.

23. Origen, *On First Principles*, Bk. IV, II, 4.

24. Especially in Contra Celsus.

25. Moises Silva, *Has the Church Misread the Bible?* (Grand Rapids; Zondervan, 1987), 58-59.

26. Origen, *On First Principles*, Bk. IV, II, 6.

27. Silva, 71-74.

28. Clarence Jordan, "The Adventures of Three Students in a Fiery Furnace," *The Twentieth Century Pulpit*, ed. James W. Cox (Nashville: Abingdon, 1978), 90-98.

29. E. D. Hirsch, Jr., *Validity in Interpretation* (New Haven: Yale University Press, 1967), 8-9.

30. Walter Kaiser, *Toward an Exegetical Theology* (Grand Rapids: Baker, 1981).

31. Willi Marxsen, *The New Testament as the Church's Book* (Philadelphia: Fortress, 1972), 9.

32. John P. Newport, "Representative Historical and Contemporary Approaches to Biblical Interpretation" *FaithMiss* (1986), 43.

33. Robert Saucy, "The Crucial Issue between Dispensational and Non-Dispensational Systems" *Criswell Theological Review* 1 (1986), 149-65.

34. Ibid., 161.

35. John Bright, *The Kingdom of God* (Nashville: Abingdon, 1953), 7.

36. See the essay by G. R. Beasley-Murray, "The Kingdom in the Old and the New Testaments."

37. Th. C. Vriezen, *An Outline of Old Testament Theology* (2nd ed.; Newton, MA: Branford, 1970), 398-404.

38. Lewis B. Smedes, *Mere Mortality: What God Expects from Ordinary People* (Grand Rapids: Eerdmans, 1983), 12-15.

39. On the legitimate function as well as the negative history of casuistry, cf. Albert R. Jonsen and Stephen Toulines, *The Abuse of Casuistry: A History of Moral Reasoning* (Berkeley: University of California Press, 1988), 11-13.

40. Cf. also Walter C. Kaiser, Jr., *Toward Old Testament Ethics* (Grand Rapids: Zondervan, 83), 34-37.

41. H. H. Rowley, *The Faith of Israel* (Philadelphia: Westminster, 1956), 149.

42. Greidanus, *The Modern Preacher and the Ancient Text* (Grand Rapids: Eerdmans, 1988), 163-68. The definition given here is my own although it does harmonize with that of Greidanus.

43. Leander E. Keck, *The Bible in the Pulpit* (Nashville: Abingdon, 1978), 100-04.

44. Carlyle Marney, "Our Present Higher Good," *To God Be the Glory: Sermons in Honor of George A. Buttrick*, ed. T. A. Gill (Nashville: Abingdon, 1973), 52-61.

45. Such a sermon is suggested in an interpretation by Thomas L. Mowbray, a pastor ("The Function in Ministry of Psalms Dealing with Anger: The Angry Psalmist" *Journal of Pastoral Counseling* [1986], 34-39).

46. F. Delitzsch, *Psalms Commentary on the Old Testament*, 3 vols., 1871 (Grand Rapids: Eerdmans, reprint 1980), 3:337.

47. One such sermon of this type is found in R. T. Kendall, *Jonah: An Exposition* (Grand Rapids: Zondervan, 1978). Entitled, "The Jonah Complex," it asserts that Jonah "needed reinstatement into the principles of the glory of God" (p. 228). That is undoubtedly true and might legitimately form part of the message. It moralizes, however, in that its *exclusive* focus is precisely Jonah's "complex" and how he could have dealt with it.

48. Greidanus, *Modern Preacher*, 165.

49. Carl G. Kromminga, "Remember Lot's Wife" *Calvin Theological Journal*, vol. 18 (1983), 38.

50. William E. Hull, "The Nature of the Bible and Its Message" *Faith and Mission*, vol. 2 (1986), 3.

51. Greidanus, *Modern Preacher*, 183.

52. John A. Broadus, *On The Preparation and Delivery of Sermons* (New and Revised edition by J. B. Weatherspoon; New York: Harper, 1870, 1944), 210.

53. Cf. David L. Larsen, *The Anatomy of Preaching: Identifying the Issues in Preaching Today* (Grand Rapids: Baker, 1989), 95-97.

54. See Greidanus, *Modern Preacher*; Haddon W. Robinson, *Biblical Preaching* (Grand Rapids: Baker, 1980), 89 f; John R. W. Stott, *Between Two Worlds*, 135-79; Merrill R. Abbey, *Preaching to the Contemporary Mind* (Nashville: Abingdon, 1963); Ronald E. Sleeth, *Persuasive Preaching* (New York: Harper, 1956); Ian Pitt-Watson, *A Primer for Preachers*, (Grand Rapids: Baker, 1986); Walter L. Liefeld, *New Testament Exposition: From Text to Sermon* (Grand Rapids: Zondervan, 1984), 96-114.

55. Broadus, *On Preparation*, 211.

56. Douglas Stuart, *Old Testament Exegesis: A Primer for Students and Pastors* (2nd ed.; Philadelphia: Westminster, 1984), 41.

57. Ibid., 47.

58. Compare verse 4; although the cleavage does not pass all the way through the hoof.

59. Compare S. I. McMillen, *None of These Diseases*, rev. ed. by David E. Stern (Old Tappan, NJ: Revell, 1984).

60. For an excellent discussion on this point, see H. Stephen Shoemaker, *The Jekyll and Hyde Syndrome* (Nashville: Broadman, 1987), 84-91.

61. J. R. Porter, *Leviticus* (Cambridge Bible Commentary; Cambridge: Cambridge University Press, 1975), 83.

62. Our arrangement follows the kind of pattern recently described by David Buttrick as "move" structure (*Homiletic: Moves and Structures* [Philadelphia: Fortress, 1988]) and by Clyde Fant as "holistic" preaching (*Preaching for Today* [Rev. ed.; New York: Harper and Row, 1987], 182-85). Both advocate

"thematic movement rather than analysis as the basis for sermon structure. A plan will consist of five to seven interrelated themes, each developed into a three to five minute segment." See also Thomas G. Long, *The Witness of Preaching* (Louisville: Westminster/John Knox, 1989), 104-11.

63. John Goldingay, *Theological Diversity and the Authority of the Old Testament* (Grand Rapids: Eerdmans, 1987).

64. Greidanus, *Modern Preacher*, 174-75.

65. David L. Bartlett, *The Shape of Scriptural Authority* (Philadelphia: Fortress, 1983). See also William C. Spohn, "The Use of Scripture in Moral Theology," *Theological Studies* 47 (1986), 89.

66. Paul Ricoeur, "Toward A Hermeneutic of the Idea of Revelation," *Essays on Biblical Interpretation*, ed. Lewis S. Mudge (Philadelphia: Fortress 1980), 73-118. Ricoeur argued that scriptural forms make different revelatory claims. Bartlett focused on "authority" rather than "revelation."

67. Expressed by the characteristic phrase "The Word of the Lord." cf. G. von Rad, *Old Testament Theology*, 2 vols. (New York: Harper and Row, 1965), 2:87.

68. Most readers will recognize the difference between "biblical" theology (the theological teaching/emphasis of a portion of Scripture) and "systematic" theology (a theological teaching/emphasis as it appears throughout the whole body of Scripture). There is an element of paradox here. This concern for preservation of diversity and integrity itself originated in the biblical theology movement which, according to Krister Stendahl ("Biblical Theology" *Interpreter's Dictionary of the Bible*, 1:419), "was swallowed up or threatened by a history of biblical thought or a history of biblical religion" so that the "question about relevance was waived." Biblical theology, in other words, has tended to abandon any hope of biblical applicability. Yet biblical preaching, of it is anything, is exposition of a distinctive theological emphasis belonging to some portion of the total Old Testament revelation.

69. Richard Lischer, "Preaching as Theology" *Currents in Theology and Mission* 8 (1981), 92-93.

70. Immanuel Kant, *Religion within the Limits of Reason Alone* (Chicago: Open Count, 1934 [1794]), 102.

71. Adolf von Harnack, *What Is Christianity?* (Torchbook; New York: Harper, 1957 [1900]), 146.

72. E. von Dobschutz, "Bible in the Church," *Encyclopedia of Religions and Ethics*, 2:580.

73. John M. Frame, *Perspectives on the Word of God: An Introduction to Christian Ethics* (Phillipsburg, NJ: Presbyterian and Reformed, 1990), 39.

74. As Frame himself implies, 29-30.

75. Peter C. Craigie, *The Book of Deuteronomy* (Grand Rapid: Eerdmans, 1976), 305.

76. C. F. Keil and F. Delitzsch, *The Pentateuch, Commentary on the Old Testament*, 3 vols. (Grand Rapids: Eerdmans, 1978), 3:419.

77. Greidanus, *Modern Preacher*, 15.

78. The two dominant words for "preach" in the New Testament make this clear. "To herald (*kerysso*) emphasizes the responsibility of messengers for a *message* not their own; while "to proclaim the gospel" (*euangelizomai*) contains the centrality of the gospel within the very definition of the word.

12

Changing Culture with Words from God:
Applying the Old Testament

James Emery White

Introduction

Kenneth Myers has written that the "challenge of living with popular culture may well be as serious for modern Christians as persecution and plagues were fore the saints of earlier centuries."[1] Langdon Gilkey adds that the "dominant question for Christianity . . . has been, What shall we do with the modern world?"[2] Yet evangelical Christianity has so emphasized confronting individual lives with the claims of the gospel that it has often neglected the decisive need for a Christian engagement of contemporary culture.[3] History teaches that significant cultural change has always been born on the wings of oratory. This has certainly been the case for all great movements of the Holy Spirit which have impacted society, for preaching has always been in the vanguard of Christianity's engagement with contemporary culture. As John R. W. Stott has suggested, the art of preaching truly stands "between two worlds," the world of the biblical text and the modern world to which we bring those words to bear.[4]

This raises a simple but profound question: how do we change culture with words from God? Specifically, in light of the focus of this book, how do we apply the Old Testament to our modern world? Let me suggest that such an enterprise involves three important steps: first, the preacher must understand the contemporary culture; second, the preacher must understand how the culture of the Old Testament was addressed by God; third, the preacher must then employ sound hermeneutical principles in order to stand between these two worlds in such a way as to continue to bring God's Word to our modern world.

Understanding Modernity

E. D. Hirsch put forth a provocative thesis in his best-selling book *Cultural Literacy*, namely that there are common denominators in factual knowledge if one is to function in contemporary society, and that these facts are cultural in orientation.[5] Regardless of whether or not one accepts Hirsch's thesis, this claim can certainly be made for the task of preaching. If preaching is to be effective, it must be culturally literate.

Three Processes of Modernity

This raises a simple but profound question: What are the forces at work in contemporary culture that are of particular relevance to the preaching task? Sociologist Peter Berger, among many others, has suggested three dominant sociological trends in contemporary American culture which have shaped modern life and thought: secularization, pluralization, and privatization.[6] These three streams characterize the modern world.

Secularization.—Secularization is the process by which "sectors of society and culture are removed from the domination of religious institutions and symbols."[7] Here is the process whereby the church is losing its influence as a shaper of life and thought in the wider social order. As Richard J. Neuhaus phrased it, we live in a "naked public square."[8] For example, whereas once the church was the dominant institution in every community, morality and truth are now more often than not the property of the media. Television may not tell you what to think, but it certainly tells us what to think about. Today we are exposed to an estimated 1500 commercial messages per day, with over 10,000 magazines, 6,000 radio stations, and 400 television stations from which to choose.[9] Howard K. Smith, for years a commentator for ABC Television, estimated that at least four-fifths of what the average citizen continues to learn about the world after leaving school "comes filtered through observations of the journalist."[10] The result of this process is that the impact of the church on contemporary culture is minimal at best. Page Smith sarcastically remarks that in our modern world, "God is not a proper topic for conversation, but 'lesbian politics' is!"[11] Secularization makes the case that the Christian faith is less real than other concerns or ideologies.

Privatization.—The second mark of modernity which Berger suggests is "individualization," or "privatization," which Berger defines as follows:

> Privatized religion is a matter of the 'choice' or 'preference' of the individual or the nuclear family, *ipso facto* lacking in common, binding quality . . . this religiosity is limited to specific enclaves of social life that may be effectively segregated from the secularized sectors of modern society.[12]

An interpreter of Berger, Os Guinness, has defined privatization as that "process by which modernization produces a cleavage between the public and the private spheres of life and focuses the private sphere as the special arena for the expansion of individual freedom and fulfillment."[13] The origin of this dynamic was the church's acceptance, during the seventeenth and eighteenth centuries, of the claim of science to the throne of public, factual truth.[14]

The practical dynamic of this stream of modernity is that one's personal faith is often suspended in relation to business, politics, or even marriage and the home. A compartmentalized faith is manifest with personal faith as one of many worlds and pockets that make-up the unrelated composite. This trend was evident to historian Theodore Roszak who, after traveling to America, remarked that Christian faith in America was one that was "socially irrelevant, even if privately engaging."[15] Perhaps this dynamic was most clearly demonstrated by the founder of McDonald's, who was quoted as saying, "I believe in God, family, and McDonald's—and in the office, that order is reversed."[16] At its worst, privatization makes the Christian faith a matter of personal preference.[17] "I believe in God. I'm not a religious fanatic. I can't remember the last time I went to church. My faith has carried me a long way. It's 'Sheilaism.' Just my own little voice."[18] Thus faith is trivialized to the realm of personal opinion or preference.

Pluralization.—The final stream within modernity, according to Berger, is "pluralization," that "the man in the street is confronted with a wide variety of religious and other reality-defining agencies that compete for his allegiance or at least attention."[19] Again, Guinness offers a good interpretation of Berger's thought, writing that pluralization is that "process by which the number of options in the private sphere of modern society rapidly multiplies at all levels, especially at the level of world views, faith and ideologies."[20] Berger speaks of the traditional role of religion as a "sacred canopy" covering the contemporary culture. Today that canopy is gone, replaced instead by millions of small tents.[21] For example, Barrett's *World Christian Encyclopedia* lists over 20,000 denominations, with over 2,000 in the United States alone. It should be noted that the process of pluralization means far more than a simple increase in the number of "faith options." Gilkey is correct when he observes that "many religions have always existed"; what is unique is a "new consciousness" that "entails a feeling of rough parity, as well as diversity, among religion. By parity I mean at least the presence of both truth and grace in other ways."[22] Harold O. J. Brown adds that by pluralism, we mean not only many and varying convictions, but "value pluralism, namely, that all convictions about values are of equal validity, which says in effect that no convictions about values have any validity."[23]

The result of this process is quite simply the devaluation of truth. Leith Anderson notes that pluralism creates a mind-set that there should be universal acceptance of diversity to the point that all values are relative.[24] The sheer number of choices and competing ideologies suggests that no one perspective or religious persuasion has the inside track on truths about God and the supernatural. This encourages what Guinness calls a "smorgasbord" mentality in regard to the construction of personal beliefs. Malise Ruthven calls it "The Divine Supermarket."[25] Barna uses the technical term "syncretism."[26] As a result, Christianity becomes simply one of many competing worldviews, no better or worse than another, which exists in the milieu of civilization.[27]

The Four Marks of Modernity

If secularization, privatization, and pluralization are the three processes of modernity, what have been the results of these processes? These three streams have, according to conventional wisdom, produced four values which characterize modernity: moral relativism, autonomous individualism, narcissistic hedonism, and reductive naturalism.[28] As Thomas Oden observes, "modernity is not just a time but a set of passions, hopes, and ideas, a mentality that prevails."[29]

Moral Relativism.—The value of "moral relativism" states that what is moral is dictated by a particular situation in light of a particular culture or social location. The usual phraseology is "what is true for you is true for you, and what is true for me is true for me." The breakdown of morals is almost epidemic; recent studies reveal that lying is now a part of our culture, a trait of American character, and that one-third of all married men and women have had at least one affair.[30] Alan Bloom, in the introduction of his best-selling *The Closing of the American Mind*, writes that there "is one thing a professor can be absolutely certain of. Almost every student entering the university believes, or says he believes, that truth is relative."[31]

Autonomous Individualism.—The value of "autonomous individualism" espouses that the individual person is autonomous in terms of destiny and accountability. Ultimate moral authority is self-generated. We ultimately answer to no one but ourselves. Thus, our choices are ours alone, determined by our personal pleasure alone. As Oden notes, the "key to 'hairesis' (root word for 'heresy') is the notion of choice—choosing for oneself, over against the apostolic tradition."[32]

Narcissistic Hedonism.—In Greek mythology, Narcissus is the character who, upon passing his reflection in the water, became so enamored with himself that he lost thought, fell in the water, and drowned. The value of "narcissistic hedonism" is the classic "I, me, mine" mentality that places personal pleasure and fulfillment at the forefront of concerns. The popular ethical expression of this mind-set is simply this: "if it makes you happy, and it doesn't hurt anyone else, then it's 'okay.'" Of course, such a philosophy offers no basis for refraining from seeking personal happiness simply because another's welfare may be jeopardized.

Reductive Naturalism.—"Reductive naturalism" is the value which states that what can be known is only that which can be empirically verified. In other words, what is real is that which can be seen, tasted, heard, smelled or touched. This is basically the view of empiricism. If it cannot be examined in a tangible, scientific manner, then it is not simply unknowable, it is meaningless. The verdict such a view imposes on religious claims is self-evident.

The Old Testament Challenge to Culture

Having taken a brief walk through the mind-set of contemporary culture, the next step is to examine the Old Testament documents for insight on how the contemporary culture of that day and time was confronted and challenged by God.[33] The distinctive form of address espoused by the prophets was "Thus says the Lord." Christopher J. H. Wright suggests that there were four principal prohibitions which God expressed to Israel that were cultural in nature: idolatry, perversion, that which was destructive of persons, and callousness to the poor.[34] These four categories will serve as a framework for an introductory understanding of how the Old Testament materials engaged the contemporary culture of its day.

Idolatry

Before entering the Promised Land, Moses reminded the people that they should "not follow other gods, the gods of the peoples around you; for the Lord your God, who is among you, is a jealous God and his anger will burn against you, and he will destroy you from the face of the land" (Deut. 6:14, NIV). The worship of the living God of Abraham, Isaac, and Jacob was the expressed purpose for the liberation of the Israelites from Egypt (Ex. 4:23). It was the first commandment issued from Mount Sinai (Ex. 20:3). The land the Israelites would inhabit was pluralistic in nature, and in light of that pluralism, God condemned any mind-set which would legitimate the plurality of "gods" as being worthy of recognition. Yet the Israelites manifested an idolatrous nature that brought condemnation from the prophets of God. The most shamefully pragmatic turn to idolatry was exhibited by Jeroboam, who instituted a religion to ensure his political stature: " . . . the king made two golden calves. He said to the people, 'It is too much for you to go up to Jerusalem. Here are your gods, O Israel, who brought you up out of Egypt'" (1 Kings 12:28, NIV). Jeroboam's actions were condemned: "By the word of the Lord a man of God came from Judah to Bethel, as Jeroboam was standing by the altar to make an offering. He cried out against the altar by the word of the Lord" (1 Kings 13:1-2a, NIV). Later, when Jeroboam's wife came to the prophet Ahijah in disguise, God's word again went forth:

> Go, tell Jeroboam that this is what the Lord, the God of Israel, says: "I raised you up from among the people and made you a leader over my people . . . but you have not been like my servant David, who kept my commands and followed me with all his heart, doing only what was right in my eyes. You have done more evil than all who lived before you. You have made for yourself other gods, idols made of metal; you have provoked me to anger and thrust me behind your back" (1 Kings 14:7-9, NIV).

Perversion

Immorality was consistently condemned by the prophetic voice of the Old Testament. Such practices as prostitution, homosexuality, beastiality, and incest were clearly denounced. God gave clear directions to Moses for the Israelites that they should "not do as they do in Egypt, where you used to live, and you must not do as they do in the land of Canaan, where I am bringing you" (Lev. 18:3, NIV). For example, God directed the Israelites not to "have sexual relations with an animal and defile yourself with it ... that is a perversion" (Lev. 18:23, NIV). Then God added, "Do not defile yourselves in any of these ways, because this is how the nations that I am going to drive out before you became defiled" (Lev. 18:24, NIV).

Destruction of the Weak and Innocent

In Deuteronomy 10:18, Moses reminded the people that God "defends the cause of the fatherless and the widow, and loves the alien, giving him food and clothing" (NIV). Anything in society that allowed for systematic oppression of the weak was to be condemned. A litany of God's attitude toward exploitation is found in Exodus:

> Do not mistreat an alien or oppress him, for you were aliens in Egypt.
> Do not take advantage of a widow or an orphan. If you do and they cry out to me, I will certainly hear their cry. My anger will be aroused, and I will kill you with the sword; your wives will become widows and your children fatherless.
> If you lend money to one of my people among you who is needy, do not be like a moneylender; charge him no interest (Ex. 22:21-25, NIV).

In Leviticus, God directed His people "not to curse the deaf or put a stumbling block in front of the blind" (Lev. 19:14, NIV). No woman was to be exploited as a result of her status in society (Ex. 21:7-11). Such instructions were alien to the practices of the culture of the ancient Near East. The challenge was to remain true to God and His Word in the midst of a fallen culture. Perhaps the area to be most guarded was the worship of God:

> You must not worship the Lord your God in their way, because in worshiping their gods, they do all kinds of detestable things the Lord hates. They even burn their sons and daughters in the fire as sacrifices to their gods (Deut. 12:31, NIV.)

Such worship practices were common in Phoenicia and other

surrounding countries. Yet Scripture says such cultural phenomenon was "detestable" and "hated" by God.

Callousness to the Poor

One of the strongest motifs throughout the Old Testament is God's consistent concern for the poor. "If there is a poor man among your brothers in any of the towns of the land that the Lord your God is giving you, do not be hardhearted or tightfisted toward your poor brother. Rather be openhanded and freely lend him whatever he needs" (Deut. 15:7-8, NIV). In Amos, God declared judgment on Israel for trampling "on the heads of the poor as upon the dust of the ground" (2:7, NIV). In Ezekiel, the sin of Sodom was that she was "arrogant, overfed and unconcerned; they did not help the poor and needy" (Ezek. 16:49, NIV). It is not that God loves the poor more than the rich, only that God protects and cares for the poor and that God's people should neither neglect the poor or support cultural practices that generate poverty or breed callousness to the poor. An example of this proclivity for the plight of the poor is found in the "Sabbatical Year." Under this provision, there would be a release of soil, slaves, and debt every seven years (Ex. 23; Deut. 15).

Applying the Old Testament

Thomas G. Long is correct when he states that "exegesis can help us in many ways, but it finally cannot do what is most important: tell us what this text wishes to say on this occasion to our congregation. The preacher must decide this, and it is a risky and exciting decision."[35] What adds to the dilemma is that the biblical texts were written both *to* a social situation as well *in* a social situation.[36] The Old Testament has a reputation for difficulty on both counts, which is something of an irony, for it is supremely the Old Testament which "reminds us of the social character of our faith."[37] As Kyle M. Yates writes, the Old Testament materials:

> throw light upon our own day and our own situation by announcing the eternal principles of divine providence which will always operate whenever similar conditions are present. It is a truism to say that in God's plan the same things are true today that were true in the Old Testament age. If we are guilty of the same sins we can be sure of reaping the same punishment. It is indeed easy for us to get the word of God for our day if, capable of analyzing our own situation, we go to the prophets to find their statement of God's prescription for a similar condition.[38]

Applying the Old Testament, which should seek to integrate both an understanding of modernity and an awareness of the Old Testament challenge to the culture of its day, begins first with sound hermeneutics. After a brief discussion of various principles of interpretation germane to the application of Old Testament materials to contemporary culture, specific themes and emphases for preaching suggested by this study will be suggested.

Hermeneutical Principles

How can the text be liberated to speak to our contemporary situation? Many expositors fear the Old Testament's apparent bondage to the specificity of its original setting. The Old Testament seems so inextricably linked to a particular culture that liberating it to speak to the our modern world appears virtually impossible. Yet as Walter Kaiser observes:

> The precise specificness and particularity in the Bible was not meant to prejudice its universal usefulness; instead, it was meant to be an aid to us in identifying with that text and [to] take it out of the realm of the abstract and put it into the real world of concrete illustration and personal attachment.[39]

Kaiser further notes that "every biblical command . . . was originally addressed to someone in some place and some particular historical situation and context."[40] Even the biblical materials themselves treat earlier presentations of God's Word as having a timeless, universal significance beyond the initial declaration, hence the gathering of the materials together as Scripture. Brevard Childs, in reference to the Decalogue, writes that "it remains an imperative directed to historical Israel, but Israel as the people of God which has been extended both in time and space beyond the first generation of those who experienced Sinai."[41]

Perhaps a good word for the use of the Old Testament in regard to contemporary culture is the word "paradigm." A paradigm is that which is used as a model for various other situations in light of a basic, unchanging principle. Thus, the Old Testament is applied to our current situation paradigmatically in light of the eternally significant principles.

The first step, therefore, is to interpret the text at hand. The general principles which are always to be followed in approaching any biblical text include, but are not limited to, the following:[42] establish the best text (use of the original language is to be preferred); place the text in its wider context (both within the book itself and the wider canonical context); investigate the historical background/context; investigate the cultural background of the text; determine the literary genre; and finally, define significant terms and phrases in terms of etymology, customary usage, and biblical usage.

Gordon Fee and Douglas Stewart add the following six principles in regard to engaging the Old Testament, particularly the law of the Old Testament:[43] First, the Old Testament law is covenant, a binding agreement between two parties. Second, the Old Testament is not our testament. Unless Old Testament law, for example, is renewed directly or by principle in the New Testament, it is not binding upon contemporary Christians (compare Rom. 6:14-15). Third, some stipulations of the Old Covenant have clearly not been renewed in the New Covenant (such as the Israelite civil and ritual laws). Fourth, part of the Old Covenant is renewed in the New Covenant (such as some aspects of the Old Testament ethical law). Fifth, all of the Old Testament is still the Word of God for us even though it is not still the command of God to us, such as the original Old Testament law for ancient Israel. Finally, only that which is explicitly renewed from the Old Testament law can be considered part of the New Testament "law of Christ" (compare Gal. 6:2). An example of this explicit renewal would be the Decalogue, as well as such passages as Deuteronomy 6:5 and Leviticus 19:18.

These principles allow the Old Testament to be appropriated with hermeneutical integrity by modern interpreters in order to be applied to specific situations and contexts present in our contemporary world, which is the second step to take for contemporary application, for interpretation without application is a truncated use of the Scriptures. The specific laws and institutions of the Old Testament were based on universal principles that are eternally valid. Kaiser adds that behind every biblical command in the Old Testament, despite its specific and particular setting, is "a definite universal that justifies the particular. It is that universal which we ought to search out as exegetes and readers of the text."[44]

Thus, applying the Old Testament to contemporary culture demands what Harry Blamires called a "Christian mind," namely that which sets:

> all earthly issues within the context of the eternal, the view which relates all human problems—social, political, cultural—to the doctrinal foundations of the Christian faith, the view which sees all things here below in terms of God's supremacy and earth's transitoriness, in terms of Heaven and Hell.[45]

The task of the preacher is to seek the significance behind the meaning of the text, and use that significance to bring the text to bear upon the modern world.[46] As Karl Barth is reported to have said, "the preacher holds the Bible in one hand and the newspaper in the other."[47]

Roy Zuck offers the following "application" principles which, though universal in usefulness, are particularly helpful in preaching and applying the Old Testament to contemporary culture:[48] First, build all application on interpretation. Second, determine what was expected of the original audience. Third, base applications on elements present-day readers share with the original audience. Fourth, recognize how God's working varies in different ages. Fifth, determine what is normative for today. Sixth, see the principle inherent in the text. Seventh, think of the principle as an implication (or extrapolation of the text, and as a bridge to application). Eighth, write out specific action-responses. Finally, rely on the Holy Spirit.

Themes for Preaching

The Old Testament's challenge to the culture of the ancient Near East sounds an uncomfortable note for our contemporary context. Old Testament principles often go against the dominant values and norms of our society. But as Martin Luther is well known to have observed, if you preach the gospel in all aspects with the exception of the issues which deal specifically with your time, you are not preaching the gospel at all. Carl F. H. Henry adds that "whoever considers the politico-economic status quo sacred or normative, or uncritically resigns himself to it, needs to reread the Bible.[49] The following are four suggestions of directions preaching the Old Testament can take to engage the four values (see above) of contemporary culture:

Functional Monotheism.—The monotheism of the Old Testament, coupled with God's strong condemnation of idolatry, provides a compelling framework for addressing the narcissistic hedonism of our day. "Functional monotheism" is living as if there really is one and only one God on the throne of our lives. Therefore, while our modern world does not offer a polytheistic world view as the ancient Near East did to the Israelites, there are many contenders for personal allegiance and worship in our modern world. The Baals of our day include money, power, sex, prestige—all forms of hedonistic self-fulfillment. And as God condemned the golden calves and Baals of ancient culture, so He condemns the false gods of our day.

Moral Absolutes.—Immorality and a personal lack of integrity continue to be an abiding cultural phenomenon. The sexual perversion of the ancient Near East was denounced by the spokesmen of God in the Old Testament, and this prophetic word is needed in our day of moral relativity. As Myers observes, "relativism is one of the dominant assumptions of modern American culture."[50] The Old Testament insistence upon absolute truth in matters of personal morality is a powerful corrective to the contemporary mind-set which reduces truth to personal choice and fulfillment. Not only is this needed in terms of sexual practice, but as Wright points out, it is also a needed word in light of the current intellectual climate in the realm of truth and falsehood (Rom. 1:18-32).[51]

The definitive word of the Old Testament prophet was "Thus says the Lord." There was clear conviction, moral courage, and solid assurance regarding the Word of the living God. This theme must be recaptured—that of the absolute trustworthiness and practical relevance of Scripture.

Sovereignty of God.—One of the base issues in our modern world, as a result of autonomous individualism, is a disavowal of the sovereignty of God. Thus, our treatment of others is often based on the selfish pursuit of our interests and desires. The Old Testament condemnation of exploitation was based on God's sovereignty.

One can draw a parallel between the exploitation of women and children in the Old Testament due to ritual prostitution and child sacrifice in such issues and pornography and abortion. The issue is not whether or not it is personally fulfilling, but whether it is sin in the eyes of God.

The sovereignty of God also serves as a correction to the materialism rampant in our society. The Old Testament can provide a biblical attitude toward wealth and possessions. It can provide a powerful corrective toward our callousness to those in underdeveloped countries. For example, it is seldom observed that while millions die each year of starvation, Americans lead the world in obesity and dollars spend in "dieting"programs.[52] Gluttony was listed by the medieval church as one of the "seven deadly sins," yet it seldom finds its place in the preaching calendar of even the most biblical of expositors. The Old Testament principles regarding economic justice ring loud and long for all cultures and societies. The theme of such preaching is not Marxist communism, or a wooden condemnation of all wealth as sinful, but rather justice and Christian concern for the poor coupled with the emphasis on the lordship of Christ over our bodies.

God as the Great "I Am."—Though not listed as a section under Old Testament challenges to the culture of the ancient Near East, the great self-declaration of God as "I Am" in Exodus 3:14, seized by Jesus in John 8:58, serves as a challenge to the contemporary value of reductive naturalism. If all that can be known is what can be empirically verified, then knowledge is severely restricted. God's self-declaration reveals the narrow world view empiricism offers. The ultimate epistemological premise is that "God is," and that all of reality can be divided between the Creator and the created.

The Reconstructionist Proposal.—In concluding this section, it should be noted that a theme finding its way into many pulpits is the call for a "theonomy" (a society ruled by the law of God), often under the banner of "Christian Reconstructionism."[53] The essential premise is that God's societal law for Israel is binding and should be implemented as the structure for contemporary society. In the words of Reconstructionist Greg Bahnsen, "Theonomists are committed to the transformation (or reconstruction) of every area of life, including the institutions and affairs of the socio-political realm, according to the holy principles of God's revealed word (the theonomy)."[54] Christian Reconstructionism can be said to be an interesting modification of the "social gospel" movement which arguably often reduced conversion to little more than social change.[55] While it is not difficult to see the attraction such a proposal holds for Bible-believing Christians, it is fraught with difficulties, often failing to draw the distinction between the meaning of the biblical text and the significance of the biblical text.[56] The enormous hermeneutical difficulties of understanding Old Testament law as that which continues to be binding on Christians living under the New Covenant are problematic as well (see above).[57] It should also be noted that there is a significant distinction between a "Christian nation" and a "nation of Christians." Only the latter is substantive and conducive to true societal change. As Christopher Wright observes, preaching the Old Testament prophetically to the modern world:

> does not mean that Christians will try to impose by law in a secular state provisions lifted directly from the laws of Moses. It does mean that they will work to bring their society nearer to conformity with the principles underlying the concrete laws of Old Testament society, because they perceive the same God to be both Redeemer and law-giver of Israel, and also Creator and Ruler of contemporary mankind.[58]

The following assessment of Christian Reconstructionism by James W. Skillen is perceptive:

> Theonomists affirm that God's Word is directly applicable to modern states and societies, but they have not adequately answered the questions about who and which institutions are responsible to enforce what parts of God's law when and how. We agree with them that civil law should not be allowed a totalitarian embrace over churches, families, businesses, schools, and many other institutions. But we disagree over the nature and scope of the state's responsibility for enforcing God's law.[59]

Special interest groups have also emerged in an effort to revise contemporary culture, such as liberation theology,[60] black theology,[61] and feminist theology.[62] The difficulty with such expressions, beyond those already mentioned in regard to Christian Reconstructionism, is their methodological starting point; rather than beginning with Scripture (revelation), they begin with praxis. Thus, the Bible becomes subservient to social action in terms of doctrinal formulation.

Emphases for Preaching

Beyond suggesting particular themes available for one's preaching from the Old Testament regarding contemporary culture, specific suggestions can be made in regard to emphases for preaching in light of the three trends which mark modernity: In regard to secularization, preaching must emphasize penetration; as a result of privatization, preaching must emphasize personification; in light of pluralization, preaching must involve itself in particularization.

Penetration.—Because of the process of secularization, preaching must take on a "penetration" mentality in regard to the modern world. It must relate the truths of the Christian to the wider world in such a way that Christianity is seen to be the all-encompassing world view it was intended to be. The focus here is on Christian discipleship in terms of a world view that is God-informed. Rather than reflecting the world and its values, preaching should be marked by an eternal, vertical perspective that engages the world but also critiques the world.

Personification.—Personification refers to the embodiment of principle and moral, truth and lesson, in such a way that one's personal faith speaks to all segments of life. The popular term is "lordship," but as with all popular terms, familiarity breeds inattention. Privatization devalues Christian faith to private preference, therefore preaching must speak of the Christian life in holistic terms. In other words, the Christian faith is not a private, personal matter, but one that is all-encompassing in scope and demand. One must think and live Christianly in every sphere of life, whether it be economics, philosophy, morals, or business. As George Barna notes, the "concept of being a Christian has become bland and generic," a trend that an emphasis on the lordship of Christ would counteract.[63]

Particularization.—Pluralization throws down the gauntlet in regard to absolute truth. As a result, preaching must be sure that it faithfully engages in the particularization of the truth of the Christian faith. Christian theology states that all truth is God's truth and that this truth is truth for all. Patterson and Kim have observed that "Americans are making up their own rules, their own laws. In effect, we're all making up our own moral codes."[64] In essence, "we choose which laws of God we believe in."[65]

Therefore, what is meant by particularization is that there are some things that are distinct about the Christian faith in light of the many competing world views and ideologies of our society. If all truth is God's truth, then all claimants for truths must therefore be judged in light of God's truth. Preaching should not hide what is unique about the gospel, but celebrate it as the light which is shining forth in a world of darkness.

Contemporary Culture	Old Testament Application
Current Values:	Preaching Themes:
Narcissistic Hedonism (Idolatry)	Functional Monotheism
Moral Relativism (Perversion)	Moral Absolutes
Autonomous Individualism (Destruction of Weak/Innocent; Callousness to the Poor)	Sovereignty of God
Reductive Naturalism (God's Self-Declaration)	God the "I Am"
Streams of Modernity:	Preaching Emphases:
Secularization	Penetration
Privatization	Personification
Pluralization	Particularization

Conclusion

The focus of this book is an effort to regain the prophetic voice of the church through effective preaching of the Old

Testament. This chapter has endeavored to address how the Word of God as found in the Old Testament challenges and can change our modern world. H. Richard Niebuhr, in his classic work *Christ and Culture*, suggested five typologies for responding to the contemporary culture.[66] First, that of "Christ against culture." Here the church sees itself as distinct and separate from culture. Culture is without value, alien to the things of God, and thus the church should seek separation. In Christian history, Tertullian might be seen as an example of this perspective.[67] The "Christ of culture" position is the opposite, exhibiting a virtual association of contemporary culture with the church. The dominant culture is not only accepted, but seen as virtually synonymous with Christianity. A leading exponent of this perspective would be Albrecht Ritschl.[68] The first of these two positions might be termed "separation," and the latter "accommodation." A third position identified by Niebuhr, "Christ above culture," attempts a synthesis between Christ and culture. Aquinas shared affinities with this perspective.[69] Here culture is drawn upward by Christ. The fourth position, "Christ and culture in paradox," is a dualist view between the world of humanity and the world of God. Martin Luther could be categorized as holding to a view similar to this perspective.[70] Humanity is sinful, God is good, and thus there is the need for grace. We are left with culture and must act in it. Therein lies the paradox. Finally, Niebuhr suggested a conversionist perspective, "Christ the transformer of culture," which understands the church to be in the world in order to transform the world. Christ is Lord over culture. Historically, John Calvin may well be the clearest example of such a mindset.[71] Society must be claimed, or redeemed, in order to create a just, Christian society.

Without entering into the subtleties of Niebuhr's classifications, let it be stated that one should be against the secularization of culture, praise God's work within that fallen culture, and yet seek the transformation of culture toward the lordship of Christ. As Charles Kraft has reflected, we view God as transcendent and absolute, yet working within culture as a vehicle to interact with human beings.[72] "True transformational change," writes Kraft, is a "change in the central conceptualizations (worldview) of a culture." The values dominant in our modern world need to be confronted by the prophetic voice of the church, a voice given birth by the Old Testament Word of God, in order to win the hearts and minds of this generation for Christ.

Notes

1. Kenneth A. Meyers, *All God's Children and Blue Suede Shoes: Christians and Popular Culture* (Westchester, Ill.: Crossway, 1989), xii.

2. Langdon Gilkey, *Through the Tempest: Theological Voyages in a Pluralistic Culture*, Selected and Edited by Jeff B. Pool (Minneapolis: Fortress, 1991), 4.

3. There are two fronts in the battle with contemporary culture: first, and the focus of this book, is the prophetic engagement of culture with the truth and claims of Christ in order to confront that culture with the ideal for its existence. This chapter sets forth the challenge of contemporary culture and something of how the Old Testament can be used to preach the truth of God within its context. Second, there is the importance of being culturally relevant, which is understanding the contemporary culture in order to communicate effectively within its confines. These two dynamics are the two most pressing needs facing expositors today.

4. John R. W. Stott, *Between Two Worlds: The Art of Preaching in the Twentieth Century* (Grand Rapids: Eerdmans, 1982).

5. E. D. Hirsch, *Cultural Literacy: What Every American Needs to Know* (New York: Vintage/Random House, 1988).

6. Peter Berger, *The Sacred Canopy: Elements of a Sociological Theory of Religion* (Garden City, N.Y.: Anchor/Doubleday, 1969). The latest treatment of these three streams of modernity from a Christian perspective can be found in Andrew Walker's *Enemy Territory* (Bristol: Walker, 1991). An excellent analysis can also be found in Robert Wuthnow's *The Struggle for America's Soul: Evangelicals, Liberals, and Secularism* (Grand Rapids: Eerdmans, 1989).

7. Ibid., p. 107. See also David Martin, *A General Theory of Secularization* (Oxford: Blackwell, 1978), and Martin E. Marty, *The Modern Schism* (London: SCM, 1969).

8. Richard John Neuhaus, *The Naked Public Square: Religion and Democracy in America* (Grand Rapids: Eerdmans, 1984).

9. George Barna, *The Frog in the Kettle: What Christians Need to Know About Life in the Year 2000* (Ventura: Regal, 1990), 53.

10. Fred Fedler, *An Introduction to the Mass Media* (New York: Harcourt, Brace, Jovanovich, Inc., 1978), 8. On the impact of technology on contemporary culture, see O. B. Hardison, Jr., *Disappearing Through the Skylight: Culture and Technology in the Twentieth Century* (New York: Viking, 1989).

11. Page Smith, *Killing the Spirit: Higher Education in America* (New York: Viking, 1990), 5. Similar sentiments can be found in Allan Bloom, *The Closing of the American Mind: How Higher Education Has Failed Democracy and Impoverished the Souls of Today's Students* (New York: Simon and Schuster, 1987).

12. Berger, *Sacred Canopy*, 133-34; cf. Peter Berger, Brigitte Berger, and Hansfried Kellner, *The Homeless Mind* (Harmondsworth, Eng.: Penguin, 1974), chap. 3.

13. Os Guinness, *The Gravedigger File: Papers on the Subversion of the Modern Church* (Downers Grove: InterVarsity, 1983), 74; cf. Thomas Luckmann, *The Invisible Religion* (New York: Macmillan, 1967). Perhaps the best investigation into this dynamic of modernity was offered by Robert Bellah, et al., in *Habits of the Heart: Individualism and Commitment in American Life* (San Francisco: Harper and Row, 1985). A recent chronicle of America's privatization of faith can be found in Phillip L. Berman's *The Search for Meaning: Americans Talk About What They Believe and Why* (New York: Ballantine, 1990).

14. On this, see the analysis offered by Lesslie Newbigin in *The Gospel in a Pluralist Society* (Grand Rapids: Eerdmans, 1990).

15. Theodore Roszak, *Where the Wasteland Ends* (Garden City, NY: Anchor, 1973), 412.

16. Quoted in *Context*, 15 (November, 1981): 6.

17. As John Naisbitt and Patricia Aburdene note in *Megatrends 2000: Ten New Directions for the 1990's* (New York: William Morrow, 1990), for contemporary society, "Spirituality, Yes. Organized Religion, No," p. 275. A similar point is made by Barna, *The Frog in the Kettle*, 41-42, 117.

18. Bellah, *Habits of the Heart*, 221.

19. Berger, *Sacred Canopy*, 127. The historical background to this stream of modernity is illuminated by Nathan O. Hatch's *The Democratization of American Christianity* (New Haven: Yale, 1989).

20. Guinness, *Gravedigger*, 93.

21. Ibid., 94. The idea of religion as a canopy serves as the motif for Martin E. Marty's recent exploration of modern American religion, *Modern American Religion: The Irony of It All, 1893-1919* (Chicago: University of Chicago Press, 1986), the first of four projected volumes on twentieth-century American religion.

22. Gilkey, *Through the Tempest*, 21.

23. Harold O. J. Brown, "Evangelicals and Social Ethics," *Evangelical Affirmations*, edited by Kenneth S. Kantzer and Carl F. H. Henry (Grand Rapids: Academie/Zondervan, 1990), 279.

24. Leith Anderson, *Dying for Change: An Arresting Look at the New Realities Confronting Churches and Para-Church Ministries* (Minneapolis: Bethany, 1990), 31-32.

25. Malise Ruthven, *The Divine Supermarket: Shopping for God in America* (New York: William Morrow, 1989).

26. Barna, *Frog in the Kettle*, 141. By syncretism, Barna means the "mix and match" mentality of pulling together different threads in various religions in order to create a personal religion that suits an individual taste.

27. It should be noted that it is the process of pluralization which leads to the individuation which underlies the process of privatization. The reason for this is that inherent within pluralism is differentiation, and diversity inevitably leads toward individuation. On this, see Benton Johnson, "Modernity and Pluralism," *Pushing the Faith: Proselytism and Civility in a Pluralistic World*, Martin E. Marty and Frederick E. Greenspahn, eds. (New York: Crossroad, 1988), 14.

28. These four marks were first suggested to my thinking by Langdon Gilkey in *Naming the Whirlwind* (Indianapolis: Bobbs-Merril, 1969), and most recently by Thomas C. Oden's *After Modernity . . . What? Agenda for Theology* (Grand Rapids: Academie/Zondervan, 1990).

29. Oden, *After Modernity . . . What?*, 52.

30. See James Patterson and Peter Kim, *The Day America Told the Truth: What People Really Believe About Everything That Really Matters* (New York: Prentice-Hall, 1991).

31. Alan Bloom, *The Closing of the American Mind: How Higher Education Has Failed Democracy and Impoverished the Souls of Today's Students* (New York: Simon and Schuster, 1987), 25.

32. Oden, *After Modernity. . . . What?*, 74, 157.

33. Perhaps the best introduction to the culture of the ancient Near East is given by James B. Pritchard, ed., *The Ancient Near East, Volume I: An Anthology of Texts and Pictures* (Princeton: Princeton University Press, 1958), and his subsequent volume, *The Ancient Near East, Volume II: A New Anthology of Texts and Pictures* (Princeton: Princeton University Press, 1975).

34. Christopher J. H. Wright, *An Eye for An Eye: The Place of Old Testament Ethics Today* (Downers Grove: InterVarsity, 1983), 187.

35. Thomas G. Long, *The Witness of Preaching* (Louisville: Westminster/ John Knox Press, 1989), 77. It should be noted that Long advises that the focus and function of the sermon, of course, should grow directly out of exegesis of the biblical text.

36. On this, see Philip Edgcumbe Hughes, "The Truth of Scripture and the Problem of Historical Relativity," *Scripture and Truth*, ed. D. A. Carson and John D. Woodbridge (Grand Rapids: Academie/Zondervan, 1983), 173-94.

37. Daniel Harrington, *Interpreting the Old Testament* (Wilmington, Del.: Michael Glazier, 1981), 123. Langdon Gilkey adds his choice of using the Old Testament to engage contemporary culture was not accidental, adding that "the New Testament is of minimal help with our problem; namely, the relation of God . . . to the historical and political events of our time," see *Through the Tempest*, 116.

38. Kyle M. Yates, *Preaching from the Prophets* (Nashville: Broadman, 1942), 1.

39. Walter C. Kaiser, Jr. *The Uses of the Old Testament in the New* (Chicago: Moody, 1985), 197.

40. Ibid., 198.

41. Brevard S. Childs, *Old Testament Theology in a Canonical Context* (Philadelphia: Fortress, 1985), 63.

42. Excellent introductions to biblical hermeneutics include, but are not limited to, the following: Gordon D. Fee and Douglas Stuart, *How to Read the Bible for All Its Worth: A Guide to Understanding the Bible* (Grand Rapids: Academie/ Zondervan, 1982); Elliot E. Johnson, *Expository Hermeneutics: An Introduction* (Grand Rapids: Academie/Zondervan, 1991); Bernard Ramm, *Protestant Biblical Interpretation: A Textbook of Hermeneutics for Conservative Protestants* (Boston: W. A. Wilde, 1956); Haddon W. Robinson, *Biblical Preaching: The Development and Delivery of Expository Messages* (Grand Rapids: Baker, 1980); John R. W. Stott, *Between Two Worlds: The Art of Preaching in the Twentieth Century* (Grand Rapids: Eerdmans, 1982); and Roy B. Zuck, *Basic Bible Interpretation: A Practical Guide to Discovering Biblical Truth* (Wheaton: Victor, 1991). See also "The Chicago Statement on Biblical Hermeneutics," *Hermeneutics, Inerrancy and the Bible*, Earl D. Radmacher and Robert D. Preus, editors (Grand Rapids: Zondervan, 1984), 881-87. For assistance with particularly problematic passages within the Old Testament, see Walter C. Kaiser, Jr., *Hard Sayings of the Old Testament* (Downers Grove: InterVarsity, 1988). For a brief overview of the history of hermeneutics, see David S. Dockery, *Biblical Interpretation Then and Now* (Grand Rapids: Baker, 1992).

43. Gordon D. Fee and Douglas Stuart, *How to Read the Bible for All Its Worth: A Guide to Understanding the Bible* (Grand Rapids: Academie/Zondervan, 1982), 136-39.

44. Kaiser, *The Uses of the Old Testament in the New*, 198.

45. Harry Blamires, *The Christian Mind* (Ann Arbor: Servant Books, 1963), 4.

46. The separation of "meaning" from "significance" is indebted to the work of E. D. Hirsch, *Validity in Interpretation* (New Haven: Yale, 1967).

47. As quoted by Ronald E. Sleeth, *God's Word and Our Words: Basic Homiletics* (Atlanta: John Knox, 1986), 39.

48. Zuck, *Basic Bible Interpretation*, 282-92.

49. Carl F. H. Henry, "Biblical Authority and the Social Crisis," *Authority and Interpretation: A Baptist Perspective* (Grand Rapids: Baker, 1987), 206.

50. Myers, *All God's Children and Blue Suede Shoes*, 29.

51. Wright, *An Eye for An Eye*, 187.

52. Though not unchallenged on many points, the most influential book in this discussion has been Ronald J. Sider's *Rich Christians in an Age of Hunger: A Biblical Study* (Second Ed.; Downers Grove: Intervarsity, 1984).

53. Foundational writings for Christian Reconstructionism usually include Greg L. Bahnsen's *Theonomy in Christian Ethics* (Nutley, N.J.: Craig, 1977), and Rousas John Rushdoony's *Institutes of Biblical Law* (Nutley, N.J.: Craig, 1973).

54. Greg Bahnsen, "The Theonomic Position," *God and Politics: Four Views on the Reformation of Civil Government*, ed. Gary Scott Smith (Phillipsburg, N.J.: Presbyterian and Reformed Publishing Co., 1989), 23.

55. See Walter Rauschenbusch, *A Theology for the Social Gospel* (Nashville: Abingdon, 1945).

56. Two thoughtful critiques and interactions of Christian Reconstructionism are William S. Barker and W. Robert Godfrey, eds., *Theonomy: A Reformed Critique* (Grand Rapids: Academie/Zondervan, 1990), and H. Wayne House and Thomas Ice, *Dominion Theology: Blessing or Curse? An Analysis of Christian Reconstructionism* (Portland: Multnomah, 1988).

57. For example, Reconstructionists assume biblical law to be binding unless they are directly rescinded, as opposed to Gordon Fee's suggestion to consider all Old Testament law rescinded by the New Testament unless directly renewed in light of Christ's fulfillment of the law.

58. Wright, *An Eye for An Eye*, 162.

59. James W. Skillen, *The Scattered Voice: Christians at Odds in the Public Square* (Grand Rapids: Zondervan, 1990), 178.

60. The foundational text for liberation theology is by Gustavo Gutierrez, *A Theology for Liberation* (Maryknoll: Orbis, 1988). See also the following introductions to liberation thought: Phillip Berryman, *Liberation Theology: The Essential Facts About the Revolutionary Movement in Latin America and Beyond* (Bloomington: Meyer Stone and New York: Pantheon/Random House, 1987); Jose Miguez Bonino, *Doing Theology in a Revolutionary Situation* (Philadelphia: Fortress, 1975); Robert McAfee Brown, *Theology in a New Key: Responding to Liberating Themes* (Philadelphia: Westminster, 1978); Jose Comblin, *The Holy Spirit and Liberation* (Maryknoll: Orbis, 1989). A thoughtful critique of liberation theology from an Evangelical perspective can be found in *Liberation Theology*, ed. Ronald H. Nash (Grand Rapids: Baker, 1984).

61. Perhaps the best introductory volume on black theology's concern with oppression is James H. Cone's *God of the Oppressed* (San Francisco: Harper and Row, 1975).

62. The foundational volume for feminist theology is probably Rosemary Radford Ruether's *Sexism and God-Talk: Toward a Feminist Theology* (Boston: Beacon, 1983). See also *Feminist Perspective on Biblical Scholarship*, edited by Adela Yarbo Collins (Chico, CA: Scholars Press, 1985). One of many evangelical assessments of feminist concerns can be found in *Women, Authority and the Bible*, ed. Alvera Mickelsen (Downers Grove: InterVarsity, 1986).

63. Barna, *Frog in the Kettle*, 113.

64. Patterson and Kim, *The Day America Told the Truth*, 6.

65. Ibid.

66. H. Richard Niebuhr, *Christ and Culture* (San Francisco: Harper and Row, 1951).

67. See *Tertullian*, Parts I-III, *Ante-Nicene Fathers*, Vol. 3 (Grand Rapids: Eerdmans). See also *Early Latin Theology*, edited by S. L. Greenslade, *Library of Christian Classics*, Vol. 5 (Philadelphia: Westminster, 1956), 21-110.

68. On Ritschl, see his *Justification and Reconciliation* (Edinburgh: T & T Clark, 1900), and *Theologie und Metaphysik*, trans. by Philip Hefner (Philadelphia; Fortress, 1972).

69. A good introduction to Aquinas can be found in *Nature and Grace, Selections from Summa Theologica*, edited by A. M. Fairweather, *Library of Christian Classics*, vol. 11 (Philadelphia: Westminster, 1954).

70. A good introduction to Luther's writings can be found in *Selected Writings of Martin Luther*, 4-vols., edited by Theodore G. Tappert (Philadelphia: Fortress, 1967).

71. On Calvin's thought, see his *Institutes of the Christian Religion*, edited by J. T. McNeill, *Library of Christian Classics*, Vol. 20-21 (Philadelphia: Westminster, 1960).

72. Charles Kraft, *Christianity in Culture: A Study in Dynamic Biblical Theologizing in Cross-Cultural Perspective* (Maryknoll: Orbis, 1979). Kraft's work is essentially a "working-out" of this principle in regard to contemporary missiological concerns of cross-cultural communication.

CONCLUSION

Where Do We Go from Here?

Integrating the Old Testament into Your Ministry

Kenneth S. Hemphill

"The confession of a Paulinist!" This could serve as an adequate and accurate subtitle to this section. Throughout the great majority of my ministry, I have been primarily a New Testament preacher, and more specifically a "Paulinist." When I look back over the last ten years of my preaching ministry, it is apparent that it is heavily weighted in the Pauline letters. I had in my repertoire a few "sugar sticks" from the Old Testament. Some were topical in nature, others biographical. My favorite Old Testament sermons were the challenging stories of crossing the Jordan and taking the promised land. These were good texts for challenging the church boldly to press on in its ministry task. Yet, I had never really attempted to integrate a systematic pattern for Old Testament preaching into my overall preaching plan.

First, my knowledge and retention of Greek far exceeds that of my Hebrew skills. This confession is in no way intended to cast aspersion on my Hebrew professor. I studied with one of the best. Truthfully, I took more Greek electives at seminary because I found it less intimidating. I have used Greek more often since graduation and thus have retained it at a higher level than my Hebrew. My impression from talking to fellow pastors is that many have parallel experiences. For this reason, we often find it easier to do our exegetical work and preaching from the New Testament.

A glance at my personal library will provide further evidence that I have leaned heavily toward the New Testament. For most books of the New Testament, I have several different commentaries. But, with few exceptions, my Old Testament commentaries are fewer in number. Many of my seminary electives were in the New Testament field and all of my graduate study was in the New Testament. For me, with my other pastoral duties, it was just easier to preach from the books which were most familiar to me and my congregation.

Another reason for avoiding the Old Testament is the intimidation created by some of the "problems" that have been raised, but not solved—at least for me—by higher critical methodology. I felt secure in my ability to grapple with and resolve the "apparent" contradictions and authorship problems of the New Testament books, but when it came to a few of the classic Old Testament problems of authorship, dating, and historical accuracy, I was a self-confessed novice. I did not want to raise questions for my congregation that I was not well-prepared to help them answer. Fortunately, conservative evangelical scholars have begun to clarify in a constructive fashion many of those passages which were once troublesome. Yet once again, it was just easier to preach from the familiar.

If you think the phrase "just easier" is beginning to sound like a refrain, you are correct. Unfortunately the busy pastor is sometimes forced to do that which is easier. In the press for time, we just grab for that familiar Pauline text and head for the pulpit. We all know that "easier" is not always best. I knew that I needed greater balance in my preaching and that I was neglecting both for myself and my congregation the rich heritage of the Old Testament.

To encourage the busy pastor to integrate the Old Testament into his regular preaching agenda, I would like to take two tracts. First I want to pull together, in a summary fashion, the significant pastoral contributions of each chapter in order for you to apply them more easily in your study. Second, I will give a few personal reflections from my continuing pilgrimage to integrate the Old Testament into my own preaching.

An Overview

This book provides a good balance for the pastor because it is scholarly yet practical. It contains a veritable treasure chest of sermon and sermon series ideas for both the novice and the experienced Old Testament expositor, providing a wonderful survey of Old Testament material. Throughout the entire book you will discover a strong emphasis on the basics: linguistic study, sound exegesis, historical-contextual background, practical application, and integrity in the accurate handling of Scripture. It will be a valuable tool for the conservative pastor who has been intimidated in his use of the Old Testament. Seldom are our congregations moved by the theology of the Yahwist redactor or the debate over the Red Sea/Reed Sea.

The following summaries in no wise do justice to the richness of each chapter, but they are included to provide a capsule reminder and to assist the reader in the utilization of this volume.

Preaching Historical Narrative

Christian proclamation is anchored in the Hebrew Scriptures and therefore requires preachers to interpret their message in continuum with the historic redemption of God's people. Therefore Christian ministers must preach the redemptive theology of the Scriptures which includes narrative theology. By narrative theology, Ken Mathews means biblical theology that is conveyed through the medium of narrative discourse.

The Primary History, Genesis through Kings, is a continuous account which traces the rise and fall of national Israel. The Secondary History, 1 and 2 Chronicles and Ezra–Nehemiah, retells the story from a later vantage point and goes beyond the Primary History to tell what happened to the faithful few who returned from Babylon. Historical narrative is also embedded in shorter accounts of the Hebrew's heroes and in poetic oracles of the Hebrew's prophets.

Mathews provides a helpful look at the relationship of historical narrative to history. Some scholars have attempted to cast doubt upon the historical reliability of the Hebrew narratives. Mathews argues that all historical events and artifacts require interpretation. These interpretative records result from a process of selection and arrangement of the materials by the author. This does not, however, render them inaccurate or less historical in nature.

While some have compared the historical narratives to fiction or mythology, Mathews points out three critical differences: (1) The primary difference lies in the commitment to reality. The historian begins with a given series of events and cannot freely disregard or distort them; (2) Historians claim that their records are authentic and submit their writings to a judgment of their facts; and (3) The primary distinction is not literary form but intention. For that reason it is wrong to question the historiography of a literary work solely on the basis of its formal similarities to fiction writing.

Mathews warns against judging biblical narrative by the conventions of modern historians. This has led to the outright rejection of some historical narratives. For example, a biblical historian's world view permits a fuller explanation for events by recognizing a dual causation for events in which providence and humanity work together in the historical process. The biblical historian claims accessibility to private knowledge not derived from public sources. The quality of divine inspiration explains the access of biblical historians to private information, but does not mean they must surrender their claim to historicity. Mathews' discussion is helpful because it gives the biblical expositor the confidence that Hebrew history is trustworthy.

The concerned expositor needs to understand the function of Hebrew history and theology. First, historical narrative enhanced the Hebrews' understanding of the nature of God as Lord of history and creation. God is a God of history and therefore the divine hand lies behind every human event. For this reason, the expositor should understand Israel's religion and the history of the ancient Near East. Second, biblical historians were not objective reporters. The preacher should be aware that he is not declaring bare historical facts, but preaching texts which are interpretations of God's acts. Scripture brings both event and its inspired interpretation together. Third, history is multifaceted in perspective and may be told from various complimentary viewpoints. The Hebrew writers were not writing a history of the ancient Near East, but they were selecting and telling events designed to express their theological understanding of how history works.

While the writers of Scripture presented a theological interpretation of history, they did so in such a way as to create aesthetically pleasing literature. For that reason, the preacher must understand the various literary features of the narratives. Form is integral to meaning. Every narrative has a deliberate arrangement of constituent parts. When the expositor understands how those parts fit together, he will be able to discover the unity, themes, and emphases of the passage. Mathews provides numerous practical examples of narrative structure.

Mathews points out four major ways that narrative served the theology of the authors: (1) Hebrew narrative depicts a God who has chosen to do nothing apart from human participation;

(2) Narrative reflects the "apparent" ambiguity of God's actions in the context of the vicissitudes of life; (3) Narrative enhances the theology of the word. The whole universe as well as Israel's history is ordered by God's spoken word; and (4) Historical narrative bears witness to God as the architect of a universal kingdom which was foreshadowed by Israel's monarchy.

This section encourages the preacher to allow the literary form of the biblical text to govern how the sermon is conceived. To preach narrative like expository discourse diminishes the power of the original writing because it neglects the form-meaning complex and detracts from the theology of the Hebrew authors. If the contemporary audience is to hear and experience biblical narrative in a manner similar to their ancient counterparts, the preacher must use narrative preaching. Narrative preaching requires following the event-line and exposing the narrational-theological features of the text. This demands sensitivity to historical awareness, literary contexts, and theological perspective(s).

Old Testament Law

The law was the glory and pride of Israel, but what place should it occupy in your preaching ministry? Robert Bergen helps the busy pastor by defining and clarifying what Israel meant by the law. Torah (law), in the context of Israelite religion referred to the written and oral instruction originating with Moses during Israel's Sinai experience. The Pentateuch was the written portion of that law. Israel saw value in both the narrative stories of the Pentateuch, as well as the legal materials, for both taught how one could live a God-pleasing life.

The Jewish rabbis recognized two distinct sets of laws: those which apply to non-Jews and those applying specifically to the Israelites. The general laws (Noachide) cover such matters as idolatry, sexual sin, human bloodshed, and theft.

The laws for the Israelites, the believing community, were more rigorous. These laws can be divided into three categories: moral, civil, and ceremonial. Moral laws address personal values such as respect for God, human life, parents, marriage, property, etc. Civil laws deal with issues like public safety, orphans, property rights, etc. Ceremonial laws address matters such as sacrifices, holy days, priesthood, dietary regulations, and purity rites. For Israel, there was no separation between religious laws and secular ones, all were of God and all were to be obeyed. Israel looked to God's law as the standard and evaluated rulers and kingdoms on the basis of their obedience to

God's law. The results of violation of the Torah were economic loss, foreign oppression, and the loss of life.

The sensitive pastor could preach a series of sermons with the relevance and vibrancy of the front page of the newspaper from these various sections of the law. With the moral confusion and ambivalence of our day, it is essential that we learn to preach from God's law.

Bergen provides a careful look at law and New Testament fulfillment that is both helpful for understanding and suggestive for preaching. The New Testament community accepted the Torah as having great value in preaching normative and authoritative behavioral guidelines. Yet the New Testament teaches that the law is utterly incapable of providing spiritual regeneration. First-century believers saw the law prefiguring and anticipating the life and ministry of Jesus Christ. Bergen proposes six specific uses of the law for New Testament believers.

1. Behavioral—It provides an invaluable guide to existence this side of eternity.

2. Analogical—The Torah presents a collection of ancient precedents for dealing with analogous modern situations. Thus it can provide insight into divine counsel.

3. Christological—The church can understand the significance of Jesus' life only when it understands the legal system established in the Torah.

4. Background—Since first-century Jewish society was forged under the hammer of Mosaic law, it provides the necessary background material to New Testament preaching.

5. Illustrative—The law provides a continual supply of good and varied illustrations.

6. Spiritual warfare—The law provides a necessary source of strength for dealing with temptation.

The preaching opportunities presented by the law are endless. One could certainly preach a series on "values clarification" that would cut across the broad stream of societal needs. One could speak to individuals and social institutions with equal clarity from the law. I could also envision a series aimed at ethical business practices. Preaching on the law could be valuable to sensitize one's church to the neglected persons in your community. Preaching from the law provides wonderful evangelistic opportunities as the law naturally leads to Christ.

Preaching Poetry

George Klein begins by correcting the popular misconception about the so called "poetic books" of the Old Testament: Job,

Psalms, Proverbs, Ecclesiastes, and Song of Solomon, noting that roughly one third of the Old Testament is poetry. Some of the best examples of biblical poetry are found outside this restrictive list. One must not fail to mention the poetry of an Isaiah or Amos, not to mention other lovely poems such as Exodus 15, Deuteronomy 32, and Judges 5.

Klein attempts to survey the most important ingredients of poetry, including figurative language and parallelism. The preacher is encouraged to recognize that figurative language can be interpreted with precision, and should not be seen as being undesirable in any way, particularly in light of the emphasis on "literal" interpretation.

The purposes of figurative language are many: embellishment, making a passage more easily recalled, and adding connotative or emotive meaning to the text. Figures of speech communicate with the audience on a more sophisticated level than prose.

This chapter introduces the major figures of speech in four major categories. Figures of Comparison emphasize something by likening it to something else. Figures of Addition or Amplification include some form of expansion of an idea in one line of poetry as compared to a former line. Figures of Subtraction or Omission represent increasing complexity as important aspects of the poetic line are omitted. Figures of Substitution are surely the most involved and sophisticated of all figurative language.

Next, Klein surveys parallelism, one of the most distinctive features of Old Testament poetry. Synonymous parallelism states the idea in one line and then restates the same thing in the next line. Antithetical parallelism, like synonymous parallelism, exhibits balanced terms as the poetic lines are compared with one another. With antithetical parallelism the terms are contrasted or in opposition. Synthetic parallelism is usually explained as parallelism in which the second line (plus the third and fourth lines, if present) add to the thought of the first line.

Before concluding with a sermonic illustration of his principles of poetic interpretation, Klein presents the different types or genres of psalms. Among the types described and identified are: the hymn, the individual and community lament, the individual and community narrative praise, and royal psalms.

Preaching the Prophets

The prophets provide a wealth of preaching opportunities. The language of the prophets is more explicitly theological and their sermonic style lend themselves readily to preaching and teaching. Yet Dan Kent warns the expositor that preaching the prophets with integrity will require work in the study. The preacher/teacher must first of all be honest to the original historical context. The prophet's primary concern was to give the Lord's message to the waiting people of his own generation. The prophet's task was not primarily predictive. They were preachers who spoke of the past, present, and future, but they did so in order to encourage the listener to turn back to the Lord.

The prophets were not systematic in their messages; they were preachers and visionaries, not academic lecturers. They preached in poetry. Yet the most important aspect of prophetic preaching was its content, not its form. The distinctive and crucial element of Hebrew prophecy was its moral element. They told who the Lord is and what He wanted His people to do.

In preaching the prophets we must follow the same general and basic principles of biblical interpretation that we apply to the entirety of Scripture. We must first be clear about context, social setting, origin, and purpose of the book. We should take the literal or normal meaning as our controlling or limiting guide for interpreting the prophets. But in preaching the literal meaning, we must recognize and interpret properly the poetic and figurative language of the prophets.

While many teachers focus on the predictive elements of the prophetic books, Kent urges us to look mainly to the moral and religious content of the message. The prophet's primary concern was to call the people of his day back to the obligations of their covenant relationship. Many of the promises and predictions were contingent on the response of the people. Many predictions were given so that they would not have to be fulfilled. While we should not attempt to find cryptic messianic allusions behind every prophetic bush, we must not neglect to declare the clear expressions of messianic expectation contained in the prophets.

The prophets provide numerous opportunities for the contemporary preacher to speak God's Word to a society in need of an anchor. The prophets give us clues for interpreting our own history in the light of God's over-arching purposes. People today need to understand their lives in the light of God's redemptive purpose. The comprehensive nature of the prophetic teaching provides ample opportunity to address the current issues of our day. The rich pictures and vivid images of the prophets such as the potter and the clay, the valley of dry bones, or the plumb line, provide wonderfully vibrant sermon ideas. The prophets, through their preaching, expose their own humanity as the struggle with the will of God. Preaching the prophets will produce both biblical and personal realism in your preaching.

Preaching Wisdom

Preaching from the Wisdom Literature is challenging both because of the structure of the material and its difficulty of interpretation. Yet the pastor must preach wisdom in order to edify his congregation through the teaching of biblical doctrine and morality. The current moral climate of the church makes the preaching of wisdom all the more essential. Divorces and domestic conflict, poor financial management, substance abuse, and simple dishonesty afflict the members of most local churches. The Wisdom Literature, properly expounded, will help the Christian learn right from wrong. More than that, Wisdom Literature teaches moral principles *as part of the life of faith.* Wisdom deals more with the practical, ordinary issues of life than does the law. That does not mean that the advice of wisdom is "secular" common sense; it is divine guidance for those who desire to please God.

For the preacher to proclaim the truths of wisdom adequately, he must accurately interpret the Wisdom Literature. Duane Garrett warns against the popular allegorization method because the texts themselves give no indication that they mean what the allegorists claim. The allegorist works under the pretense of preaching a passage, but ignores the real message of the text. The topical approach which searches the Wisdom Literature for verses on particular topics has been popular, particularly with regard to Proverbs and Ecclesiastes. Garrett accepts the validity of the topical approach, but expresses serious reservations about its use, because it obscures the complexities and tensions in the biblical text and virtually declares the book, in its present form, unusable for sermons.

Garrett prefers the contextual approach that takes a single, connected passage of Scripture and expounds the meaning of that text. It assumes that the task of the preacher is to explain the meaning of the Bible *as it is written, in its literary, and historical context.* This demands that the pastor must first understand the book as a whole before he begins to expound any individual text. The next step is to examine the structure of the book and thus mark off boundaries of individual units in the book. When the expositor has chosen a sermon text, he must observe both its external and internal context. The external context is the text before and after. The internal context is the structure and outline of the passage itself. Beginning from this point, the normal steps of exegesis follow. As the pastor moves to preparation and presentation he must keep two goals in focus. He must teach the lesson of the text itself. Second he must preach Christ.

The Wisdom Literature, Proverbs, Ecclesiastes, Job, and the Song of Solomon are very diverse, and thus Garrett gives a helpful look at the individual wisdom books. He suggests preaching from Job with the central question being: "Why should a person serve God?" This question enables the preacher to focus on major themes such as the dangers of pharisaical orthodoxy, the value of knowing God for His own sake, the need for compassion, and the greatness of God's power.

Garrett also gives the preacher a boost in his exposition from the Proverbs by giving direction for understanding its organizational unity. The Book of Ecclesiastes is discussed in the light of its genre and intended audience. He sees the original readers as members of the aristocracy. Thus, he sees Ecclesiastes as a refutation of international wisdom and as the most evangelical book of all wisdom literature. He argues that the pastor can find here a clear rejection of pagan or "New Age" notions of eternal life. In looking at the Song, Garrett rejects both the allegorical and historical methods of interpretation. He believes it must be understood as love poetry. With this theme in mind, Garrett suggests several preaching themes.

This chapter reminds us of the timeless value of Scripture. The Wisdom Literature enables the expositor to address contemporary issues from the timeless wisdom of God's revelation. This chapter, along with the helpful footnotes, will enable the serious preacher to discover new opportunities for biblical preaching.

The New Testament Use of the Old Testament

The Christian church was born on the day of Pentecost with sacred Scriptures: the Law, the Prophets, and the Writings. The earliest Christians were Jews, and the Scriptures were the literary foundation of their confession of faith in the crucified and risen Messiah, Jesus. The distinctive difference between the Jews who became Christians and those who rejected the messianic claims being made about Jesus centered around the proper reading of the Scriptures. The non-Christian Jews saw no expectation of a crucified Messiah, whereas the Christians declared that the ancient Scriptures did predict such a Messiah. Thus, the Christian reading of Scripture would often differ dramatically from the interpretive traditions of their Jewish heritage, but they were convinced that their new readings were coherent and consistent with the divine purposes accomplished in the history of Israel as revealed in the sacred texts.

Robert Sloan thus postulates that the use of the Old Testament by the New Testament writers is important for our understanding of New Testament theology. He further suggests that we must read the Old Testament as the New Testament writers read the theological conclusion that Jesus is the Christ. He cautions, however, that the question is more difficult to answer in terms of the interpretive methods they used to read the ancient texts.

Sloan first surveys the literary phenomena which occur in the various New Testament readings of the Old Testament. He looks at various instances where a New Testament author incorporates material from the Old Testament into his own text. The material may be a phrase, a verbal or conceptual parallel, and/or a direct quote. It must be understood that there is a correspondence, at some level, between the two texts in question. The correspondence may be prophecy-fulfillment, thematic correlation, or analogy between the situation of the writer/readers and the ancient text. The correspondence between the two bodies of literature resulted in the fact that historically prior material was in some way incorporated into the historically more recent text.

The most obvious type of intertextual relationship between the Old Testament and New Testament occurs when a New Testament author explicitly cites an Old Testament text. He points to the Gospel of Matthew as a prime example of explicit citation. Typological correspondence is also common in the New Testament. Typology is a method of interpretation whereby a larger level of correspondence is established between persons and events. One example of typological interpretation is found in 1 Corinthians 10:6 where Israel's sins teach that we should not crave the evil things they also craved. The use of phrases, allusions, and echoes of Old Testament texts in the New Testament is difficult to analyze or describe because it involves smaller units of verbal correspondence. These are sometimes specific references, although not necessarily verbatim, while at times they are simply allusions to the biblical language. It is not always clear to what extent the original context of the older material is important for understanding the point being made in the later text.

Some Old Testament texts were chosen by New Testament writers because of the occurrence of certain "catchwords." The gathering together of certain Old Testament texts to be used together in a single New Testament context often occurs by virtue of the recurrence of a single "catchword." Such is the case for the various "stone" passages from the Old Testament. The use of the word "rest" in Hebrews 3–4 is an example of the "catchword" which becomes central for holding together a collection of Old Testament texts. There are other instances where a single word in a given Old Testament text is the centerpiece of an interpretive maneuver made by the author. At other times the New Testament author appeals to the general witness of the Scriptures without any indication that he has in mind any particular text, word, story, or event in mind. This general appeal is often noted by a phrase like, "according to the Scriptures."

Sloan provides a helpful discussion of what he terms, "surprising shifts." This occurs when a New Testament writer has a surprising and innovative use of Old Testament materials. For example, what stands in Hosea 13:14 as a summons to death to come forward and do its worst, because of the disobedience of God's people, is dramatically transformed in the context of 1 Corinthians 15 into a triumphal crowing on the part of Paul against the powers of death and the grave. Another innovative, interpretive twist is seen in Paul's application of Old Testament texts which refer to Israel, to Gentile Christians. The warrant for such shifts lies in the theological givens. Such innovative readings should not be referred to as "spiritualizing" or "allegorizing." This is an issue of hermeneutical direction, that is, from Christian theology to scriptural reading.

Sloan helpfully explains the two major theological uses of Scripture found in the New Testament—the Christocentric and the ecclesiocentric. The New Testament writers frequently use Old Testament passages with a clear Christ-centered interpretation. Matthew's Gospel alone includes at least ten events in the life of Jesus which are supported by explicitly introduced Old Testament citations. Another important matter is that of interpreting Old Testament passages in a church-centered manner. Romans clearly illustrates this pattern of interpretation. Paul utilized numerous Old Testament passages which teach that Jew and Gentile alike participate in sin and may alike participate in God's mercy. Thus, the Jews and Gentiles alike, as those who believe in Jesus, are true heirs of the scriptural promises and together constitute the people of God. Sloan argues that we too must read the ancient Scriptures with a view to their Christ-centered and church-centered functions.

Sloan concludes that the "original intent" of a passage did not always determine the meaning a New Testament writer derived from it. Nevertheless, they did interpret Scripture under two extrinsic controls. First, one control was the message of and/or the central events related to the death, burial, and exaltation of Jesus. Second, they saw themselves to be in continuity with the scriptural people of God. Thus, we can say that for the New Testament writers: (1) the Scriptures of Israel are the living Word of the living God and (2) the Scriptures of Israel have a certain eschatological/prophetic character.

Sloan argues that given the divine event of the resurrection, the interpretation of the Old Testament in a Christocentric and ecclesiocentric manner is apt and understands the original scriptural vision. He believes that the New Testament writers drew legitimate conclusions to certain trajectories already begun within the theology and history of the Old Testament itself. While acknowledging that the New Testament writers obviously went beyond the intentionality of the original writers, they do so in an appropriate manner. Yet we cannot conclude that the texts have complete elasticity. Some interpretations fit while others do not. The fitness of a given text depends upon its original intention and its adaptability to, via the medium of a creative mind, the constraints of the given, historically affirmed truths of the Christian faith. The authors of the New Testament had a body of sacred texts which they believed were divinely given, prophetic in character, and susceptible to interpretive and inspired reinterpretation. Sloan argues that we cannot reduplicate their methods because their prophetic insights represent a historically particularized set of interpretive acts which, in salvation-history, are as unique as the gospel events themselves. This conclusion is based upon the uniqueness of the role of the apostles and early Christian prophets, whose offices have closed.

Since we are beneficiaries of their readings, we may live in their light. Our readings of the Old Testament must be focused in the light of the New Testament writers' readings of the Old Testament. To attempt to read the Old Testament as if the New Testament had not been written is historically naive and is as audacious as the attempt to add to the New Testament. Through the prism of the apostolic literature we can appreciate more fully the glorious Light of God which first shone in the Scriptures of the ancient Hebrews, later burst forth into the world of human flesh, and is still reflected in the liege and worship of the church. This light must be preached because it still brings illumination.

Typological Exegesis

David Dockery gives the preacher great assistance in understanding one of the most misunderstood and misapplied principles of biblical interpretation. Many view typology as an unacceptable hermeneutic, a methodology no modern interpreter would dare practice. Others see typology as their primary interpretive guide when attempting to prepare an Old Testament text for presentation to a contemporary audience. Dockery attempts to steer a middle course between these two extremes.

Without attempting to portray every Old Testament text as explicitly messianic, "Typological Exegesis" reminds the reader that the New Testament, including Christ Himself, saw the Old Testament through Christological eyes. Christ was seen as the "fulfillment" of the Scriptures, the Old Testament.

Next, Dockery surveys the diverse hermeneutical methods current at the time the New Testament was written. With the common assumption that the "Old" Testament was inspired Scripture, Jewish interpretation during New Testament times encouraged the idea that there were numerous legitimate interpretations of any text. The five most common Jewish approaches to interpretation included the literal, typological, allegorical, pesher, and midrash. Dockery illustrates how the apostles, Luke, Paul, Peter, and the Book of Hebrews all utilize these well-known Jewish hermeneutical approaches.

A literal hermeneutic will uncover the historical meaning of an Old Testament text to its author. However, a typological approach, without becoming fanciful, will add cohesion to the relationship between the Old and New Testaments, producing a Christological framework for interpretation in keeping with the spirit in which the New Testament authors read the Old.

The Kingdom of God in the Old and New Testaments

The kingdom of God represents God putting forth His almighty royal power to judge and to save. The use of this phrase represents God's action in the world in fulfillment of His saving purpose.

It is curious that the phrase "kingdom of God" does not occur in the Old Testament since it is clear that the reality is present throughout. The declaration of the royal psalms, "the Lord reigns" is fundamental to the Old Testament. Beasley-Murray argues that the most crucial revelation of the kingship of God in the Old Testament took place in the Exodus event. The name "I am who I am" suggests that God is active for His people. The events of the exodus showed that His working is royal and powerful in judgment and salvation.

Beasley-Murray sees a sustained application of the hope of a second exodus, when God would deliver His people from tyranny and give them a greater inheritance in a kingdom of salvation. The description of the Servant of the Lord, who will be exalted as Savior and Lord of all peoples by virtue of His redeeming death and resurrection, furthers the emphasis on the kingdom of God.

In accord with the concept of the kingdom resulting from a new exodus, God's redeeming action is described in terms of His coming. Two basic ideas are expressed: the Lord comes forth to intervene in the affairs of this world, and the elements of nature tremble in fear before the God of creation. Beasley-Murray points out five significant characteristics of the kingdom of God: (1) the kingdom of God is represented as a kingdom for humanity in this world. God comes to earth to save His people; (2) the kingdom of God is for all nations; (3) righteousness will prevail in God's kingdom; (4) peace is integral to the kingdom of God because it is the most inclusive term for the salvation of the kingdom; and (5) along with peace, joy is the great characteristic of the kingdom.

The place of the Messiah in the kingdom of God in Old Testament writing is somewhat ambivalent. The Messiah is representative of God in His kingdom and in whom God is uniquely present and through whom He acts. God is typically set forth as the Deliverer; he comes for judgment and salvation, and thus establishes the kingdom. Then with the kingdom, He gives the Messiah to be ruler for Him.

The great theme of the intertestamental literature was the coming of the kingdom of God, with an increased emphasis on the transcendental element in God's work. The literature represents God as coming from above to bring wickedness on earth to an end and introduce the new age of righteousness and life. It was thus considered inevitable that the coming of God would issue in a judgment of all generations of mankind, followed by a kingdom of God in a transformed world. The writings of the Qumran community are of interest in that they echo a belief that two messiahs will be raised up by God, the one a priest and the other a king. The earliest statement of the proclamation of Jesus concerning the kingdom of God occurs in Mark 1:14-15. Beasley-Murray argues that this passage teaches that with Christ the kingdom has arrived. Jesus proclaims not an end, but a beginning of a kingdom of God that will culminate in a recreated creation.

The New Testament clearly proclaims that the kingdom is present in the ministry of Jesus. When the Pharisees inquired concerning the coming of the kingdom (Luke 17:20), Jesus declared that the kingdom would not be visible. His statement that the kingdom is within you may mean that it is among the Jews since the King was literally among them. Yet it is also possible that it may mean, "within your reach." This would indicate that it was within the power of the hearers of Jesus to enter the kingdom and receive its blessing.

Jesus Himself provided the link between the present and the future of the kingdom. Jesus thus fulfills various prophetic strains; the sufferings of the Righteous Man, the Servant of the Lord, the Prophet, and the Martyr for God's truth. The intent of the New Covenant made in the body and blood of our Lord is salvation in the kingdom of God, mediated by His total redeeming activity as the Son of Man.

The gospel Paul preached was fundamentally the same as that of the apostles of Jesus. For him the decisive points in redemptive history are the resurrection of Christ, His coming, and the end. The ultimate end is when God will be all in all.

The teaching of the kingdom in the Book of Revelation is consistent with that of the Gospels. The theme of the central vision (ch. 5) indicates that the turn of the ages happened when the Lamb was slain and lived again. Revelation portrays the kingdom inaugurated through the death and resurrection of Christ as now brought to victory at the coming of Christ.

The pastor concerned to preach the gospel must preach the kingdom of God. Since Jesus Himself is the kingdom, the pastor should focus on His teaching on the kingdom. The expositor will then be occupied with the Lord and not with the land of Gog and Magog.

The Renewal of the Promise of Rest

David Garland points the biblical expositor to the canonical approach to Scripture as a model for using the Old Testament in our contemporary preaching. The canonical approach to Scripture emphasizes the final form of the text as the authoritative Word for the church rather than probing behind the text to investigate various stages in its composition. This approach asks what the text said to the living community of faith in the past and what it says to the community of faith in the present. The meaning of a text may thus eclipse what was intended for the original addressees as it speaks afresh to a new audience. The canonical approach also requires us to take seriously the text in its canonical context. What does this text say in light of what other books in the Bible say? The canonical approach to interpretation will force the expositor to give due consideration to the Old Testament.

Garland gives a helpful demonstration of the canonical method by his analysis of Hebrews 3:7–4:13. The focus of Hebrews as a whole concerns Christians who had spiritual anemia. They were losing their zest for living the Christian life and were growing dangerously weak in their commitment. The writer of Hebrews cited Psalm 95 as a word of warning that speaks directly to their present situation. He drew an analogy between the church called out by Jesus and the people of Israel called out into the wilderness by Moses. The author made this comparison because of his conviction that Old Testament Scripture was directly relevant to his generation. Scripture was not an object to be analyzed, but the voice of God to be heard and honored, trusted and done.

Psalm 95 was interpreted as God's Word that was still applicable to the people of God, but whose fulfillment was possible only then through what Christ had accomplished. The psalm was used in the preparation of the people for their worship and their entry into the sanctuary. The warning draws upon Exodus 17:1-7, an account of Israel's crisis and rebellion at Rephidim. The combination of belligerence, doubt, and ingratitude caused that generation to forfeit the promise of rest in the land of Canaan. Thus, the desert generation became a cautionary example for the church of the first-century Hebrew Christians.

Hebrews, then, presents an extended exhortation based on the failures of the wilderness generation. The writer denounced the fathers for putting God to the test, thus provoking God's wrath. To test God is to impugn God's power and faithfulness to fulfill His promises. The testing of God also entails trying to force God's hand to serve our own interests. The wilderness generation was also characterized as having hardened their hearts. Garland points out that the word "today" is a refrain throughout this passage in Hebrews. Thus, the attention to the Old Testament example helps clarify the urgency of responding today. The promised land was in sight, but they hesitated because of fear and unbelief and forfeited their "today." Thus, they forfeited the opportunity to enter the land of rest. The "coming to rest" is a persistent theme of the Old Testament. It is one aspect of God's presence. In many of the early passages, *rest* refers to a secure dwelling place, freedom from war, and relief from affliction—refuge on this earth.

In Psalm 95 rest is reinterpreted to mean entering into the sanctuary. Yet within the psalm are the seeds for an even greater understanding of rest which was picked up in Hebrews. The writer of Hebrews concluded that God was still offering His promise in his day and that the warning of failing to enter that rest was still applicable. The entry into the presence of God and thus true rest is made possible only by Christ. One enters God's rest by faith, but that faith can be sapped by persecution and suffering or crippled by fear. The people of God have been mobilized for a heavenward journey, and we cannot shift into neutral and coast into God's rest. The word "today" reverberates through this passage and reminds us that God's call is ever present and ever urgent. Today is the day of decision, because God's call always requires a response and has a time limit. The lesson of Rephidim is that God does not extend the opportunity indefinitely.

Garland's example of canonical interpretation gives us further opportunity and cause to study and preach from great Old Testament themes. He calls us to declare the whole counsel of God with a modern day urgency. This section should stir the imagination of the expositor and prompt him to see the relevance and immediacy of Old Testament exposition.

Preaching in the Present Tense

We need not ask how we can make the Old Testament come alive for our people, we need to ask how we can get ourselves out of the way so that the pulsating life of God's Word can come through in all its power. Al Fasol argues that the Old Testament is alive with action which has the power to give life to the hearers.

The first step in getting out of the way involves the selection of a text, which becomes the fabric from which the sermon is woven. A proper text may vary in length from a portion of a verse to an entire chapter, but it should form a complete literary unit of thought. Fortunately, the biblical writers used various literary devices to show the reader when a literary unit of thought begins and ends. The repetition of key words, brief introductions, changes in time, and place of occasion provide adequate clues to help the expositor determine an appropriate unit of thought.

Once the text has been selected the next step is to interpret the text. The historical context and the linguistic nature of the text are important in interpretation. Beyond this the contemporary preacher must always concern himself with the movement from then to now. Fasol suggests that we deal with the then of Scripture by first summarizing the text in a brief, interpretative, past tense statement—the eternal truth of the text. Having completed this task, we can deal with the now of Scripture by writing a present tense sentence application of the text—the truth for today. These two truth statements should guide the preacher throughout sermon development, often providing a title for the sermon. The outline should then show a clear relationship to the title.

Fasol provides several examples of this methodology using familiar Old Testament passages. He then suggests several Old Testament series. Fasol gives four practical guidelines for preaching an effective series of sermons: (1) make a list of the absolutely essential verses, events, persons, and doctrines that must be included in the survey; (2) from this list find a unifying theme that will give unity to the series; (3) make each sermon in the series a sermon unto itself; and (4) do not preach everything you know about every text. Stick to the essential matters.

The expositor who wants to preach a biographical sermon should be thoroughly familiar with the historical/cultural background of the text. Second, he should not sanctify nor assassinate the biblical character. The pastor will find this chapter both helpful and suggestive. It is filled with practical helps as well as sermon outlines from the Old Testament. These should be used as models for developing one's own sermon series.

Changing the Church with Words from God

Every preacher wants to know how he can preach the Old Testament so that it can contribute meaningfully to the life and ministry of the church without violating the integrity of the Old Testament itself. Richard Wells provides helpful insight plus practical suggestions that will prove helpful to the busy pastor.

Wells first addresses problems that the Old Testament poses for authentic preaching. The authority of the Old Testament was not an issue for the New Testament community, but modern critical scholarship has caused the contemporary church to question its authority. When the church views the word of the Bible solely as a historical document from the past to be studied by scientific and rational methods, it loses its power and becomes the exclusive province of the critically trained scholar.

The average preacher can become intimidated by the scholarly
science and thus avoid authentic Old Testament preaching.
Wells argues that we must first reclaim the authority of the
Old Testament before we can preach it as living and active to
transform people's lives.

The major concern of this chapter is the issue of applicability. Once again there is a stern warning against allegorizing
the Old Testament while ignoring its historical context. Wells
follows Vriezen in spelling out five limitations of application:
(1) the Old Testament is historically limited in that it reflects
life and ideas of its own time. To bridge this gap we should look
for the governing theological principle; (2) There are national
limitations in that a preponderance of regulatory material concerns Israel and not the nations; (3) the commands of the Old
Testament lend themselves to legalism; (4) because law regulated acts it invited casuistry rather than spiritual religion;
and (5) the Old Testament bears some evidence of "eudaemonism," the belief in material reward for right religion. Yet
Israel never divorced the "good life" from communion with God.

These limitations often fuse in our preaching by "moralizing." In this case the exclusive focus of a sermon becomes behavior, attitude, or psychological state. Because such preaching
addresses contemporary categories, we are attempted to excuse
it on the basis of relevance. Such moralizing, however, distorts
authentic biblical preaching by transforming the Bible into an
assortment of moral precepts. Further, it idolizes the past, obscures the proper relation of law and gospel, and assumes that
the fundamental task of the sermon is to tell people what to do.
While application may suggest behavioral principles, the thrust
of the sermon must be "God's cause and work in the world and
its history."

Having pointed out possible pitfalls, Wells devotes the second part of his chapter to the nature of Old Testament and
New Testament preaching with a focus on application. Wells
defines application as discovering the theological teaching of a
passage and "setting it to use" in a contemporary setting. Application denotes the specific way a topic will or should impact
the lives people are living. In order to avoid moralizing, Wells
points to four stages of development suggested by Greidanus:
(1) concentrate on the original message; (2) recognize the discontinuity or changes over time which affect interpretation of a
text; (3) identify the continuity inherent in the "one faithful
God" and in the "one covenant people"; and (4) focus on the

goal of the text. We must ask what do we encounter today that is similar or related to the issue of this passage.

Good application will evaluate the universal, human condition, analyze the world in terms of its relevant cultural context and discover the narrative teaching of Scripture. Yet good application differs from ethics in three ways. First, ethics distills a biblical teaching to its exact applicability to a carefully defined ethical problem. Second, preaching, unlike ethics, endeavors to apply a theological truth-claim rather than a behavioral-claim. Third, ethics calls for a behavioral response and preaching calls for a response to the gospel.

Changing Culture with Words of God

The heart of the preaching task is to take the truth of the Bible and relate it to the modern world. This is also the most difficult task the preacher faces, especially in terms of the Old Testament. How do we apply the Old Testament to contemporary culture? James Emery White capably assists this task by first detailing the characteristics of the modern world. If the modern world is not understood, it cannot be addressed. White finds three "streams" that are currently flowing in modern society: secularization, privatization, and pluralization. These three streams have formed four dominant "mind-sets" in contemporary life: moral relativism, autonomous individualism, narcissistic hedonism, and reductive naturalism. Through an examination of how the Old Testament addressed similar concerns in its own day and time, White finds paradigms by which to approach and challenge our contemporary situation through Old Testament themes. He also engages many of the current approaches to using the Old Testament to confront contemporary culture, such as the Reconstructionist proposal, providing insight and guidelines for the proper application of Old Testament teachings. Though these discussions may sound intimidating, White offers insightful and practical examples and helpful definitions that make this chapter a useful guide to a difficult topic.

Personal Reflection for Pastoral Application

How do I take the insights gained from the reading of this book and improve my preaching ministry? That is the practical question that moves us from theory to practice. The good news is that one can do it with great personal benefit, as well as for one's entire congregation. I speak to you from experience. I have just recently completed a sixteen week series on the names of God taken from a variety of Old Testament passages. This was my third major Old Testament series in the last several years. My first series was on the Book of Nehemiah and the second was from the Book of Proverbs. I must confess that it has been a truly refreshing and stimulating experience both for me and for the entire congregation.

The Value of Old Testament Preaching

This section may appear to be so obvious as not to need stating. Yet my conversation with a number of colleagues leads me to the conclusion that all of us may need a little prompting to make regular Old Testament exposition a higher priority.

The first value is to the pastor himself. The preparation for exposition enriches ones own personal life. I have gained a new appreciation of the rich heritage of Scripture. I have been challenged by passages hitherto neglected. My appreciation for the sovereign activity of God in people's affairs throughout history has been sharpened by my study of the Old Testament.

Regular preaching from the Old Testament has, I believe, improved my total preaching ministry. It has provided freshness, variety, balance, and depth to my regular preaching schedule. People sometimes ask if I am a "full gospel" preacher. I understand that their question carries a certain agenda, but I can now answer with an enthusiastic "yes." I respond, "I preach from the entire counsel of God's Word, Old and New." Preaching from the Old Testament has also given additional richness to my New Testament exposition by providing a rich treasury of illustrative material. I am a "reformed Paulinist."

The values to one's congregation are multiple as well. Old Testament exposition helps a congregation put biblical faith in historical perspective. For many of our people the Bible is a wonderful, but somewhat fanciful book. I was rudely awakened to this reality while teaching at Wingate College. I was teaching a required Old Testament survey course to a moderately inspired classroom of freshmen. One particularly bright young man who asked perceptive questions throughout the semester remained somewhat skeptical about the reality of Christian commitment. One day, when I was lecturing on a historical narrative in the Old Testament, I happened to mention the name of a pagan king who was preparing to do battle with Israel. I noticed that a light turned on in this young man's mind. I could see the sparkle in his eyes. After class he approached me with the exclamation: "This stuff really happened in the real world!" "Why yes," I replied, "it did." He left that class a changed young man because, for the first time, the Bible became a living book of reliable history for him. That event made me realize that, for this young man, and countless others like him, the Bible is a wonderful book full of good stories whose historical value is on a par with the tales of the Knights of the Roundtable. For all he knew the biblical lands were approached through a wardrobe like the mythical Narnia of C. S. Lewis fame.

Old Testament exposition opens up a whole new arena of opportunity for spiritual growth to your congregation. Most have been exposed to Psalms and Proverbs, but for many the rest of the Old Testament remains an enigma. The historical foundations, real life experiences, and faith building events provided by Old Testament exposition is essential to personal spiritual growth and to church growth. One's congregation will have a clearer understanding of the inter-connectedness of the Old and New Testaments. They will better understand the teachings of Jesus and Paul which are couched in Jewish history and tradition. Many of the Old Testament characters are wonderful role models for adults and children alike. Old Testament sermons often appear to be more easily retained and applied by the various age groups in every church family. Good exposition of the Old Testament helps one's people to discover for themselves what has been the "missing half" of their Bible.

Requirements of the Pastor

Adequate preparation time is essential.—Sound Old Testament exposition requires that the pastor not be content to take the easy way out. It requires disciplined study and therefore it requires good time management. When pressed for time, we tend to go with the familiar. A few years ago I picked up an idea that has provided rich dividends in my own preaching ministry. I take an entire week early in January to do sermon planning for the entire year. I get away from the church by myself for a time of prayer and preparation. My primary objective during this week is to project a year's worth of preaching. I am committed to biblical exposition and I prefer to preach sermons in series. Therefore, I first attempt to develop a broad outline of the series that I plan to preach during the coming year.

For example, if I am planning to do a series of messages on the Book of Jeremiah, I would spend a majority of the week acquainting myself with background issues such as authorship, date, historical context, and the like. Then I would read through the book several times in different translations. Often I alternate reading the book with listening to a translation on tape. My next step is to outline the book. This broad outline of the book will usually determine my preaching blocks for the series of messages. Once I feel that I have a good handle on the total book, I begin to work through the individual messages. All I attempt to accomplish during this week-long retreat is to put on paper a purpose statement, a title, a simple outline, and any illustrations that come to mind. If any resources come immediately to mind, I write those down. At this point I allocate from 10-30 minutes per message. There is no attempt at thoroughness. Upon return, the sheets are placed in individual folders and they become my sermon starters for each week. Often I discover that my initial reactions to a text are my best ones, but I feel the freedom to change anything or everything as the occasion demands and the Spirit leads.

Let me suggest one further idea for time-saving sermon preparation. In a time management book, I encountered the suggestion that one could save time by grouping work. I have found this principle especially applicable to sermon preparation for a series. Once I get my resource materials out and get the creative juices flowing, I find it easier to stay at the task. I thus attempt to set aside significant blocks of time to prepare several consecutive sermons. I do my work on computer and thus I find it easy to go back into the text the week that I plan to preach a particular sermon and revise and illustrate it where necessary.

Careful study of the background material is essential to creative and sound Old Testament exposition.—One must put the text in its historical and contextual context. Be sure to get a clear picture of the entire book or series before beginning any one particular message. These steps will help avoid some of the pitfalls of Old Testament preaching such as over-spiritualizing a text or even projecting one's own agenda onto a text. Authentic biblical preaching must first faithfully interpret the text in its original historical contextual setting before making any hermeneutical application. The application and invitation must emerge naturally from the text.

Sound exegesis of the text must permeate Old Testament preaching.—Here lies the rub for many pastors. Biblical Hebrew is a nearly forgotten or poorly learned art for many pastors. Take heart my friend. There are several new tools on the market that greatly assist the pastor to understand the significance of biblical Hebrew. Here are a couple of suggestions.

Bruce Einspahr's *Index to Brown, Driver & Briggs' Hebrew Lexicon* (Moody) and John Owens' *Analytical Key to the Old Testament*, vol. 1: Genesis–Joshua, vol. 3: Ezra–Song of Solomon, and vol. 4: Isaiah–Malachi (Baker; vol. 2, forthcoming) are both excellent tools to guide the neophyte through a Hebrew passage gently and efficiently.

A lack of knowledge of Hebrew does not invalidate one's ability to preach sound, biblical sermons from the Old Testament. Most good commentaries will greatly assist the pastor in making good decisions about difficult exegetical problems. Thus, while a working knowledge of Hebrew is certainly helpful, the lack of such skill should not keep you from Old Testament sermonizing.

The application of the text should emerge naturally from the text and not be forced upon it.—Once the pastor has determined the original meaning and intent of a text, he is well prepared to decide how the text can be applied to the church today. This is the easiest step for me because I find myself so greatly convicted or moved by the text that I apply the text out of my personal experience. The expositor cannot adequately preach any text he has not first personally experienced. My best application comes from the work of the Holy Spirit in my own life.

To get started, consider a series of messages from a short book.—Some prophetic books are easy to begin with because they are often sermonic in nature. A series on a specific book will allow you to spend adequate time on historical-situation context that will provide carry over for the entire series. You may want to attempt a connected series such as one on the names of God revealed in the Old Testament. I preached a single message on each name such as Yahweh, Elohim, Adonai, and the compound names like Jehovah-Jireh. To conclude this series I did a summary message demonstrating the progressive nature of the revelation of the character of God through the giving of His names. Another good series could be one on personal revival in the Old Testament.[1] There are several other suggestions of potential sermon series in this book. I have given greater emphasis to sermon series because a series allows the preacher to save on preparation time and gives an inner connectedness and continuity to his messages. This does not imply that one cannot preach a single message from the Old Testament.

There are many passages that are appropriate on their own and may speak to a specific situation. For instance, while I was writing this chapter, I was impressed to preach a single message on Psalm 46. This message was most appropriate and comforting in a military community the Sunday after the war in the Gulf became reality.

One must first choose the text or the series of texts from which one intends to preach.—Every message should be based in a primary text, even if other texts are used for illustration of completeness. People will not follow a "sword drill" message, comprised of linking text after text. In the series mentioned on the names of God, I would often illustrate a particular name from several texts, but I remained anchored in a primary text. The primary text was either the first occurrence of a particular name of the most explicit use of a name. Frequently I would end the message in the New Testament by showing how this name found fulfillment in Christ.

Multiple factors come together in the selection of a text or series. I look first to the needs of the church. These are best determined by the pastor through personal contact with his people. What are the hurts, fears, struggles, needs, and aspirations of your congregation? The pastor must know his people to answer such questions. In determining answers to these questions, one will often be drawn to a particular text. I also find my text from that which God is saying to me. I have frequently discovered that God began a work in my life in order to do that same work in our church through my preaching.

I have kept careful chronological records of my preaching over my entire ministry at a particular church in order to ensure theological and biblical balance over the long haul. I want to assure that I am preaching the "whole counsel of God." I ask trusted and mature laypersons to give input if they sense that my preaching has become unbalanced. Such checkpoints ensure that I do not come down too heavily in one area of doctrine to the neglect of other essential doctrinal issues.

All of these methods for selecting a text presume that the pastor is seeking the guidance of the Holy Spirit in the entire process of selection, preparation, and delivery of the message.

Make sure that the series has a unifying theme.—If one chooses to do a series of messages, one should ensure that each message has a central purpose and that each message can stand alone. Yet the entire series should have a unifying thread, a common denominator. In a long series it is helpful to do short summary statements from time to time. This will help people to remember the truths already learned in previous messages or to catch up with missed messages. These should be kept brief and be integrated into the introduction.

Just do it!—One of the popular phrases of our day is "Just do it." "Dive in!" "Get started!" Preaching from the Old Testament becomes easier and more natural with practice. Make sure your preaching is clear, biblical, practical, and relevant. Put yourself into your text. Seek the internal unity and order of the text and allow it to guide you. Always include a strong and clear call for action, for decision. But the first step is to get started.

Notes

1. A book that provides a good starting point for preaching on Old Testament revivals is Walter C. Kaiser, Jr., *Quest for Renewal* (Chicago: Moody, 1986).